MARTHE ROBERT is not a professional psychologist but a literary scholar and a brilliant biographer. Born in Paris, she was educated at the Sorbonne. Mme. Robert now lives in Paris with her husband, who is a doctor. She is the author of highly acclaimed biographies of Heinrich von Kleist and Franz Kafka, and a frequent contributor to intellectual and literary periodicals. In her latest book, THE PSYCHOANALYTIC REVOLUTION, "Marthe Robert crams into less than 400 pages an outline of Freud's own life and inner turmoil, his relationship with other scientists and the Viennese society of his day, a fairly detailed account of the growth of his own ideas about mental illness and the nature of the human mind, as well as the sometimes hysterical squabblings of the early psychoanalysts. . . . Her account can serve as a quick guide for the constant allusions to Freud and his ideas that any reader finds in any field of literature." *The Chicago Tribune*

THE PSYCHOANALYTIC REVOLUTION

Sigmund Freud's Life and Achievement

Marthe Robert

Translated by Kenneth Morgan

DISCUS BOOKS
PUBLISHED BY AVON

AVON BOOKS
A division of
The Hearst Corporation
959 Eighth Avenue
New York, New York 10019

Published by arrangement with Harcourt, Brace & World, Inc.
Library of Congress Catalog Card Number: 66-15017.

Originally published in France under the title *La Revolution Psychanalytique,* Payot, Paris, 1964

First Printing (Discus Edition), September, 1968

Cover photo courtesy of National Library of Medicine, Bethesda, Maryland

Printed in the U.S.A.

CONTENTS

The publishers wish to acknowledge permission to quote extensively from the following works:

The Life and Work of Sigmund Freud by Ernest Jones; *The Basic Writings of Sigmund Freud; Autobiographical Study* by Sigmund Freud; *Letters of Sigmund Freud; The Origins of Psychoanalysis,* Letters to Wilhelm Fliess, Drafts and Notes: 1887–1902; *Psychoanalysis and Faith,* The Letters of Sigmund Freud and Oskar Pfister; the *Standard Edition of the Complete Works of Sigmund Freud,* translated from the German, under the general editorship of James Strachey. Of these volume 4 is by arrangement with Allen & Unwin Ltd., volume 6 is by arrangement with Ernest Benn Ltd., and volume 8 is by arrangement with Routledge & Kegan Paul Ltd.; *The Collected Papers of Sigmund Freud; The Interpretation of Dreams.*

ABBREVIATIONS

Ernest Jones — *The Life and Work of Sigmund Freud* by Ernest Jones, 3 volumes, New York, Basic Books, Inc., 1957.

Basic Writings — The material on pp. 185, 186, 187, 188, 294, 296-99 is from *The Basic Writings of Sigmund Freud,* trans. and ed. by Dr. A. A. Brill. Copyright 1938 by Random House, Inc. Copyright renewed 1965 by Gioia B. Bernheim and Edmund Brill. Reprinted by permission.

Autobiographical Study — *Autobiographical Study*. Copyright 1935 and 1952 by W. W. Norton & Company, Inc. Copyright renewed 1963 by James Strachey.

Letters — *Letters of Sigmund Freud,* selected and edited by Ernst L. Freud, New York, Basic Books, Inc., 1960.

Origins — *The Origins of Psychoanalysis,* Letters to Wilhelm Fliess, Drafts and Notes: 1887–1902 by Sigmund Freud, edited by Marie Bonaparte, Anna Freud and Ernst Kris, New York, Basic Books, Inc., 1954.

Psychoanalysis and Faith — *Psychoanalysis and Faith,* The Letters of Sigmund Freud and Oskar Pfister, edited by Heinrich Meng and Ernst L. Freud, New York, Basic Books, Inc., 1963.

Std Edn	*Standard Edition of the Complete Works of Sigmund Freud* in 23 volumes, London, Hogarth Press, 1964. The footnote references to *The Interpretation of Dreams* also refer to the American edition of *The Interpretation of Dreams* by Sigmund Freud, translated and edited by James Strachey, New York, Basic Books, Inc., 1955 The following references are to material that also appears in *The Collected Papers of Sigmund Freud,* 5 volumes, edited by Ernest Jones, M.D., New York, Basic Books, Inc., 1959: pp. 16 (4), 55 (1), 57 (1), 83 (2), 148 (2), 149 (2), 151 (1), 156 (1, 2), 160 (1), 166 (1), 169 (1), 195 (1), 199 (1), 200 (1), 205 (1, 2), 235 (1), 237 (1), 243 (1), 244 (1,2), 246 (1,2), 252 (2), 255 (1), 257 (1, 2, 3), 265 (1, 2), 267 (1, 3), 268 (1), 269 (1, 2), 271 (1, 2), 282 (2), 283 (1), 284 (2), 286 (1), 301 (1), 345 (1), 364 (1, 2).

1

FREUD'S ORIGINS AND CHILDHOOD

One day in 1885 Sigmund Freud, then twenty-nine, decided to destroy all his intimate papers—diaries, letters, scientific manuscripts—and congratulated himself on having neatly tricked his future biographers, not at that time a very dangerous species as its existence still belonged only to the realm of chimera. Dreaming of fame yet mistrusting it, the young scientist elaborated this theme in a letter to his fiancée:

'I have destroyed all my notes of the past 14 years, as well as letters, scientific excerpts and the manuscripts of my papers. . . . All my thoughts and feelings about the world in general and about myself in particular have been found unworthy of further existence. They will now have to be thought all over again, and I certainly had accumulated some scribbling. But that stuff settles round me like sand-drifts round the Sphinx. . . . I couldn't have matured or died without worrying about who would get hold of those old papers. . . . As for the biographers, let them worry, we have no desire to make it too easy for them. Each one of them will be right in his opinion of "The Development of the Hero", and I am already looking forward to seeing them go astray. . . .'[1]

This letter was prophetic. Freud has certainly had the biographers which his fame merited and he has not made their task easy. This man, who perfected an infallible method of understanding the enigma of every individual life—including his own—always took great pains to protect his personal life from the legitimate curiosity of his successors and the malice of his innumerable opponents. He undoubtedly made himself a subject of investigation and gave the public some of the results of his self-analysis, reserving, however, his right to suspend the interpretation when it involved his private life too closely. Thus he pro-

[1] To Martha Bernays, April 28, 1885, *Letters*, pp. 140–1.

vided about himself a body of material which, of its kind, was unique but incomplete, so as to safeguard the privacy to which he believed he was entitled in spite of the indiscretion inevitably associated with his own method and also, as he clearly stated, because he did not believe that biographies reveal the truth:

'Anyone turning biographer commits himself to lies, to concealment, to hypocrisy, to flattery, and even to hiding his own lack of understanding, for biographical truth is not to be had, and even if it were it couldn't be used.'[1]

That should discourage amateur psychoanalysts who are in a hurry to decipher Freud with the method he has given them. No psychoanalysis performed after the event, supposing such a thing were technically possible, will fill in the gaps which the master deliberately left in his account of the deeper side of his life. In any case, it would not answer the most disturbing question raised by the sudden appearance of a really important discovery: why was it necessary to wait so many centuries for a discovery which, after all, was simply waiting to be brought to light and which anyone could have made? Why was Freud the one who was called to proclaim what men knew without realizing it and to which art, philosophy and literature have alluded ever since? What destined him to fill this exceptional role, what conjunction of historical, social, family and psychological circumstances led him to play this role and therefore change the face of his age? Freud's life will not, any more than any other life, provide satisfactory answers to these striking questions, but it will at least demonstrate in an exemplary way *how* an idea, an intuition which, after all, was like millions of others which have crossed the human mind, became a decisive force from the very fact that he took it with passionate seriousness and had the courage to persevere with it.

Freud always felt there was a connection between his origins and the particular cast of his mind which, in other ages, would have brought him more serious forms of persecution than criticism and derision. He brings this out clearly at the beginning of his autobiography:

I was born on May 6th, 1856, at Freiberg in Moravia, a

[1] To Arnold Zweig, May 31, 1936, *Letters,* p. 430.

small town in what is now Czechoslovakia. My parents were Jews, and I have remained a Jew myself. I have reason to believe that my father's family were settled for a long time on the Rhine (at Cologne), that, as a result of a persecution of the Jews during the fourteenth or fifteenth century, they fled eastwards, and that, in the course of the nineteenth century, they migrated back from Lithuania through Galicia into German Austria . . .'[1]

Opening the account of his scientific development by recalling his Jewish origin, Freud stressed what he owed to it: both the relentless hostility of the traditionally anti-Jewish Viennese circles against which he had to fight for much of his life, and the strength to defy public opinion and to accept, like his ancestors, a sort of intellectual exile. Brought up by a believing but broad-minded father, Freud, himself a radical atheist, always declared his adherence to Judaism—a decentralized but profound Judaism of which he felt himself to be the direct heir. He often spoke about this in his letters to his fiancée, as in this passage in which he draws a portrait of himself:

'One would hardly guess it from looking at me, and yet even at school I was always the bold oppositionist, always on hand when an extreme had to be defended and usually ready to atone for it. As I moved up into the favoured position of head boy, where I remained for years and was generally trusted, people no longer had any reason to complain about me. You know what Breuer told me one evening? I was so moved by what he said that in return I disclosed to him the secret of our engagement. He told me he had discovered that hidden under the surface of timidity there lay in me an extremely daring and fearless human being. I had always thought so, but never dared tell anyone. I have often felt as though I had inherited all the defiance and all the passions with which our ancestors defended their Temple and could gladly sacrifice my life for one great moment in history. . . .'[2]

On another occasion he again explained to Martha Bernays, his future wife, that Judaism was the solid basis on which he intended to build their life:

[1] *An Autobiographical Study, Std Edn* XX, pp. 7–8.

[2] To Martha Bernays, February 2, 1886, *Letters,* p. 202.

'And as for us, this is what I believe: even if the form wherein the old Jews were happy no longer offers us any shelter, something of the core, of the essence of meaningful and life-affirming Judaism will not be absent from our home. . . .'[1]

Freud was well aware of the singular nature of his relations with Judaism. He explains them with his usual clarity in an address to B'nai B'rith, the liberal Jewish Association to which he belonged all his life and of which he was an active member for many years:

'That you were Jews could only be agreeable to me; for I was myself a Jew, and it had always seemed to me not only unworthy but positively senseless to deny the fact. What bound me to Jewry was (I am ashamed to admit) neither faith nor national pride, for I have always been an unbeliever and was brought up without any religion though not without a respect for what are called the "ethical" standards of human civilization. Whenever I felt an inclination to national enthusiasm I strove to suppress it as being harmful and wrong, alarmed by the warning examples of the peoples among whom we Jews live. But plenty of other things remained over to make the attraction of Jewry and Jews irresistible—many obscure emotional forces, which were the more powerful the less they could be expressed in words, as well as a clear consciousness of inner identity, the safe privacy of a common mental construction. And beyond this there was a perception that it was to my Jewish nature alone that I owed two characteristics that had become indispensable to me in the difficult course of my life. Because I was a Jew I found myself free from many prejudices which restricted others in the use of their intellect; and as a Jew I was prepared to join the Opposition and to do without agreement with the "compact majority" . . . .'[2]

Given such a deeply-rooted feeling, it can be imagined how greatly Freud suffered from Viennese anti-Semitism which, before being carried to extremes by the Nazis, flourished more or less openly and meant that all his life he was a target if not for actual persecution, at least for indignities or hypocritical attacks. The memory of one of

[1] To Martha Bernays, July 23, 1882, *Letters*, p. 22.
[2] *Std Edn* XX, pp. 273–4.

these humiliations already suffered by his father takes on a sad meaning in a passage from *The Interpretation of Dreams*:

'At that point I was brought up against the event in my youth whose power was still being shown in all these emotions and dreams. I may have been ten or twelve years old when my father began to take me with him on his walks and reveal to me in his talk his views upon things in the world we live in. Thus it was on one such occasion, that he told me a story to show me how much better things were now than they had been in his days. "When I was a young man", he said, "I went for a walk one Saturday in the streets of your birthplace; I was well dressed, and had a new fur cap on my head. A Christian came up to me and with a single blow knocked off my cap into the mud and shouted: 'Jew! get off the pavement!' " "And what did you do?" I asked. "I went into the roadway and picked up my cap," was his quiet reply. . . .'[1]

A counterpart to this unforgettable scene was another incident, many years later, from which Freud emerged with a sense of triumph and which, in a way, redressed the earlier wrong. One day, while travelling by train, he had opened the window of his compartment which, according to him, was stuffy. Someone protested and insisted on his closing it. Freud refused to close it unless another window were opened. It was the beginning of a very painful episode which he relates at length in a letter to Martha:

'While the discussion ensued and the man said he was prepared to open the ventilation slit instead of the window, there came a shout from the background: "He's a dirty Jew!"—And with this the whole situation took on a different colour. My first opponent also turned anti-Semitic and declared: "We Christians consider other people, you'd better think less of your precious self," etc., and muttering abuses befitting his education, my second opponent announced that he was going to climb over the seats to show me, etc. Even a year ago I would have been speechless with agitation; but now I am different; I was not in the least frightened of that mob, asked the one to keep to himself his empty phrases which inspired no respect in me, and the other to step up and take what was coming to

[1] *The Interpretation of Dreams, Std Edn,* IV, p. 197.

him. I was quite prepared to kill him, but he did not step up; I was glad I refrained from joining in the abuse, something one must always leave to the others. . . .'[1]

Faced with a situation which could be combated only by bandying answers which were themselves degrading, the young Freud developed at a precociously early age the ambition, the burning thirst for fame which is undoubtedly one of the outstanding features of his character. There can be no doubt that he regarded the achievement of fame and the accomplishment of great things in the field of action or thought as one of the most effective ways of forcing the world to recognize him and accord him a place in it. For a long time the desire to defeat people's malevolence by a sort of heroism was for him definitely more important than even the goal of his ambition.

Ernest Jones tells us in his *Life and Work of Sigmund Freud* that the young Freud passionately admired Bonaparte and Masséna and that he was for a time attracted to a military career. It is probable that in his case the attraction was not so much the career itself as the two great prestige figures, both of them heroes and self-made men.

According to a legend which is devoid of all foundation, Masséna was of Jewish origin. As for Napoleon, a liberator of the Jews and a model for self-made men, Europe's little Jews did not need to be particularly bellicose to make him their hero.

Freud who, like all strong natures, had an inexhaustible faculty for admiration, embraced in one single feeling of veneration all free, audacious and solitary men who, one way or another, came into conflict with the prejudices of their age. Along with Bonaparte, Masséna, Hannibal, the Semitic hero, and many others who, later, were his direct masters, Freud always felt for Cromwell, also a liberator of the Jews and a revolutionary hero, such profound admiration that he named one of his sons 'Oliver' in his honour.

And so anti-Semitism, plus a poverty which sometimes assumed alarming proportions, was a considerable factor in the formation of Freud's character and the way he confronted his own society. Although this situation, so common to his age in that part of Europe, might have had a detrimental effect on the fate of Freudian science—we

[1] To Martha Bernays, December 16, 1883, *Letters,* p. 78.

shall see how later—it is clear that we cannot look to it for the explanation of the mental event which gave rise to psychoanalysis. If such an explanation exists, it is to be found rather in Freud's family group, in his relations with his first circle of friends, the emotional experiences of his childhood—all things which, according to him, permanently affect the individual, give him his gifts, his weaknesses and his aspirations and determine his successes and his failures.

The man who discovered the secret laws of the human family and unravelled its secret drama could draw his experience only from himself, his childhood and his own family. It can be assumed that the Freud family, the first to be understood, analysed and laid bare, was able to play this role only because it was in some way naturally fitted for this.

In fact, Sigismund Freud—Sigismund was his real name which he changed to Sigmund when he was twenty-two—was born and grew up in a family remarkable for the unusual complexity of its parental relationships. Jakob Freud, his father, had married twice, the first time at the age of seventeen. He had two sons by this first marriage, Emmanuel and Philipp, and after his wife died he re-married, this time a young woman of twenty, Amalie Nathansohn, Freud's mother, who therefore belonged to the same generation as her step-sons. When, in his turn, Emmanuel, the older half-brother, married and had children, the two families lived in the greatest intimacy, which was intensified by their having houses next door to one another. It is easy to imagine the psychological complications that could result from this paradoxical situation. The young Freud's playmate, the first friend to whom he became passionately attached, was the son of his half-brother Emmanuel, and was therefore Freud's nephew, and his nephew was a year older than himself. His mother and his half-brother Philipp, being of exactly the same age, the child was inevitably tempted to pair them off so that Jakob, his father, assumed the role of grandfather which, in view of his age, he could logically have been. Psychoanalytically speaking this gathering of the three generations in the same family milieu was to entail more than one enigma for the little boy. In his biography of Freud, Ernest Jones describes the most striking consequences of all this:

'As seen through a child's eyes it was not unnatural that

he should pair off Jakob and Nannie, the two forbidding authorities. Then came Emmanuel with his wife, and there remained Philipp and Amalie who were just of an age. All this appeared very tidy and logical, but still there was the awkward fact that Jakob, not Philipp, slept in the same bed as Amalie. It was all very puzzling.

'What we have called the logical pairing off would have a deeper psychological advantage and motivation. By removing his father to a more remote order in the household he would absolve him from rivalry about the mother and from the mischief of creating unwelcome children. There is every reason to think that Freud's conscious attitude to his father consistently remained, despite the latter's representing authority and frustration, one of affection, admiration, and respect. Any hostile component was thoroughly displaced on to the figures of Philipp and John. It therefore came as a great shock to Freud when forty years later he discovered his own Oedipus complex, and had to admit to himself that his unconscious had taken a very different attitude towards his father from that of his consciousness. It was no chance that this insight came about only a year or two after his father's death.

'In tracing, as best we can, the genesis of Freud's original discoveries we may therefore legitimately consider that the greatest of them—namely the universality of the Oedipus complex—was potently facilitated by his own unusual family constellation, the spur it gave to his curiosity and the opportunity it afforded of a complete repression. . . .'[1]

Freud was thus the eldest of a family numbering eight children in all, and this, in a home which very soon lost its early prosperity and often knew hardship, must have strengthened in the child, then in the young man, a sense of responsibility and a tendency to adopt a paternal attitude.

Manès Sperber saw an important clue to Freud's personality in what he calls the 'Joseph complex'.[2] In fact Freud often identified himself with the biblical Joseph who, like himself, was the son of a Jacob and an interpreter of dreams. What is more, the Christian name of 'Joseph' played a special part in his life. Freud himself ob-

[1] Ernest Jones, I, p. 11.

[2] Manès Sperber, *Misère de la psychologie. Preuves,* No. 46, December 1954.

served that it often occurred in his dreams. The only uncle he mentioned was called Josef, Josef Paneth was for a time one of his closest friends, Josef Breuer, who started him on psychoanalysis, he long considered to be in the front rank of scientists and, finally, it was another Joseph —Josef Popper-Lynkeus—who almost forestalled him in expounding his theory.

In a letter to Thomas Mann, Freud noted the same significance which the name 'Joseph' held for another great man—Napoleon, who also identified himself closely with the biblical Joseph. According to him it was not for political reasons but because of this unconscious link that he embarked on his fantastic Egyptian expedition. [1]

In spite of these complicated family relationships, Freud seems to have had a happy childhood, at least as long as his parents lived in Freiberg, for their trials and tribulations did not begin until they went to Vienna. Deeply loved by a mother who was young, lively and pretty, Freud felt himself to be her pride and particular favourite. This gave him a feeling of confidence which, in spite of the vicissitudes of his career, proved almost unshakable. Later, he maintained that 'when you have definitely been your mother's favourite child, you keep for life that feeling of triumph, that sense of confidence in success which almost invariably ensures it'. [2]

Freud says he resembled his father and that he had to some extent inherited his turn of mind. Freud's father was a lovable, broad-minded man who was not lacking in authority although, apparently, rather irresponsible in business. Freud described him as being like Dickens's Mr Micawber—always trusting in a providential solution to his financial difficulties. A wool merchant, he had done badly in Freiberg and had to move to Vienna; but whether through lack of means or bad luck or irresponsibility, he seems never to have restored his fortunes and his numerous family lived in a chronic state of poverty. Nobody held this against him. Freud helped his family, whatever their circumstances, as much as his own precarious means would allow. But the poverty which cast a shadow over his childhood and youth remained the really damaging thing in his life.

Freud's parents are almost totally absent from the pub-

[1] Cf. chap. 28, *Moses* and Exile.

[2] *A Childhood Recollection from Dichtung und Wahrheit, Std Edn*, XVII.

lished analyses of his childhood memories. It is easy to understand why. When he began to analyse his dreams in order to clarify certain obscure points in his theory, his father had just died and he was suffering from a violent mental disturbance, the real origin of which he naturally did not realize at the time. Analyzing his dreams made him see his childhood and his relationships with his parents in a completely unexpected light, and this revelation caused a shock for which he was no better prepared than the next man. People forget this today when they criticize Freud for being reticent about certain matters. At the age of forty-two, a husband and father, with a long career already behind him, he was led for scientific reasons and also, no doubt, by the need to know himself in a moment of crisis, to relive his past right back to his very earliest childhood. He did not know what was awaiting him, but he set out to discover it: it was humanity's great drama, its great scandal to which, in remembrance of the ancient tragedy, he gave the name of 'Oedipus complex'. It can be assumed that others had reached this forbidden frontier before him: but, terrified, they had retreated while he alone, without help or confirmation from outside, overcame the horror of his discovery at the cost of an inner struggle about which he kept silent and decided to press forward. He then discovered, deep within himself, a child with feelings of hostility towards his father, an incestuous love for his mother, death-wishes and marks of the savage. There is absolutely no reason to believe that he accepted the scandalous truth without a struggle. On the contrary, his whole way of thinking, his character, his puritanical morality were all bound to make him reject his discovery about himself and to disbelieve the evidence. In fact his reluctance to unveil the dark world into which he had just penetrated was so great that, in the letters to the only friend to whom he confided the results of his analysis, he described his memories about his mother in Latin. Elsewhere he explained his reluctance by a favourite quotation from Goethe: 'You are not going to share your precious knowledge with these rogues'.

Freud therefore deliberately omitted the figures of his parents from *The Interpretation of Dreams,* our main source of information about his childhood. On the other hand we do catch occasional glimpses of the important figures belonging to his distant past who, recurring in his dreams, provided material which was indispensable for his interpretation. His nephew John, his first companion in his war-like and erotic games, who, he realized, was the model of all his friendships; Pauline, his niece with whom he was in love; Nannie, the old and hideously ugly nanny —she was also a thief—who terrified him with her descriptions of the torments of hell and who had been arrested on his own father's orders; Uncle Josef, who had been in trouble with the law, causing Freud's father to go grey before his time—all these people bring back to life for us the loves, the unhappiness, the games and the drama of Freud's childhood.

On the whole a commonplace childhood in which the most important events might easily have passed un-noticed by the adults—the jealousy roused by the birth of a brother or a sister, a misdeed punished by his father, violence to a little girl in which his half-brother had been his accomplice, rivalry with his half-brother Philipp. A childhood which was happy, too, aglow with the warmth of an intimate family life, in contact with nature and as free as was possible to find in those days. This was true at least of the first three years, and Freud has taught that those are the most decisive years and that, whatever happens subsequently, they leave an indelible mark on a person's whole life.

The Freud family's departure for Leipzig, then its final move to Vienna, brought a painful change in the life of little Sigmund, who did not exchange the freedom and gaiety of country life for the tough existence of the capital without a pang of regret. Freud remembered the journey to Leipzig as a terrifying event. At Breslau station he saw gas flames for the first time and they made him think of souls burning in hell. The agony of their departure, tearing him from his native city, the fear of the unknown, the fear, too, that he might not be able to find his mother again in new and hostile surroundings, all this set up a profound travel phobia which could be cured only by analysis. Not to mention another feeling of which he could never rid himself—a mixture of love and intense aversion for the city where he was going to spend the rest of his life—Vienna.

Freud's Vienna bore hardly any resemblance to the popular picture then prevalent in England and elsewhere—the Vienna of waltzes and the beautiful blue Danube. It was a hard city, divided into water-tight castes proud of their way of life and fixed in their prejudices. The middle class accepted neither people nor ideas from outside, and if Vienna became, as she did, such an astonishing cradle of revolution, her official élites undoubtedly made a purely negative contribution by driving to even greater lengths of non-conformity those aesthetic and intellectual circles which were incensed by their meanness. As far as Freud is concerned, Vienna benefits undeservedly from his fame, for during the thirty-eight years he lived there she did nothing but harass and snub him. Then, when it was no longer possible to deride him, she treated him with scornful indifference. It is a fact that Freud never received the slightest official recognition, never became a Professor at the University; and his ostracism by Viennese scientific circles undoubtedly had something to do with the remarkable fact that despite the repeated efforts of leading international figures he never received the Nobel Prize either. The Mayor, Lüger, a declared anti-Semite who presided over the city's destiny for many years and who Freud could see was definitely a personal enemy, might well stand as the symbol for that reactionary and retrograde Vienna which, even when Freud was being fêted all over the world, immured herself in her own resentment.

It can well be imagined that in conditions as materially and morally distressing as these, Freud should often have thought of emigrating. He did, in fact, dream more than once of leaving Vienna and going to live in England where his brother Emmanuel and family had settled. A journey which Freud made to England in his youth had left him with the memory of a free country, one favourable to intellectual work and offering the chance of a dignified life—in a word, a life which was the opposite of his own.

But in spite of this legitimate antipathy, Vienna held him and he clung to Vienna. Whenever events provided the best of reasons for going, Freud refused to leave—he even used the word 'desert'—the city. And so he shared Vienna's fate in the blackest moments of her history, during the First World War and after, when Austria was dying of hunger and he himself, with no patients and no money, faced starvation. Even in 1938, when the invasion of Austria by the Nazis had become inevitable, he still refused to listen to those who urged him to leave. It took the desperate efforts of his English and French pupils, in particular Ernest Jones and Marie Bonaparte, to get him eventually to agree to go into exile. And so he found a final refuge in England, but quite differently from the way he had dreamed. And it was London which, giving him a welcome full of warmth and emotion, made up for Vienna's ingratitude.

2

STUDIES AND VOCATION

We are better informed about the first three years of Freud's life than about his later childhood because, attaching decisive importance to this remote period of his life, he had to try to reconstruct it patiently in the course of his self-analysis. There is, perhaps, another reason as well. Freud—who once wrote to the mayor of his native city that he still felt living deep within himself 'the happy Freiberg child, the young mother's first-born son who had received his first indelible impressions from its air and its soil' [1]—had, however, such bitter memories of his early years in Vienna that he would never speak about them. The narrowness of city life, the misery which cramped living conditions as well as material difficulties were bound to bring to a large family, all left him with a painful feeling of distress which from the very beginning aggravated his tendency to neurasthenia. Of those dark days he recalls only two or three notable incidents, to which he attributes certain features in his character. The first is connected with his love of books:

'It had once amused my father to hand over a book with *coloured plates* (an account of a journey through Persia) for me and my eldest sister to destroy. Not easy to justify from the educational point of view! I had been five years old at the time and my sister not yet three; and the picture of the two of us blissfully pulling the book to pieces (leaf by leaf, like an *artichoke,* I found myself saying) was almost the only plastic memory that I retained from that period of my life. Then, when I became a student, I had developed a passion for collecting and owning books. . . . I had always, from the time I first began to think about myself, referred this first passion of mine back to the childhood memory I have mentioned. Or rather, I had recognized that the childhood scene was a "screen memory" for my later bibliophile propensities.' [2]

[1] Letter to the Mayor of Pribor-Freiberg, October 25, 1931.

[2] *The Interpretation of Dreams, Std Edn* IV, pp. 172–3.

A later incident is described in *The Interpretation of Dreams:*

'When I was seven or eight years old there was another domestic scene, which I can remember very clearly. One evening before going to sleep I disregarded the rules which modesty lays down and obeyed the calls of nature in my parents' bedroom while they were present. In the course of his reprimand my father let fall the words: "The boy will come to nothing." This must have been a frightful blow to my ambition, for references to this scene are still constantly recurring in my dreams and are always linked with an enumeration of my achievements and successes, as though I wanted to say: "You see, I *have* come to something." '[1]

A love of books, and a desire to become somebody and to prove his worth are certainly two marked features which help to explain the future scientist's precocious seriousness and his studious childhood. Taught first by his father, a self-educated man who was probably very intelligent, Freud accepted at a very early age the almost sacred value which Jewish tradition attaches to learning. His father had undoubtedly moved a long way from a strictly orthodox position, but study still meant as much to him as it meant to the old teachers of the Talmud. This comes out clearly in the dedication he wrote in Hebrew in his own Bible, which he gave to Sigmund as a thirty-fifth birthday present:

'My dear Son,

'It was in the seventh year of your age that the spirit of God began to move you to learning. I would say the spirit of God speaketh to you: "Read in My Book; there will be opened to thee sources of knowledge and of the intellect." It is the Book of Books; it is the well that wise men have digged and from which lawgivers have drawn the waters of their knowledge.

'Thou hast seen in this Book the vision of the Almighty, thou hast heard willingly, thou hast done and hast tried to fly high upon the wings of the Holy Spirit. Since then I have preserved the same Bible. Now, on your thirty-fifth birthday I have brought it out from its retirement and I send it to you as a token of love from your old father.'[2]

[1] *Ibid.*, p. 216.

[2] Ernest Jones, I, p. 19.

Freud always admitted candidly that his early reading of the Bible had a profound influence on his intellectual and moral development. One has only to read what he wrote about Joseph, and, more particularly, about Moses in the two works he devoted to this great figure to feel that, in Freud's case, interest in science was based on a natural bent. From one point of view it can be said that he followed Moses' solitary road in reverse and that the book, so shockingly irreligious, is in its way the ultimate commentary on Mosaic Law.

Jakob Freud's instruction must have been sound, for Sigmund went to a grammar school at the age of nine. He was a year ahead of his class-mates and throughout his eight years at school he was always top of the class. This zeal for work was undoubtedly due to an insatiable intellectual curiosity, but much later Freud realized that there were more complex reasons and these prompted him to write *Some Reflections on Schoolboy Psychology*. This 'Psychology', which he wrote on the occasion of the fiftieth anniversary of his old school, is worth quoting both as a piece of autobiography and as a fine example of Freud's gift for explaining the most abstract phenomena with all the vividness and skill of a novelist:

'It gives you a queer feeling if, late in life, you are ordered once again to write a school essay. But you obey automatically, like the old soldier who, at the word "Attention!", cannot help dropping whatever he may have in his hands and who finds his little fingers pressed along the seams of his trousers. It is strange how readily you obey the orders, as though nothing in particular had happened in the last half-century. But in fact you have grown old in the interval, you are on the eve of your sixtieth birthday, and your physical feelings, as well as your mirror, show unmistakably how far your life's candle is burnt down.

'As little as ten years ago, perhaps, you may have had moments at which you suddenly felt quite young again. As you walked through the streets of Vienna—already a grey-beard, and weighed down by all the cares of family life—you might come unexpectedly on some well-preserved, elderly gentleman and would greet him humbly almost, because you had recognized him as one of your former schoolmasters. But afterwards you would stop and reflect: "Was that really he? or only someone deceptively like him? How youthful he looks! And how old you yourself have grown! How old can he be to-day? Can it be possible that the men who used to stand for us as types of adulthood were really so little older than we were?"

'At such moments as these, I used to find, the present time seemed to sink into obscurity and the years between ten and eighteen would rise from the corners of my memory, with all their guesses and illusions, their painful distortions and heartening successes—my first glimpses of an extinct civilization (which in my case was to bring me as much consolation as anything else in the struggles of life), my first contacts with the sciences, among which it seemed open to me to choose to which of them I should dedicate what were no doubt my inestimable services. And I seem to remember that through the whole of this time there ran a premonition of a task ahead, till it found open expression in my school-leaving essay as a wish that I might during the course of my life contribute something to our human knowledge.

'Later I became a physician—or a psychologist, rather—and was able to create a new psychological discipline, something that is known as "psycho-analysis", which is followed to-day with excited interest, and is greeted with praise and blame, by physicians and enquirers in neighbouring, and in distant foreign lands—but least of all, of course, in our own country.

'As a psycho-analyst I am bound to be concerned more with emotional than intellectual processes, with unconscious than with conscious mental life. My emotion at meeting my old schoolmaster warns me to make a first admission: it is hard to decide whether what affected us more and was of greater importance to us was our concern with the sciences that we were taught or with the personalities of our teachers. It is true, at least, that this second concern was a perpetual undercurrent in all of us, and that in many of us the path to the sciences led only through our teachers. Some of us stopped half-way along that path, and for a few—why not admit as much?—it was on that account blocked for good and all.

'We courted them or turned our backs on them, we imagined sympathies and antipathies in them which probably had no existence, we studied their characters and on theirs we formed or misformed our own. They called up our fiercest opposition and forced us to complete submission; we peered into their little weaknesses, and took pride in their excellences, their knowledge and their justice. At bottom we felt a great affection for them if they gave us any ground for it, though I cannot tell how many of them were aware of this. But it cannot be denied that our position in regard to them was a quite remarkable one and one which may well have had its inconvenience for those concerned. We were from the very first equally inclined to love and to hate them, to criticize and respect them. Psychoanalysis has given the name of "ambivalence" to this readiness to contradictory attitudes, and it has no difficulty in pointing to the source of ambivalent feelings of such a kind. . . .'[1]

Freud goes on to give the psychoanalytical explanation of this ambivalent attitude which always characterized his own relations with his masters, his friends and, later, with his students. Then he concludes, with a touch of sadness:

'So that we can now understand our relation to our schoolmasters. These men, not all of whom were in fact fathers themselves, became our substitute fathers. That was why, even though they were still quite young, they struck us as so mature and so unattainably adult. We transferred on to them the respect and expectations attaching to the omniscient father of our childhood, and we then began to treat them as we treated our fathers at home. We confronted them with the ambivalence that we had acquired in our own families and with its help we struggled with them as we had been in the habit of struggling with our fathers in the flesh. Unless we take into account our nurseries and our family homes our behaviour to our schoolmasters would be not only incomprehensible but inexcusable.'[2]

Freud says that the School Leaving Examination had an important bearing on his life since it allowed him to discover the general direction his work was to take. True, the subject set for the essay—'Considerations involved in the Choice of a Profession'—was in itself a help. The candidate, then seventeen, seems to have taken it with the utmost seriousness. One of the few surviving letters from this period of his youth, addressed to Emil Fluss, his childhood friend, shows the maturity of mind he brought to the examination and was already bringing to his life:

[1] *Some Reflections on Schoolboy Psychology, Std Edn* XIII, pp. 241–2.

[2] *Ibid.*, p. 244.

'Finally, my German paper was stamped with an *exc.* It was a most ethical subject on "Considerations involved in the Choice of a Profession", and I repeated more or less what I wrote to you a couple of weeks ago, although you failed to confirm it with an *exc.* Incidentally, my professor told me—and he is the first person who has dared to tell me this—that I possess what Herder so nicely calls an *idiotic* style—i.e. a style at once correct and characteristic. I was suitably impressed by this amazing fact and don't hesitate to disseminate the happy event, the first of its kind, as widely as possible—to you, for instance, who until now have probably remained unaware that you have been exchanging letters with a German stylist. And now I advise you as a friend, not as an interested party, to preserve them—have them bound—take good care of them—one never knows.' [1]

This letter breathes the joy and pride which comes from having succeeded brilliantly at something which, fundamentally, had little to do with his plans for a scientific career but to which he attached the greatest importance, as all his subsequent work proved. Freud had a passionate love of writing. His work reveals a love of words, a need to write and to bring people to life, making him, as he himself once said, more akin to the novelist than the doctor. Did he have literary ambitions which he never confessed to anybody and which, perhaps, he dared not admit even to himself? Many things give us grounds for believing this was the case—his marked taste for symbols, the secret play of words and language, the signs and the imaginary constructions. If this is true, psychoanalysis would, by a paradox, owe its existence to a vocation whose course had mysteriously been changed. . . .

For Freud the choice of a profession was not just an essay subject; already, because of his family's material circumstances, it was a serious cause for anxiety. In the same letter he unburdens himself to his boyhood friend and from a discussion about the exam goes on to make some observations which seem to anticipate his psychology:

'You take my "worries about the future" too lightly. People who fear nothing but mediocrity, you say, are safe. Safe from what? I ask. Surely not safe and secure from

1 To Emil Fluss, June 16, 1873, *Letters,* p. 4.

being mediocre? What does it matter whether we fear something or not? Isn't the main question whether what we fear exists? Admittedly more powerful intellects are also seized with doubts about themselves; does it therefore follow that anyone who doubts his virtues is of powerful intellect? In intellect he may be a weakling yet at the same time an honest man by education, habit, or even self-torment. I don't mean to suggest that if you find yourself in a doubtful situation, you should mercilessly dissect your feelings, but if you do you will see how little about yourself you're sure of. The magnificence of the world rests after all on this wealth of possibilities, except that it is unfortunately not a firm basis for self-knowledge. . . .'[1]

Freud's anxieties, which give this adolescent letter a precocious seriousness, revolved especially round the precarious circumstances of his family. He had decided to become a doctor but thought that was asking very heavy, perhaps unfair, sacrifices of his father. His father, however, willingly accepted these and he even promised Sigmund a trip to England if he were successful. In point of fact material difficulties cropped up and it was another two years before he was able to go. And so Freud was nineteen when he first went to Manchester to stay with his half-brother Emmanuel, who had settled there. England, as has been said, was and for a long time remained the land of his dreams. He went back to Vienna with an even greater admiration for Cromwell, one of his childhood heroes, and feeling a secret envy for his half-brother's children whom he saw happy and free and safe from the never-ending vexations that Vienna's Jews had to suffer. There was an even more secret reason underlying Freud's envy: he regretted not being the son of the brother who was twenty years older than himself and who, he believed, would have made life easier for him.

We should naturally like to know whether this adolescence, so precociously studious and serious, was nevertheless relieved by the joy of some love affair. But we know very little about that, as Freud took very good care that his emotional life, especially before his marriage, should not come to light. The only known incident was discovered through the astuteness of one of Freud's followers, in spite of all the precautions Freud had taken to give it an

[1] *Ibid.*, p. 5.

anonymous character. Freud described it in an article entitled 'Screen Memories' in which, as Dr. Bernfeld[1] has clearly demonstrated, he attributed his own affair to a fictitious case. The history of this little article, which is very interesting in itself, shows how anxious Freud was to protect himself and gives some idea of what he must have had to overcome later to analyse and publish his own dreams.

The article appeared in 1899 in a psychiatric review. Normally it would have appeared again later in the *Collected Essays on the Theory of Neuroses* or in *The Psychopathology of Everyday Life.* Ten years later Freud put into *The Interpretation of Dreams* a remark about the scar on his face which gave a clue to the real identity of his pseudo-patient. But, in 1925, when his first complete works were about to be published, he withdrew the remark which could have betrayed him, at the risk of making the relevant passage unintelligible. This is all the more surprising as the incident itself is hardly important enough to justify such an action.

At the age of sixteen Freud had fallen in love with Gisela, the sister of his friend Fluss, while on a visit to his native city. He had been afraid to declare his love and, after a few days, the girl had left. The young man was shattered and he began to wander about the forests, imagining what his life would have been like if his parents had stayed in Freiberg instead of exposing him to the harsh existence of Vienna. Later this episode became associated in his mind with a family plan of which he had got to hear. His father and half-brother had thought of making him go into business instead of letting him take up a scientific career. He would then have lived in Manchester, married Pauline, his half-brother's daughter and his childhood playmate, and he would have led once more a free and simple life, very different from the one awaiting him at home. The dream described in the article contained, therefore, a violent reproach towards his father. In addition, the figures of the two girls were merged in one erotic desire, from which Freud naturally discovered that it really concerned his mother. Thus the apparently innocuous episode revealed the two aspects of his Oedipus complex and that is doubtless why he was so anxious to keep it secret.

[1] Siegfried Bernfeld: 'An Unknown Biographical Fragment by Freud', American *Imago,* 4, No. 1, 1946, quoted by Ernest Jones, Vol. I.

We can see that in spite of his determination to take up a scientific career, Freud sometimes yearned for a simple, easy life. But he did not settle in the country, he did not become a business man, nor did he marry his niece Pauline, for the girl he had seen in Manchester had never won his heart. And so a disappointment in love and a marriage which never materialized left him free to do the work which could not possibly have been foreseen and which was to lead to his discoveries. And Ernest Jones is perhaps right to conclude that if Pauline's charms had equalled those of the country girl, much might have been different in our world.

Most of Freud's biographers still find certain disturbing features about Freud's vocation which, after innumerable vicissitudes, culminated in the creation of something completely new. Why did this man, they ask, who during his childhood and adolescence admired particularly historical figures who were the very embodiment of power and action, why did this man suddenly decide to take up medicine and devote himself to biological research? That is to take his childish aspirations a little too literally. They forget that in such dreams desire and the youthful longing for an ideal probably count for much more than the actual content of the dream. The most that can be concluded from the fact that Freud indiscriminately lumped together Hannibal, Napoleon, Masséna and Cromwell, not forgetting Goethe and Shakespeare, is that he felt an imperative need to achieve great and original things and that he aspired, like them, to discover, make known and dominate new aspects of reality. Scientific research, although less spectacular than military conquest or political domination, might well conform to a similar pattern. On the other hand, one feature about Freud's vocation is still obscure—his choice of medicine, a profession for which he had neither liking nor, as he himself admitted, any particular aptitude. Freud often noted this contradiction, but he made no attempt to explain it. Thus, at the very beginning of his autobiography, he wrote:

'Although we lived in very limited circumstances, my father insisted that, in my choice of a profession, I should follow my own inclinations alone. Neither at that time, nor indeed in my later life, did I feel any particular predilection for the career of a doctor. I was moved, rather, by a sort of curiosity, which was, however, directed more towards human concerns than towards natural objects; nor had I grasped the importance of observation as one of the best means of gratifying it.' [1]

In another work, devoted specifically to the relationship between psychoanalysis and medicine, Freud gave a slightly different version:

'After forty-one years of medical activity, my self-knowledge tells me that I have never really been a doctor in the proper sense. I became a doctor through being compelled to deviate from my original purpose; and the triumph of my life lies in my having, after a long and roundabout journey, found my way back to my earliest path. . . .' [2]

It must be admitted that there is a discrepancy between these two accounts. What were the original plans which Freud said he sacrificed? Were they connected with the human relationships to which he felt drawn or, on the contrary, with the natural sciences which were his original field of research? Freud never provided a clear explanation, at least publicly. But he expressed the essence of his thought in a letter which he wrote to his friend Wilhelm Fliess when he felt he was at last approaching his true goal:

'If we are both granted a few more years of quiet work, we shall certainly leave behind something which will justify our existence. That feeling strengthens me against all daily cares and worries. When I was young, the only thing I longed for was philosophical knowledge, and now that I am going over from medicine to psychology I am in the process of attaining it. I have become a therapist against my will. . . .' [3]

Philosophy, therefore, was the secret reason why Freud took such a complicated road. But why did he not openly admit it? Why did he not become a philospher, which would have been the simplest way to satisfy his immense thirst for knowledge? This strange attitude intrigued one

[1] *An Autobiographical Study, Std Edn* XX, p. 8.
[2] *The Question of Lay Analysis, Std Edn* XX, p. 253.
[3] To Wilhelm Fliess, April 2, 1896, *Letters,* pp. 231–2.

of his biographers, Fritz Wittels,[1] who finally gave two explanations. One was that Freud had been brought up to distrust philosophy which, in his day, was in a pretty sorry state; the other was his fear of his own tendency towards speculation, which he seemed to think dangerous unless it were kept severely in check. Attracted by the abysses of thought on which the idea current in his day and his own intellectual ethic laid a sort of taboo, Freud seems to have decided on a compromise: to guard against the temptations of speculative imagination he chose arid laboratory work, the naturalist's patient observation which leaves to others the construction of systems and the formulation of theories. And so psychoanalysis would appear to have been born of this severe repression which he precociously imposed on his visionary nature.

If Wittels' thesis is correct—and many things in Freud's work seem to bear it out—it is understandable that the young man, still undecided about his real aim in life, should have been launched on his career not by a scientist but by no less a poet than Goethe himself. Freud has often described how he went and registered at the Medical Faculty after hearing an essay by Goethe entitled 'Nature' read aloud at a lecture. No doubt the dithyrambic passage, in which nature is invoked as an inexhaustible and all-loving mother in whom every contradiction is resolved does not seem all that appropriate as a factor in determining a scientific career, but one only needs to read a few lines to understand why it is so closely linked with Freud's destiny and, therefore, with psychoanalysis:

NATURE

'One obeys her even when one resists her, one acts with her even when one thinks one is defying her.

'She has neither language nor speech, but she creates hearts and tongues that she may feel and speak.

'Her crown is love. She can be approached through that alone. She digs ditches between beings and everything aspires to intertwine. She has isolated everything so that she may reunite everything. With a few draughts from the cup of love she redeems a whole life of misery.

'She is everything. She rewards and she punishes herself, she rejoices and she torments herself. She is rough and

[1] Fritz Wittels, *Der Antiphilosoph Freud, Almanach der Psychoanalyse*, 1931, pp. 16–50.

gentle, lovable and terrible, feeble and omnipotent. Everything exists in her at all times. She knows neither past nor future. The present is her eternity. She is good. I praise her and all her works. She is wise and serene. No explanation can be wrung from her, there is no gift which she does not willingly give. She is cunning, but to good purpose, and it is best not to see her cunning.

'She is whole and yet always incomplete. What she does she can always do.

'To every man she appears in a form of her own. She lies hidden in a thousand names and a thousand terms and yet always remains the same.

'She has put me here. She will also take me hence. I trust her. She can lead me as she likes. She will not hate her handiwork. It is I who have spoken of her. No, it is she who has spoken both the true and the false. Everything is her fault, everything is her merit.' [1]

[1] *Über die Natur,* in Wittels: 'Freud und Goethe, Psychoanalytische Bewegung', II, Jahrgang 1930, pp. 430–66.

3

BEGINNINGS OF FREUD'S MEDICAL CAREER

Because of the contradictory forces driving him towards medicine and, at the same time, away from its normal goal—medical practice—Freud nearly became an eternal student and a wash-out, as his fellow-student jokingly described him. Although he was poor and knew he would have to earn his living he was in no particular hurry to obtain his degree and he dragged out his studies for eight years. The one thing of which he seems to have been sure was that he wanted, at all costs, to avoid having to practice. Why, then, did he take up medicine?

He would undoubtedly have explained his shifts and evasions by a little Jewish story which he liked to quote in support of his intuitions: 'Where are you going, Izzy' 'I don't know. Ask my horse.' Perhaps he did not know what led him, from the very first year in his medical studies, to disperse his efforts so that they extended to zoology, chemistry, botany, mineralogy and even to other subjects—but his horse knew.

One of the courses which Freud followed—although there was scarcely any practical reason for his doing so—was that given by the philosopher Franz Brentano, whose brilliant lectures drew all Vienna at the time. Once a week, for nearly three years, he attended these lectures. The only reasonable explanation is that he wanted to, since compulsory attendance at philosophy lectures had just been abolished for medical students in Vienna. In 1876 he even went to three series of lectures which Brentano gave on Aristotle and that was at a time when his other studies were taking up all his time. It was on Brentano's recommendation that, a little later, he got the job of translating a work by the philosopher John Stuart Mill—another occupation which had no connection whatsoever with his own studies.

Brentano's lectures were Freud's only direct contact with the philosophy of his day. What did he get from them which may have permanently influenced his thought?

Brentano enjoyed considerable notoriety at the time. He advanced new ideas in psychology which brought him into conflict with Theodor Fechner, who held that sensations were the result of measurable stimuli and could therefore be calculated according to a formula. Brentano based his psychology on a division of psychical life into three distinct sectors—representations, affective movements, judgements—of which only the latter was responsible for ethical knowledge and consequently for a person's moral conduct. It may be worth noting that this so-called 'descriptive' psychology made a deep impression on the mind of the young Franz Kafka who, in his day, assiduously attended the lectures given by Brentano's followers in Prague. It would be rash to try to say just how much it influenced Freud's subsequent conception of the psychical apparatus, since Freud never mentioned Brentano as one of the teachers to whom he felt indebted. It may possibly have helped him not to overcome, but to moderate the fanatical materialism which characterized him at the beginning of his university life. We know that this change did occur, from what Freud says about it in *The Interpretation of Dreams,* although he made no attempt to explain the reason for it. He merely emphasized that he once defended his materialistic views with unusual vehemence during a student discussion in which, ironically enough, his opponent was Victor Adler, the future leader of the Social Democrats in Vienna. Freud remembered the incident vividly because, for the first and last time in his life, it almost ended in a duel:

'There was a discussion in a *German* students' club on the relation of philosophy to the natural sciences. I was a green youngster, full of materialistic theories, and thrust myself forward to give expression to an extremely one-sided point of view. Thereupon someone who was my senior and my superior, someone who has since then shown his ability as a leader of men and an organizer of large groups (and who also, incidentally, bears a name derived from the Animal Kingdom), stood up and gave us a good talking-to: he too, he told us, had fed swine in his youth and returned repentant to his father's house. *I fired up* (as I did in the dream) and replied boorishly (*"saugrob"*, literally "swinishly gross") that since I now knew that he had fed swine in his youth I was no longer *surprised* at the tone of his speeches. (In the dream I was *surprised* at my

German-nationalist attitude.) There was a general uproar and I was called upon from many sides to withdraw my remarks, but I refused to do so. The man I had insulted was too sensible to look upon the incident as a *challenge,* and let the affair drop. . . .'[1]

Clearly, Freud's intellectual development was not plain sailing. After first being inspired by Goethe's pantheistic dithyramb on Nature and, presumably, by the monist and mystical speculations of the *Naturphilosophie,* he went through a period of rather narrow materialism, like many other young people at the end of the century who considered experimental science to be a guarantee of honesty. Once over this phase of fanatical materialism, he underwent the influence of those who were then his teachers—and some of them were strong personalities—without, however, discovering or even suspecting what was the right road for him to follow. With a voracious appetite for knowledge, great ambition, a need to bow to some form of authority and, at the same time, to retain his freedom, Freud was not too sure which direction to take. His curiosity was boundless, everything attracted him, even disciplines for which he felt he had no talent, such as biology and chemistry, at which he was hopeless. Later, the memory of these adventurous studies visibly caused him a certain uneasiness. He no doubt saw them as a sort of dilettantism, although his first original works are remarkably free of this. Or he saw them as a mark of typical Viennese muddle, that *Schlamperei* to which he knew he was prone. That is why he was so grateful to the first teacher who made him stick at a definite and specific task and guided his thinking.

Freud regarded Ernst Brücke—to whom, to use his own words, he 'stuck like glue' for six years—as the 'greatest authority he had ever met'. The old professor lectured at the University and directed the Institute of Physiology, which Freud entered in 1876, after he had been a student for three years. Brücke was a scientist on the grand scale and an altogether remarkable man. Ernest Jones depicts him as a shy man with a Berlin accent, a large and expressive head, a Prussian sense of order and with 'terrible blue eyes' which still haunted Freud's dreams twenty years later:

[1] *The Interpretation of Dreams, Std Edn* IV, pp. 212–3.

'A conscientious and indefatigable worker himself, he exacted the same standard from his assistants and students. Here is a typical anecdote. A student who in one of his papers had written: "Superficial observation reveals . . ." had his paper returned with the objectionable line violently crossed out and Brücke's comment on the margin: "One is not to observe superficially. . . ." But this man was completely free of vanity, intrigue, and lust for power. To the student who proved his ability he was a most benevolent father, extending counsel and protection far beyond scientific matters. He respected the student's own ideas, encouraged original work, and sponsored talents even if they deviated considerably from his own opinions. It is said that no pupil or friend ever became unfaithful to him. . . .'[1]

The history of the scientific movement represented by Brücke, Du Bois-Reymond and Helmholtz, the most famous of them all, is worth recalling. Between 1840 and 1845 the three men had formed a small group which a little later became 'The Berlin Physics Society'. They are said to have remained in very close touch all their lives and to have kept the promise they made to one another to ensure that what Du Bois-Reymond somewhat pathetically called 'the truth' should triumph:

'Brücke and I pledged a solemn oath to put into effect the truth: "No other forces than the common physical-chemical ones are active within the organism. In those cases which cannot at the time be explained by these forces one has either to find the specific way or form of their action by means of the physical-mathematical method or to assume new forces equal in dignity to the chemical-physical forces inherent in matter, reducible to the force of attraction and repulsion".'[2]

The solemn pledge to see that truth should triumph, the ideal of absolute intellectual integrity, the sort of self-discipline honoured by the Helmholtz school, all these denote a passion for science, an enthusiasm and a self-denial which came very near to being a religious faith. There can be no doubt that Freud's youthful fervour originated in this faith, which took the place of the old beliefs, and that, in spite of the heresy for which he was later responsible, he retained it all his life. That was his strength, for science

[1] Ernest Jones, I, p. 44.

[2] *Ibid.*, pp. 40–1.

always remained for him the supreme authority, the only one to which he felt responsible: it may also have been a weakness, or at the very best a reason why his discoveries came so slowly.

Be that as it may, it was in Brücke's laboratory that Freud first felt himself in possession of his scientific powers and, what is to his master's great credit, was able to enjoy an inner calm, which he had hardly known during his first years at the University. The University had, in fact, disappointed and damaged him for reasons which he analysed very clearly in his autobiography:

'When, in 1873, I first joined the University, I experienced some appreciable disappointments. Above all, I found that I was expected to feel myself inferior and an alien because I was a Jew. I refused absolutely to do the first of these things. I have never been able to see why I should feel ashamed of my descent or, as people were beginning to say, of my "race". I put up, without much regret, with my non-acceptance into the community; for it seemed to me that in spite of this exclusion an active fellow-worker could not fail to find some nook or cranny in the framework of humanity. These first impressions at the University, however, had one consequence which was afterwards to prove important; for at an early age I was made familiar with the fate of being in the Opposition and of being put under the ban of the "compact majority". The foundations were thus laid for a certain degree of independence of judgement.' [1]

And Freud concluded with a tribute to his old teacher who had succeeded in putting an end to his early scientific confusion and to the discrimination of which he had been a victim:

'I was compelled, moreover, during my first years at the University, to make the discovery that the peculiarities and limitations of my gifts denied me all success in many of the departments of science into which my youthful eagerness had plunged me. Thus I learned the truth of Mephistopheles' warning:

'Vergebens, dass ihr ringsum wissenschaftlich schweift,
Ein jeder lernt nur, was er lernen kann.[2]

'At length, in Ernst Brücke's physiological laboratory, I

[1] *An Autobiographical Study, Std Edn* XX, p. 9.

[2] 'It is in vain that you range around from science to science: each man learns only what he can learn.'—*Faust,* Part I.

found rest and satisfaction—and men, too, whom I could respect and take as my models.'[1]

Apart from Brücke, the people to whom Freud is referring here were his two assistants at the Institute of Physiology, Sigmund Exner and Ernst von Fleischl-Marxow. Exner, who was to succeed his master in the Chair of Physiology, was a scientist of stature whom Freud admired without, however, liking. But from the very first he sought the friendship of Fleischl-Marxow, an extremely brilliant, handsome and original young man with a fascinating personality. This refined, highly gifted aristocrat was a figure one would never have associated with the horrible fate that was to be his. At the age of twenty-five he had contracted a serious infection while doing research in pathological anatomy. His right thumb had to be amputated and ever since he had suffered from continued growth of neuromas, which necessitated a whole series of operations. His existence was no more than a slow death plagued by intolerable pain. For reasons which we shall have to come back to his death was a terrible blow to Freud.

Ernst von Fleischl-Marxow appears more than once in *The Interpretation of Dreams* and the reason becomes plain when we read one of Freud's letters to his fiancée in which he speaks of his friend whom he saw, with an envy of which he was most conscious, as the incarnation of the ideal human being:

'Yesterday I went to see my friend, Ernst v. Fleischl, whom hitherto, so long as I did not know Marty, I envied in every respect. But now I have an advantage over him. I believe he has been engaged for 10 or 12 years to a girl of his own age, who was prepared to wait for him indefinitely, but with whom he has now fallen out, for reasons unknown to me. He is a thoroughly excellent person in whom natute and education have combined to do their best. Wealthy, skilled in all games and sports, with the stamp of genius in his manly features, good-looking, refined, endowed with many talents and capable of forming an original judgement about most things, he has always been my ideal and I was not satisfied until we became friends and I could properly enjoy his value and abilities. On this occasion I brought him a criticism of a pamphlet by him, he taught me the Japanese game "Go" and as-

[1] *An Autobiographical Study, Std Edn* XX, p. 9.

tounded me with the news that he was learning Sanskrit.'[1]

This letter, with its portrait of Fleischl, ends on a note of violent jealousy. In the presence of his friend Freud felt himself to be poor, dependent and without any future except one he might carve out by force from a hostile society. If he, too, had to make his fiancée wait, it was not for higher reasons, but because his extreme poverty prevented him from setting up a home. It must be noted, however, that his outlook was that of his age, which saw nothing extraordinary in a young woman being engaged for twelve years before getting married.

Freud used to say that his two years with Brücke had been the best years of his youth. In any case they were years of hard work during which he acquired sound scientific principles and began to give his research a more personal direction. The result was three papers—two on nerve roots and the spinal ganglions of the petromyzon,[2] the third on the nerve cells of the crayfish—all of them published in the *Bulletin* of the Academy of Science. During this period his most original contribution to the histology of the nerve cell was an improved method of preparing nervous tissue for examination, then the discovery of a new procedure, the use of gold chloride to colour tissues. These two procedures made little stir outside the Vienna Institute. But specialists declare that his first papers show clearly that Freud was already on the way to a great discovery—that of the neurone theory which was made shortly afterwards. Thus, even as a young man, he nearly gave his name to a major discovery. And this happened a second time when, a few years later, he almost achieved fame with his work on cocaine.

Freud finally passed his medical examinations, perhaps to follow the example of all the physiologists in the Institute who were doctors and had sometimes practised. He took his first examination in 1880, although two years before he was still writing to a friend that, faced with the alternative of 'skinning animals or torturing people',[3] he had chosen the first course. Did the cruelty which is unavoidable in medicine in the end have something to do with his aversion? The fact is, it was alien to his nature

[1] To Martha Bernays, June 27, 1882, *Letters*, pp. 11–12.

[2] *Über Spinalganglien und Rückenmark des Petromyzon*, a paper read to the Academy of Science, Vienna, 1877.

[3] To W. Knöpfmacher, August 6, 1878, *Letters*, p. 7.

and he showed this by inventing a method of treatment based on the principle of the physician's benevolent neutrality rather than his active intervention.

Bearing in mind the close links between psychoanalysis and guilt and punishment, it is amusing to remember that the only examination Freud ever failed was in forensic medicine. Apart from that he gained his diploma with ease and found himself with the title of doctor without, however, having lost any of his uncertainty. At first the diploma made no difference to his programme. He continued to work at Brücke's Institute, apparently without making any plan or perhaps secretly hoping he would one day succeed Brücke in the Chair of Physiology. But his hopes were dashed by an event which completely changed the whole course of his life:

'The turning-point came in 1882, when my teacher, for whom I felt the highest possible esteem, corrected my father's generous improvidence by strongly advising me, in view of my bad financial position, to abandon my theoretical career. I followed his advice, left the physiological laboratory and entered the General Hospital. . . .'[1]

It must be admitted that Freud's explanation is not altogether convincing. Who will in fact believe that he did not know how precarious his circumstances were and that someone else had to remind him of this? Theoretical research in those days was the privilege of moneyed people and it was not a matter of chance that the poor scholar, a popular theme at the time, was everywhere looked on as something of a hero, even a martyr. Freud could only reckon on his father's help, but his father was old. After 1873 he had lost all his remaining money in a financial crash and often had to borrow to keep his large family from starving. It is unlikely that Freud did not take this situation into account in his plans for the future. Why then did Brücke's warning suddenly take on such importance?

The reason is undoubtedly that it brought Freud face to face with a sad truth. Brücke's two assistants were young, and even if Fleischl, doomed to a premature death, was not a serious competitor, there remained Sigmund Exner, who would normally have succeeded his master. In these circumstances any hope of obtaining the Chair of Physiology was more or less an illusion. Much later Freud was to

[1] *An Autobiographical Study, Std Edn* XX, p. 10.

contratulate himself on not having clung to this hope. In fact he was sixty-nine before Brücke's Chair finally fell vacant and he could officially have had it.

But there was a further reason for his docile acceptance of Brücke's advice and for the abruptness of his decision. He had fallen madly in love and, three months after making the girl's acquaintance, he secretly became engaged. Now, getting established was no longer something abstract. He had to solve the problem in a practical way and this was only possible if he practised his profession. But nowhere in his autobiography does Freud tell us that this was the real reason for his volte-face. No doubt he found it painful to admit that in his youth the passion of love had once, at least, triumphed over intellectual passion.

There will be much to say about Freud's passionate engagement, which lasted five years and brought him both unexpected happiness and much suffering. The two young people had, in fact, to part shortly after their secret engagement and their relationship was reduced almost entirely to a flow of anxious letters, which they exchanged to damp their impatience. Freud's letters have been preserved. It will be seen that apart from their unequalled value for the understanding of his subsequent work, they still deserve to take a place in literature along with the finest love letters.

Having resigned himself to the inevitability of medicine out of love and, as he said, 'with an ever-growing heaviness of heart', Freud came up against a new difficulty. His research had been no real preparation for actual practice. Certain branches of medicine were a closed book to him and, in general, he lacked any clinical knowledge. He decided, therefore, to spend more time in a hospital to remedy this and to experience direct contact with the sick. On July 31, 1882 he inscribed himself in the General Hospital of Vienna, where he worked for three years.

After doing a period of general medicine, which once more convinced him that he was not born to be a doctor, he transferred to Meynert's Psychiatric Clinic, where he was immediately appointed a house-surgeon. Freud speaks of his new chief, whose lectures were the only ones he had found interesting when he was a student, as 'the great Meynert in whose footsteps I followed with such veneration.' Freud spent nearly five months with him and it was a period of great importance since it was the only purely psychiatric experience he had. It was while he was with Meynert that Freud, for the first time, seriously devoted himself to one branch of medicine. Neurology gradually became his speciality, and he began to show an interest in psychiatry, thus approaching the field of activity which was to become his own. But Freud's quest, which gave the pre-psychoanalytical period its rather adventurous character, was not at an end. If Freud was really a seeker, the thing he was seeking was fundamentally science itself, a science able to broaden the medical thinking of his time, which he considered to be narrow and no more than moderately effective. Before successfully establishing his own, he kept on looking for new methods of treatment by which he hoped to escape from the depressing inaction which was far too often the doctor's, and especially the neurologist's lot. This anxiety for therapeutic efficiency was at the root of the cocaine affair, which, this time, took him right outside the field in which he was working. He first mentioned the drug in 1884 in a letter to Martha:

'I am also toying now with a project and a hope which I will tell you about; perhaps nothing will come of this, either. It is a therapeutic experiment. I have been reading about cocaine, the effective ingredient of coca leaves, which some Indian tribes chew in order to make themselves resistant to privation and fatigue. A German has tested this stuff on soldiers and reported that it has really rendered them strong and capable of endurance. I have now ordered some of it and for obvious reasons am going to try it out on cases of heart disease, then on nervous exhaustion, particularly in the awful condition following withdrawal of morphine (as in the case of Dr Fleischl). There may be any number of other people experimenting on it already, perhaps it won't work. But I am certainly going to try it and, as you know, if one tries something often enough and goes on wanting it, one day it may succeed. We need no more than one stroke of luck of this kind to consider setting up house. But, my little woman, do not be too convinced that it will come off this time. As you know, an explorer's temperament requires two basic qualities: optimism in attempt, criticism in work. . . .'[1]

Freud tried cocaine successfully on himself and the result far exceeded his expectation. All his letters at the time spoke of the drug with an enthusiasm which was not often to appear again in his writing:

[1] To Martha Bernays, April 21, 1884, *Letters*, pp. 107–8.

'If it goes well I will write an essay on it and I expect it will win its place in therapeutics, by the side of morphia and superior to it. I have other hopes and intentions about it. I take very small doses of it regularly against depression and against indigestion, and with the most brilliant success. I hope it will be able to abolish the most intractable vomiting, even when this is due to severe pain; in short it is only now that I feel I am a doctor. . . . If things go on in this way we need have no concern about being able to come together and to stay in Vienna. . . .'[1]

Here, once more, are the two obsessions which haunted Freud during this difficult period, to find an efficacious therapy and, by means of this, to earn enough to marry and live decently. This double preoccupation, together with the state of euphoria induced by cocaine, certainly did much to lull his sense of caution. He wrote his article, an essay remarkable for its brilliant literary qualities, but above all he spoke in defence of the drug and distributed it freely with the zeal of a propagandist, without ever in the least suspecting its disadvantages. Blinded by his need for haste, Freud saw in cocaine what he wanted to find—a cure for suffering. Scientifically speaking, the irresponsibility he showed in this matter is not altogether inexplicable: the history of pharmacology has provided similar examples in the past and even today would still provide many others. Morally, at any rate, it had distressing consequences for Freud.

The first was the set-back to his research. Freud had, in fact, confined himself exclusively to studying the analgesic effects of cocaine and, therefore, its internal use, but ignoring its anaesthetic properties which, we now know, constitute its only real value. In his article he had, it is true, indicated this aspect of research and had even spoken about it in the presence of Koller, the man who actually used cocaine as a local anaesthetic and, as a result, won all the fame. But Freud had never pursued this line to its end and this greatly troubled him as he could, up to a point, reproach himself with dilettantism.

We can imagine his feelings about the tremendous sensation which Koller's discovery created in the world. His disappointment was certainly very bitter and many years later he let something of it colour the rather tendentious version he gave of the affair:

[1] Letter to Martha Bernays, May 25, 1884, Ernest Jones, I, p. 81.

'. . . It was the fault of my *fiancée* that I was not already famous at that early age. A side interest, though it was a deep one, had led me in 1884 to obtain from Merck some of what was then the little-known alkaloid cocaine and to study its physiological action. While I was in the middle of this work, an opportunity arose for making a journey to visit my *fiancée,* from whom I had been parted for two years. I hastily wound up my investigation of cocaine and contented myself in my book on the subject with prophesying that further uses for it would soon be found. I suggested, however, to my friend Königstein, the ophthalmologist, that he should investigate the question of how far the anaesthetizing properties of cocaine were applicable in diseases of the eye. When I returned from my holiday I found that not he, but another of my friends, Carl Koller (now in New York), whom I had also spoken to about cocaine, had made the decisive experiments upon animals' eyes and had demonstrated them at the Ophthalmological Congress at Heidelberg. Koller is therefore rightly regarded as the discoverer of local anaesthesia by cocaine, which has become so important in minor surgery; but I bore my *fiancée* no grudge for her interruption of my work. . . .'[1]

Infuriating as it was for Freud, the cocaine affair did not, however, damage his scientific reputation. After all, he had played the role of forerunner by boldly launching a treatment about which little was known at the time. Against that was the fact that it involved his moral responsibility and that was the sphere in which it must have affected him most of all. From 1884, in fact, he had widely prescribed the new alkaloid, had used it extensively in his immediate circle and, in particular, had induced his friend Fleischl to take it regularly as a treatment for morphine poisoning. The consequences were those which are known today. Freud had not foreseen them and he was all the more shattered as they affected not an ordinary person but someone quite exceptional, the friend of whom he said: 'I admire and love him with an intellectual passion, if I may so express myself. His going[2] will affect me as the destruction of a sacred temple would have affected an

[1] *An Autobiographical Study, Std Edn* XX, p. 14.

[2] It was obvious that Fleischl's incurable disease would end in his early death.

Ancient Greek. What I love in him is not so much the human being as an unparalleled example of creation. . . .'

Freud watched this man, whose life was so dear to him, wage day after day an unremitting fight against suffering and deterioration. Sincerely convinced of the virtues of cocaine, he gave his friend the new remedy which, at first, seemed to be successful. But gradually things got worse, the drug no longer afforded any relief, Fleischl increased the doses but the symptoms recurred with increasing severity. The failure of the treatment was obvious and cocaine now added to the sick man's torment by causing attacks of delirium tremens which Freud witnessed with something like terror. He thought that whatever might happen later, he would never experience anything more horrible than the nights he spent at his friend's bedside.

Of course, cocaine did not kill Fleischl. It did not even hasten his end, since the unhappy scientist's agony went on for another six long years. But attention was drawn to the drug and in 1886 numerous cases of cocaine poisoning led to a violent outcry in Germany. Opinion was undoubtedly divided. Some people regarded the suspect alkaloid as the third scourge of humanity, others attacked Freud while praising the literary quality of his article. And one famous writer [1] rallied to Freud's support, as so many others did later. But public opinion remained severely critical. The man who advocated cocaine was looked on as a criminal, and Freud probably held much the same view. This unhappy affair provoked a veritable crisis in his life, as is proved by one of his best-known dreams [2] which is full of allusions to injections and poisonous substances. If it did not seriously discredit him socially, it did at least affect his reputation in scientific circles. And the affair was not forgotten. When Freud returned from Paris a few months later as an enthusiastic champion of Charcot's new ideas on hysteria, the Viennese doctors treated him as a charlatan or derided him. And Vienna fell into the habit of thinking of him as a disgrace.

[1] Arthur Schnitzler, novelist and doctor, who defended Freud against the detractors of cocaine, *Internationale klinische Rundschau,* 1888, Vol. III, p. 23. Schnitzler was the most famous Austrian author and a friend of Freud. He kept in touch with him all his life.

[2] The dream about Irma's injection, *The Interpretation of Dreams, Std Edn* VI, pp. 106 ff.

4

FREUD AND CHARCOT

From the beginning of his medical career, Freud had dreamed of obtaining the title of *Privatdozent*. This has no exact equivalent in England. A *Privatdozent* is not entitled to attend faculty meetings, nor does he receive a salary, but he is allowed to hold a certain number of classes, usually on topics outside the regular curriculum. This distinction, much sought after in Austria as well as in Germany and Central Europe, was essential to anyone wanting to make himself a University career. Freud wrote a thesis about work he was doing on the anatomy of the marrow and submitted his application in January 1885 to a board composed of his former teachers. His application was supported by Brücke who ended his report with a glowing description of the young research worker:

'Dr Freud is a man with a good general education, of quiet and serious character, an excellent worker in the field of neuro-anatomy, of fine dexterity, clear vision, comprehensive knowledge, and a cautious method of deduction, with the gift for well-organized written expression. His findings enjoy recognition and confirmation, his style of lecturing is transparent and secure. In him the qualities of a scientific researcher and of a well-qualified teacher are so well united that the Committee submits the suggestion that the Honorable College resolve on his admission to the further habilitation tests.' [1]

And so Freud became a *Privatdozent* in neurology, but for the time being it made hardly any difference to his circumstances. He had left Meynert's Clinic, all his efforts to secure a post as an assistant with an adequate salary had failed and as he was still impoverished he accepted a job as *locum tenens* in a private psychiatric establishment in the suburbs. There he was fed and he earned a hundred

[1] Ernest Jones, I, p. 80.

florins a month. He liked the place, its atmosphere was courteous and pleasant and, as in all such establishments in those days, the so-called medical work was non-existent:

'The medical treatment is of course negligible, confined to their secondary surgical and internal complaints; the rest consists of supervision, nursing, diet, and non-interference. The kitchen of course is in the (big) house. The mildest cases lunch with the director, the doctor and the inspector. Needless to say, they are all rich people: counts, countesses, barons, etc. The *pièces de résistance* are two Highnesses, Prince S. and Prince M. The latter, as you may remember, is a son of Marie Louise, wife of Napoleon, and thus, like our Emperor, a grandson of Emperor Franz. You cannot imagine how dilapidated these princes and counts look, although they are not actually feeble-minded, rather a mixture of feeble-minded and eccentric. . . .'[1]

Freud might have resigned himself to spending the rest of his life in this distinguished establishment, looking after a few incurable aristocrats. But something happened which saved him from having to give this prospect his serious consideration. This was the award of a scholarship which, more than he realized at the time, was to change the whole course of his plans.

This scholarship, given by the Ministry for post-graduate study abroad, was worth 600 florins. Freud would be able to use it as he liked and it would enable him to realize one of his most cherished dreams, which was to go to Paris, learn about French science and return to Vienna with some of the prestige which French science enjoyed in the world at large. He therefore decided to try his luck and began to look round for patrons, a move which was indispensable in a country where everything was done by favouritism. His case was hotly discussed, there were two other candidates and, as time went by, Freud believed less and less in his chances of success. He dreamed every night about the scholarship which he thought would help him to win fame and hasten the day when he could marry. At last, after a month in which he was torn by alternating hope and uncertainty, he was able to share his triumph with his fiancée:

[1] To Martha Bernays, June 8, 1885, *Letters*, p. 151.

'Oh, how wonderful it will be! I am coming with money and staying a long time and bringing something beautiful for you and then go on to Paris and become a great scholar and then come back to Vienna with a huge, enormous halo, and then we will soon be married, and I will cure all the incurable nervous cases and through you I shall be healthy and I will go on kissing you till you are strong and gay and happy. . . .'[1]

This prophecy, dictated to Freud by his desire, had a happy ending, except on one score: fame was to keep him waiting a long time yet, and what was brewing in the historic rooms of the Salpêtrière was not the comfortable career of a successful doctor, but the uproar and the scandal over hysteria which drove him to become a revolutionary and left him more solitary than ever.

Freud arrived in Paris in October 1885, after having spent six weeks with his fiancée at Wandsbeck. The beginning of his stay was not very happy. He found the French capital bewildering, the Parisians rather intimidating. He was ashamed of his bad French and, above all, he was terrified at the cost of living. His scholarship, in fact, was not enough to cover his expenses and then, living with the utmost frugality, he once more ran into debt. A feeling of isolation, money worries, the thought of his family, which he had left in such appalling poverty in Vienna that one of his sisters had to take a job as a nurse-maid, all ruined his first days in Paris—something which he had certainly forgotten when, much later, in *The Interpretation of Dreams* he wrote: 'Paris had been for many years the goal of my longings, and the bliss with which I first set foot on its pavements I took as a guarantee that I should attain the fulfillment of other wishes also.'

There is, in fact, hardly any sign of this bliss in his first letters. On the contrary, Paris angered him, the luxury and extravagance of the beautiful and elegant districts provoked in him the reaction of a poor man, as he shows in an otherwise well-observed description of a walk down the Champs-Elysées:

'Elegant ladies walk here with expressions suggesting that they deny the existence in this world of anyone but themselves and their husbands or are at least graciously trying

[1] To Martha Bernays, June 20, 1885, *Letters,* p. 154.

to ignore it; one side of the avenue is formed by an extensive park in which the prettiest children spin their tops, ride on merry-go-rounds, watch the Punch-&-Judy show, or drive themselves about in little carriages drawn by goats. On the benches sit wet-nurses feeding their babies, and nursemaids to whom the children dash screaming after they have had a quarrel. I couldn't help thinking of poor Mitzi and grew very, very furious and full of revolutionary thoughts. . . .'[1]

But Freud did not go to France just to add to the literature about Paris, although he did so with much talent in many of his letters. His objective was the Salpêtrière, where he went on October 21st and found everything better than he had expected. He was given the key to a set of pigeon holes in the laboratory, an overall against a deposit of three francs and a receipt made out to 'Herr Freud, medical student'. The same day he had the pleasure of meeting Charcot and immediately described the great man for Martha's benefit:

'At 10 o'clock M. Charcot arrived, a tall man of 58, wearing a top hat, with dark, strangely soft eyes (or rather one is, the other is expressionless and has an inward cast), long wisps of hair stuck behind his ears, clean shaven, very expressive features with full protruding lips—in short, like a worldly priest from whom one expects a ready wit and an appreciation of good living. . . .'[2]

Apart from the top hat, the similarity between Charcot as seen by Freud and the Charcot of popular photographs is striking. The meeting of these two men who were so very different, the one world famous and at the height of his powers, the other obscure and feeling his way towards a goal of which he as yet knew nothing, was to mark a turning point in the history of scientific thought. The meeting made an extraordinary impression on Freud, who had a vague presentiment of the consequences it would have for his work:

'I am really very comfortably installed now and I think I am changing a great deal. I will tell you in detail what is

[1] To Martha Bernays, October 19, 1885, *Letters,* pp. 172–3.

[2] To Martha Bernays, October 21, 1885, *ibid.,* p. 175.

affecting me. Charcot, who is one of the greatest of physicians and a man whose common sense borders on genius, is simply wrecking all my aims and opinions. I sometimes come out of his lectures as from out of Notre-Dame, with an entirely new idea about perfection. But he exhausts me; when I come away from him I no longer have any desire to work at my own silly things; it is three whole days since I have done any work, and I have no feelings of guilt. My brain is sated as after an evening in the theatre. Whether the seed will ever bear any fruit, I don't know; but what I do know is that no other human being has ever affected me in the same way. . . .'[1]

Charcot greeted the young foreigner with great courtesy, shaking him by the hand and bidding him welcome. Freud commented: 'Despite my feeling for independence I was very proud of this mark of attention, since he is not only a man to whom I have to be subordinate, but a man to whom I am gladly so. . . .'[2] Freud reveals a great deal about himself in his relations with Charcot and the Paris medical world and, for the first time, he no longer felt he was being treated as an intruder, as he felt in Vienna, but as a free man who is not going to be asked where he comes from. That he should be so moved by the friendly hand-shake of a leading authority speaks volumes for the way he was treated at home. In Paris he became aware of his inferior status, his lack of self-confidence, his instinctive distrust of other people and of the strange contrast between his intellectual courage and his social timidity. In his long daily letters to Martha he devoted most space to this attempt at analysis, which he was to pursue blindly for some years, up to the time when dreams furnished him with an unsuspected means of self-knowledge. For the moment he referred to his poverty, the slowness of his progress, his lack of charm, his hyper-sensitiveness and his nervousness. With a lucidity which was devoid of all complacency, he described himself time and time again as being torn between the feelings of an outcast and the ambitions of a self-made man, yet refusing to yield one way or the other and having already chosen at heart what was to be the only way by which he could attain success: effort, hardship and unremitting intellectual labour.

[1] To Martha Bernays, November 24, 1885, ibid., pp. 184–5.
[2] Ernest Jones, I, p. 185.

Weighing up his difficulties and his chances, he asked his fiancée:

'Do you really find my appearance so attractive? Well, this I very much doubt. I believe people see something alien in me and the real reason for this is that in my youth I was never young and now that I am entering the age of maturity I cannot mature properly. There was a time when I was all ambition and eager to learn, when day after day I felt aggrieved that Nature in a benevolent mood hadn't stamped my face with that mark of genius which now and again she bestows on men. Now for a long time I have known that I am not a genius and cannot understand how I ever could have wanted to be one. I am not even very gifted; my whole capacity for work probably springs from my character and from the absence of outstanding intellectual weaknesses. But I know that this combination is very conducive to slow success, and that given favourable conditions I could achieve more than Nothnagel, to whom I consider myself superior, and might possibly reach the level of Charcot. By which I don't mean to say that I will get as far as that, for these favourable conditions no longer come my way, and I don't possess the genius, the power, to bring them about. Oh, how I run on! I really wanted to say something quite different. I wanted to explain the reason for my inaccessibility to and gruffness with strangers, which you mentioned. It is simply the result of suspicion due to my having learned that common or bad people treat me badly, but this is bound to disappear to the extent to which I grow stronger and more independent, and don't have to fear them any more. I always comfort myself with the fact that people subordinate to or on a par with me have never considered me unpleasant, only superiors or people otherwise above me. . . .'[1]

Paris, then, affected Freud in opposite ways. On the one hand he felt lonely, poor, awkward in a provincial way among a crowd which he found disconcerting, evil and capable, at any moment, of dangerous outbursts: on the other the city fascinated him, forced him to come out of his shell and take up outside interests. This man, who had never before so much as discussed politics, took a keen interest in the electoral fight, the party groupings which that year excited Parisian passions. He walked a lot, observed

[1] To Martha Bernays, February 2, 1886, ibid., p. 202.

everything with great shrewdness and humour, spent a fortune on theatres and wrote about Sarah Bernhardt with emotion, irony and great lyrical feeling. In a word, as he realized, Paris both scared and inspired him:

'I am under the full impact of Paris and, waxing very poetical, could compare it to a vast overdressed Sphinx who gobbles up every foreigner unable to solve her riddles. But I will save all this for verbal effusions. Suffice it to say that the city and its inhabitants strike me as uncanny; the people seem to me of a different species from ourselves; I feel they are all possessed of a thousand demons; instead of "Monsieur" and "Voilà l'Echo de Paris" I hear them yelling "A la lanterne" and "A bas" this man and that. I don't think they know the meaning of shame or fear; the women no less than the men crowd round nudities as much as they do round corpses in the morgue or the ghastly posters in the streets announcing a new novel in this or that newspaper and simultaneously showing a sample of its content. They are people given to psychical epidemics, historical mass convulsions and they haven't changed since Victor Hugo wrote *Notre-Dame*. . . . As you realise, my heart is German provincial, and it hasn't accompanied me here. . . . Paris is simply one long confused dream, and I shall be very glad to wake up. . . .'[1]

At other times Freud thought very differently about Paris life—he only needed to emerge from his dejection, overcome his shyness or win some small success. Thus he was very proud of having had the temerity to ask Charcot's permission to translate one of his books and when the latter invited him to one of his soirées he felt elated. The first one bored him, the third delighted him and, he said, fired him with enthusiasm. Some fifty people were there, artists, French and foreign medical celebrities, one of Alphonse Daudet's sons, Mlle. Charcot, who was almost ridiculously like her brilliant father and with whom, for that reason no doubt, he fell a little in love:

'And now you will be anxious to know how I fared in this distinguished company. Very well. I approached Lépine, whose work I knew and had a long conversation with him,

[1] Letter to Minna Bernays, his future sister-in-law, December 3, 1885, ibid., pp. 187–8.

then I talked to Strauss and Giles de la Tourette and accepted a cup of coffee from Mme. Charcot, later on I drank beer, smoked like a chimney, and felt very much at ease without the slightest mishap occurring. . . .'[1]

Freud's letters would provide excellent raw material for a little chronicle of the French medical upper class which the young foreigner admired not only for its scientific brilliance, but also for its urbanity, its humanism and its especial gift for combining refinement with a genuinely democratic spirit. Freud describes, vividly and affectionately, the great doctors he met at the Salpêtrière and at Charcot's home—Babinski, Brouardel, Richet, the great histologist Ranvier, the famous psychiatrist Giles de la Tourette, all the celebrities in the world of science whose simplicity and naturalness fascinated him. Shortly after he left Paris, in February 1886, Freud wrote to his fiancée that he would die if he had to return to Vienna straight away. But within a short time of arriving in Berlin he exclaimed, parodying Schiller: 'How different it was in France.'[2]

Freud left Paris on February 23, 1886. He was to go back three times—in 1889, after his visit to Nancy; in 1910, for a psychoanalytical congress; and in 1938, when he left Vienna to escape from the Nazis. But he never saw Charcot again.

Freud has left an admirable document about his scientific work in Paris and the profound influence which the Salpêtrière had on his later development. It is the neurological paper which he wrote about Charcot in 1893 and in which, breaking the conventions usual in this sort of composition, he paid the Master a tribute glowing with intelligence and truth. This article, one of the finest of his pre-psychoanalytical period, deserves to be quoted almost in entirety, as it throws so much light on Freud's attitude to science:

'He took an honest, human delight in his own great success and used to enjoy talking of his beginnings and the road he had travelled. His scientific curiosity, he said, had been aroused early, when he was still a young *interne,* by the mass of material presented by the facts of neuropa-

[1] To Martha Bernays, January 20, 1886, ibid., p. 196.

[2] Letter to Martha Bernays, March 19, 1886, ibid., p. 214.

thology, material which was not in the least understood at the time. In those days, whenever he went the rounds with his senior in one of the departments of the Salpêtrière (the institution for the care of women) amid all the wilderness of paralyses, spasms and convulsions for which forty years ago there was neither name nor understanding, he would say: *"Faudrait y retourner et y rester"*, and he kept his word. When he became *médecin des hôpitaux,* he at once took steps to enter the Salpêtrière in one of the departments for nervous patients. Having got there, he stayed where he was instead of doing what French senior physicians are entitled to do—transferring in regular succession from one department to another and from hospital to hospital, and at the same time changing their speciality as well.

'Thus his first impression and the resolution it led him to were decisive for the whole of his further development. His having a great number of chronic nervous patients at his disposal enabled him to make use of his own special gifts. He was not a reflective man, not a thinker: he had the nature of an artist—he was, as he himself said, a *"visuel"*, a man who sees. Here is what he himself told us about his method of working. He used to look again and again at the things he did not understand, to deepen his impression of them day by day, till suddenly an understanding of them dawned on him. In his mind's eye the apparent chaos presented by the continual repetition of the same symptoms then gave way to order: the new nosological pictures emerged, characterized by the constant combination of certain groups of symptoms. The complete and extreme cases, the "types", could be brought into prominence with the help of a certain sort of schematic planning, and, with these types as a point of departure, the eye could travel over the long series of ill-defined cases—the *"formes frustes"*—which, branching off from one or other characteristic feature of the type, melt away into indistinctness. He called this kind of intellectual work, in which he had no equal, "practising nosography", and he took pride in it. He might be heard to say that the greatest satisfaction a man could have was to see something new—that is, to recognize it as new; and he remarked again and again on the difficulty and value of this kind of "seeing". He would ask why it was that in medicine people only see what they have already learned to see. He would say that it was wonderful how one was suddenly able to see new things—new states of illness—which must probably be as old as the human race; and that he had to confess to himself that he now saw a number of things which he had overlooked for thirty years in his hospital wards. No physician needs to be told what a wealth of forms were acquired by neuropathology through him, and what increased precision and sureness of diagnosis were made possible by his observations. But the pupil who spent many hours with him going round the wards of the Salpêtrière—that museum of clinical facts, the names and peculiar characteristics of which were for the most part derived from him—would be reminded of Cuvier, whose statue, standing in front of the Jardin des Plantes, shows that great comprehender and describer of the animal world surrounded by a multitude of animal forms; or else he would recall the myth of Adam, who, when God brought the creatures of Paradise before him to be distinguished and named, may have experienced to the fullest degree that intellectual enjoyment which Charcot praised so highly.'[1]

Nothing is more significant than the passage in which Freud, anticipating his own scientific achievement, brings together the great modern naturalist and the Biblical Adam, both scientists, both creators of words, both poets by virtue of the supreme human privilege of distributing and naming the things of this world. He did not see the French naturalist's beautiful classifications or Charcot's verbal inventions as simple technical commodities, but as the model for the poetic science of which he already had the vision, if not the key:

'He was a tireless worker, and always, I believe, the busiest in the whole institute. His private consultations, to which patients flocked "from Samarkand and the Antilles", could not keep him from his teaching activities or his researches. There is no doubt that this throng of people did not turn to him solely because he was a famous discoverer but quite as much because he was a great physician and friend of man, who could always find an answer to a problem and who, when the present state of science did not allow him to *know*, was able to make a good guess. He has often been blamed for his therapeutic method which, with its multiplicity of prescriptions, could

[1] *Charcot* (1893, *Wiener medizinische Zeitschrift* No. 37), *Std Edn* III, pp. 11–13.

not but offend a rationalistic conscience. But he was simply continuing the procedures which were customary at that time and place, without deceiving himself much about their efficacy. He was, however, not pessimistic in his therapeutic expectations, and repeatedly showed readiness to try new methods of treatment in his clinic: their short-lived success was to find its explanation elsewhere.

'As a teacher, Charcot was positively fascinating. Each of his lectures was a little work of art in construction and composition; it was perfect in form and made such an impression that for the rest of the day one could not get the sound of what he had said out of one's ears or the thought of what he had demonstrated out of one's mind. He seldom demonstrated a single patient, but mostly a series of similar or contrasting cases which he compared with one another. In the hall in which he gave his lectures there hung a picture which showed "citizen" Pinel having the chains taken off the poor madmen in the Salpêtrière. The Salpêtrière, which had witnessed so many horrors during the Revolution, had also been the scene of this most humane of all revolutions. . . . At about the time at which the clinic was established and at which he gave up the Chair of Pathological Anatomy, a change occurred in the direction of Charcot's scientific pursuits, and to this we owe the finest of his work. He now pronounced that the theory of organic nervous illnesses was for the time being fairly complete, and he began to turn his attention almost exclusively to hysteria, which thus all at once became the focus of general interest. This, the most enigmatic of all nervous diseases, for the evaluation of which medicine had not yet found a serviceable angle of approach, had just then fallen into thorough discredit; and this discredit extended not only to the patients but to the physicians who concerned themselves with the neurosis. It was held that in hysteria anything was possible, and no credence was given to a hysteric about anything. The first thing that Charcot's work did was to restore its dignity to the topic. Little by little, people gave up the scornful smile with which the patient could at that time feel certain of being met. She was no longer necessarily a malingerer, for Charcot had thrown the whole weight of his authority on the side of the genuineness and objectivity of hysterical phenomena. Charcot had repeated on a small scale the act of liberation in memory of which Pinel's portrait hung in the lecture hall of the Salpêtrière. Once the blind fear of being made a fool of by the unfortunate patient had been given up—a fear which till then had stood in the way of a serious study of the neurosis—the question could arise as to what method of approach would lead most quickly to a solution of the problem. . . .'[1]

Freud concluded his article with an impartial criticism of the Master's theoretical work. He perceived those elements which would endure, and those which advances in medical thought would quickly sweep away. Actually it was Freud who was to deal this splendid edifice its hardest blow. Two years later he published *Studies on Hysteria* and upset all accepted ideas on the subject for which Charcot had fired his enthusiasm. Thus he turned against the man who had shown him the way. But he remained faithful to his teaching, for in spreading his revolutionary ideas on hysteria he, too, was preparing to free mankind from its chains.

[1] Ibid., pp. 17–19.

5

ENGAGEMENT AND MARRIAGE

During Freud's long life nobody knew anything about his love life, about the passions which might have stirred him in his youth; nor about the conflicts he may have had to overcome before becoming Sigmund Freud, the man who was looked on by some people as a devil incarnate and by others as a legendary sage. Had he known any woman other than his wife? Had he married for love or convenience? The inventor of the modern Eros, the libido, maintained an absolute silence on this point, a silence which bad faith and calumny alone dared to break. But the American neurologist who explained the doctrine of the libido and so-called Freudian pansexualism by its author's sexual turpitude and 'Viennese' immorality had, in the end, very little success even with the detractors of psychoanalysis. The generally accepted picture of Freud was like the one described, for instance, by Stefan Zweig in his essay in *Mental Healers.*

'For half a century Sigmund Freud shut his private life away behind the severe-looking door of a Vienna apartment. One would be almost tempted to say he had no private life, since it went on so modestly in the background. An almost unseen official figure, a mode of life of almost bourgeois regularity, unbroken by any startling changes or happenings (the exceptions all took place in the intellectual sphere) and never a single personal statement which might lend itself to anecdote or raise an eyebrow. Seventy years in the same city, more than forty years in the same house. Consultations always in the same room, reading in the same arm-chair, writing always in the same study. Father of six children, a man who had no personal needs, his only love his profession and his vocation. A man who never gave a minute of his time to seeking worldly vanities, position or honours, who never put the creator above his creation, and in whom the rhythm of life was subordinated absolutely and exclusively to that of never-ending, patient work.'

In his lifetime Freud never said, did or published anything to modify this austere, ascetic portrait. But, people will say, it is the portrait of an old man and it would be inconceivable, even monstrous that, in his youth at least, Freud should not have experienced personally the passion of love which he in particular has taught us to understand as the most powerful motive-force of human action and the source of all life. The inventor of psychoanalysis cannot have been just an impassive observer of the human drama of which he discovered the hidden depths. Where else but in his own life would he have acquired the certitude and the courage to fight alone for his ideas?'

It takes a very long search through Freud's writings to glean any information about certain events in his life, his relations with his friends and relatives and about the conflicts which caused him suffering. The two richest sources for this side of his life are *The Psychopathology of Everyday Life* and *The Interpretation of Dreams,* and even there Freud spoke about himself only because it was necessary in order to prove his theory. When, however, he did so it was with the greatest frankness. He neither toned down nor altered what he knew to be his basic character. Whatever the cost to himself, he portrayed himself exactly as he saw himself in the mirror of his dreams—envious, jealous, coveting love and esteem, tyrannous, capable of the most contradictory emotions, so that he found he could (unconsciously, of course) long for the death of his dearest friend. But he never even alluded to what he is reproached with seeing everywhere. He never spoke of his own sexuality, he never associated one of his dreams with an erotic desire or a woman. André Breton criticized him for his stubborn determination to keep silent, calling it illogical, even dishonest. Freud answered the letter but not the criticism. He clearly no more understood the surrealists' rigorism than he understood their poetry.[1]

Thus the man who affirmed the sexual etiology not only of mental illness but also of the creations of the human mind and the supreme products of human culture; the scandalous man whose adversaries said that he 'profaned everything past, poisoned everything present, killed everything future'—this man would seem to have been incapable of overcoming in his own life the prejudice of his age,

1 André Breton: *Les Vases Communicants,* Gallimard, 1932, Appendix 200–7.

that very thing which he kept on showing in his books to be hypocrisy and a serious cause of disturbance. While this is certainly paradoxical, why should it be so shocking? No revolutionary, however radical, has ever eradicated in himself all his prejudices and weaknesses; most audacities go side by side with strange pusillanimities, as the history of 'enlightened' philosophies and rationalist movements abundantly prove. Like all men, Freud inherited the morality of his family *milieu* and of the lower middle class from which he sprang—a morality which was both simple and rigid, in which Goodness was held to lie in the repression of the instincts and in which Evil was almost completely synonymous with sexual liberty or licence. When the study of neuroses led Freud to discover the fundamental principles of psychoanalysis he was forty years old, his youth was past and his adult life, if not his adult thought, had already been following a course which he had no reason to renounce. That he did not think it good to let the public in on his own personal conflicts is unimportant compared with the courage needed to analyse himself and, against the prompting of his shyness, his modesty (even call it false modesty), calmly to state truths which—and let there be no doubt on this point—he found just as scandalous or upsetting as anyone else did. Like all great achievements, Freud's ideas were hard won, in the face of prejudice, fear and conformity. They forced people seriously and for the first time to draw a distinction between two things which had been confused for centuries: the sexual etiquette of an age and a society, and morality, a mysterious phenomenon which is only just beginning to be studied. Freud was nearly sixty when he realized with some astonishment that all his life he had been a good and moral man, without, however, knowing what was the origin of these qualities or in what name he had developed them:

'I should add that I stand in no awe whatever of the Almighty. If we were ever to meet I should have more reproaches to make to Him than He would to me. I would ask Him why He hadn't endowed me with a better intellectual equipment, and He couldn't complain that I have failed to make the best use of my so-called freedom. (Incidentally, I know that every individual represents a chunk of life energy, but I don't see what energy has to do with freedom—i.e. not being conditioned by circumstances.)

'I think I ought to tell you that I have always been dissatisfied with my intellectual endowment and that I know precisely in what respects, but that I consider myself a very moral human being who can subscribe to Th. Vischer's excellent maxim: "What is moral is self-evident." I believe that when it comes to a sense of justice and consideration for others, to the dislike of making others suffer or taking advantage of them, I can measure myself with the best people I have known. I have never done anything mean or malicious, nor have I felt any temptation to do so, with the result that I am not in the least proud of it. I am taking the notion of morality in its social, not its sexual, sense. Sexual morality as defined by society, in its most extreme form, that of America, strikes me as very contemptible. I stand for an infinitely freer sexual life, although I myself have made very little use of such freedom. Only so far as I considered myself entitled to. . . .'[1]

Fifteen years after the founding of psychoanalysis Freud finally effected the essential separation between sexual morality and the true ethic of human relations. Having established that the great issue of Good and Evil has nothing to do with sexuality, there remains the problem of what constitutes this moral sense, which he called obvious and natural. Whence does it come? What has put it in man's heart? Why, if it is natural, is it distributed unequally between people? Later Freud tried to solve this problem as well. He explained the genesis of the moral sense—called the Super-Ego—by the complex relationship between a child and the ideal image of its parents. In 1915 he simply affirmed his own goodness and confessed his ignorance about the rest:

'When I ask myself why I have always aspired to behave honourably, to spare others and to be kind wherever possible, and why I didn't cease doing so when I realized that in this way one comes to harm and becomes an anvil because other people are brutal and unreliable, then indeed I have no answer. Sensible this certainly was not. In my youth I didn't feel any special ethical aspirations, nor does the conclusion that I am better than others give me any recognizable satisfaction! You are perhaps the first person to whom I have boasted in this fashion. So one could cite

[1] To James Putnam, July 8, 1915, *Letters*, p. 308.

just my case as a proof for your assertion that such an urge towards the ideal forms a considerable part of our inheritance. If only more of this precious inheritance could be found in other human beings! . . . But as I have said before, I know nothing about this. . . .'[1]

This letter to James Putnam, an American psychoanalyst who had attempted to establish the connection between psychoanalysis, morality and religion, throws light on what may well be the main reason for Freud's silence about his private life—the desire to spare his family and friends any suffering, and the refusal to expose to public curiosity the woman who, after being the passion of his youth, had shared his hardships and endured the disadvantages that went with his fame. Freud could not prevent the unpleasant polemics which his ideas provoked; but at least he tried his best to shield his nearest and dearest from the consequences.

Posterity's image of him, therefore, would have been that of a scientist who was austere, almost disembodied from science and abstract thought if Martha Freud, his wife, had not throughout her life kept the letters he wrote to her at the time of their long engagement. These letters, which number nine hundred, could not be studied and published until after her death, in 1951, twelve years after Freud's own death. They are an extraordinarily charming collection and fill in all the details missing from the conventional, legendary portrait of the man. Madly in love with the girl to whom he had hardly dared declare his feelings, Freud naturally spoke mainly about his love. But what he put down on paper in the course of nearly five years is not only worthy of a place in an anthology of the literature of love: he put into them so much life, truth, and humour that they are also an important part of his work.

To judge from her photographs, Martha Bernays would not seem to be the sort of person to justify such an outburst of passion. She was a slim, dainty girl with delicate, but rather ordinary features. However, she enjoyed great success with men and at the beginning of their engagement Freud was constantly consumed with jealousy. However enchanted he may have been, her fiancé did not consider

[1] Ibid., pp. 308–9.

her beautiful, and with what was somewhat disconcerting frankness for a man in love, he confessed to her:

'I know you are not beautiful in a painter's or sculptor's sense; if you insist on strict correctness in the use of words then I must confess you are not beautiful. But I was not flattering you in what I said; I cannot flatter; I can, it is true, be mistaken. What I meant to convey was how much the magic of your being expresses itself in your countenance and your body, how much there is visible in your appearance that reveals how sweet, generous, and reasonable you are. I myself have always been rather insensitive to formal beauty. But if there is any vanity left in your little head I will not conceal from you that some people declare you to be beautiful, even strikingly so. I have no opinion on the matter. . . .'[1]

Martha Bernays came from a Hamburg family which was steeped in Jewish culture. Her grandfather, who was related to Heinrich Heine, had been the Chief Rabbi of the city and had defended orthodoxy against the liberal movement which, in the first quarter of the nineteenth century, had severely shaken Judaism. The Bernays family had remained strictly orthodox. From the first this was a source of conflict between her and Freud, who grew indignant over the ritual restrictions on food imposed on his beloved as he naturally considered such practices to be absurd and bad for her health. For a long time Martha refused to oppose her mother and give up her religious customs. But in the end she gave way and Freud's atheism triumphed over family tradition. But religion was not the main cause of disagreement between the lovers. There were others, the most serious being Freud's jealousy and his categorical need to torment himself.

Reading these letters with their varying moods, fears and day-to-day worries, we get a clear picture of the two sides of the man who wrote them. One sombre, passionate, inclined to self-torment and superstition, sometimes tender to the point of sentimentality, and yet blessed with a sense of humour, in a word marked with the sign by which Thomas Mann later recognized the fraternity of the Romantics; the

[1] Letter to Martha Bernays, August 2, 1882, Ernest Jones, I, p. 102.

other reasonable and somewhat argumentative, always ready to recognize his mistakes, provided they were proved to him, and with a tendency to lay down the law and to draw a lesson from everything. These two aspects of Freud's nature appear alternately, sometimes even both together in the same letter, but always absolute and unadulterated. Naturally it was the romantic Freud that Martha got to know first:

'I knew it was only after you had gone that I would realise the full extent of my happiness and, alas! the degree of my loss as well. I cannot grasp it, and if that elegant little box and that sweet picture were not lying in front of me, I would think it was all a beguiling dream and be afraid to wake up. . . . Your lovely photograph. At first, when I had the original in front of me I did not think so much of it; but now, the more I stare at it the more it resembles the beloved object; I expect the pale cheeks to flush the colour our roses were, the delicate arms to detach themselves from the surface and seize my hand; but the precious picture does not move, it just seems to say: Patience! Patience! I am but a symbol, a shadow cast on paper, the real person is going to return and then you may neglect me again. . . .

'And all the while I kept thinking that somewhere I had read about a man who carried his sweetheart about with him in a little box, and having racked my brain for a long time I realised that it must be "the New Melusina", the fairy tale in Goethe's *Wilhelm Meister's Wanderings*, which I remembered only vaguely. For the first time in years I took down the book and found my suspicion confirmed. But I found more than I was looking for. The most tantalising, superficial allusions kept appearing here and there, behind the story's every feature lurked a reference to ourselves, and when I remembered what store my girl sets by my being taller than she is I had to throw the book away, half-amused, half-annoyed, and comfort myself with the thought that my Martha is not a mermaid but a lovely human being. As yet we don't see humour in the same things, which is why you may possibly be disappointed when you read this little story. And I would prefer not to tell you all the crazy and serious thoughts that crossed my mind while reading it.' [1]

[1] To Martha Bernays, June 19, 1882, *Letters*, pp. 7–8.

This young man who sent his beloved a rose every day, treated her like a princess in a fairy-tale and even once wrote her a letter in mediaeval style, could also prove exacting, possessive and stubborn as soon as his ideas on life were involved. His letters then took on a harsh, argumentative tone which, more often than not, half-camouflaged his jealousy:

'My beloved girl, a month ago today my delighted eyes spied you sitting on the veranda of the Philippses' house and you didn't recognize me, and two months ago you had just become my fiancée. Since then little, very little has happened to make the union for which we are striving a reality. And yet we have made some use of this time. We were strangers to one another, had to get to know each other, experience things together—this we have achieved; and if we both keep healthy and some demon does not disrupt our feelings for one another, the ensuing monthly memorials should find us well on the way towards our longed-for desire. For you, poor darling, hope for the future must compensate you for the many sacrifices you are imposing on yourself at the moment; for me, the courage to court you has already found reward in the awareness of my sweetest good fortune. If I may repeat a request today, please don't be taciturn or reticent with me, rather share with me any minor or even major discontent which we can straighten out and bear together as honest friends and good pals. I have always acted like this, sometimes at the expense of your delicate nature, and you have told me that you agree. If in doing so I must have often hurt your feelings, I know you have not misunderstood my efforts to make you my own as intimately as possible, and if this be egotistical, love after all cannot be anything but egotistical. . . .'[1]

The main reason for disagreement between the two young people was, of course, Freud's jealous nature. His efforts to make Martha break off all her attachments were unremitting. He constantly demanded that she should choose between him and people she loved or had loved. The very thought of her having had a previous fiancé made him ill, a childhood friend who was a little too pressing in his attentions gave rise to a violent quarrel,

[1] To Martha Bernays, August 17, 1882, ibid., pp. 24–5.

even his fiancée's brother and mother became dangerous rivals whom he resolved to supplant. And throughout this period in which the most petty conflicts were aggravated by separation, Freud already revealed a characteristic which later became very familiar to his followers: those he loved had to return his love, and nothing angered him more than a disregard for the rules of correspondence. If that happened he would quarrel even with a friend. Jung's extreme negligence on this score is said to have been one of the reasons why he lost Freud's affection. Martha's shortcoming was never as serious, but she was threatened with the same penalty:

'I am beginning these notes without waiting for your answer, my girl, in order to tell you more about myself and my activities than our personal contact would allow. I am going to be very frank and confidential with you, as is right for two people who have joined hands for life in love and friendship. But as I don't want to keep on writing without receiving an answer I will stop as soon as you fail to respond. Continuous inner monologues about a beloved person that are not corrected or refreshed by that person lead to false opinions about the mutual relationship, and even to estrangement when one meets again and finds things to be different from what one had thought. Nor shall I always be very affectionate, sometimes I will be serious and outspoken, as is only right between friends and as friendship demands. . . .'[1]

Freud found separation all the more intolerable for his being unable to do much towards curtailing it. During the four and a half years that their engagement lasted he went to see Martha only six times, because he could not afford the fare. He could only make the journey from Vienna to Hamburg if he borrowed from his friends; but he was already up to the ears in debt and a journey was a folly which compromised his whole financial position and, even more, his work. This situation could only aggravate the young people's emotional difficulties. It sharpened Freud's passion, and his jealousy as well; at the same time it increased his fear of being thrown over and of never being able to achieve the married happiness which, at that moment, seemed to him an unattainable ideal. 'Oh Martha

[1] To Martha Bernays, September 25, 1882, ibid., pp. 28–29.

darling,' he exclaimed one day, 'how poor we are!' They were indeed poor. Their poverty was so extreme that it assumed in Freud's eyes the dimensions of a Biblical trial. He hardly dared hope to be luckier than Jacob, who had to wait seven years for his wife:

'My precious beloved darling, when I think that you are my bride and have been so for 3½ years, I see myself in turn as worthy of envy and pity. Like the wind, you say? It is half the engagement time of our patriarchs, but they lived to an incredible age and God was on their side. . . .'[1]

Love, money worries, fears for the future and scientific preoccupations are the predominating topics of this impatient correspondence which, to some extent, made the young people's separation more bearable. But they were by no means the only topics. Freud also wrote to Martha in order to share with her his ideas on life, his opinons on affairs and people. He loved to discuss at length his favourite books, which he gave her as presents as soon as he could scrape together a bit of money. Thus his letters give us a very accurate picture of his literary tastes. They even contain real little critical articles in which he expressed highly individual ideas on the aesthetic value of the works and, above all, they show the love and gift for interpretation which he was to develop in such a masterly way later, in his psychoanalytical writings:

'You must have noticed that all writers and artists have a "mannerism", a stereotyped series of motives and arrangements which indicate the limits of their art: that is why it is so easy to parody them . . . To these mannerisms belong with Dickens those flawless girls, selfless and good, so good that they are quite colourless; then the fact that all the good people immediately become friends as soon as they meet and work together throughout the whole book; then the sharp distinction between virtue and vice which doesn't exist in life (where should I be for example?); finally, his easy toleration of feeble-mindedness, represented in almost every novel by one or two blockheads or crazy people, who belong to the side of the "good ones", and so on. Oh, I had almost forgotten the philanthropist,

[1] To Martha Bernays, November 19, 1885, ibid., p. 184.

who has such a frightful lot of money and is available for any noble purpose. Copperfield has the least of all this. The characters are individualized; they are sinful without being abominable. . . .'[1]

The book to which most space is devoted in the correspondence of this period is Cervantes' *Don Quixote.* Freud had sent Martha an edition illustrated by Gustave Doré which he had been given by one of his friends. The girl disliked the masterpiece, being shocked by its crudity. Freud apologized, but admitted he found the book so fascinating that he almost forgot his own work. And for several days he returned to the subject, clearly feeling that some secret bond existed between the book and himself:

'Don't you find it very touching to read how a great person, himself an idealist, makes fun of his ideals? Before we were so fortunate as to apprehend the deep truths in our love we were all noble knights passing through the world caught in a dream, misinterpreting the simplest things, magnifying commonplaces into something noble and rare, and thereby cutting a sad figure. Therefore we men always read with respect about what we once were and in part still remain. . . .'[2]

It is clear that if Freud was not a psychologist in the current meaning of the word—and he was anything but one in his daily life—he was already analysing himself with rare perception. And just as he felt caught in a Don Quixote-like conflict between dream and reality—a conflict which was to demand of him nothing less than the invention of a new science for its resolution—so he revealed his secret resemblance to the intellectual ascetic, the hermit Antony whose story is told by Flaubert in *The Temptation of St Antony:*

'I was already deeply moved by the splendid panorama, and now on top of it all came this book which in the most condensed fashion and with unsurpassable vividness throws at one's head the whole trashy world: for it calls

[1] Letter to Martha Bernays, October 5, 1883, Ernest Jones, I, p. 174.

[2] Letter to Martha Bernays, August 23, 1883, Ernest Jones, I, p. 175.

up not only the great problems of knowledge, but the real riddles of life, all the conflicts of feelings and impulses; and it confirms the awareness of our perplexity in the mysteriousness that reigns everywhere. These questions, it is true, are always there, and one should always be thinking of them. What one does, however, is confine oneself to a narrow aim every hour and every day and get used to the idea that to concern oneself with these enigmas is the task of a special hour, in the belief that they exist only in those special hours. Then they suddenly assail one in the morning and rob one of one's composure and one's spirits. . . .'[1]

One is sometimes inclined to think that the Freudian revolution was carried out in one fell swoop round about 1895 and marked a complete break with the past life and thought of its instigator. The letters to Martha show this to be quite untrue. While doing pathology Freud's mind was already active in the sphere in which he was to become famous. The conflict from which he was suffering without yet knowing its cause exploded a few years later, on his father's death. It had not been resolved, merely masked or attenuated by his approaching marriage.

The two young people decided to set a time-limit to their interminable wait. Whatever happened they would get married in 1887, after an engagement of exactly five years. In actual fact they were able to do so six months earlier, thanks to an uncle and an aunt of Martha who made them a present of a modest sum of money, just enough to set up house. Freud, moreover, was at the end of his tether. He spent the last days of his separation from Martha in a painful state of excitement:

'Then I shall breathe again, my darling, and willingly let myself be once more harassed and economize, and if we sometimes have to rack our brains to know where this or that is coming from what will it matter? After all, we shall be two together and far removed from the direst poverty which doesn't prevent so many people from loving each other, instead of consoling ourselves with the thought of a future which could never be so beautiful as what had been sacrificed for it. How long does one stay young, how long healthy, how long does one stay pliable enough to adapt oneself to the changing mood of the other? You would be

[1] Letter to Martha Bernays, July 26, 1883, ibid.

an old maid if I let you wait until I can save up to pay for everything, and you would have forgotten how to laugh. I miss you so much since I am back, so that I hardly live like a decent human being. I miss you in every way, because I have taken you to myself in every respect, as sweetheart, as wife, as comrade, as working companion, and I have to live in the most painful privation. I cannot employ my time, I do not enjoy anything, for weeks I haven't borne a cheerful expression, and in short I am so unhappy. . . .'[1]

Their marriage had to be delayed a little because Freud, who thought he would not do his conscription until the following year, was called up for the big manoeuvres. After that he had to settle the ticklish problem of the ceremony. Freud was so appalled by the complicated rites of a Jewish marriage that he thought of becoming a Protestant, since every Austrian citizen was held to have a religion, whatever his opinions and religious practices. Then he felt reassured. As he was getting married in Germany where, unlike Austria, civil marriage was recognized, he thought he would be spared the religious ceremony. He was wrong! Wherever it took place, a civil marriage was invalid in Austria. So he had to resign himself to the ceremony after all. It took place according to the Jewish rites, after Freud had stayed the night with an uncle to learn the Hebrew prayers which he had to recite next day. It was the last time he conformed to a convention which ran counter to his ideas.

On October 1, 1886, the young couple came back from their honeymoon and returned to Vienna where, for a long time, they lived in straitened circumstances. Except for Freud's travels and occasionally at holiday times, they were hardly ever separated again. They did not leave Vienna until the eve of the Second World War, after living together for fifty-five years, during which time Martha had only one rival—science, just as her fiancé had predicted. All the same he was wrong on one point. Martha's only rival was not the classic anatomy of the brain but the study of neuroses, and then the stormy subject of psychoanalysis on which Freud, for the rest of his life, was to concentrate all his passion.

[1] Letter to Martha Bernays, June 1886, ibid., pp. 146–7.

6

HYSTERIA

On Sunday, April 25, 1886, Easter Day, the following announcement appeared in a Viennese paper: 'Dr Sigmund Freud, Lecturer in Neuropathology in the University of Vienna, has returned from spending six months in Paris and now resides at 7, Rathausstrasse.'

And so Freud opened his first consulting room on a Sunday, and on Easter Sunday at that, the slackest working day in the whole Viennese year. It was a strange idea and since it is natural to seek an explanation for everything in Freud's life, which seems to have been predestined to explanation, one wonders what could possibly have suggestd this particular day to Freud, whose practical decisions were normally more inspired.

Was it the memory of the old nurse who, on Easter Day, used to take him to Mass in Freiberg? A wish to defy society by challenging its most established customs? Or was it one of those semi-superstitious beliefs to which Freud long remained attached, giving them, more or less successfully, a rational explanation? We do not know what that day, April 25th, meant to Freud, but in view of its importance and solemnity it is highly likely that he had a good reason for choosing it.

He had, in fact, long felt hesitant and doubtful about his plans for settling in Vienna. Before actually doing so, Freud had considered all sorts of solutions: emigrating to England or America, living in the country or in a small provincial town. In the end he decided to try his luck in the capital, a risky adventure for an impecunious doctor who could not count on much support.

A month before his marriage he left his first lodgings and moved into a larger flat where, at first, patients were in no hurry to come. Freud had warned his wife that they would almost certainly have a hard life. This was indeed the case and, for some time, their wedding presents found their way, one by one, to the pawn-broker. From mid-day, surgery time, the young couple waited for the patients whom they irreverently referred to as 'Negroes', an allusion to a cartoon they had seen in a paper showing a picture of a lion yawning and saying: 'Mid-day already and not a Negro!' [1] Gradually, however, the 'Negroes' came, sent by Freud's former teachers or by the close friends who had long been helping him with money and advice. And so, after all, all the terrifying monthly bills could be met.

Freud had set up as a specialist in 'nervous illnesses,' but he very quickly saw that neurology, as he had been taught it, could do little for the majority of his patients. These were not generally suffering from any organic lesions of the nervous system. They were 'nervous cases' (today they would be called neurotics), that is, people who cluttered up all branches of medicine without really belonging to any particular one. This peculiarly disinherited crowd wandered from one doctor to another, vainly trying every kind of treatment and exhausting everyone with their sufferings and their complaints. Now Freud wanted to live from his practice and he told himself that his best hope of success lay in proving himself efficient in a field in which his colleagues had come to the conclusion that they were completely powerless. This wish to cure seems to be natural to a doctor, but it can hardly have been all that common since Freud was the first in his particular field to make it the basis of his scientific effort.

Faced with patients of a type he had not been taught how to treat, Freud gave them the attention and curiosity which he had seen exemplified in Charcot while he was at the Salpêtrière. The great French master had certainly not provided him with the efficient therapy which he now felt he needed; but he had at least given hysteria a new scientific importance which, as Freud could see for himself every day, was not merely theoretical. Returning home from Paris bursting with ideas and eager to propagate them, Freud thought he would have no difficulty in convincing his colleagues; but his first contact with the Vienna Society of Physicians quickly disillusioned him:

'The duty devolved upon me of giving a report before the "Gesellschaft der Ärzte" (Society of Medicine) upon what I had seen and learnt with Charcot. But I met with a bad reception. Persons of authority, such as the chairman (Bamberger, the physician), declared that what I said was

[1] Ernest Jones, Vol. I.

incredible. Meynert urged me to find some cases in Vienna similar to those which I had described and to present them before the Society. I tried to do so; but the senior physicians in whose departments I found any such cases refused to allow me to observe them or to work at them. One of them, an old surgeon, actually broke out with the exclamation: "But, my dear sir, how can you talk such nonsense? *Hysteron* (*sic*) means the uterus. So how can a man be hysterical?" I objected in vain that what I wanted was not to have my diagnosis approved, but to have the case put at my disposal. At length, outside the hospital, I came upon a case of classical hysterical hemianaesthesia in a man, and demonstrated it before the "Gesellschaft der Ärzte". This time I was applauded, but no further interest was taken in me. The impression that the high authorities had rejected my innovations remained unshaken; and, with my hysteria in men and my production of hysterical paralyses by suggestion, I found myself forced into the Opposition. As I was soon afterwards excluded from the laboratory of cerebral anatomy and for a whole session had nowhere to deliver my lectures, I withdrew from academic life and ceased to attend the learned societies. It is a whole generation since I have visited the "Gesellschaft der Ärzte. . . ."'[1]

If the failure of this first report did not impair Freud's relations with the Society of Physicians as radically as, much later, he thought he remembered that it had, it was nevertheless decisive as it forced him to work on his own to achieve his double task of treating the strange illnesses confronting him and, in order to do that, discovering a way of understanding them at all costs. As he had to earn a living at once, he began using the inadequate therapeutic methods available at the time:

'My therapeutic arsenal contained only two weapons, electrotherapy and hypnotism, for prescribing a visit to a hydropathic establishment after a single consultation was an inadequate source of income. My knowledge of electrotherapy was derived from W. Erb's text-book [1882], which provided detailed instructions for the treatment of all the symptoms of nervous diseases. Unluckily I was soon driven to see that following these instructions was of no

[1] *An Autobiographical Study, Std Edn* XX, p. 15.

help whatever and that what I had taken for an epitome of exact observations was merely the construction of phantasy. The realization that the work of the greatest name in German neuropathology had no more relation to reality than some "Egyptian" dreambook, such as is sold in cheap book-shops, was painful, but it helped to rid me of another shred of the innocent faith in authority from which I was not yet free. So I put my electrical apparatus aside. . . .'[1]

After that Freud kept mainly to hypnosis, which did nothing to reconcile the psychiatrists, who regarded hypnosis as sheer charlatanism and the 'mesmerists', as they were called, as being quite beyond the pale. In Paris he had seen Charcot use hypnosis to create symptoms and then remove them. Then he got to know the work of the Nancy school which used suggestion with or without hypnosis for therapeutic purposes. Trying to exploit to the full every possible technique, even those which were most decried, Freud, quite unintentionally, moved further and further away from organic nervous illnesses:

'But that was of little importance. For on the one hand the prospects in the treatment of such disorders were in any case never promising, while on the other hand, in the private practice of a physician working in a large town, the quantity of such patients was nothing compared to the crowds of neurotics, whose number seemed further multiplied by the manner in which they hurried, with their troubles unsolved, from one physician to another. And apart from this, there was something positively seductive in working with hypnotism. For the first time there was a sense of having overcome one's helplessness; and it was highly flattering to enjoy the reputation of being a miracle-worker. It was not until later that I was to discover the drawbacks of the procedure. . . .'[2]

The reader must have noticed Freud's courageous frankness in bringing into the open the interested motives about which the history of science generally maintains a bashful silence. He pursued his research because he needed money and from a sense of his own power, two factors which al-

[1] Ibid., p. 16.
[2] Ibid., p. 17.

ways, in some form, underlie every great human achievement. Like every idea and every science, psychoanalysis had obscure and elementary origins which had nothing in common with its eventual aim. The only difference is that psychoanalsis was the first and, so far, is still almost the only one to admit this.

The imperfection of his therapeutic methods pre-occupied Freud constantly during his first years of practice. He very quickly saw that it was not possible to hypnotize every patient and that with those who submitted the hypnotic state was not always as deep as was desirable. And so, during the summer of 1889, he decided to go and spend a few weeks at Nancy to perfect his technique:

'I witnessed the moving spectacle of old Liébault working among the poor women and children of the labouring classes, I was a spectator of Bernheim's astonishing experiments upon his hospital patients and I received the profoundest impression of the possibility that there could be powerful mental processes which nevertheless remained hidden from the consciousness of men. . . .'[1]

While he was with Charcot, Freud had become convinced that hysterical disturbances—for instance, contractures and paralysis—did not fit into any definite sector of anatomy, but corresponded to an image, a mental representation of the arm or the limb. In an *Etude comparative des paralysies motrices organiques et hystériques,* written and published in French, he said that 'hysteria behaves in its paralyses and other manifestations as though anatomy did not exist, or as though it were totally ignorant of it.' And at Nancy Bernheim allowed him to establish another major fact—that hysterical cases knew things connected with the cause of their illness, but were in some way unaware of them. By themselves they could neither re-discover nor express what remained mysteriously hidden from their consciousness. Hypnosis and suggestion were only ways of making them remember. But then an annoying problem arose: Why did certain cases respond to suggestion while others remained unaffected or only half responded?

'Thinking it would be instructive, I had persuaded one of my patients to follow me to Nancy. She was a very highly

[1] Ibid., p. 17.

gifted hysteric, a woman of good birth, who had been handed over to me because no one knew what to do with her. By hypnotic influence I had made it possible for her to lead a tolerable existence and I was always able to take her out of the misery of her condition. But she always relapsed again after a short time, and in my ignorance I attributed this to the fact that her hypnosis had never reached the stage of somnambulism with amnesia. Bernheim now attempted several times to bring this about, but he too failed. He frankly admitted to me that his great therapeutic successes by means of suggestion were only achieved in his hospital practice and not with his private patients. I had many stimulating conversations with him, and undertook to translate into German his two works upon suggestion and its therapeutic effects. . . .'[1]

Freud was not yet in a position to form hypotheses on the genesis of the illness. For the moment he established that hysterics behaved as though they had no knowledge of anatomy—which was only a step towards his future conception of the 'symbolism' of hysterical symptoms—and also that they acted as though they were moved by images concealed from their own consciousness. Moreover, he was very worried by the unpredictable, apparently capricious nature of the therapeutic effects he happened to obtain. Worried, but by no means discouraged or annoyed as most of his colleagues clearly were. The unevenness of his results and the need to explain them were the very things which drove him to persevere.

We recognize here the most distinctive feature of this period, which was so important for the maturing of Freud's ideas: willingness to accept everything, to receive everything at first without rejecting *a priori* anything which might perhaps serve as a guide. Just as he allowed himself to be penetrated by Charcot's and Bernheim's conceptions and appointed himself their interpreter in his own language (it was in this period that he translated Charcot's *Polyclinique* and Bernheim's two works on suggestion), in the same way he laid himself completely open to the new experiences offered by his patients. This receptivity, which was as emotional as it was intellectual and was altogether revolutionary compared with the usual attitude of psychiatrists, offered Freud's genius its great opportunity.

[1] Ibid., pp. 17–18.

It allowed Freud to take up and exploit a surprising discovery made not by him but by a friend and colleague, Dr Josef Breuer, who was forty years his senior and with whom he had long been on close terms. In September 1882 Breuer had informed Freud about some completely unexpected observations that he had been able to make of a case, which had somehow not been published, of a hysterical girl whom he had treated for two years and who, he said, had left him almost cured. Freud immediately became passionately interested in the case, which seemed to him to reveal great possibilities for both therapeutics and the theory of neurosis. He read the history of the treatment which Breuer had partly written up, and, during the next few years, studied it with much greater enthusiasm than the person who had been primarily concerned and who, strangely, seemed rather to want to forget it. He also spoke about it to Charcot while he was in Paris as he thought Charcot would naturally be interested in such a rich and detailed case history. But, contrary to all expectation, Charcot was merely indifferent.

The history of Anna O . . ., which has since become famous in the annals of psychiatry, began to preoccupy Freud again when, faced with similar cases, he found himself more and more disappointed by the therapeutic arsenal available. Electrotherapy was a delusion, hypnosis was not always practicable, suggestion cured the symptoms and then, in accordance with some unfathomable law, made them re-appear. He therefore decided to try the method of which Breuer had told him—an empirical method if ever there was one, created less by the doctor's ideas than by the unpredictable development of the treatment and, what was quite new, by the intelligent collaboration of the patient. The tenacity which Freud showed in this case in spite of his friend's peculiar reticence provided psychoanalysis with its first tool and thereby determined its destiny.

Anna O . . ., her real name was Bertha Pappenheim, fully deserves her scientific fame, since it was to her we owe Breuer's method, which she very aptly described as 'the talking cure' and as 'chimney-sweeping'. At the time of her treatment she was a girl of twenty-one, extremely intelligent, with even a touch of genius; and she was fascinating as well, a fact which only added to her doctor's difficulties. She had consulted Breuer, who was not a psychiatrist, because of a very painful nervous cough; but in addition, she was suffering from disturbances as spectacular as they were varied, and all these had appeared after her father's death: the paralysis of three limbs with contractures and unconsciousness; complicated disturbances of speech and sight; inability to feed herself etc. In addition she was liable to two distinct states of consciousness, behaving normally in one but like a spoiled and naughty child in the other. Transition from one state to the other was brought about by a sort of self-hypnosis from which she emerged perfectly lucid, with her intellectuals powers unimpaired. On top of this Anna O . . . had, throughout the treatment, completely forgotten her mother tongue, which was German, and could only express herself in English. English had become so natural to her that she was able to translate any French or Italian book without making a mistake.

Breuer's visits took place in the evening, when the girl was lucid and she would tell him everything she had suffered during the day and also describe her terrible hallucinations, after which she felt relief. One day she described in detail the conditions in which one of her symptoms had appeared, and to Breuer's astonishment, the mere telling was enough to make the symptom disappear, as though exorcised by some magic formula. Anna O . . . at once realized the importance of this unexpected phenomenon: and of her own accord she continued the 'chimney-sweeping' to which Breuer afterwards gave the scientific term of 'catharis', or purging of the soul.

For a long time Freud was struck by the obscurities which still clouded the history of the illness, especially those connected with what had clearly been the rather hasty ending of the treatment by the doctor. What had happened? Why did Breuer show such an aversion to discussing the case? Why, above all, having found such a promising therapeutic method, had he lost all interest in hysteria? Freud could only answer these questions when he himself had penetrated more deeply into the obscure realm of neurosis. But even then he did not publish all the details he had been able to learn, out of consideration for the man whom he had loved and admired so long, before coming to regard him as an enemy of his ideas. Breuer's secret, which is today an open secret for psychoanalysts, has been revealed by Ernest Jones in his biography of Freud, *The Life and Work of Sigmund Freud*:

'Freud has related to me a fuller account that he described

in his writings of the peculiar circumstances surrounding the end of this novel treatment. It would seem that Breuer had developed what we should nowadays call a strong countertransference to his interesting patient. At all events he was so engrossed that his wife became bored at listening to no other topic, and before long she became jealous. She did not display this openly, but became unhappy and morose. It was a long time before Breuer, with his thoughts elsewhere, divined the meaning of her state of mind. It provoked a violent reaction in him, perhaps compounded of love and guilt, and he decided to bring the treatment to an end. He announced this to Anna O . . . , who was by now much better, and bade her good-bye. But that evening he was fetched back to find her in a greatly excited state, apparently as ill as ever. The patient, who according to him had appeared to be an asexual being and had never made any allusion to such a forbidden topic throughout the treatment, was now in the throes of an hysterical childbirth (pseudocyesis), the logical termination of a phantom pregnancy that had been invisibly developing in response to Breuer's ministrations. Though profoundly shocked, he managed to calm her down by hypnotizing her, and then fled the house in a cold sweat. . . .'[1]

Anna O . . ., one imagines, was very far from being cured. For a long time she continued to suffer from her disturbances, then her condition gradually improved and she succeeded in leading an active life in which she found scope for her energy and gifts. She became the first social worker in Germany, and seems to have been one of the first in the world. She never married, she kept her religious faith, and she devoted herself to the cause of women's emancipation and travelled all over Eastern Europe to help children whose parents had perished in the pogroms.

For Breuer, one can imagine, hysteria had become a thorny subject about which he would doubtless have liked to keep silent. Ten years later, when Freud and he were collaborating in the study of certain cases, Breuer consulted his friend about one case of hysteria which was worrying him. A mere description of the symptoms was enough for Freud to diagnose a typical phantom preg-

[1] Ernest Jones, I, p. 224. Cf. also chap. 28, Freud's letter to Stefan Zweig on the same subject.

nancy. Breur could not face the repetition of a situation which had seriously upset him in the past. Without saying a word, he seized his hat and walking stick and, once again, fled.

Freud had, however, succeeded in persuading Breuer to resume with him the systematic study of what he called 'the great neurosis'. There followed a collaboration which lasted five years—from 1890 to 1895—the year in which the two men published jointly their *Studies on Hysteria*. The book, generally held to be the first work in the literature of psychoanalysis, contained the case histories of five patients, including Anna O . . ., brilliantly described by Breuer, and four case histories described by Freud, in which it is possible to follow the slow evolution of his technique. Actually Breuer's cathartic method by no means solved every problem. It demanded the use of hypnosis and Freud was becoming increasingly convinced that this was not always possible nor, perhaps, even desirable. The hypnotic state seemed, indeed, to disguise certain phenomena which Freud was beginning to suspect were of decisive importance: for instance, what he called 'transference', a body of violent, contradictory and ambiguous emotion which the patient had formerly felt about his parents and which he now unconsciously switched to the person of his doctor. Determined not only to treat but also to fathom the profound nature of the illness, Freud gradually gave up hypnotism and, in the third case in *Studies on Hysteria* used instead a technique of concentration. For the first time he was fully satisfied with the results of this method, which he called 'psychic analysis' in order to mark the beginning of his independence.

The patient was made to lie down with her eyes closed and Freud asked her to concentrate on a particular symptom and to try to recall everything which might explain its origin. Sometimes nothing came. Then Freud laid his hand on the patient's forehead, telling her that certain memories, certain thoughts would not fail to surge up. Whenever the patient remained silent, he repeated his attempt until she told him what had come into her mind, which she did with the remark: "I could have told you that the first time, but I did not think it was what you wanted to know.' Convinced that this was the obstruction, Freud then urged her to tell him everything which was passing through her mind, without choosing or pre-judging or censoring her thoughts. It was the first step towards the technique of 'free association', to which Freud was led by the logic of his observations and, very often, by his patients' intelligent initiative.

For a long time Freud had been accumulating proofs of the importance that must be given to sexual factors in causing neuroses. This discovery was unexpected and at first he was deeply shocked. His revulsion was so great that it was as though he had himself forgotten his most conclusive observations. His theory of the sexual etiology of neurosis, far from originating in any preconceived idea, was, in fact, born of a struggle against his own prejudices:

'As regards the controversial matter itself, I will only remark that the singling out of the sexual factor in the etiology of hysteria springs at least from no preconceived opinion on my part. The two investigators as whose pupil I began my studies of hysteria, Charcot and Breuer, were far from having any such presupposition; in fact they had a personal disinclination to it which I originally shared. . . .' [1]

At first Freud was convinced that his discovery was entirely his own. But later he remembered certain remarks by well-known doctors who seemed to have had a similar idea, or at least a similar intuition. He had once heard Breuer say that hysteria often had some connection with the secrets of the marriage bed. Another time he had heard Charcot tell his assistant Brouardel that *'la chose génitale'* was always a factor in certain cases of neurotic disturbance.[2] A year later, the famous gynaecologist Chrobak had expressed the same idea even more crudely when he passed on to Freud a hysterical case. It is true that two of the doctors in question categorically denied the remarks, and if Charcot had also been asked he would probably have done the same.

It was 1895 before Freud actually put forward what he already considered to be a certainty. As he had had the utmost difficulty in obtaining Breuer's collaboration in *Studies on Hysteria*, he had agreed that the role given to sexuality should be a minor one. Not that Breuer refused to recognize sexuality; but, for one thing, the subject was far too closely associated with a painful personal experience for him to be able to handle it with complete frankness,

[1] *Etiology of Hysteria, Std Edn* III, p. 199.

[2] Cf. *History of the Psychoanalytic Movement, Std Edn* XIV, p. 13.

and, for another, some of Freud's conclusions seemed to him premature, too exclusive, too compromising scientifically. Hence his evasive attitude, which did not make the two men's tasks any easier and helped to spoil their friendship. He had finally recognized the reality of 'transference', the phenomenon which had upset him so much in his relations with Anna O . . . and which Freud was now beginning to see had real therapeutic value. But the sexual etiology of neurosis continued to shock him. He defended it in public, but confessed to Freud that, in spite of everything, he could not really bring himself to believe it. And so the twenty-year-old friendship between pupil and master slowly began to cool and in the end collapsed in utter ruin. It was the first of the sensational quarrels which were to mark Freud's career and were one aspect of the history of psychoanalysis.

Studies on Hysteria was badly received in the medical world. Breuer became disheartened, but Freud turned to mockery as a defence against the stupidity of the critics, an enemy which was hardly ever to stop hounding him for the rest of his long life. As so often was the case later, the only intelligent criticism came not from a scientist, but from a writer and dramatic critic whose review, entitled 'Surgery of the Soul', appeared in the most important Viennese newspaper. Alfred von Bergner, Professor of the History of Literature in the University of Vienna and later Director of the Imperial Theatre, said in particular:

'We dimly conceive the idea that it may one day become possible to approach the innermost secret of personality. The theory itself,' he continued, 'is in fact nothing but the kind of psychology used by poets. . . .'[1]

This article is a landmark in the chequered history of psychoanalysis and literature. Freud, who in *Studies on Hysteria* wrote that his case histories had more in common with the novel than with medical observation, found it a satisfying compensation. He had yet to learn that literature would often prove to be his most faithful and sometimes his only support in the face of general hostility and malevolence.

In 1896 the break with Breuer became complete. Another friend came to assume an exclusive importance in

[1] *Neue Freie Presse,* December 2, 1895. Ernest Jones, I, p. 278.

Freud's life, a friend from whom he was also to separate in dramatic circumstances. In the same year he categorically affirmed the sexual etiology of what he henceforth called 'psychoneurosis'. And for the first time he used the word 'psychoanalysis'. This is also interesting in connection with an article first written and published in French:

'As regards the second class of major neuroses, hysteria and obsessional neurosis, the solution of the aetiological problem is of surprising simplicity and uniformity. I owe my results to a new method of psycho-analysis, Josef Breuer's exploratory procedure; it is a little intricate, but it is irreplaceable, so fertile has it shown itself to be in throwing light upon the obscure paths of unconscious ideation. By means of that procedure—this is not the place in which to describe it—hysterical symptoms are traced back to their origin, which is always found in some event of the subject's sexual life appropriate for the production of a distressing emotion. Travelling backwards into the patient's past, step by step, and always guided by the organic train of symptoms and of memories and thoughts aroused, I finally reached the starting-point of the pathological process; and I was obliged to see that at bottom the same thing was present in all the cases submitted to analysis—the action of an agent which must be accepted as the specific cause of hysteria. . . .'[1]

[1] *L'Hérédité et l' Etiologie des Névroses* (1893, in French). *Std Edn* III, pp. 151–2.

7

THE BIRTH OF PSYCHOANALYSIS

In *The Interpretation of Dreams* Freud disclosed what had guided him in the way he named his children. He was determined that their names should not be chosen according to the fashion of the day or a family tradition, but to perpetuate the memory of people he loved, generally his masters and friends. He said this principle made his children 'ghosts'[1] and placed him outside perishable time by conferring on him a kind of immortality. It was also undoubtedly the equivalent of an act of piety.

Freud followed this rule scrupulously for his six children. Of his three sons he called one Jean-Martin, in tribute to Charcot's memory, not Luther's as has sometimes been claimed; another Oliver, in memory of Cromwell, one of his favourite boyhood heroes; and the third Ernest to remind him of his old teacher Brücke, whose name, he used to say, would remain dear to him all his life.

Although they did not have such illustrious sponsors, his daughters did not escape the rule. The eldest, Mathilde, bore the name of Frau Breuer, of whom Freud was very fond; the second, Sophie, was named after Frau Paneth, the wife of Josef Paneth whose figure haunts the pages of *The Interpretation of Dreams*; and the youngest, Anna, bore the same of a daughter of his schoolteacher, Hammerschlag, who had taught him Hebrew and the Scriptures. At the height of his passionate relationship with Fliess he had decided to call his next son Wilhelm. But he did not have a son and in spite of his enthusiasm for his friend he could not bring himself to call a daughter of his Wilhelmine.

Children, therefore, represented for Freud a living link with love, friendship and the admiration inspired by certain great men. Later, his first followers discovered that in his dreams he often associated them with psychoanalysis, the future of which was for a long time a source of great

[1] Cf. the dream 'Non Vixit' in chap. 10.

anxiety to him. He used to call his children his pride and wealth—which he may have thought in his best moments but did not dare say in his books.

The friendship which Freud thus honoured in the person of his children was a big factor in his life. After his marriage, which brought him the peace and joy of loving parenthood, it was the only passion which continued to dominate him, and it was all the more tyrannical for being bound up with his research and the evolution of his ideas. Freud, it would seem, simply had to love and admire a man who was both close to him and superior to him, from whom he expected not only support and affectionate help, but a kind of inspiration, an example that would stimulate him. Thus his enthusiastic admiration for Ernst von Fleischl had stimulated his work at the Institute of Physiology; and Josef Breuer, whose kindness, intelligence and moral courage were indeed remarkable, had inspired Freud's first discoveries about hysteria. However, this deep form of manly devotion was not the ordinary relic left over from adolescence: Freud experienced it in his maturity and still felt it in his old age, although with time it took on a more paternal character. In the period we are now considering it had grown so excessive that it probably precipitated, if it did not actually cause the birth of psychoanalysis. We shall soon see how.

Like all passions, Freud's friendship was both generous and unjust, violent and extravagant, fertile and pregnant with misunderstandings, even conflicts for the two parties concerned. In addition it was interested, in the higher as well as in the common meaning of the word. Freud, it seems, needed to be indebted to his friends in some way; and his debt was not only intellectual, for his material circumstances, always precarious and sometimes desperate, often obliged him to accept, if not ask for financial help. He has explained that, at first, he found the idea of borrowing from his friends extremely painful: but Hammerschlag, who was very poor himself, managed to persuade him that there was nothing humiliating about it, that material help from his closest friends was simply a mark of confidence in his future success.[1] And so for years

[1] We see here a modern form of the traditional solidarity which made it a duty for the more affluent members of the Jewish community to help poor students and subsidize the Talmudic schools. In eastern Europe impecunious students were fed in rotation by the eminent and the wealthy. The dividing line between those who lived

Freud had Fleischl, Paneth and others who regularly came to his assistance as 'bankers'; but his main protector was Breuer, who for a very long time lent him or gave him a certain sum of money every month. It is highly likely that none of them reckoned on being repaid. In any case, Fleischl and Paneth died before Freud could pay them back. And when he quarrelled with Breuer he still owed him a large amount of money, which no doubt added to his resentment.

This being the situation, we shall not be surprised to learn that Freud sometimes considered himself a *Schnorrer*, that lovable, cynical parasite who is part and parcel of Jewish life and who, according to tradition, pays his share with his wit and his jokes. We shall also understand why the peculiar association between *debt* and *friendship* which long characterized his personal relations is one of the commonest and saddest themes running through *The Interpretation of Dreams.*

Nowhere did Freud's feelings appear so contradictory, so extreme and baffling as in his friendship with Wilhelm Fliess, which lasted for twelve years and also ended in a sensational break. The word 'passion' is not too strong to describe this extraordinary attachment which, for a long period of time, lay at the centre of Freud's life and determined once and for all the course of his work. A letter dated January 1, 1896, one of many like it, will illustrate the point:

'People like you should not die out, my dear friend; we others need the like of you too much. How much have I to thank you for in consolation, understanding, stimulation in my loneliness, in the meaning of life you have given me, and lastly in health which no one else could have brought back to me. It is essentially your example that has enabled me to gain the intellectual strength to trust my own judgment . . . and to face with deliberate resignation, as you do, all the hardships the future may have in store. For all that accept my simple thanks.'[1]

---

on their meal tickets and the *Schnorrer* (sponger), a typical figure in so many Jewish stories, was often vague. In certain passages in *The Interpretation of Dreams* (cf. chap. 10, the dream about the *table d'hôte*) Freud hints that he often feared he might cross this line.

[1] Letter to Fliess, January 1, 1896, Ernest Jones, I, p. 328. The letter was accompanied by an important manuscript on defence neuroses, which Freud had entitled 'Christmas Tale'.

The man whom Freud was thanking in these disturbing and extravagant terms exercised an amazing influence on him for more than six years. He dragged him into an extraordinary adventure, of which many aspects still remain enigmatic. At the age of forty, with a large part of his life behind him, a wife whom he loved and six children to whom he was passionately devoted, Freud put his fate into the hands of a man he considered a genius, but whose talent was probably inferior. And he did so in such an emotional way that his whole existence came to depend on his friend's judgement and ideas as well as on his affection. The affair lasted too long for it to be called an infatuation. It was much more like a magic spell, and so strong that every normal countermeasure was ineffective. Freud only broke free by risking the boldest measure a man has ever tried on himself—self-analysis.

Fliess lived in Berlin, Freud in Vienna; and although the two men did their utmost in order to see one another often, the essence of their relationship is contained in a very intimate correspondence, in which each revealed to the other his innermost thoughts. These letters, which show the birth of psychoanalysis in an extremely dramatic light, themselves had a chequered history. Freud had destroyed Fliess's letters: it was only through a combination of complicated circumstances, and very much in spite of himself, that his own were preserved.

Some years after Fliess's death, in 1928, his widow sold Freud's 284 letters and the notes and manuscripts which were with them to a Berlin bookseller. Frau Fliess, knowing that Freud would destroy the letters if they fell into his hands, sold them on the express condition that, whatever happened, the bookseller should not let Freud get hold of them. The bookseller, driven out by the Nazi regime, was a refugee in Paris for a time and offered the lot to Marie Bonaparte, who immediately bought them for £ 100. When she got back to Vienna, where she was one of Freud's pupils, Marie Bonaparte told him about her providential acquisition and read him some of the letters to convince him of their scientific interest. Freud was indignant at the way the deal had been concluded and tried to buy back some of the letters so as to have the right to destroy them. But Marie Bonaparte had the courage to refuse. She managed to keep them and to save them from destruction through all the difficulties of the war. It was only after Freud's death that they finally reached England, where Anna Freud and Ernest Kris began to go through them.

Freud's letters provide us with only an imperfect knowledge of Fliess's personality, but they do afford a glimpse of an intrepid mind, capable of vast speculations and apparently very self-assured. Fliess was a man who was undoubtedly fascinating and impressive on account of his scientific knowledge and the richness of his literary culture, but inclined to extremes and so enamoured of his own ideas that nothing could make him give them up. A product of the liberal Berlin school and without the usual prejudices of the doctors of the time, he was undoubtedly seen by Freud as representing all the breadth of outlook which Freud found lacking in Vienna.

Fliess was not a psychiatrist but a specialist in diseases of the nose and throat. He worked all his life in Berlin where, unlike Freud, he had a large practice. However, his speciality was merely the pivot for his broad medical and scientific views, which took him far beyond the domain of medicine and into the field of biology. In that respect he was already converging on Freud, who, likewise, had only turned to medicine as a way of attaining other ends.

Without going into the details of the half-serious, half-extravagant theories by which Fliess made a name for himself, a word or two must be said about them, for they closely concern the tough problems which Freud was then trying to solve. Fliess is known mainly for two conceptions which are nowadays given little credit but which were for some time much discussed. One concerns a new clinical entity, 'nasal reflex neurosis', the other is the famous 'periods theory', which has nothing whatsoever to do with the exact biology which he dreamed of founding, but with mysticism or with psychopathology.

The syndrome of 'nasal reflex neurosis' consisted of three different kinds of symptoms: headaches, neuralgic pains widely distributed from the cardiac to the lumbar region, and functional disturbances which mainly affected digestion, circulation and respiration. Fliess had discovered that he could make all these symptoms disappear by applying cocaine to the mucous membrane of the nose. From that he deduced that, however numerous and diverse, they were homogeneous and owed their existence to one zone alone—the nose. The etiology of the nasal reflex neurosis was two-fold: it could be either organic, due for example to an infectious state, or functional, and then the cause was to be sought in vaso-motor disturbances of sexual origin. In the latter case Fliess's syndrome was like that of neurasthenia, which Freud classified among the neuroses which have not a psychical origin but one connected with bad bodily, particularly bad sexual hygiene.

The periodic law sprang from the alleged observation of a relationship between the zone of the female genital organs and the nose. Excited by the problems of menstruation which suggested to him an incredible profusion of ideas, Fliess came to believe that periodicity was the fundamental law of all the vital activities of human beings, animals and even the whole universe. He expounded his ideas in this way:

'Woman's menstrual bleeding is the expression of a process which affects both sexes and the beginning of which goes back beyond puberty. . . . The facts before us compel us to emphasize another factor. They teach us that, apart from the menstrual process of the twenty-eight day type, yet another group of periodic phenomena exists with a twenty-three day cycle, to which people of all ages and both sexes are subject. . . .'[1]

Fliess saw an intimate connection between these periodic processes and masculine and feminine sexual characteristics. He argued that this proved his theory of the bisexuality of human beings and allowed some very bold conclusions:

'This knowledge, once acquired, leads one to think that the development of our organism is produced in fits and starts in the course of these sexual periods and that, consequently, the day of our death is just as fixed as the day of our birth. The disturbances due to illness are subject to the same laws as the periodic phenomena themselves. . . . The mother transmits her periods to her child and, following the first period transmitted, determines its sex. The periods continue afterwards in the child and then, following the same rhythm, down through succeeding generations. They cannot be re-created, any more than energy it-

[1] 'Relationship between the nose and the female genital organs from the biological point of view,' Vienna, 1897. *Origins*, p. 7.

The same ideas are expressed in later works: *Der Ablauf des Lebens* (The Rhythm of Life) Vienna, 1923; *Vom Leben und vom Tod* (Life and Death), Jena, 1924; *Das Jahr im Lebendigen* (The Year in Living Things), Jena, 1924; etc.

self. their rhythm is not modified as long as organized beings continue to reproduce themselves sexually. These rhythms concern not only the human species but also animals and undoubtedly also the whole organized universe. The astonishing precision with which the interval of twenty-eight or twenty-three days is maintained, according to the case, allows one to suppose that a connection exists between the astronomical conditions and the creation of organisms. . . .'[1]

Neither Freud nor Fliess seems to have suspected that the idea of bisexuality was far from being new and that it had engaged the attention of more than one mind before then. Fliess believed he was its inventor and set great store by it. Sometime later, in an article which was almost libellous, he publicly accused Freud of divulging his discovery to one of his pupils and of thus betraying his secret.[2]

Note that Freud long believed in the periodic law and that he attempted, without any great success, to use it in his own work. Thus he tried to explain by the periods twenty-eight and twenty-three the distinctions to be drawn between neurasthenia and anxiety neurosis; and he got it into his head that the sum of the two prophetic numbers —fifty-one—gave him the exact date of his death. At the time when Fliess, who was falling more and more into a confused mysticism of numbers, extended his calculations to the entire cosmos, Freud went so far as to call him the 'Kepler of biology'.

The two men had become acquainted in 1887, through Breuer, when Fliess was on a study trip to Vienna. At that time Fliess had not yet published anything and Freud was only just beginning to tackle the problem of hysteria. The two men were therefore in a similar position, both bubbling over with ideas and impatient to find proofs for them. That was not the only resemblance between them. Both belonged to the Jewish lower middle class, both were poor (but Fliess married into money shortly afterwards), both stood on the fringe of the medical thought of their time and both possessed the same solid classical culture and had many similar tastes. In addition they had a common scientific outlook which could be expected to engender a

1 Ibid.

2 *In eigener Sache* (In my own Cause). Gegen Weininger und Swoboda, Berlin, 1906, pp. 214–8. Cf. chap. 12.

mutual liking. Fleiss was, in fact, a follower of Helmholtz's school, of which Freud's teacher, Brücke, was considered to be its ambassador in Vienna. And there is a perfectly good reason why Freud once made a significant pun on the name 'Brücke' (bridge) in a dream: the old scientist was a 'bridge' between Vienna and Berlin, just as he was between Freud and his new friend.

As has been said, Freud's scientific thought was linked to a physiological doctrine solidly based on the physical sciences and this would seem to be ideally suitable for measuring all phenomena. This physiology, which became the starting point of psychoanalytical theories, was also what inspired Fliess in his search for an 'exact biological science' as he called it in the sub-title of one of his books. That provided a solid basis for collaboration and gave Freud reason to hope that he would see his own intuitions confirmed by an extensive knowledge which he was not sure he himself possessed.

The interest was mutual, for if Freud could find, for example, a direct connection between the theory of the nasal reflex neurosis and the problem of the differential diagnosis of hysterical and somatic disturbances—a problem which had continually absorbed him since his stay in Paris—Fliess for his part could not but be attracted by the ideas of Freud who was trying to preserve a link between the conceptions of psychology and those of physiology and physics. However, the two scientists' share in this exchange of ideas was very unequal. Fliess acted as though he could do without it, while Freud was for a long time convinced that he was the only one to gain anything from it.

It is also certain that Freud was carried away by the courage of the Berlin doctor who, instead of rejecting sexuality, made it the centre of his thinking. After the disappointment of Breuer's pusillanimity, this freedom of mind, cutting clean through Viennese pettiness, restored his faith in his old ideal of collaboration and friendship. Moreover, it was when Breuer had gone completely out of his life that Freud's relations with Fliess took on their most passionate note.

Freud's first letters were still somewhat formal although, driven on by an intense need to break his scientific isolation, he spoke freely in them of his ideas, his least solid hypotheses and of the obstacles which were blocking his path. Gradually, however, the tone became more familiar, the two men used one another's Christian names (which Freud hardly ever did again) and their correspondence became more voluminous. Soon letters were not enough. They decided to meet for a thorough-going exchange of ideas and they gave these meetings the half-serious, half-ironic title of 'congresses'. At first their congresses took place in Vienna and Berlin, then they went more and more frequently to a neutral city, such as Munich, Dresden, Salzburg, Nuremberg, Breslau, Aussee, Innsbruck. After the last 'congress', which took place in the Tyrol in 1900, Freud and Fliess never met again.

Between 1890 and 1900 the letters showed that the 'congresses' assumed an ever-increasing importance in Freud's personal life. At first to miss a meeting with Fliess caused him no more than normal disappointment:

'I am writing to you to-day to tell you, very much against the grain, that I cannot come to Berlin; not that I care about Berlin or the congress, but I am so disappointed that I shall not be able to see you there. What has upset my plans is not one big thing, but a combination of little ones, as can so easily happen in the case of a doctor and a family man. Going to Berlin would clash with everything. On the professional side my most important patient is going through a kind of nervous crisis . . . and on the family side all sorts of things have been going wrong with the children (I now have a son as well as a daughter); and my wife, who generally never objects to my going away for a short time, does not want me to go away just now; and so on and so forth. In short, it cannot be done and, as I look forward to this trip as a great treat, I must be ready to give it up when called upon.

'I do so most unwillingly, because I expected a great deal from meeting you. Though otherwise quite satisfied, happy if you like, I feel very isolated, scientifically blunted, stagnant and resigned. When I talked to you, and saw that you thought something of me, I actually started thinking something of myself, and the picture of confident energy which you offered was not without its effect. I should also have profited professionally from meeting you, and perhaps I should also have benefited from the Berlin atmosphere, because for years now I have been without anyone who could teach me anything and have settled down more or less exclusively to the treatment of the neuroses. . . . Do not lose patience with me for not having answered you and now for refusing your extremely kind invitation. Let me know that there is some prospect of seeing you for a few days, so that I shall not feel that I am losing your friendship.'[1]

Some years later Freud looked forward to a coming 'congress' with the joy of someone who 'is at last going to satisfy his hunger and thirst.' After a meeting in Nuremberg he was 'in a continual state of euphoria and worked like a young man.' One day, unable to keep a meeting as arranged, he explained to Fliess what this 'abstinence' meant to him:

'After each of our congresses I have been newly fortified for weeks, new ideas press forward, pleasure in the hard work was restored, and the flickering hope of finding one's way through the jungle burned for a while steadily and brilliantly. This time of abstinence teaches one nothing, since I have always known what our meetings meant to me.'[2]

Or he confessed his absolute dependence on the man he regarded as 'the supreme judge' of his writings:

'I can write nothing if I have no public at all, but I am perfectly content to write only for you.'[3]

Without knowing Fliess's letters it is hardly possible to appreciate the value of his judgement on the works of which Freud sent him the manuscripts. The latter never questioned it: praise sent him 'wild with joy',[4] criticism plunged him into despair. It can be assumed, however, that when Freud came to think that the links between his psychology and physiology and physics were looser than he had first believed—for instance, when he discovered infantile sexuality—Fliess had some difficulty in followng him along a path so far removed from his own. On one

[1] Letter to Fliess, August 1, 1890. *Origins,* pp. 59–60.

[2] Ernest Jones, I, p. 302.

[3] Ibid., letter of May 18, 1898.

[4] In 1900 Freud began to understand the reasons for his dependence on Fliess. In a letter dated May 7 he said: 'But as far as I am concerned nothing can take the place of contacts with a friend; it is a need which corresponds to something in me, perhaps something feminine. . . .' *Origins,* p. 318.

point at least he seems to have been a most competent critic: in all matters concerning Freud's literary style and composition he was most exacting. His suggestions and criticism, by which Freud laid great store, were undoubtedly the most positive part of his influence which, in other respects, was highly dubious.

Literature also took up a large part of the correspondence between the two men, who had common tastes and were often keen on the same books.

Freud repeatedly quoted Shakespeare to his friend and recommended him to read Kipling; Fliess, for his part, introduced Freud to the work of Conrad Ferdinand Meyer, the great Swiss writer. This author became a life-long favourite with Freud and it was he who first gave Freud the idea of applying the technique of analysis to a literary work, namely *The Woman Judge*. He sent Fliess an interpretation which was obviously incomplete, but it was written in a style which already possessed all the attractiveness to be found in his future essays on aesthetics.[1]

In a general way this correspondence provides a mass of indispensable information about Freud's life during those ten years which, in many respects, represent a serious crisis in his life. In it Freud speaks about his family, describes his children's smallest doings, his successes or his failures with his few patients, the things that stand out in his daily round, or the difficulties he encountered on his travels. We see him recalling the distressing time when, on Fliess's orders, he tried to stop smoking and give up his beloved cigars. Then there is his passion for archaeology which absorbed him more and more as time went on and of which Fliess, who was less fascinated by the past then Freud was, disapproved as being an expensive and useless hobby.

The two friends also held passionate discussions on contemporary politics. The Dreyfus affair incensed them, Zola took their breath away: 'What a wonderful man,' Freud

[1] There can be no doubt that it concerns the romanticized rejection of a memory to do with the writer's relationship with his sister. Nevertheless one thing strikes us, namely that this rejection happens exactly as in a neurosis. All neurotics invent what is called a family romance (in paranoia it becomes conscious). On the one hand this romance flatters megalomania, on the other it constitutes a defence against incest. If your sister is not your mother's child, you can no longer be blamed.' *Origins*, pp. 255–6.

said, 'one could get on with him!' But nothing excited him more than the elections for the Vienna City Council in which the Liberals waged a furious campaign against the leader of the Christian Social Party, Dr Karl Lüger, a declared anti-Semite whom Freud looked on as a personal enemy. Lüger was elected Mayor of Vienna three times within the two years 1895 and 1896, but his election was not confirmed by the Emperor until 1897. He retained his position until his death in 1910, so that Freud, who voted only when the Liberals put up a candidate, did not have the pleasure of seeing him defeated.

It now remains to be seen how Freud liberated himself from the extraordinary emotional and intellectual bondage in which Fliess had kept him for ten years. In 1896 Freud's father died, and this event, in itself undramatic in view of the old man's great age, produced in Freud such a profound disturbance that he was led to seek its origin. During the summer of 1897 he decided to apply to his own case the investigating technique he was using on his patients. It was a painful task, more dangerous than he had imagined, demanding not only courage but a sort of ascetic self-discipline. It was a long time before Freud realized that if Fliess was stimulating his efforts, Fliess was also preventing him from carrying them through to a logical conclusion. One day in 1900 he saw that in spite of his compulsive need to see Fliess, some obscure feeling was urging him to avoid the meeting and, sadly, he told him so:

'There has never been a period in which the wish that we lived in the same place as you and your family has affected me so deeply and constantly as in the past six months. You know I have been going through a deep inner crisis, and if we met you would see how it has aged me. So I was deeply touched when I was told of your proposal that we should meet at Easter. Anyone who did not understand the more subtle resolution of contradictions would think it incomprehensible that I am not hastening to assent to the proposal. In point of fact it is more probable that I shall avoid you—not only because of my almost childish yearning for the spring and the beauties of nature, which I should willingly sacrifice for the pleasure of your company for three days. But there are other, inner reasons, an accumulation of imponderables, which weigh heavily on me. . . . Inwardly I am deeply impoverished. I have had to demolish all my castles in the air, and I have just plucked up enough courage to start rebuilding them. During the catastrophic collapse you would have been invaluable to me; in the present stage I should hardly be able to make myself intelligible to you. I conquered my depression with the aid of a special intellectual diet, and now, under the influence of the distraction, it is slowly healing. In your company I should inevitably attempt to grasp everything consciously and tell you all about it, we should talk rationally and scientifically, and your fine and positive biological discoveries would rouse my innermost (impersonal) envy. The upshot would be that I should unburden my woes to you for the whole five days and come back agitated and dissatisfied for the summer, for which I shall probably need all my composure. No one can help me in what oppresses me, it is my cross, which I must bear, and heaven knows my back is getting noticeably bent under it. . . .'[1]

[1] Letter to Fliess, *Origins,* p. 314.

8

SELF-ANALYSIS

Anyone reading *The Interpretation of Dreams* or Freud's *Autobiography* might come to the conclusion that Freud achieved his discoveries after long and unremitting labour and that, although beset by all sorts of difficulties and obstacles, he remained, except on rare occasions, the impassive man of science. Nothing is further from the truth. The proof lies in the most vivid and moving document he left the world. His letters to Wilhelm Fliess[1] bear witness to the hard personal struggle to which psychoanalysis more than any other of man's discoveries owed its birth.

The most significant letters in this respect are clearly those in which Freud, from 1897 onwards, describes the various phases of his self-analysis, his inspiring progress and all the risks attendant on his inner work. But before this date the correspondence with Fliess shows how Freud, in order to correct certain errors which were obstructing his research, came to be seriously involved, thereby losing the scientist's so-call serenity. It takes us into the dark regions in which he long struggled, aided only by his intense thirst for knowledge, and of which, for understandable reasons, his subsequent work retains no more than an occasional shadowy hint.

An example is the mistake which, at one juncture, most hindered his understanding of hysterical phenomena. In his autobiography he merely said:

'Before going further into the question of infantile sexuality I must mention an error into which I fell for a while and which might well have had fatal consequences for the whole of my work. Under the pressure of the technical procedure which I used at that time, the majority of my patients reproduced from their childhood scenes in which they were sexually seduced by some grown-up person.

[1] Most of these letters are published in Freud's letters to Wilhelm Fliess, with the notes and work-plans which Freud sent to his friend.

With female patients the part of seducer was almost always assigned to their father. I believed these stories, and consequently supposed that I had discovered the roots of the subsequent neurosis in these experiences of sexual seduction in childhood. My confidence was strengthened by a few cases in which relations of this kind with a father, uncle, or elder brother had continued up to an age at which memory was to be trusted. If the reader feels inclined to shake his head at my credulity, I cannot altogether blame him; though I may plead that this was at a time when I was intentionally keeping my critical faculty in abeyance so as to preserve an unprejudiced and receptive attitude towards the many novelties which were coming to my notice every day. When, however, I was at last obliged to recognize that these scenes of seduction had never taken place, and that they were only phantasies which my patients had made up or which I myself had perhaps forced upon them, I was for some time completely at a loss.'[1]

In actual fact—and the letters written to Fliess bear this out—Freud was not just temporarily bewildered: he was profoundly disturbed for several years by the improbability of his theory. It was only after he began to analyse himself that he unravelled the obscure reasons for his credulity: the child's seduction, which he imputed to the father (i.e. also to his own father) masked the child's (i.e. Freud's own) incestuous desires, the full reality of which he was to understand a little later. The revelation, which arose out of the analysis of his own dreams, forced him to abandon the seduction theory at the risk of compromising all his work, as from 1893 onwards the idea of precocious seduction had been the very basis of his own conception of hysteria:

'Now I do not know where I am, as I have failed to reach theoretical understanding of repression and its play of forces. . . . Were I depressed, jaded, unclear in my mind, such doubts might be taken for signs of weakness. But as I am in just the opposite state, I must acknowledge them to be the result of earnest and effective intellectual labour, and I am proud that after penetrating so far I am still capable of such criticism. . . . It is curious that I feel not in

[1] *An Autobiographical Study, Std Edn* XX, pp. 33–4.

the least disgraced, though the occasion might seem to require it. Certainly I shall not tell it in Gath, or publish it in the streets of Askalon, in the land of the Philistines—but between ourselves I have a feeling more of triumph than of defeat (which cannot be right.).'[1]

Despite the intellectual exhilaration inspired by this setback, Freud was scared by what this involved:

'The hope of eternal fame was so beautiful, and so was that of certain wealth, complete independence, travel, and removing the children from the sphere of worries which spoiled my own youth. All that depended on whether hysteria succeeded or not. Now I can be quiet and modest again and go on worrying and saving, and one of the stories from my collection[2] occurs to me: "Rebecca, you can take off your wedding-gown, you're not a bride any longer!'"[3]

The following letter, written on October 3, 1897, marks a historic date. It contains the first allusion to Freud's most sensational discovery, the one which gave him the key to the secret drama of every childhood, a long-forgotten but fatal drama which he called the 'Oedipus complex', in memory of the Greek hero. What patient observation of his cases had given him an inkling of he now experienced by making a prodigious descent into his own self:

'For the last four days my self-analysis, which I regard as indispensable for clearing up the whole problem, has been making progress in dreams and yielding the most valuable conclusions and evidence. At certain points I have the impression of having come to the end, and so far I have always known where the next night of dreams would continue. To describe it in writing is more difficult than anything else, and besides it is far too extensive. I can only say that in my case my father played no active role, though I certainly projected on to him an analogy from myself; that my "primary originator" [of neurosis] was an ugly, elderly but clever woman who told me a great deal

[1] Letter to Fliess, September 21, 1897, *Origins,* pp. 216–7.

[2] The anthology of Jewish anecdotes which Freud had begun and which provided him with much material for *Jokes and Their Relation to the Unconscious.*

[3] *Origins,* pp. 217–8.

about God and hell, and gave me a high opinion of my own capacities; that later (between the ages of two and two-and-a-half) libido towards *matrem* was aroused; the occasion must have been the journey with her from Leipzig to Vienna, during which we spent a night together and I must have had the opportunity of seeing her *nudam*. . . . I still have not got to the scenes which lie at the bottom of all this. If they emerge, and I succeed in resolving my hysteria, I shall have to thank the memory of the old woman who provided me at such an early age with the means for living and surviving. You see how the old liking breaks through again. I cannot give you any idea of the intellectual beauty of the work. . . .'[1]

It is certain that the *intellectual* beauty of his work gave Freud the courage to advance into the alarming regions where he had long seen his patients struggling. This beauty, however, was powerless to save him from the anguished involved in his course, and so for four or five years he was a prey to the anxiety, the depression and the sudden changes of mood which characterized the inner life of his patients.

Freud had felt the absolute necessity for this analysis, the most difficult of all, about a year before, when he came up against the completely unexpected disturbance he suffered as a result of his father's death. The old man was eighty, Freud forty, but that in no way tempered the violence of the shock, nor the feeling of guilt which the analysis of a typical dream showed him to lie at the root of his grief.

'I find it so difficult to put pen to paper at the moment that I have even put off writing to you to thank you for the moving things you said in your letter. By one of the obscure routes behind the official consciousness the old man's death affected me deeply. I valued him highly and understood him very well indeed, and with his peculiar mixture of deep wisdom and imaginative light-heartedness he meant a great deal in my life. By the time he died his life had long been over, but at a death the whole past stirs within one. . . .

'I must tell you about a very pretty dream I had on the

[1] Ibid., pp. 218–20.

night after the funeral. I found myself in a shop where there was a notice up saying:

You are requested
to close your eyes.

I recognized the place as the barber's to which I go every day. On the day of the funeral I was kept waiting, and therefore arrived at the house of mourning rather late. The family were displeased with me, because I had arranged for the funeral to be quiet and simple, which they later agreed was the best thing. They also took my lateness in rather bad part. The phrase on the notice-board has a double meaning. It means "one should do one's duty towards the dead" in two senses—an apology, as though I had not done my duty and my conduct needed overlooking, and the actual duty itself. The dream was thus an outlet for the feeling of self-reproach which a death generally leaves among the survivors. . . .'[1]

After that Fliess received almost daily the most conclusive results of this astonishing inner adventure which led Freud beyond the *official* world of consciousness into unexplored regions where he sometimes felt lost, sometimes full of enthusiasm and at others disheartened by the very magnitude of his task. Obliged to be both analyst and analysed and lacking the help of someone who might have played for him the role he played for his patients, Freud could only confide in the friend whose face he had long idealized and the mere thought of whom brought him encouragement. It was Fliess to whom he confided his woes, described the sad moods which sometimes left him feeling empty and numb and disclosed the intimate meaning of his dreams and the slow genesis of his theories:

'Last night's dream produced the following under the most remarkable disguises:

'She was my instructress in sexual matters, and chided me for being clumsy and not being able to do anything (that is always the way with neurotic impotence: anxiety over incapacity at school gets its sexual reinforcement in

[1] Ibid., November 2, 1896, pp. 170–1. The same dream is told with a variation in *The Interpretation of Dreams*. There the order is expressed in a double formula: 'Please close your eye/your eyes.' In German 'ein Auge zudrücken' means 'to shut one's eyes to something.'

this way). I saw the skull of a small animal which I thought of as a "pig" in the dream, though it was associated in the dream with your wish of two years ago that I might find a skull on the Lido to enlighten me, as Goethe once did. But I did not find it. Thus it was "a little *Schafskopf*".[1] The whole dream was full of the most wounding references to my present uselessness as a therapist. Perhaps the origin of my tendency to believe in the incurability of hysteria should be sought here. Also she washed me in reddish water in which she had previously washed herself (not very difficult to interpret; I find nothing of the kind in my chain of memories, and so I take it for a genuine rediscovery); and she encouraged me to steal "Zehners" (ten-Kreuzer pieces) to give to her. A long chain of association connects these first silver Zehners to the heap of paper ten-florin notes which I saw in the dream as Martha's housekeeping money. The dream can be summed up as "bad treatment", just as the old woman got money from me for her bad treatment of me. . . . A severe critic might say that all this was phantasy projected into the past instead of being determined by the past. The *experimenta crucis* would decide the matter against him. The reddish water seems a point of this kind. Where do all patients derive the horrible perverse details which are often as alien to their experience as to their knowledge?'[2]

Fascinating as it was, the strange world in which Freud was attempting to find his way failed to destroy his critical spirit. He undoubtedly had faith in his method of interpretation and it seemed to him that he 'was burning'; but he was far from being content with an arbitrary structure—a charge which has often been levelled against him—and he tried to find an unimpeachable witness who would corroborate his results. He found her, in fact, in the person of his mother. It was the first verification, with the help of objective data, of a psychoanalytical reconstruction of the past:

'All this is the more valuable from my point of view because I have succeeded in finding a number of real points of reference. I asked my mother whether she remembered my nurse. "Of course", she said, "an elderly woman, very shrewd indeed. She was always taking you to church.

[1] Literally 'sheep's head', fool.

[2] Ibid., October 4, 1897, pp. 220–1.

When you came home you used to preach, and tell us all about how God conducted His affairs. At the time I was in bed when Anna was being born," (Anna is two-and-a-half years younger) "she turned out to be a thief, and all the shiny Kreuzers and Zehners and toys that had been given you were found among her things. Your brother Philipp went himself to fetch the policeman, and she got ten months." Now see how that confirms the conclusions from my dream interpretation. . . .'[1]

This guilt which Freud felt unconsciously toward his patients and which, undoubtedly, was not alien to his complex relations with medicine, is one of the commonest themes in his dreams. As in the celebrated dream about Irma's injection, the mistake is confused with an alleged professional error still weighing heavily on the doctor's conscience.

In fact, it seems that Freud felt guilty in some way in every direction: toward his patients, who had to pay him although he could not guarantee to cure them; toward morality, for the new course his psychology had taken was sweeping him toward the forbidden regions of sexuality and barbarous instinct; and finally towards science, which could accuse him of drawing arbitrary conclusions from slender hypotheses. This supreme authority, which Freud held to be so important, was at the time represented by a brilliant friend who, unlike himself, was living on the *terra firma* of biology. And so it was for Fliess's benefit that, after analysing a dream, Freud attempted to justify his conclusions one by one:

'It might be objected that these coincidences are not conclusive, because I might have heard that the nurse was a thief in later childhood and to all appearances forgotten the fact until it emerged in the dream. I think myself that that must have been the case. But I have another unexceptionable and amusing piece of evidence. If the woman disappeared so suddenly, I said to myself, some impression of the event must have been left inside me. Where was it now? Then a scene occurred to me which for the last twenty-nine years had been turning up from time to time in my conscious memory without my understanding it. I was crying my heart out, because my mother was nowhere to be found. My brother Philipp (who is twenty years

[1] Ibid., October 15, 1897, pp. 221–2.

older than I) opened a cupboard for me, and when I found that mother was not there either I cried still more, until she came through the door, looking slim and beautiful. What can that mean? Why should my brother open the cupboard for me when he knew that my mother was not inside it and that opening it therefore could not quieten me? Now I suddenly understand. I must have begged him to open the cupboard. When I could not find my mother, I feared she must have vanished, like my nurse not long before. I must have heard that the old woman had been locked, or rather "boxed" up, because my brother Philipp, who is now sixty-three, was fond of such humorous expressions, and still is to the present day. The fact that I turned to him shows that I was well aware of his part in my nurse's disappearance. . . .'[1]

Freud, however, was far from being satisfied with his results. He did, of course, correct a mistake which was greatly prejudicial to the pursuit of his work. He knew now that if the alleged precocious seduction of hysterics was not necessarily based on a biographical fact, it is none the less rooted in reality, in the incestuous desires of the child who, in his very earliest years, really does behave like a little Oedipus. But such a discovery raises even more questions than it answers. He saw that it would take him a long way and that, willy-nilly, he had to follow it to the end.

'If the analysis goes on as I expect, I shall write it all out systematically and lay the results before you. So far I have found nothing completely new, but all the complications to which by now I am used. It is no easy matter. Being entirely honest with oneself is a good exercise. Only one idea of general value has occurred to me. I have found love of the mother and jealousy of the father in my own case too, and now believe it to be a general phenomenon of early childhood, even if it does not always occur so early as in children who have been made hysterics. (Similarly with the "romanticization of origins" in the case of paranoiacs—heroes, founders of religion). If that is the case, the gripping power of *Oedipus Rex,* in spite of all the rational objections to the inexorable fate that the story

[1] Ibid. Freud told this story of the cupboard and the nurse as an example of 'screen memory' in *The Psychopathology of Everyday Life*. See *Std Edn* VI, pp. 49–51.

presupposes, becomes intelligible, and one can understand why later fate dramas were such failures. Our feelings rise against any arbitrary individual fate such as shown in the *Ahnfrau*,[1] etc., but the Greek myth seizes on a compulsion which everyone recognizes because he has felt traces of it in himself. Every member of the audience was once a budding Oedipus in phantasy, and this dream-fulfilment played out in reality causes everyone to recoil in horror, with the full measure of repression which separates his infantile from his present state. . . .'[2]

From this moment Freud searched literature for the proofs which neither his own analysis nor the analysis of his all too few patients could yet provide. He had hardly laid bare the secret of the Greek tragedy before Shakespeare seemed to confirm his ideas:

'The idea has passed through my head that the same thing may lie at the root of *Hamlet*. I am not thinking of Shakespeare's conscious intentions, but supposing rather that he was impelled to write it by a real event because his own unconscious understood that of his hero. How can one explain the hysteric Hamlet's phrase "So conscience doth make cowards of us all", and his hesitation to avenge his father by killing his uncle, when he himself so casually sends his courtiers to their death and despatches Laertes so quickly? How better than by the torment roused in him by the obscure memory that he himself had meditated the same deed against his father because of passion for his mother—"use every man after his desert, and who should 'scape whipping?" His conscience is his unconscious feeling of guilt. And are not his sexual coldness when talking to Ophelia, his rejection of the instinct to beget children, and finally his transference of the deed from his father to Ophelia, typically hysterical? And does he not finally succeed, in just the same remarkable way as my hysterics do, in bringing down his punishment on himself and suffering the same fate as his father, being poisoned by the same rival?'[3]

[1] *Die Ahnfrau*, the title of a play by Franz Grillparzer.

[2] *Origins*, pp. 223–4.

[3] Ibid. This letter provided the first version of the parts of *The Interpretation of Dreams* dealing with *Oedipus Rex* and *Hamlet*.

Although he did not yet expressly link the vital element in poetic creation with the unconscious part of psychical life, Freud could already perceive the enormous wealth of material available in great art, especially literature, in which man, in all ages, has fulfilled his most unrealizable dreams. From that moment he felt that psychoanalysis and literature are in some strange way inter-related, that both draw on the same sources and that they can enrich each other. Of course, this idea could only occur to a man whose own taste and culture led him to set a high, perhaps an excessively high value on art. But it also afforded a certain consolation. It partly compensated for the scientific isolation from which he was suffering such agonies at the time and it also helped to comfort him by showing him that the monstrous things of which he had proof within himself had already been experienced and described by other men who were universally recognized as geniuses.

To appreciate the results of this unprecedented analysis, which created a new, systematic, scientific form of self-knowledge, we should naturally have to know more about Freud's inner life and about what brought him suffering and disturbance. In his letters to Fliess, Freud often spoke of his 'psychoneurosis', which he called 'hysteria', although this should perhaps be seen rather as what he later called 'anxiety hysteria'. As in all cases of this kind, the clinical picture of the neurosis was not so straightforward as to produce an infallible diagnosis. Although Freud was very pre-occupied with nosological questions at this period, it is certain that he thought less about labelling his own disturbances than he did of gaining from them more understanding to help and possibly cure his patients. Certain of these disturbances probably belong to the sphere of what is now called psychosomatic medicine: dreadful migrane; an extremely painful nasal infection which twice drove him to be operated on by Fliess, who was a specialist in this field and who suffered from the same trouble; or digestive disturbances and a marked propensity to fatigue. Others, however, were manifestly of psychical origin: train phobia, of which he provided an analysis and which was not strictly a phobia since it did not prevent him from travelling; inhibitions like the one which for years kept him from going to Rome, although this city was the object of one of his oldest dreams; sudden changes of mood, fits of depression and anxiety and, above all, obsessive ideas revolving round death, taking the form of a fear of accidents or a longing for early death. In a word, the rather motley and altogether common-place picture to which psychoanalysts have long been accustomed.

In his letters to Fliess Freud complained a great deal about these disturbances which made him like his own patients, although much later he bore without a word of complaint the incurable illness which, for sixteen years, made almost every day of his life one long agony. But even in the worst moments his painful affective states never prevented him from working.

The letters to Fliess inform us about the self-analysis only up to 1902, the year when the break between the two men occurred. There is reason to believe that it was continued and that Freud had to resume it at certain intervals over a long period of time. He never claimed that it was completely successful.

If by cure is meant what bodily medicine can rightly promise in its most favourable cases, Freud was certainly not cured. But the mind cannot be treated like the body and a cure for the mind would be nothing less than total perfection. What is more, Freud analysed himself on his own, without the help of an objective analyst and without being able to study transference manifestations, which are of decisive importance in any treatment. Left incomplete, Freud's self-analysis was bound to leave untouched neurotic characteristics which were not without influence subsequently on certain of Freud's conclusions, and on the history of the psychoanalytical movement. We can, however, well believe that it had been deep enough to give him the inner peace he needed for his tremendous work and to give him that fine countenance, at once stern and wise, with which he faced the world for the remaining forty years of his life.

9

THE INTERPRETATION OF DREAMS

The Interpretation of Dreams is considered to be Freud's major work and, so far, one of the most solid pillars of psychoanalysis. Freud himself felt that this work sprang from an exceptional inspiration and that, even if parts of his other books had one day to be corrected, this one, with its freshness and its truth, would remain intact.

It would be an exaggeration to say that *The Interpretation of Dreams* was the fruit of a chance discovery. But there is something in this, since Freud discovered the significance of dreams while seeking to fathom the why and the wherefore of neuroses. It is true that at quite an early stage the two lines of research had become so closely connected that they were bound to influence each other: neurosis had revealed to him the importance of dreams, and dreams gave him the key to neuroses.

It was a decisive modification of his therapeutic technique which enabled Freud to perceive the enormous value of the dream as a psychical phenomenon. We remember that his 'psychical analysis' (based at first on hypnosis and suggestion, both of which were subsequently abandoned) employed certain practices. The doctor admonished, or urged or questioned the patient, pressed on his forehead with his hand, and all this was done with the aim of rousing in the patient's mind an idea connected with the cause of his symptom. But one day a patient asked Freud not to interrupt the course of her thoughts and Freud took the hint. Henceforth he refrained from interrupting and thus gradually moved towards the technique called 'free association', to which psychoanalysis owes its originality.

The moment free association became the rule, patients began spontaneously to give an account of their dreams, so that Freud was led to treat the productions of nocturnal life as he did the other symptoms evoked in the conversation. Hysterics had, in a way, pushed him into this position since, from an inner necessity, they associated together all the ideas which came into their minds simultaneously.

Another clinical observation had also encouraged Freud in his research. This was the fact that an analogy existed between dreams and the hallucinatory states that went with certain mental illnesses such as 'acute hallucinatory psychosis' (Meynert's 'amentia'). Struck by the idea held by some psychiatrists that oneirical delusion was a way of fulfilling a hidden wish, Freud began to suspect that it might be the same with dreams and that the nocturnal part of our life, although absurd and anarchical, was no less meaningful or directed than our waking life.

His intuition was only really confirmed by the first complete analysis which he made of one of his dreams, on Wednesday, July 24, 1895, a historic day, as he himself noted half-seriously. The dream in question was the one called 'Irma's injection'. Freud had written down his interpretation of it in a café in a suburb of Vienna, the Bellevue Restaurant, where he wondered if a commemorative tablet would ever be put up with the inscription: 'In this house, on the 24th of July, 1895, the secret of dreams was revealed to Dr. Sigmund Freud.'[1] No marble plaque commemorates this extraordinary event which, like many others which were also important, passed quite unnoticed at the time. But the fame of *The Interpretation of Dreams,* which has continued undimmed for more than sixty years, deserves a whole monument to itself.

Freud would not have devoted himself to the problem of dreams with such passion if he had not had a personal inclination for the subject. He was, in fact, a great dreamer himself and, it would seem, had always assiduously written down his dreams in one of the note books which he destroyed one day along with his other papers. His dreams fascinated him. What is more he manifestly gave them a sort of credence and, in a letter to Martha for example, we find him vaguely attributing a prophetic meaning to them. Even then he made some observations which are very similar to his future work: he described at length to Martha a typical example of 'the dream within the dream' and was amazed to find that certain dreams, such as the one in which he passed the examination for his doctorate, recur periodically, sometimes over a number of years.

[1] Letter to Fliess, June 12, 1900, *Origins,* p. 321.

For Freud, then, dreams were not only a scientific subject but, as always with this man who was anxious to gain a keeper knowledge of himself, a source of questions closely bound up with his life. In that respect he was more like the traditional oneiromancers than the scientists of his day who, as a whole, denied that dreams had any value and relegated the ancient beliefs to the realm of superstition.

In calling his book *The Interpretation of Dreams* Freud showed clearly which camp he intended to join: as an interpreter of night's enigmas he followed all who from time immemorial had taken dreams to be secret messages, divine or otherwise, and held their revelations to be valuable for the conduct of life. Like them, Freud declared that dreams have a meaning and that this meaning directly concerns the dreamer himself.

The title of the book proclaimed and mapped out Freud's whole plan. Freud's aim was not, in fact, to create a science of dream life as understood by the writers of his day. He studied the immense literature on this subject, as he tells us in the first chapter of his book, and, apart from a few exceptions, found it to be appallingly superficial. His wish was, rather, to show that dreams are not only a sort of tremor which disturbs the sleeping mind, but a significant phenomenon possessing the fullness and something of the dignity of the other psychical activities. In a word he wanted to belie the proverb and say 'All dreams are truth'.

Writing *The Interpretation of Dreams* was several years' work. Freud said he had voluntarily delayed publication for four or five years, preferring to publish the book with more numerous and more solid proofs. But his memory led him astray. His letters to Fliess show that he did not conceive of the idea until 1897, two months after he had started to analyze himself. Moreover, we can well believe that from the beginning these two tasks reinforced each other, since Freud found the first and by far the most important material for the book in the analysis of his own dreams, which he was undertaking systematically at the time. Actually the very planning of the work coincided with a crisis, and Freud finally forced himself to write in an attempt to overcome the very painful state of mind into which he had been plunged by his father's death. He therefore became his own subject, and when he expounded his ideas it was himself he was exposing to public curiosity. This unpleasant necessity is a better explanation for his hesitation than mere scientific scruple. If he kept his discovery to himself for a long time it was because it laid his own self utterly bare.

In the letters to Fliess we can follow the risks of this self-imposed task which Freud undertook at first as a sort of mental hygiene and which gradually came to engross him. In 1897, when he was obliged to recognize the inaccuracy of his seduction theory, he hoped that dreams would still save the edifice he had built. Then he stopped writing to study the vast literature on the subject and was delighted to find that no writer had anticipated his conclusions. He hated the idea of having to write a history of the problems of dreams but he could not avoid it; and as he also wanted to include a chapter about general psychology, the whole project had to be re-cast. For two years he worked without a thought of publication but on May 28, 1889, he suddenly made up his mind and immediately told Fliess:

'The dreams, however, have suddenly taken shape without any special reason, but this time for good. I have decided that all the efforts at disguise will not do, and that giving it all up will not do either, because I cannot afford to keep to myself the finest—and probably the only lasting—discovery that I have made. In this dilemma I have followed the rabbi's line in the story of the cock and the hen. Do you know it? A man and wife who owned one cock and one hen decided to celebrate a festival by having a fowl for dinner, but they could not make up their mind which to kill, so they consulted the rabbi. "Rabbi, what are we to do, we've only one cock and one hen. If we kill the cock, the hen will pine, and if we kill the hen the cock will pine. But we want to have a fowl for dinner on the festival. Rabbi, what are we to do?" "Well, kill the cock," the rabbi said. "But then the hen will pine." "Yes, that's true; then kill the hen." "But rabbi, then the cock will pine." "Let it pine!" said the rabbi.

'So the dreams will be done. . . . Alas! That the gods should have set up the existing literature on a subject to frighten off the would-be contributor to it! The first time I tackled it I got stuck, but this time I shall work my way through it; there is nothing that matters in it anyway.

None of my works has been so completely my own as this. . . .'[1]

No sooner had Freud decided to publish the book than he felt utterly discouraged. Writing the history of dreams was exacting and tedious work which he found in no way inspiring. His predecessors in this field had absolutely nothing to teach him and in the end he felt that the poverty of their ideas cheapened the value of his own and he almost gave the whole thing up in disgust:

'Some of the specimens of the literature on the subject make me wish for the first time that I had never had anything to do with it. One of them is named Spitta . . . I am over the hill now. Naturally one gets deeper and deeper into the thing, and there comes a point where you have to break off. Once again the whole thing resolves itself into a commonplace. There is *one* wish that every dream is intended to fulfil, though it assumes various forms. That is the wish to sleep. You dream to avoid having to wake up, because you want to sleep. *Tant de bruit . . . !*'[2]

The chapter devoted to an examination of the literature on dreams was a source of embarrassment to Freud. Written at the insistence of Fliess, who considered it essential in order to forestall the attacks of specialists, it seemed to be extraneous to the work as a whole. Freud did not know where to put it, Fliess did not want it either in the middle or at the beginning. Freud at first agreed with him, then decided to make it the first chapter of the book:

'You feel about it as I do; the secret must be that we do not want it at all. But, if we do not want to put a weapon into the hands of the "learned", we must put up with it somewhere. The whole thing is planned on the model of an imaginary walk. First comes the dark wood of the authorities (who cannot see the trees), where there is no clear view and it is very easy to go astray. Then there is a cavernous defile through which I lead my readers—my specimen with its peculiarities, its details, its indiscretions, and its bad jokes—and then, all at once, the high ground and

[1] Letter to Fliess, May 28, 1899, *Origins*, p. 281.

[2] Ibid., June 9, 1899, pp. 282–3.

the prospect, and the question: "Which way do you want to go?" '[1]

In addition to the historical chapter, which he felt to be absolutely necessary, Freud added a chapter on psychology which, for other reasons, caused him more worry. This chapter, which deals with oneirical processes and ends the book, is considered to be the most difficult and most abstract he ever wrote. Freud said he wrote it 'like a dream', but in a letter to Fliess he declared it to be hopelessly imperfect:

'Notes are already beginning to pile up for the last and most ticklish chapter, the psychological one, the scope and arrangement of which I still do not see. I also have to do some reading for it. The psychologists will have enough to rail at in any case, but a thing like this must take its own course. . . . So it will contain 2,467 mistakes—which I will leave in it. . . .'[2]

The number 2,467 which Freud thought he had left in chapter 7 of *The Interpretation of Dreams* called for an explanation, but Freud did not think of doing this immediately. It was only when he assembled material for *The Psychopathology of Everyday Life* that he was struck by this apparently absurd figure which, according to his theory, must have a definite meaning. He then made a dazzling analysis of his 2,467 mistakes, an analysis which must be quoted in full to prove one of his most well-founded ideas, without which psychoanalysis would be partly incomprehensible—his absolute belief in the mind's determinism:

'You will find that in the letter I put down the number 2,467 as a bold arbitrary estimate of the number of mistakes which will be found in the dream book. What I meant was some very big number; but that particular one emerged. However, nothing in the mind is arbitrary or undetermined. You will therefore rightly expect that the unconscious had hastened to determine the number which was left open by consciousness. Now, immediately before, I had read in the newspaper that a General E. M. had re-

[1] Ibid., August 6, 1899, p. 290.
[2] Ibid., August 27, 1899, p. 293.

tired from the post of Master of Ordnance. I should explain that I am interested in this man. While I was serving as a medical officer-cadet he came to the sick quarters one day (he was then a colonel) and said to the medical officer: "You must make me well in a week, because I have some work to do for which the Emperor is waiting." After that episode I decided to follow his career, and lo and behold! now he has reached the end of it, having become Master of Ordnance, and is already (1889) on the retired list. I wanted to work out how long he had taken over this. Assuming that it was in 1882 that I saw him in hospital, it must have been seventeen years. I told my wife this and she remarked: "Oughtn't you to be on the retired list too, then?" "Heaven forbid!" I exclaimed. After this conversation I sat down to write to you. But the earlier train of thought went on in my mind, and with good reason. I had miscalculated; I have a fixed point in my memory to prove it. I celebrated my majority, i.e. my twenty-fourth birthday, under military arrest (having been absent without leave). So that was in 1880, or nineteen years ago. That gives you the "24" in 2,467. Now take my present age—43—add 24, and you have 67. In other words, in answer to the question whether *I* meant to retire too, my wish gave me another twenty-four years' work. I was obviously annoyed at having failed to get very far myself during the period in which I have followed Colonel M.'s career; and yet I was celebrating a kind of triumph over his career being at an end, while I still have everything in front of me. So one can say with justice that not even the number 2,467 which I threw out unthinkingly was without its determinants from the unconscious.'[1]

To the end Freud had very mixed feelings about his book. Sometimes the idea of leaving *The Interpretation of Dreams* to posterity consoled him for many hours of sadness; at other times he grieved over the serious defects in the work and asked Fliess, who corrected the proofs, to

[1] *The Psychopathology of Everyday Life, Std Edn* VI, ch. 12. The passage begins: 'In a letter to a friend I informed him that I had finished reading the proof-sheets of *The Interpretation of Dreams,* and that I did not intend to make any further changes in it, "even if it contained 2,467 mistakes!" I immediately attempted to explain the number to myself and added this little analysis as a postscript to the letter. It will be best to quote it now as I wrote it when I caught myself doing it. . . .'

help him to eliminate the most obvious ones. All in all, the form in which he described the dreams left him dissatisfied:

'What I dislike about it is the style. I was quite unable to express myself with noble simplicity, but lapsed into a facetious, circumlocutory straining after the picturesque. I know that, but the part of me that knows it and appraises it is unfortunately not the part that is productive. . . .'[1]

The final manuscript was sent to the publishers in September, 1899. At the end of October Wilhelm Fliess received a copy and on November 4, 1899, the book was on sale. But whether the publisher was superstitious or impressed by the imminent birth of a new century or whether he understood the prophetic character of the book, he preferred to date it 1900.

For eighteen months the press was almost completely silent about *The Interpretation of Dreams*. No scientific review marked its publication and apart from a eulogistic notice in the *Berliner Tagblatt* the daily papers ignored it. The statements by a few scientists who said anything were all negative. One was afraid that 'uncritical minds would be delighted to join in this play with ideas and would end up in complete mysticism and chaotic arbitrariness'; one Berlin professor lamented that 'the author's artistic imagination has triumphed over the scientific research worker's thinking;' and in 1907 a certain Professor Hoche, of Freiburg, ranked Freud's work beside 'the well-known dream-books, printed on bad paper, which may be found in cooks' drawers'.[2] And so for ten years the book went unsold and passed unnoticed.

[1] Letter to Fliess, September 11, 1899, *Origins*, p. 297. Cf. a letter of September 21 in which Freud said: 'Hidden somewhere within me is a certain feeling for form, an appreciation of beauty, that is to say a sort of perfection, and the involved sentences in my book on dreams, with their circumlocutions and clumsiness of expression, fell seriously short of one of my ideals. I do not think I am wrong in thinking that this lack of form indicates a lack of mastery of the subject. . . .'

[2] Ernest Jones, Vol. I. Referring to the public's reception of *The Interpretation of Dreams* Freud said in a letter to Fliess, March 23, 1900: 'The reception it has been given, at least up to now, has not exactly delighted me. It has been very little understood; the praises are like alms, most people obviously find the work distasteful. No one round me seems to have the slightest suspicion of its impor-

For Freud, however, *The Interpretation of Dreams* had more decisive consequences than any other of his books. It was the fruit of a long inner labour which had allowed him to emerge from a grave personal crisis with more fortitude, more self-confidence and equanimity about other people's opinions. Above all, it attracted the attention of a few young people who soon formed the first nucleus of his followers and at last ended his isolation.

The Interpretation of Dreams has gone through nine editions in thirty years, and Freud amplified it several times with dreams and observations sent to him by his pupils. Even in conception it is a complex work and so vast that the unprepared reader may well be afraid of getting lost. Moreover, Freud very soon felt the need to gather the main ideas together in a shorter account so as to put it within the reach of the non-technical but cultured public by whom he hoped to be better understood than by the scientific world. In 1901 therefore he produced a short but extremely clear version—a sort of popular version, but one from which none of his ideas were missing. And it is this little book, entitled *On Dreams,*[1] which will be used to present briefly the Freudian theory of dreams, a major part of psychoanalytical doctrine and the instrument of its day-to-day work.

According to Freud's theory, dreams are not a useless, unhealthy or morbid and rubbishy product of psychic activity, as most psycholgists of his day believed. They are phenomena whose absurdity and incoherence disappear as soon as we know how to interpret them with the aid of a suitable scientific method. Wiser than the scientists, the ancients and the common people had a profound intuition of their truth. They were mistaken only in believing that dreams had a prophetic value; for dreams predict nothing, they express a wish and immediately ensure its realization.

What the dreamer remembers on awakening is the 'manifest dream content'. The material which the dream

---

tance. I explain this to myself by saying that I am fifteen or twenty years in advance of my time.' Elsewhere the failure of the book inspired in him painful doubts about himself. He wrote in a letter to Fliess, June 7, 1900: 'No critic is more capable than I of grasping the disparity which exists between the problems and the solution I provide and, for my just punishment, none of the unexplored psychical regions into which I have been the first to penetrate will bear my name nor be subject to my laws.' *Origins*, p. 313 ff.

[1] *On Dreams, Std Edn* V.

provides in the course of analysis is called its 'latent content'. The process by which the latent dream is transformed into the manifest dream is 'the dream work'. Analysis exactly reverses this process. Looked at from the standpoint of the connection between latent content and manifest content, dreams can be divided into three categories.

First there are the clear and reasonable dreams which seem to be taken directly from our conscious life. They are frequent, short and without any great interest for us because there is nothing in them that strikes the imagination. However, their dream character is incontestable and we should never confuse them with products of the waking state.

The second group consists of reasonable dreams whose meaning, although perfectly clear, nevertheless astonishes us because nothing in us justifies this kind of preoccupation. They are the dreams which make us exclaim on waking: 'Where can this idea have come from?'

The third group comprises precisely those dreams which have suggested to psychologists the idea of reduced and useless psychical activity. They are in fact obscure, absurd, incoherent. They are the dreams which contain the enigmas, the analysis of which succeeds in penetrating to the meaning by replacing the manifest content by the latent content. It is to be noticed that the more obscure the dream is, the more it seems to resist analysis and the more it seems to oppose reconstruction of the thought hidden in it.

To the category of clear dreams belong all children's dreams, which are simply wish fulfilments. Freud became convinced of this by noting the dreams of his own children. His little daughter Anna became ill through eating strawberries and was not allowed to eat much. The same night she had a dream in which she first said her name, then: 'strawberry, bread and butter, pudding. . . .' And so the child dreams she is eating and going to get the very things she expects not to be allowed.

Even when children's dreams become complicated it is still always easy to reduce them to the satisfaction of a wish. Freud's little eight-year-old son dreamed that he was standing by Achilles in the chariot driven by Diomedes. His father knew that the evening before he had been absorbed in reading the legends of the Greek heroes. Excited by the two heroes he doubtless regretted not having lived in their times.

Adults' dreams can take on the features of children's dreams in certain situations of extreme need. Freud found confirmation of this in the books of the explorer Nansen.[1] While wintering amid the ice the members of the expedition, condemned to a meagre and monotonous diet, dreamed every night of huge meals, mountains of tobacco and the joys of their far-off homes.

All child-type dreams can be expressed by a wish—'Oh, if only the boat-trip had lasted longer!' 'If only I were up and dressed!' 'Why didn't I have the luck to be born in the days of the Greeks!' But dreams bring something more than this optative mood: they show us the wish fulfilled, they present the fulfilment in a visual form. In other words they transform an idea into an *image* and a wish into an actual *situation*: even the simplest of children's dreams must undergo this transposition.

For an idea to force its way into a dream it must be of such a kind that it can be transformed into an image and give rise to a dramatic situation. That is the principle which is valid for all types of dreams, whether they are clear or enigmatical, coherent or apparently fantastic. The complexity and obscurity of the scenario which generally characterize adults' dreams do not, however, in any way change the profound meaning of the dream products, which is always the fulfilment of a wish. The striking discrepancy, with adults, between the manifest dream content and the latent dream content merely shows that what is here involved is the fulfilment of a *disguised,* or a *hidden,* or a *repressed* wish.

But how do the latent dream thoughts succeed in disguising themselves sufficiently to become unrecognizable and, when the sleeper awakens, appear alien to his consciousness? The answer is that there are a certain number of technical processes which are not exclusive to dreams, but are active in other forms of psychic activity, in partic-

[1] *The Interpretation of Dreams, Std Edn* IV, p. 191. Also letter to Fliess, August 20, 1898, *Origins,* p. 260. 'I shall make very good use of Nansen's dreams as they are perfectly transparent. My own experience has taught me that he went through the ordinary psychical state of a person who is attempting something new, who must appeal to the trust of the others and who, probably on a false track, is going to discover new things, but not as much as he had imagined. I know this state because I have experienced it.'

ular in the work of the imagination. The first of these means, we have seen, is the transformation of abstract concepts into images and situations. There are several others, each contributing in its own way to the tendentious arrangement which Freud was the first to realize was the model of the secret way art functions.

Dreams function partly by means of a compression, or *condensation* of their primitive elements, which explains why latent ideas discovered in the course of analysis are always more numerous than the ideas of the manifest content. In fact, the people and objects seen in dreams are usually of composite form, hybrids produced by the fusion or the superimposition of completely dissimilar features. They are creations disconcerting to the waking state, but in all respects comparable to those which are found frequently in popular fables or myths. The only difference is that the mythical figures are permanent and stable, whereas dreams must somehow start functioning again every night.

Freud has given a nice example of this process of condensation. It is the dream in which he saw himself sitting in a railway compartment with a top hat of transparent glass in his lap. This absurd object results from the fusion of two images—the hat, obviously connected with the head of its owner; and a glass cylinder, also rather like a top hat in shape, such as protects an incandescent mantle, which brought its inventor, Dr Auer von Welsbach, a compatriot of Freud, fame and fortune. And Freud said to himself:

'I should like to make a discovery which would make me as rich and independent. I should like to travel instead of stopping in Vienna. In the dream I was travelling with my discovery, the hat in the shape of a glass cylinder, a discovery which, it is true, was not as yet of any great practical use. . . .'[1]

Dreams also function through a process of *displacement*, the main result of this being a reversal or an exchange of the values involved. What was strong and important in the latest thought of the dream is transferred to a weak, insignificant object, so that a fact originally moving becomes banal and, inversely, trivial items take on an intense color-

[1] *On Dreams*, *Std Edn* V, p. 652.

ation and a central place in the story. Dreams are capable of treating an accessory detail as a serious event, of dissociating situations from the affective states which normally accompany them, or of disguising, in some odd corner, the very element which constitutes their most pressing thought. Nothing contributes more to the absurdity of dreams than this deceitful shift of emphasis.

The third process is by far the most obvious. It consists in the replacing of objects, people and situations by images likely to delineate them in a purely analogical fashion. This is the *symbolism* of dreams which in all ages has struck men's imagination and justified the systematic deciphering of night's enigmas. Everything—signs, allusions, play on words, even utter nonsense—can be utilized by dreams to express the wish which they bear without, however, betraying it by making it intelligible. But the symbol is not the product of the dream work. On the contrary, it is the main driving force. The symbol provides the material for condensation, displacement and for the setting in which the situation is played out.

But, people will ask, what forces dreams to such tortuous elaboration? Why are adult dreams not expressed as naïvely as children's dreams? In other words, to what does this strange phenomenon of repression, which forces the wish to be fulfilled in a veiled form, correspond? The answer is not furnished by the dream itself but by a general characteristic of our psychical make-up:

'Our hypothesis is that in our mental apparatus there are two thought-constructing agencies, of which the second enjoys the privilege of having free access to consciousness for its products, whereas the activity of the first is in itself unconscious and can only reach consciousness by way of the second. On the frontier between the two agencies, where the first passes over to the second, there is a censorship, which only allows what is agreeable to it to pass through and holds back everything else. According to our definition, then, what is rejected by the censorship is in a state of repression. . . .'[1]

We see that the wishes most severely rejected by the censorship are precisely those which individual and collective morality represses with the same rigour—erotic

[1] Ibid., p. 676.

desires which are all the more incompatible with the demands of the adult Ego as they spring from an indestructible infantile background. Behind the actual erotic desires which are in some way fulfilled in dreams by a trick, Freud in fact discovered the first wish, the scandalous wish to commit incest and murder, which every adult has forgotten but which links him for ever with his past. It was a revelation which explained for the first time the universal and the eternal nature of the drama of Oedipus:

'His destiny moves us only because it might have been ours—because the oracle laid the same curse upon us before our birth as upon him. It is the fate of all of us, perhaps, to direct our first sexual impulse towards our mother and our first hatred and our first murderous wish against our father. Our dreams convince us that that is so. King Oedipus, who slew his father Laïus married his mother Jocasta, merely shows us the fulfilment of our own childhood wishes. But, more fortunate than he, we have meanwhile succeeded, in so far as we have not become psychoneurotics, in detaching our sexual impulses from our mothers and in forgetting our jealousy of our fathers. Here is one in whom these primeval wishes of our childhood have been fulfilled, and we shrink back from him with the whole force of the repression by which those wishes have since that time been held down within us. . . . Like Oedipus, we live in ignorance of these wishes, repugnant to morality, which have been forced upon us by Nature, and after their revelation we may all of us well seek to close our eyes to the scenes of our childhood. . . .'[1]

[1] *The Interpretation of Dreams, Std Edn* IV, pp. 262–3.

10

TWO OF FREUD'S DREAMS

There is no better way of understanding Freudian dream analysis than to follow step by step the extraordinary inner prospecting which Freud invites his readers to share by recounting his own dreams in order to discover their meaning and to hunt down in turn all the riddles they contain. A dream interpreted by Freud is an adventure in which one is both witness and hero, a drama which one at first watches with indifference or amusement but which later becomes a personal affair and its outcome a matter of concern.

Above all it is a lesson which allows one to grasp in the act, so to speak, the very technique of psychoanalysis, which thereby becomes more living and of more immediate practical use than any purely theoretical account. Dream analysis had been the indispensable instrument for Freud's self-analysis; for the reader today it is still the royal road to the heart of his books.

To give a completely concrete idea of the method which Freud, from 1895, had begun to apply to the treatment of his patients, two of his own dreams have been selected from among the innumerable examples which go to make up the subject matter of *The Interpretation of Dreams.* The first has been chosen because of its simplicity and the easy, familiar style used to describe the analysis, the second because of the wonderful intellectual structure which is built up from it and the aesthetic emotion which it produces.

The *table d'hôte* dream does not, strictly, belong to *The Interpretation of Dreams.* It is recounted in the little book already mentioned, *On Dreams,* in which Freud assembles and sets out in the simplest way the principles of his enormous dream Summa. He retraces all the stages, all the details of the path which the dreamer himself had followed at the moment of awakening:

'Company at table or table d'hôte . . . spinach was being

eaten . . . Frau E. L. was sitting beside me; she was turning her whole attention to me and laid her hand on my knee in an intimate manner. I removed her hand unresponsively. She then said: "But you've always had such beautiful eyes." . . . I then had an indistinct picture of two eyes, as though it were a drawing or like the outline of a pair of spectacles. . . .

'This was the whole of the dream, or at least all that I could remember of it. It seemed to me obscure and meaningless, but above all surprising. Frau E. L. is a person with whom I have hardly at any time been on friendly terms, nor, so far as I know, have I ever wished to have any closer relations with her. I have not seen her for a long time, and her name had not, I believe, been mentioned during the last few days. The dream-process was not accompanied by affects of any kind.

'Reflecting over this dream brought me no nearer to understanding it. I determined, however, to set down without any premeditation or criticism the associations which presented themselves to my self-observation. As I have found, it is advisable for this purpose to divide a dream into its elements and to find the associations attaching to each of these fragments separately.

'*Company at table or table d'hôte.* This at once reminded me of an episode which occurred late yesterday evening. I came away from a small party in the company of a friend who offered to take a cab and drive me home in it. "I prefer taking a cab with a taximeter," he said, "it occupies one's mind so agreeably; one always has something to look at." When we had taken our places in the cab and the driver had set the dial, so that the first charge of sixty hellers [equivalent at the time to *6d* or 12½ cents] became visible, I carried the joke further. "We've only just got in," I said, "and already we owe him sixty hellers. A cab with a taximeter always reminds me of a table d'hôte. It makes me avaricious and selfish, because it keeps on reminding me what I owe. My debt seems to be growing too fast, and I'm afraid of getting the worst of the bargain; and in just the same way at a table d'hôte I can't avoid feeling in a comic way that I'm getting too little, and must keep an eye on my own interests." I went on to quote, somewhat discursively:

You lead us into life,
You make the poor creature guilty.

'And now a second association to "table d'hôte". A few

weeks ago, while we were at table in a hotel at a mountain resort in the Tyrol, I was very much annoyed because I thought my wife was not being sufficiently reserved towards some people sitting near us whose acquaintance I had no desire at all to make. I asked her to concern herself more with me than with these strangers. This was again *as though I were getting the worst of the bargain at the table d'hôte.* I was struck too by the contrast between my wife's behaviour at table and that of Frau E. L. in the dream, who "turned her whole attention to me".

'To proceed. I now saw that the events in the dream were a reproduction of a small episode of a precisely similar kind which occurred between my wife and me at the time at which I was secretly courting her. The caress which she gave me under the table-cloth was her reply to a pressing love letter. In the dream, however, my wife was replaced by a comparative stranger—E. L.

'Frau E. L. is the daughter of a man to whom I was once *in debt.* I could not help noticing that this revealed an unsuspected connection between parts of the content of the dream and my associations. If one follows the train of association starting out from one element of a dream's content, one is soon brought back to another of its elements. My associations to the dream were bringing to light connections which were not visible in the dream itself.

'If a person expects one to keep an eye on his interests without any advantage to oneself, his artlessness is apt to provoke the scornful question: "Do you suppose I'm going to do this or that for the sake of your *beaux yeux* [*beautiful eyes*]?" That being so, Frau E. L.'s speech in the dream, "You've always had such beautiful eyes", can only have meant: "People have always done everything for you for love; you have always had everything *without paying for it.*" The truth is, of course, just the contrary. I have always paid dearly for whatever advantage I have had from other people. The fact that my friend took me home yesterday in a cab *without my paying for it* must, after all, have made an impression on me.

'Incidentally, the friend whose guests we were yesterday has often put me in his debt. Only recently I allowed an opportunity of repaying him to slip by. He has had only one present from me—an antique bowl, round which there are *eyes* painted: what is known as an "*occhiale*", to avert the *evil eye.* Moreover he is an *eye surgeon.* The same evening I asked him after a woman patient, whom I had sent on to him for consultation to fit her with *spectacles*.

'As I now perceived, almost all the elements of the dream's content had been brought into the new context. For the sake of consistency, however, the further question might be asked of why *spinach,* of all things, was being served in the dream. The answer was that *spinach* reminded me of an episode which occurred not long ago at our family table, when one of the children—and precisely the one who really deserves to be admired for his *beautiful eyes*—refused to eat any spinach. I myself behaved in just the same way when I was a child; for a long time I detested spinach, till eventually my taste changed and promoted that vegetable into one of my favourite foods. My own early life and my child's were thus brought together by the mention of this dish. "You ought to be glad to have spinach," the little *gourmet's* mother exclaimed; "there are children who would be only too pleased to have spinach." Thus I was reminded of the duties of parents to their children. Goethe's words:

> You lead us into life,
> You make the poor creature guilty

gained a fresh meaning in this connection.

'I will pause here to survey the results I had so far reached in my dream-analysis. By following the associations which arose from the separate elements of the dream divorced from their context, I arrived at a number of thoughts and recollections, which I could not fail to recognize as important products of my mental life. This material revealed by the analysis of the dream was intimately connected with the dream's content, yet the connection was of such a kind that I could never have inferred the fresh material from that content. The dream was unemotional, disconnected and unintelligible; but while I was producing the thoughts behind the dream, I was aware of intense and well founded affective impulses; the thoughts themselves fell at once into logical chains, in which certain central ideas made their appearance more than once. Thus, the contrast between "selfish" and "unselfish", and the elements "being in debt" and "without paying for it" were central ideas of this kind, not represented in the dream itself. I might draw closer together the threads in the material revealed by the analysis, and I might then show that they converge upon a single nodal point, but considerations of a personal and not of a scientific nature prevent my doing so in public. I should be obliged to betray many things which had better remain my secret, for on my way to discovering the solution of the dream all kinds of things were revealed which I was unwilling to admit even to myself.'[1]

The 'Non Vixit' dream which comes next is one of the most moving and also one of the most brilliant in *The Interpretation of Dreams.* The interpretation is more exhaustive than in the preceding dream, although Freud's usual reticence is still in evidence. With its suspense, its shadows which gradually fade and its continual twists and turns it is a veritable little drama with a strikingly beautiful development. And it is especially fitting that it should be included here as the characters who appear in it are already known to us. They are the masters and friends who had played a leading role in Freud's life and to whom he was still bound by feelings as contradictory as they were profound:

'*I had gone to Brücke's laboratory at night, and, in response to a gentle knock on the door, I opened it to* (the late) *Professor Fleischl, who came in with a number of strangers and, after exchanging a few words, sat down at his table.* This was followed by a second dream. *My friend Fl.*[2] *had come to Vienna unobtrusively in July. I met him in the street in conversation with my* (deceased) *friend P.,*[2] *and went with them to some place where they sat opposite each other as though they were at a small table. I sat in front at its narrow end. Fl. spoke about his sister and said that in three quarters of an hour she was dead, and added some such words as "that was the threshold". As P. failed to understand him, Fl. turned to me and asked me how much I had told P. about his affairs. Whereupon, overcome by strange emotions, I tried to explain to Fl. that P. could not understand anything at all, of course, because he was not alive. But what I actually said—and I myself noticed the mistake—was,* "NON VIXIT." *I then gave P. a piercing look. Under my gaze he turned pale; his form grew indistinct and his eyes a sickly blue—and finally he melted away. I was highly delighted at this and I now realized that Ernst Fleischl, too, had been no more than an apparition, a "revenant"* ["ghost"—literally, "one who

[1] *On Dreams, Std Edn* V, pp. 636–40.

[2] Fl.=Fliess; P=Josef Paneth.

returns"]; *and it seemed to me quite possible that people of that kind only existed as long as one liked and could be got rid of if someone else wished it.'* [1]

Freud puts forward this splendid example because it contains a veritable repertory of the riddles which occur in dreams. Highly typical elements are the fact that the dreamer himself criticizes his mistake that the dead are presented in the dream as dead and that relations with them are perfectly normal and finally the absurd discord between the terrifying ending and the extreme satisfaction which this gives to the dreamer.

'I would give a great deal to be able to present the complete solution of its conundrums. But in point of fact I am incapable of doing so—of doing, that is to say, what I did in the dream, of sacrificing to my ambition people whom I greatly value.' [2]

Freud therefore confines himself to interpreting a few elements selected from among the most significant ones, which he considers from two points of view. First he elucidates the problem of *non vixit* and of the natural presence of the dead in the dream: then he explains the absurd happiness which he feels after having dissolved his friend.

'The central feature of the dream was a scene in which I annihilated P. with a look. His eyes changed to a strange and uncanny blue and he melted away. This scene was unmistakably copied from one which I had actually experienced. At the time I have in mind I had been a demonstrator at the Physiological Institute and was due to start work early in the morning. It came to Brücke's ears that I sometimes reached the students' laboratory late. One morning he turned up punctually at the hour of opening and awaited my arrival. His words were brief and to the point. But it was not they that mattered. What overwhelmed me were the terrible blue eyes with which he looked at me and by which I was reduced to nothing—just as P. was in the dream, where, to my relief, the roles were reversed. No one who can remember the great man's eyes, which retained their striking beauty even in his old age,

[1] *The Interpretation of Dreams, Std Edn* V, p. 421.
[2] Ibid., p. 422.

and who has ever seen him in anger, will find it difficult to picture the young sinner's emotions.

'It was a long time, however, before I succeeded in tracing the origins of the *"Non vixit"* with which I passed judgement in the dream. But at last it occurred to me that these two words possessed their high degree of clarity in the dream, not as words heard or spoken, but as words *seen*. I then knew at once where they came from. On the pedestal of the Kaiser Josef Memorial in the Hofburg [Imperial Palace] in Vienna the following impressive words are inscribed:

Saluti patriae vixit
non diu sed totus.

'I extracted from this inscription just enough to fit in with a hostile train of ideas among the dream-thoughts, just enough to imply that "this fellow has no say in the matter—he isn't even alive". And this reminded me that I had the dream only a few days after the unveiling of the memorial to Fleischl in the cloisters of the University. At that time I had seen the Brücke memorial once again and must have reflected (unconsciously) with regret on the fact that the premature death of my brilliant friend P., whose whole life had been devoted to science, had robbed him of a well-merited claim to a memorial in the same precincts. Accordingly, I gave him this memorial in my dream; and, incidentally, as I remembered, his first name was Josef.

'By the rules of dream-interpretation I was even now not entitled to pass from the *Non vixit* derived from my recollection of the Kaiser Josef Memorial to the *Non vivit* required by the sense of the dream-thoughts. There must have been some other element in the dream thoughts which would help to make the transition possible. It then struck me as noticeable that in the sense in the dream there was a convergence of a hostile and an affectionate current of feeling towards my friend P., the former being on the surface and the latter concealed, but both of them being represented in the single phrase *Non vixit*. As he had deserved well of science I built him a memorial; but as he was guilty of an evil wish (which was expressed at the end of the dream) I annihilated him. I noticed that this last sentence had a quite special cadence, and I must have had some model in my mind. Where was an antithesis of this sort to be found, a juxtaposition like this of two opposite reactions towards a single person, both of them claiming to be completely justified and yet not incompatible? Only in one passage in literature—but a passage which makes a profound impression on the reader: in Brutus's speech of self-justification in Shakespeare's *Julius Caesar* [iii, 2], "As Caesar loved me, I weep for him; as he was fortunate, I rejoice at it; as he was valiant, I honour him; but, as he was ambitious I slew him." Were not the formal structure of these sentences and their antithetical meaning precisely the same as in the dream-thought I had uncovered? Thus I had been playing the part of Brutus in the dream. If only I could find one other piece of evidence in the content of the dream to confirm this surprising collateral connecting link! A possible one occurred to me. *"My friend Fl. came to Vienna in July."* There was no basis in reality for this detail of the dream. So far as I knew my friend Fl. had never been in Vienna in July. But the month of July was named after Julius Caesar and might therefore very well represent the allusion I wanted to the intermediate thought of my playing the part of Brutus.'[1]

Freud continued the interpretation of this dream in a later chapter which dealt with the affective states accompanying the development of the events of the dream. The point now to be elucidated is the complex connection which these states of different quality bear to the manifest dream content:

'I have not yet related the exciting cause of the dream. It was of great importance and led deep into an understanding of the dream. I had heard from my friend in Berlin, whom I have referred to as "Fl." [i.e. Fliess], that he was about to undergo an operation and that I should get further news of his condition from some of his relatives in Vienna. The first reports I received after the operation were not reassuring and made me feel anxious. I should have much preferred to go to him myself but just at that time I was the victim of a painful complaint which made movement of any kind a torture to me. The dream-thoughts now informed me that I feared for my friend's life. His only sister, whom I had never known, had, as I was aware, died in early youth after a very brief illness. (In the dream *Fl. spoke about his sister and said that in three quarters of an hour she was dead*. (I must have imagined that his constitution was not much more resistant than his sister's and that, after getting some much worse news of him, I should make the journey after all—and arrive *too late,* for which I might never cease to reproach myself. ([a]) This reproach for coming too late became the central point of the dream but was represented by a scene in which Brücke, the honoured teacher of my student years, levelled this reproach at me with a terrible look from his blue eyes. It will soon appear what it was that caused the situation [in regard to Fl.] to be switched on to these lines. The scene [with Brücke] itself could not be reproduced by the dream in the form in which I experienced it. The other figure in the dream was allowed to keep the blue eyes, but the annihilating role was allotted to me—a reversal which was obviously the work of wish-fulfilment. My anxiety about my friend's recovery, my self-reproaches for not going to see him, the shame I felt about this—*he had come to Vienna* (to see me) *"unobtrusively"*—the need I felt to consider that I was excused by my illness—all of this combined to produce the emotional storm which was clearly perceived in my sleep and which raged in this region of the dream-thoughts.

'But there was something else in the exciting cause of the dream, which had a quite opposite effect upon me. Along with unfavourable reports during the first few days after the operation, I was given a warning not to discuss the matter with anyone. I had felt offended by this because it implied an unnecessary distrust of my discretion. I was quite aware that these instructions had not emanated from my friend but were due to tactlessness or over-anxiety on the part of the intermediary, but I was very disagreeably affected by the veiled reproach because it was not wholly without justification. As we all know, it is only reproaches which have something in them that "stick"; it is only they that upset us. What I have in mind does not relate, it is true, to this friend, but to a much earlier period of my life. On that occasion I caused trouble between two friends (both of whom had chosen to honour me, too, with that name) by quite unnecessarily telling one of them, in the course of conversation, what the other had said about him. At that time, too, reproaches had been levelled at me, and they were still in my memory. One of the two friends concerned was Professor Fleischl; I may describe the other by

[a] The phantasm arising out of the unconscious thought of the dream which demand *non vivit* in place of *non vixit:* 'You have come too late, he is no longer alive'.

his first name of "Josef"—which was also that of P., my friend and opponent in the dream.[1]

'The reproach of being unable to keep anything to myself was attested in the dream by the element "unobtrusive" and by Fl.'s question as to *how much I had told P. about his affairs*. But it was the intervention of this memory [of my early indiscretion and its consequences] that transported the reproach against me for coming too late from the present time to the period at which I had worked in Brücke's laboratory. And, by turning the second person in the scene of annihilation in the dream into a Josef I made the scene represent not only the reproach against me for coming too late but also the far more strongly repressed reproach that I was unable to keep a secret. Here the processes of condensation and displacement at work in the dream, as well as the reasons for them, are strikingly visible.

'My present-day anger, which was only slight, over the warning I had been given not to give anything away [about Fl.'s illness] received reinforcements from sources in the depth of my mind and thus swelled into a current of hostile feelings against persons of whom I was in reality fond. The source of this reinforcement flowed from my childhood. I have already shown how my warm friendships as well as my enmities with contemporaries went back to my relations in childhood with a nephew who was a year my senior; how he was my superior, how I early learned to defend myself against him, how we were inseparable friends, and how, according to the testimony of our elders, we sometimes fought with each other—and made complaints to them about each other. All my friends have in a certain sense been re-incarnations of this first figure who "früh sich einst dem trüben Blick gezeigt"[2]: they have been *revenants*. My nephew himself re-appeared in my boyhood, and at that time we acted the parts of Caesar and Brutus together. My emotional life has always insisted that I should have an intimate friend and a hated enemy. I have always been able to provide myself afresh with both, and it has not infrequently happened that the ideal situation of childhood has been so completely reproduced that friend and enemy have come together in a sin-

[1] Probably Paneth again.

[2] 'Long since appeared before my troubled gaze' (Goethe, dedication).

gle individual—though not, of course, both at once. . . .'

At this point in his story—for all interpretation is a story, a little adventure novel as much as an analysis—Freud shows some reserve about going any further, having reached those remote regions of childhood where a person is revealed in his entirety. He uses an almost impersonal style to explain the origin of his ghosts and the enormous power they have retained over him:

'I do not propose at this point to discuss how it is that in such circumstances as these a recent occasion for the generation of an affect can hark back to an infantile situation and be replaced by that situation as far as the production of affect is concerned. This question forms part of the psychology of unconscious thinking, and would find its proper place in a psychological elucidation of the neuroses. For the purposes of dream-interpretation let us assume that a childhood memory arose, or was constructed in phantasy, with some such content as the following. The two children had a dispute about some object. (What the object was may be left an open question, though the memory or pseudo-memory had a quite specific one in view.) Each of them claimed to have *got there before the other* and therefore to have a better right to it. They came to blows and might prevailed over right. On the evidence of the dream, I may myself have been aware that I was in the wrong (*"I myself noticed the mistake"*). However, this time I was the stronger and remained in possession of the field. The vanquished party hurried to his grandfather—my father—and complained about me, and I defended myself in the words which I know from my father's account: "I hit him 'cos he hit me." This memory, or more probably phantasy, which came into my mind while I was analysing the dream—without further evidence I myself could not tell how—constituted an intermediate element in the dream-thoughts, which gathered up the emotions raging in them as a well collects the water that flows into it. From this point the dream-thoughts proceeded along some such lines as these: "It serves you right if you had to make way for me. Why did you try to push *me* out of the way? I don't need you, I can easily find someone else to play with," and so on. These thoughts now entered upon the paths which led to their representation in the dream. There had been a time when I had had to reproach my friend Josef [P.] for an attitude of this same kind: *"Ote-toi que je m'y mette!"* He had followed in my footsteps as demonstrator in Brücke's laboratory, but promotion there was slow and tedious. Neither of Brücke's two assistants was inclined to budge from his place, and youth was impatient. My friend, who knew that he could not expect to live long,[1] and whom no bonds of intimacy attached to his immediate superior, sometimes gave loud expression to his impatience, and, since this superior [Fleischl] was seriously ill, P.'s wish to have him out of the way might have an uglier meaning than the mere hope for the man's promotion. Not unnaturally, a few years earlier, I myself had nourished a still livelier wish to fill a vacancy. Wherever there is rank and promotion the way lies open for wishes that call for suppression. Shakespeare's Prince Hal could not, even at his father's sick-bed, resist the temptation of trying on the crown. But, as was to be expected, the dream punished my friend, and not me, for this callous wish. . . .'[2]

From the vague events of childhood Freud's dream passes on to death, to the death of others, to his own death and to the inadmissible joy of always being the survivor, the central and certainly the most painful theme of the whole enigma:

'It cannot be denied that to interpret and report one's dreams demands a high degree of self-discipline. One is bound to emerge as the only villain among the crowd of noble characters who share one's life. Thus it seemed to me quite natural that the *revenants* should only exist for just so long as one likes and should be removable at a wish. We have seen what my friend Josef was punished for. But the *revenants* were a series of reincarnations of the friend of my childhood. It was therefore also a source of satisfaction to me that I had always been able to find successive substitutes for that figure; and I felt I should be able to find a substitute for the friend whom I was now on the point of losing: no one was irreplaceable.

'But what had become of the dream-censorship? Why

[1] Josef Paneth had died of tuberculosis at a very early age; the 'assistant' is Professor von Fleischl-Marxow whom everyone knew to be doomed and whose post Freud had also coveted. (Cf. chap. 3).

[2] Ibid., pp. 483–4.

had it not raised the most energetic objections against this blatantly egotistic train of thought? And why had it not transformed the satisfaction attached to that train of thought into severe unpleasure? The explanation was, I think, that other, unobjectionable trains of thought in connection with the same people found simultaneous satisfaction and screened with *their* affect the affect which arose from the forbidden infantile source. In another stratum of my thoughts, during the ceremonial unveiling of the memorial, I had reflected thus: "What a number of valued friends I have lost, some through death, some through a breach of our friendship! How fortunate that I have found a substitute for them and that I have gained one [1] who means more to me than ever the others could, and that, at a time of life when new friendships cannot easily be formed, I shall never lose his." My satisfaction at having found a substitute for these lost friends could be allowed to enter the dream without interference; but there slipped in, along with it, the hostile satisfaction derived from the infantile source. It is no doubt true that infantile affection served to reinforce my contemporary and justified affection. But hatred, too, succeeded in getting itself represented.

'In addition to this, however, the dream contained a clear allusion to another train of thought which could legitimately lead to satisfaction. A short time before, after long expectation a daughter had been born to my friend [Fl.]. I was aware of how deeply he had mourned the sister he had so early lost and I wrote and told him I was sure he would transfer the love he felt for her on to the child, and that the baby girl would allow him at last to forget his irreparable loss.

'Thus this group of thoughts was connected once again with the intermediate thought in the latent content of the dream from which the associative paths diverged in contrary directions: "No one is irreplaceable!" "There are nothing but *revenants*: all those we have lost come back!" And now the associative links between the contradictory components of the dream-thoughts were drawn closer by the chance fact that my friend's baby daughter had the same name as the little girl I used to play with as a child,[2]

1 Fliess, whom Freud was not going to 'keep' all his life but, on the contrary, was soon to lose as a friend.

2 Fliess had remained inconsolable at the premature death of his young sister Pauline. He had just had a daughter whom he had

who was of my age and the sister of my earliest friend and opponent. It gave me great *satisfaction* when I heard that the baby was to be called "Pauline". And as an allusion to this coincidence, I had replaced one Josef by another in the dream and found it impossible to suppress the similarity between the opening letters of the names "Fleischl" and "Fl.". From here my thoughts went on to the subject of the names of my own children. I had insisted on their names being chosen, not according to the fashion of the moment, but in memory of people I have been fond of. Their names made the children into *revenants*. And after all, I reflected, was not having children our only path to immortality? . . .'[1]

---

named Pauline. Pauline was also Freud's niece, his nephew John's sister, with whom he had an amorous attachment in his childhood. (Cf. chap. 2, p. 32).

[1] Ibid., pp. 485–7.

11

DREAMS AND REALITY

At first neither the advent of the century nor the publication of *The Interpretation of Dreams* made any great difference to Freud's material existence. It remained as precarious as ever and sometimes the future looked very black indeed. In addition to his six children Freud was partly responsible for his mother and his spinster sisters, not counting his sister-in-law, Minna Bernays, who, after her fiancé's death, came to live with Freud and his family and stayed with them for the rest of her life. With such crushing family burdens and an extremely uncertain income, making ends meet was bound to be a serious problem. At the turn of the century Freud often despaired of success and, in his moments of depression, even doubted whether he would ever be anything but poverty-stricken.

In 1897 his letters to Fliess began to betray his anxiety. That year he realized that he had been wrong in putting forward the 'precocious seduction' of hysterics as a reality and if this error did not seriously shake the foundations of his psychology it did, nevertheless, shake his faith in his own therapeutic ability. This doubt about himself adversely affected both his relationship with his patients and his work. This was largely the reason for the fluctuation in the number of his patients which, at times, reached alarming proportions.

In addition, Freud's relations with those of his colleagues who were in a position to swell his practice suffered increasingly as people came to know, or thought they came to know his ideas. Who would compromise himself by exposing a lady or a young society girl to his disgusting methods? His colleagues took good care not to do so and Freud found himself deprived of an important source of patients. And one day in 1897 he commented sadly that he had only three cases in hand—two which he agreed to treat for nothing and, this being the time of his self-analysis, his own!

At other times, however, patients descended on him, he

said, like an avalanche and then he did ten or twelve psychotherapies a day and felt positively exhausted. Then once more his consulting room would be empty so that he had all the time in the world to 'dream', but did not know how he was going to live. Towards the end of 1899 the situation was so bad that Freud decided to seek a post in a hydrotherapeutic establishment as this would at least bring in a regular salary. But for some reason nothing came of this.

It was undoubtedly to put an end to this alarming uncertainty that, in 1897, he submitted his name for the title of Associate Professor, a purely honorary title; it involved no specific duties at the University but would raise his prestige in the eyes of Viennese society which was infatuated with questions of distinction and rank. Freud's first approach to three professors, including Nothnagel, one of his former teachers, was completely unsuccessful for reasons which were primarily connected with anti-Semitism in official circles and also largely, no doubt, with Freud's reputation in the matter of sexuality. As these reasons were never openly admitted and as Freud everywhere came up against silence, he soon gave up his efforts.

Every year therefore he perceived bitterly that his name failed to appear on the lists of promotions. In 1900 every name submitted to the Minister was accepted save his own. He merely had the consolation of seeing, at long last, recognition given to Königstein, the oculist, to whom he had formerly entrusted his experiments with cocaine. And matters would have undoubtedly stayed like that if an apparently innocuous event had not inspired Freud with the desire and the courage to take up the struggle once again.

This event was as remote as it was possible to be from the professional sphere on which, on Freud's own admission, he was soon afterwards to have a profound influence. This event was Freud's first visit to Rome, which he made in 1901. It was a journey he had not been able to make until then because of an extremely strange inner disposition which he was able to overcome only through analysis. The apparently very ordinary fact of his having been able to break the sort of spell which had always before stopped him, against his wish, at the gates of the city acquired immense value for him. It confirmed his psychological theory and his ideas on dreams and thereby already brought him something like a guarantee of success.

We have already noted the strange mixture of feelings

which journeys aroused in Freud, especially train journeys, a source of violent anxiety which he sometimes had difficulty in controlling. On the one hand travel was a veritable passion, one of the few which he felt all his life, along with a passion for cards and archaeology.[1] On the other hand journeys were the object of a sort of phobia which, if not strong enough to prevent the plan from being carried out, was at least strong enough to make his journeys very painful experiences. In the case of Rome the situation was frankly humiliating. He had set off several times with hope and a high heart but each time he had to stop by Lake Trasimeno, as though he had no right to go any further. He was therefore forced to recognize that the city he so yearned to see was for him a place of mysterious taboo or an inaccessible Promised Land.

During the last years of the century Wilhelm Fliess was naturally the centre of these plans for going to Rome, which came up at each 'congress'. To go with Fliess to the Eternal City, to exchange ideas on eternal things was a happiness to which Freud had long looked forward. But it was not to happen like this. He journeyed to Rome alone when Fliess was near to departing this life. The fact is that his 'Berlin friend', as he calls him in the following passage from *The Interpretation of Dreams,* was not connected with the real Rome but with that symbolic Rome which he tells us, with a reserve which is fraught with irony, he could not enter for 'reasons of health':

'In another instance it became apparent that, though the wish which instigated the dream was a present-day one, it had received a powerful reinforcement from memories that stretched far back into childhood. What I have in mind is a series of dreams which are based upon a longing to visit Rome. For a long time to come, no doubt, I shall have to continue to satisfy that longing in my dreams: for at the season of the year when it is possible for me to travel, residence in Rome must be avoided for reasons of health. For instance, I dreamt once that I was looking out of a railway-carriage window at the Tiber and the Ponte Sant'Angelo. The train began to move off, and it occurred to me that I had not so much as set foot in the city. The view that I had seen in my dream was taken from a well-

[1] Later, Freud made much of these 'passions' to counter Stefan Zweig's over-flattering portrait. Cf. chap. 28.

known engraving which I had caught sight of for a moment the day before in the sitting-room of one of my patients. Another time someone led me to the top of a hill and showed me Rome half-shrouded in mist; it was so far away that I was surprised at my view of it being so clear. There was more in the content of this dream than I feel prepared to detail; but the theme of "the promised land seen from afar" was obvious in it. The town which I saw in this way for the first time, shrouded in mist, was—Lübeck, and the prototype of the hill was—at Gleichenberg. In a third dream I had at last got to Rome, as the dream itself informed me; but I was disappointed to find that the scenery was far from being of an urban character. *There was a narrow stream of dark water; on one side of it were black cliffs and on the other meadows with big white flowers. I noticed a Herr Zucker* (whom I knew slightly) *and determined to ask him the way to the city.* I was clearly making a vain attempt to see in my dream a city which I had never seen in my waking life. Breaking up the landscape in the dream into its elements, I found that the white flowers took me to Ravenna, which I have visited and which, for a time at least, superseded Rome as capital of Italy. In the marshes round Ravenna we found the loveliest water-lilies growing in black water. Because we had had such difficulty in picking them out of the water, the dream made them grow in meadows like the narcissi at our own Aussee. The dark cliff, so close to the water, reminded me vividly of the valley of the Tepl near Karlsbad. "*Karlsbad*" enabled me to explain the curious detail of my having asked Herr Zucker the way. The material out of which the dream was woven included at this point two of those facetious Jewish anecdotes which contain so much profound and often bitter worldly wisdom and which we so greatly enjoy quoting in our talk and letters. Here is the first one: the "*constitution*" story. An impecunious Jew had stowed himself away without a ticket in the fast train to *Karlsbad.* He was caught, and each time tickets were inspected he was taken out of the train and treated more and more severely. At one of the stations on his *via dolorosa* he met an acquaintance, who asked him where he was travelling to. "To Karlsbad," was his reply, "if my constitution can stand it." My memory then passed on to another story: of a Jew who could not speak French and had been recommended when he was in Paris to ask the way to the rue Richelieu. Paris itself had for many long years been another goal of my longings; and the blissful feelings with which I first set foot on its pavement seemed to me a guarantee that others of my wishes would be fulfilled as well. "Asking the way", moreover was a direct allusion to *Rome,* since it is well known that all roads lead there. Again, the name *Zucker* [sugar] was once more an allusion to *Karlsbad;* for we are in the habit of prescribing treatment there for anyone suffering from the *constitutional* complaint of diabetes. The instigation to this dream had been a proposal made by my friend in Berlin that we should meet in Prague at Easter. What we were going to discuss there would have included something with a further connection with "sugar" and "diabetes".'[1]

The reader must have noticed Freud's liking for Jewish anecdotes and the skill with which he applies them to his own circumstances. In fact he saw in these humble products of the mind not only a 'profound and bitter wisdom' but a psychological enigma similar to those which stimulated his thought. Thus, before 1900, he had begun to make a collection of them, and this became the nucleus of *Jokes and Their Relation to the Unconscious,* one of his books which are richest in ideas. During the black years we are now speaking of 'Jewish anecdotes' constantly come crowding into his writings and naturally they are not always particularly gay. If Fliess wants to know his own feeling about *The Interpretation of Dreams,* he replies with the story of Uncle Jonah who is going to be married: 'Well, Uncle, what's your fiancée like?' 'It's a matter of taste. I don't like her.' And all through his letters there runs the little gate-crasher on the Karlsbad train who so perfectly expresses his fears that he will not be able to withstand the constant blows of misfortune much longer. His 'constitution' may not even be able to stand the journey to Karlsbad so how dare he go to Rome?

'It was on my last journey to Italy, which, among other places, took me past Lake Trasimeno, that finally—after having seen the Tiber and sadly turned back when I was only fifty miles from Rome—I discovered the way in which my longing for the eternal city had been reinforced by impressions from my youth. I was in the act of making

[1] *The Interpretation of Dreams, Std Edn* IV, pp. 193–5.

a plan to by-pass Rome next year and travel to Naples, when a sentence occurred to me which I must have read in one of our classical authors: "Which of the two, it may be debated, walked up and down his study with the greater impatience after he had formed his plan of going to Rome—Winckelmann, the Vice-Principal, or Hannibal, the Commander-in-Chief?" I had actually been following in Hannibal's footsteps. Like him, I had been fated not to see Rome and he too had moved into the Campagna when everyone had expected him in Rome. But Hannibal, whom I had come to resemble in these respects, had been the favourite hero of my later school days. Like so many boys at that age, I had sympathized in the Punic Wars not with the Romans but with the Carthaginians. And when in the higher classes I began to understand for the first time what it meant to belong to an alien race, and anti-Semitic feelings among the other boys warned me that I must take up a definite position, the figure of the Semitic general rose still higher in my esteem. To my youthful mind Hannibal and Rome symbolized the conflict between the tenacity of Jewry and the organization of the Catholic church. And the increasing importance of the effects of the anti-Semitic movement upon our emotional life helped to fix the thoughts and feelings of those early days. Thus the wish to go to Rome had become in my dream-life a cloak and symbol for a number of other passionate wishes. Their realization was to be pursued with all the perseverance and single-mindedness of the Carthaginian, though their fulfilment seemed at the moment just as little favoured by destiny as was Hannibal's lifelong wish to enter Rome. . . .'[1]

Here Freud links up with his memories an episode which has already been described and which had left an indelible impression on him. It was the scene in which his father, Jakob Freud, was humiliated by a Christian who threw his new hat into the mud and made him pick it up. In place of this degrading scene, the deeply hurt boy had substituted a different incident, one which would restore his pride. This was the episode in which Hamilcar made his son Hannibal swear to take vengeance on the Romans. Thus, little Sigmund had identified himself with Hannibal to avenge his father for the affront which he ascribed to

[1] Ibid., pp. 196–7.

Rome. And this identification had been so close that, in his maturity, the Carthaginian still haunted his dreams and prevented him from reaching his goal.

Freud did not dwell on the deep reasons for this strange inhibition, which he mastered through his self-analysis when he was forty-two. His reticence, which is perhaps why the essential feature in his connections with Rome is left rather shadowy, has naturally aroused the curiosity of many writers and given rise to a whole host of more or less extravagant hypotheses. It should be noted that most of these interpretations play on the opposition which appears here between Rome and Judaism. Freud, so runs the argument, had a secret admiration for the Pope (hence the importance of his master Brücke whose name means 'bridge' and is very like 'pontiff'), an unacknowledged yearning for the Holy Trinity (because he had a habit of going up three steps at a time) and finally an unconscious wish to be converted to Roman Catholicism in order to make a place for himself in the world. It goes without saying that neither Freud's life nor his most completely analysed dreams provide the slightest confirmation for such conclusions.

Though he may not have revealed the secret of his love and his aversion for Rome—two extreme and intimately connected emotions—Freud did nevertheless definitely guide his reader towards the simplest explanation which, for him, was also the most difficult to publish. In a note in *The Interpretation of Dreams*[1] he suggested there was a link between his own inhibitions and certain ancient beliefs connected with the maternal symbol of the city. The oracle given to the Tarquins predicted that the first of them to 'kiss' his mother would become the master of Rome; Julius Caesar dreamed that he had relations with his mother and concluded that he would possess the world; and Herodotus tells how Hippias led the Barbarians at Marathon after dreaming that he was sleeping with his mother—and in fact he did reach Athens and regain his authority. To explain his own dreams Freud clearly proposes to use these 'Oedipian' dreams which he called sincere because they all betray the sleeper's profound wish.

We can now understand the seemingly excessive, almost ridiculous importance he attached to his first journey to Rome, a climactic event, he said, to which he attributed

[1] Ibid., V, p. 398*n*.

an immediate effect on his social status. At the age of forty-five, after struggling for years to avoid recognizing the truth hidden behind his dreams and his strange symptoms, he reached a crucial point in his knowledge of himself and at the same time was able to enter Rome. The end of that long inner epic which outwardly was just an ordinary tourist adventure gave him hope of triumphing in other fields as well if he but dared grasp the weapons essential for the fight.

The only account we have of that memorable journey is a letter to Wilhelm Fliess in which Freud finally spoke of the real Rome and showed himself half disappointed:

'I ought to write to you about Rome, but it is difficult. It was an overwhelming experience for me, and, as you know, the fulfilment of a long-cherished wish. It was slightly disappointing, as all such fulfilments are when one has waited for them too long, but it was a high-spot in my life all the same. But, while I contemplated ancient Rome undisturbed (I could have worshipped the humble and mutilated remnant of the Temple of Minerva near the forum of Nerva), I found I could not freely enjoy the second Rome; I was disturbed by its meaning, and, being incapable of putting out of my mind my own misery and all the other misery which I know to exist, I found almost intolerable the lie of the salvation of mankind which rears its head so proudly to heaven:

'I found the third, Italian, Rome hopeful and likeable. . . .'[1]

Once back in Vienna, Freud took his own affairs seriously in hand. If he wanted to obtain the title of professor he must somehow break or at least circumvent the resistance of the Minister, Wilhelm von Hartel. He therefore looked round for solid support and found some which, this time, finally allowed him to succeed. The matter took the form of a bargain. Freud's protectress, Baroness Ferstel, who was being treated by him, bought Freud's appointment with a picture which she gave to the Minister as a present. On March 11th Freud sent to Fliess, who had congratulated him, an exact and very amusing account of the mysterious deal:

[1] Letter to Wilhelm Fliess, September 19, 1901, *Origins*, pp. 235–6.

'Just think what an "excellency" can do! He can even cause me again to hear your welcome voice in a letter.[1] But as you talk about such grand things in connection with the news—recognition, mastery, etc.—my usual compulsion to honesty which is so detrimental to my interests makes me feel it incumbent on me to tell you exactly how it finally came about.

'It was my own doing, in fact. When I got back from Rome, my zest for life and work had somewhat grown and my zest for martyrdom had somewhat diminished. I found that my practice had melted away and I withdrew my last work from publication because in you I had recently lost my only remaining audience.[2] I reflected that waiting for recognition might take up a good portion of the remainder of my life, and that in the meantime none of my fellow-men were likely to trouble about me. And I wanted to see Rome again and look after my patients and keep my children happy. So I made up my mind to break with my strict scruples and take appropriate steps, as others do after all. One must look somewhere for one's salvation, and the salvation I chose was the title of professor. . . .'[3]

Freud then tells in great detail the steps he made himself take. One of his former teachers, Exner, who had succeeded Brücke as Professor of Physiology and was connected with the Ministry of Education, had let him understand that the Minister had been warned against him. And so Freud decided to appeal to an old friend and patient, the wife of a member of the Aulic Council, the philosopher Theodor Gomperz, who in his youth had given him the job of translating one of John Stuart Mill's books. Frau Gomperz went and saw the Minister and told him how long Freud had waited: 'Four years!' said the Minister, 'And who is it?' Freud then solicited the support of two other medical authorities but the Minister turned a deaf ear and once more Freud's attempt seemed doomed to failure.

At this point a very influential lady, the Baroness von

[1] Although the two men had not yet completely fallen out, Fliess was now writing less and less.

[2] Looking through the curtain and seeing only two people in the orchestra stalls for a benefit performance, Nestroy is said to have exclaimed: 'I know one of the audience, he's got a free ticket. Perhaps the other one has as well!'

[3] Letter to Fliess, September 11, 1902, *Origins*, p. 342.

Ferstel, undoubtedly in a spirit of rivalry, decided to act alone, employing methods which her experience of the world had taught her were the only ones that would be effective in a society with a strong sense of hierarchy and such passionately held prejudices:

'She did not rest until she had made the Minister's acquaintance at a party, made herself agreeable to him, and secured a promise from him through a mutual woman friend that he would give a professorship to the doctor who had cured her. But, being sufficiently well-informed to know that a first promise from him meant nothing at all, she approached him personally, and I believe that if a certain Böcklin had been in her possession instead of in that of her aunt . . . I should have been appointed three months earlier. As it is, his Excellency will have to satisfy himself with a modern picture for the gallery which he intended to open, naturally not for himself. Anyway, in the end the Minister most graciously announced to my patient while he was having dinner at her house that the appointment had gone to the Emperor for signature, and that she would be the first to hear when the matter was completed.

'So one day she came to her appointment beaming and waving an express letter from the Minister. It was done. The Wiener Zeitung has not yet published it, but the news spread quickly from the Ministry. The public enthusiasm is immense. Congratulations and bouquets keep pouring in, as if the role of sexuality had been suddenly recognized by His Majesty, the interpretation of dreams confirmed by the Council of Ministers, and the necessity of the psychoanalytic therapy of hysteria carried by a two-thirds majority in Parliament.

'I have obviously become reputable again, and my shyest admirers now greet me from a distance in the street.'[1]

After stating, not without some bitterness, that he had done his first 'bowing and scraping' to Authority and that he now had good grounds for expecting a reward, Freud concluded with a look into his own heart. It was his last confidence to Wilhelm Fliess:

[1] Ibid., pp. 343–4.

'In the whole affair there is one person with very long ears, who was not sufficiently allowed for in your letter, and that is myself. If I had taken those few steps three years ago I should have been appointed three years earlier, and should have spared myself much. Others are just as clever, without having to go to Rome first. That, then, was the glorious process to which, among other things, I owe your kind letter. Please keep the contents of this one to yourself.' [1]

That letter concluded the ten years' intensive correspondence between Freud and Fliess in which Freud depicted his own character with an incorruptible love of truth and with the skill of a born writer. Fliess's letters had been becoming less and less frequent, and soon Freud stopped writing altogether. He had done his utmost to prolong this friendship beneath which, unknown to him, violent infantile passions had smouldered for so long. Disillusioned by his self-analysis, he now knew the nature of his attachment. In addition, he saw that the man whom he had most admired in the world, his only 'public', did not understand or really accept his ideas. And so, in order to achieve complete self-conquest, he resigned himself to losing his last friend.

[1] Ibid., p. 344.

12

FREUD AND SCIENCE

On several occasions Freud recalled the difficulties he had to overcome over a period of ten years before he was able to put an end to his scientific exile. Thus he said in his autobiography:

'For more than ten years after my separation from Breuer I had no followers. I was completely isolated. In Vienna I was shunned; abroad no notice was taken of me. My *Interpretation of Dreams,* published in 1900, was scarcely reviewed in the technical journals. In my paper "On the History of the Psycho-Analytic Movement" I mentioned as an instance of the attitude adopted by psychiatric circles in Vienna a conversation with an assistant at the Clinic, who had written a book against my theories but had never read my *Interpretation of Dreams.* He had been told at the Clinic that it was not worth while. The man in question, who has since become a professor, had gone so far as to repudiate my report of the conversation and to throw doubts in general upon the accuracy of my recollection. I can only say that I stand by every word of the account I then gave.'[1]

In the work to which he is referring here, the *History of the Psycho-Analytic Movement*[2] written in 1914, Freud disclosed the profound reasons for this humiliating attitude which, in Vienna at least, persisted for many years. His faith in science was so great that it was a long time before he really fathomed these reasons:

'I treated my discoveries as ordinary contributions to science and hoped they would be received in the same spirit. But the silence which my communications met with, the void which formed itself about me, the hints that were conveyed to me, gradually made me realize that assertions

1 *An Autobiographical Study, Std Edn* XX, p. 48.
2 *Std Edn* XIV.

on the part played by sexuality in the aetiology of the neuroses cannot count upon meeting with the same kind of treatment as other communications. I understood that from now onwards I was one of those who have "disturbed the sleep of the world", as Hebbel says, and that I could not reckon upon objectivity and tolerance. . . .'[1]

If Freud could not hope for objectivity or indulgence on the part of scientific circles because they did not think him worth reading, he could certainly not expect them from the general public, which approached his books merely with unhealthy or malicious curiosity. He noticed this one day in 1900 on the occasion of a lecture he was to give to the Philosophical Society and which, after incredible arguments and negotiations, was finally cancelled.

As a rule Freud did not speak in public apart from the lectures he delivered at the University. The only place where he sometimes lectured was in the B'nai B'rith Society, the Jewish liberal association which he joined towards 1897 and to which he belonged all his life. There he was, in fact, assured of public sympathy and good will and a genuine thirst for knowledge. But elsewhere he could assume that his audience came, if not with openly malevolent intent at least with unpleasant ulterior motives.

On one occasion Freud had accepted—but without any enthusiasm—the Philosophical Society's invitation and while preparing his lecture he reversed his decision as he thought his subject would be out of place in a mixed and probably not very serious audience.

'So I wrote a letter calling it off. That was the first week. Thereupon a delegation of two called on me and pressed me to deliver it after all. I warned them very seriously to do nothing of the sort, and suggested that they should come and hear the lecture themselves one evening at my house (second week). During the third week I gave the two of them the lecture. They said it was wonderful and that their audience would take no exception to it, etc. The lecture was therefore arranged for the fourth week. A few hours beforehand, however, I received an express letter, saying that some members had objected after all and asking me to be kind enough to start by illustrating my theory with inoffensive examples and then announce that I was coming to objectionable matter and make a pause, during

[1] Ibid., pp. 21–2.

which the ladies could leave the hall. Of course I immediately cried off, and the letter in which I did so at any rate did not lack pepper and salt. Such is scientific life in Vienna!'[1]

Freud at first believed that his scientific integrity, the accuracy and the high tone of his works would in the end triumph over the reputation he had acquired as a result of the scientists' scorn and the public's excited ignorance. But if he was not read what was the good of all his excellences? What point was there to the minute examination of the literature of dreams which he had put at the beginning of his book and the patient observations which he rightly considered to be irrefutable proofs? Disheartened, he finally resigned himself to the paradoxical situation which put him on a par with a sort of magician of doubtful morality. And he tried to reconcile himself to his fate:

'I pictured the future as follows: I should probably succeed in maintaining myself by means of the therapeutic success of the new procedure, but science would ignore me entirely during my lifetime; some decades later, someone else would infallibly come upon the same things—for which the time was now ripe—would achieve recognition for them and bring me honour as a forerunner whose failure had been inevitable. Meanwhile, like Robinson Crusoe, I settled down as comfortably as possible on my desert island. . . .'[2]

When he wrote those lines—it was in 1914, more than ten years after the period he is recalling—Freud seemed rather to have forgotten the sufferings he had experienced as a result of his scientific isolation, the main theme of his letters to Fliess. This was the time when he had just broken with Jung and saw the collapse of the great hopes he had based on the man who was so different from him in every respect. A few years earlier the great Swiss psychiatrist Bleuler and his most brilliant pupils had quite unexpectedly come out in support of Freud's ideas. Freud had seen this as marking the end of the Viennese 'spell' which weighed so heavily on the fate of psychoanalysis, and as the end of the moral and social 'ghetto' which he had built

[1] Letter to Fliess, February 15, 1901, *Origins*, p. 329.

[2] *History of the Psycho-Analytic Movement, Std Edn* XIV, p. 22.

against his wish round the new science and in which its first followers, Jews like himself, necessarily remained confined. With Switzerland, European science, a free intellectual world that knew neither frontiers nor race discrimination, was at last being opened up to his researches. Jung was younger, stronger and better equipped than he was to impose their common ideas. Jung would be his spiritual heir and, under his protection, psychoanalysis could, without compromising itself, find a field of action commensurate with its importance.

We shall soon see that this hope was founded on very serious illusions. Many elements in Jung's personality might well have alarmed Freud from the first, and had, in fact, perturbed most of his Viennese followers. Jung was of a vigorous nature in whom brilliant intellectual gifts were allied to a vast culture and a fine imagination. But this robustness concealed singular weaknesses, if what Professor Etiemble calls the capital sin of our age, anti-Semitism, must so be regarded. Jung—and it is a fact which cannot be passed over in silence—was and remained an anti-Semite, as is proved by the articles he wrote during the war for the German Psychiatric Society, then directed by Göring's nephew.[1] Freud knew this and confided to one of his most loyal friends, Pastor Oskar Pfister, that Jung had overcome this unpleasant disposition in his particular case, in some way out of love for him. Imagine Freud's disappointment when he had to admit that he was wrong and that the man he loved like a son, far from opening wide for him the doors of science, had joined the ranks of his enemies.

This disappointment explains why Freud looked back with regret on the immediate past of psychoanalysis, a period in which his total solitude, painful as it was, at least meant that he was spared the anguish of internal dissensions and left his mind free:

'When I look back to those lonely years, away from the pressures and confusions of to-day, it seems like a glorious heroic age. My "splendid isolation" was not without its advantages and charms. I did not have to read any publications, nor listen to any ill-informed opponents; I was not subject to influence from any quarter; there was nothing to hustle me. I learnt to restrain speculative tendencies and to

[1] Cf. chap. 28.

follow the unforgotten advice of my master, Charcot: to look at the same things again and again until they themselves begin to speak. My publications, which I was able to place with a little trouble, could always lag far behind my knowledge, and could be postponed as long as I pleased, since there was no doubtful "priority" to be defended. . . .'[1]

Consequently Freud often idealized what Fliess, to console him, used to call his 'splendid isolation'. The reasons he gives here for his regret are quite remarkable. They reveal clearly the many contradictions which throughout his life complicated his relations with science and by that very fact gave his work its greatest singularity.

It cannot be doubted that science, or at least that higher form of science of which he regarded Brücke and Charcot as being living embodiments, was for Freud a universal authority capable of destroying the particular limitations and discriminations from which, because of his origins, he personally had to suffer so much. Recognition by the scientific world of his time would have meant having a normal status, entering a human society which judged things according to their value and not by utterly irrational forms of discrimination against which there was neither proof nor defence. Freud very quickly perceived that his abnormal position as a semi-tolerated Jew was being reproduced exactly, although on different pretexts, in the realm of science, and in the very sphere where he hoped to gain his freedom. Instead of welcoming his ideas and discussing them frankly, they were dismissed with a word or a humiliating gesture, exactly as though the Empire were settling his case by placing an ignominious label on his person. This repetition of his early position, which seemed to seal his fate, gravely compromised the future of psychoanalysis, his invention which, in an ironic allusion to Christian Science, was already being called the 'Jewish Science'.

Freud therefore had very mixed feelings about the authority which he still regarded as the highest and most legitimate. On the one hand science was confused with the truth he wished to serve and to which he had to account; on the other hand it had rejected him and thrown him back into an exile in which his faith and integrity were

[1] *History of the Psycho-Analytic Movement, Std Edn* XIV, p. 22.

very poorly rewarded. Because it abandoned him in this way science inspired in Freud a violent resentment from which he seems never quite to have recovered. From his closely knit love and hatred there follow naturally certain peculiarities of the psychoanalytical movement and, in an even more striking way, certain features of Freud's work.

Thus with Freud the ideal of an unassailable scientific integrity went hand in hand with the desire to affirm his singularity and to be rid of all constraint. These two demands were not easy to reconcile because scientific integrity, for example, compelled Freud to submit to a number of conventions—notably in questions of 'priority'; but in view of his strong feeling of the immediacy and novelty of his ideas he did so only with impatience and sometimes incompletely. The few violations of the scientific code of which he was guilty, out of ignorance, thoughtlessness or weariness, were in themselves of no great consequence, but they weighed heavily on his scrupulous conscience to judge by the frequency in his work and especially in the dreams he relates of themes more or less concerned with the theft of ideas.

Freud seems to have been predestined to be caught up in these questions of priority. They were, of course, by no means unimportant to him but his contradictory feelings towards science sometimes led him to treat them lightly, at the risk of laying himself open to criticism. To begin with he owed the first form of his method of treatment to Josef Breuer, who had himself abandoned it; and in *The Psychopathology of Everyday Life* we can see how annoyed he is when, at some meeting or other, the 'Breuer-Freud' method gave rise to a speech blunder, which, of course, often happens.[1] But the most unpleasant incidents which befell him in this connection undoubtedly arose out of *The Interpretation of Dreams,* the book of which he said that no other had been so completely his own and which he was forced to defend many times against the charge of dishonesty.

In Freud's letters to Fliess we saw how burdensome he found the task of making the huge compilation which precedes the exposition of his own ideas. Was it this boredom, the aversion inspired by his predecessors or the fear of seeing himself forestalled, a fear he expresses at least once in a letter? In any case his list of the books on

[1] See *The Psychopathology of Everyday Life, Std Edn* VI, ch. 9.

dreams revealed a few oversights and his bibliography had one or two very obvious gaps. Naturally that was all corrected as far as possible in subsequent editions but Freud was never satisfied and twenty years later he wrote to Pastor Pfister as though to anticipate his eventual reproaches:

'I am really very ignorant about my predecessors in the interpretation of dreams, and if we are ever to meet in the next world I shall certain have a bad reception as a plagiarist. But it is so pleasurable to examine things for oneself at first hand instead of consulting the literature about them. . . .'[1]

Later still the question as to who was first with the ideas on dreams led to a slight quarrel between Freud and André Breton, who was one of the first people in France to make use of Freud's ideas. In *Les Vases Communicants* Breton had written that Freudian dream symbolism merely repeated the ideas of Volkelt, a writer of the end of the last century about whom the bibliography of *The Interpretation of Dreams* remained, he said, 'rather significantly silent'. Freud replied immediately, without bothering to read the book through:

'Dear Sir, I can assure you that I shall carefully read your little book *Les Vases Communicants* in which the explanation of dreams plays such an important part. As yet I have not reached very far in this study, but I write to you now because on p. 19 I come across one of your "impertinences" which I cannot readily follow.

'You take me to task for not having mentioned Volkelt in the bibliography, the man who discovered the symbolism of the dream though I have made use of his ideas. That is serious and goes altogether counter to my usual method.

'In point of fact it was not Volkelt who discovered the symbolism of the dream, but Scherner, whose book appeared in 1861, whereas Volkelt's dates from 1878. Both authors are referred to several times in the corresponding parts of my text, and they appear together in the place where Volkelt is mentioned as Scherner's supporter. *Both* names appear in the bibliography. I must now be allowed to ask you for an explanation.

[1] Letter to Pfister, July 12, 1909, *Psychoanalysis & Faith,* p. 26.

'In your justification I have just discovered that the name Volkelt does not in fact appear in the bibliography of the French translation (Meyerson, 1926). . . .'[1]

After more than thirty years Freud should really have been past worrying about a manifestly wild accusation which could then scarcely harm his reputation. However, he was so shattered by it that the very next day he wrote Breton a second letter in which he tried to justify everybody—Breton, himself and his translator.

From this rather unnecessary haste André Breton, who had read *The Psychopathology of Everyday Life,* at once realized that he must have touched a sensitive spot. This was truer than he thought. Freud was one of those profound people in whom nothing fades with the passage of time and who are always rethinking their life. At the age of seventy-six the criticism of a young man who was also passionately honest revived in Freud the memories of old quarrels in which he had been sometimes the accuser, sometimes the accused and sometimes, he thought, the guilty party. Shortly before his break with Jung he had criticized him strongly for having used his work in an article without quoting his name. And at an even earlier period he was involved in a lamentable matter of priority, in which his accuser was Wilhelm Fliess, the man whose friendship had meant so much in his life.

This somewhat complicated affair was connected with the question of bisexuality, which Fliess claimed to be his by right and which, after 1897, the two men had discussed when they held their Breslau 'congress'. Some years later Freud suffered from a strange fit of amnesia on this matter which he analyzed in *The Psychopathology of Everyday Life:*

'One day in the summer of 1901 I remarked to a friend with whom I used at that time to have a lively exchange of scientific ideas, "These problems of the neuroses are only to be solved if we base ourselves wholly and completely on the assumption of the original bisexuality of the individual." To which he replied, "That's what I told you two and a half years ago at Breslau when we went for that evening walk. But you wouldn't hear of it then." It is painful to be requested in this way to surrender one's originality. I

[1] Op. cit.

could not recall any such conversation or this pronouncement of my friend's. One of us must have been mistaken and on the *"cui prodest?"* principle it must have been myself. Indeed in the course of the next week I remembered the whole incident, which was just as my friend had tried to recall it to me; I even recollected the answer I had given him at the time: "I've not accepted that yet; I'm not inclined to go into the question." But since then I have grown a little more tolerant when, in reading medical literature, I come across one of the few ideas with which my name can be associated, and find that my name has not been mentioned. . . .'[1]

The last assertion was not altogether sincere. Not only did Freud not become calmer about matters of scientific priority but ten years later, when he reproached Jung for behaving in the same way to him he suddenly fainted. The incident occurred in Munich, a city which Freud had first visited when Fliess was once ill and which, ever since then, had remained intimately associated with that period of his life.

There was a further lamentable epilogue to the bisexuality affair. In 1903 a young Viennese philosopher, Otto Weininger, had published a book entitled *Sex and Character*[2] in which he emphasized the idea of bisexuality. Having heard that Weininger was on close terms with a young psychologist named Swododa, who was one of Freud's pupils, Fliess immediately thought Weininger got his idea from him.

Questioned about it, Freud declared that Swoboda was not a pupil, but a patient of his. During a session he mentioned to him that human beings have a bisexual constitution, without telling him anything more about the theory. But Fliess was not satisfied. Was it true or not that Freud had had a conversation with Swoboda and had given him to read a manuscript by Fliess on the subject?

Freud then stopped dodging. He confessed he had done so and said he had been compelled by an obscure wish to rob Fliess of his original idea, a wish which was connected with the extremely complex motives underlying their friendship. Fliess was incensed, not touched by this. He

[1] *The Psychopathology of Everyday Life, Std Edn* VI, pp. 143–4.
[2] Otto Weininger: *Geschlecht und Charakter,* Vienna, 1903.

broke finally with Freud and two years later defied Freud by publishing a number of his most intimate letters.

In 1905 he even got one of his friends to publish a pamphlet in which Freud, Swoboda and Weininger were publicly accused of plagiarism. As Weininger had committed suicide a year after the publication of his book, only Freud and Swoboda could defend themselves. Freud did so by writing to the press, Swoboda by publishing a book in which he explained and discussed the claims of Fliess, who himself became suspect because he obviously thought he was being persecuted. Juridically the matter was undoubtedly ambiguous. Morally it was for Freud one of those painful experiences which he kept coming up against all his life and from which he gained a new insight into human beings as well as an increased knowledge of himself.

Freud was not blessed with more than average health or mental balance. His heroism—it was no less than that—lay simply in his refusal to rid himself of his inner burden by forgetting it, denying it or dressing it up with clever artistic touches. None of the things which caused him suffering or disturbance, none of the riddles he had set himself ever disappeared from his life. At the age of eighty he wrote Romain Rolland an admirable letter in which he offered him, as a birthday present, the analysis of his first trip to Athens thirty years before! [1] And when he was very old, remembering a man who had also opened up a new road through the labyrinth of dreams, he did not hesitate to debate publicly the obscure question of intellectual ownership which had disturbed and pursued him all his life.

The article entitled *Josef Popper-Lynkeus and the Theory of Dreams* [2] is one of the two papers which Freud devoted to the scientist who, as it happens, was neither a doctor nor a psychologist, but a physicist whose book had appeared in 1899 and was therefore to some extent deprived of his fame by *The Interpretation of Dreams*. The article Freud wrote twenty-three years later is at once a moving tribute to Popper-Lynkeus and a penetrating analysis of the situation:

'There is much of interest to be said on the subject of ap-

[1] *A Disturbance of Memory on the Acropolis* (letter to Romain Rolland), *Std Edn* XXII, pp. 239 ff.; cf. also chap. 13.

[2] *Std Edn* XIX, pp. 261–3.

parent scientific originality. When some new idea comes up in science, which is hailed at first as a discovery and is also as a rule disputed as such, objective research soon afterwards reveals that after all it was in fact no novelty. Usually the discovery has already been made repeatedly and has afterwards been forgotten, often at very long intervals of time. Or at least it has had forerunners, had been obscurely surmised or incompletely enunciated. This is too well known to call for further discussion.

'But the subjective side or originality also deserves consideration. A scientific worker may sometimes ask himself what was the source of the ideas peculiar to himself which he has applied to his material. As regards some of them he will discover without much reflection the hints from which they were derived, the statements made by other people which he has picked out and modified and whose implications he has elaborated. But as regards others of his ideas he can make no such acknowledgements; he can only suppose that these thoughts and lines of approach were generated—he cannot tell how—in his own mental activity, and it is on them that he bases his claim to originality.

'Careful psychological investigation, however, diminishes this claim still further. It reveals hidden and long-forgotten sources which gave the stimulus to the apparently original ideas, and it replaces the ostensible new creation by a revival of something forgotten applied to fresh material. There is nothing to regret in this; we had no right to expect that what was "original" could be untraceable and undetermined.

'In my case, too, the originality of many of the new ideas employed by me in the interpretation of dreams and in psychoanalysis has evaporated in this way. I am ignorant of the source of only one of these ideas. It was no less than the key to my view of dreams and helped me to solve their riddles, so far as it has been possible to solve them hitherto. I started out from the strange, confused and senseless character of so many dreams, and hit upon the notion that dreams were bound to become like that because something was struggling for expression in them which was opposed by a resistance from other mental forces. In dreams hidden impulses were stirring which stood in contradiction to what might be called the dreamer's official ethical and aesthetic creed; the dreamer was thus ashamed of these impulses, turned away from them and refused to acknowledge them in day-time, and if during the night he could not withhold expression of some kind from them, he submitted them to a "dream-distortion" which made the content of the dream appear confused and senseless. To the mental force in human beings which keeps watch on this internal contradiction and distorts the dream's primitive instinctual impulses in favour of conventional or of higher moral standards, I gave the name of "dream-censorship".

'Precisely this essential part of my theory of dreams was, however, discovered by Popper-Lynkeus independently. I will ask the reader to compare the following quotation from a story called "Träumen wie Wachen" ["Dreaming like Waking"] in his *Phantasien eines Realisten* [*Phantasies of a Realist*] which was certainly written in ignorance of the theory of dreams which I published in 1900, just as I myself was then in ignorance of Lynkeus's *Phantasien. . . .*'[1]

'Of a man who has the remarkable ability of never having an absurd dream. . . . That marvellous ability of having a dream-life which is like your waking-life is due to your virtues, your goodness, your fairness of mind, your love of the truth: it is the moral transparency of your nature which allows me to understand everything about you.

' "On thinking carefully about it," the other replied, "I should imagine that all men are like me and that nobody ever dreams an absurd dream! A dream which one remembers clearly and which one can describe, a dream which is not the delirium caused by fever always has a meaning. And it must be so! For anything contradictory would destroy coherence. That time and space should sometimes be turned topsy turvy in no way detracts from the true dream content for undoubtedly neither the one nor the other were important for its essential tenor. Don't we often do the same in the waking state? Think of the stories, think of all the pictures which are full of meaning and of which only an ignoramus would say: 'That's absurd because it's impossible!"

' "If only one knew how to interpret dreams correctly as you have just interpreted mine!" the friend said.

'It's certainly not easy, but if the dreamer pays some attention he should always be able to. Why is it usually a

[1] 'Träumen wie Wachen' in *Phantasien eines Realisten,* Vienna, 1899. *Std Edn* XIX, pp. 261–2.

failure? It seems that there is something hidden in our dreams, lubricity of a special, higher nature, a certain dissimulation which is difficult to imagine in your case. That is why your dreams so often seem to be meaningless or even to be nonsense. But at bottom it is not true. No, and it cannot be otherwise since the same man is involved, whether he is awake or dreaming. . . .'

'I believe that what enabled *me* to discover the cause of dream-distortion was my moral courage. In the case of Popper it was the purity, love of truth and moral serenity of his nature.'[1]

[1] *Josef Popper-Lynkeus and the Theory of Dreams, Std Edn* XIX, p. 263.

13

THE BIRTH OF THE MOVEMENT

In spite of the documents available about this period, it is still not very easy to reconstruct exactly the beginnings of what was to become the Vienna Psycho-Analytical Society. The reason is undoubtedly that neither Freud nor the group which had formed round him were aware that they were creating a movement whose history would one day have to be written. In *The History of the Psycho-Analytic Movement*, a work dating from 1914, Freud confined himself to recalling briefly how a few young people gradually gathered round him and put an end to the isolation which he had believed would always be his lot:

'From the year 1902 onwards, a number of young doctors gathered round me with the express intention of learning, practising and spreading the knowledge of psycho-analysis. The stimulus came from a colleague who had himself experienced the beneficial effects of analytic therapy. Regular meetings took place on certain evenings at my house, discussions were held according to certain rules and the participants endeavoured to find their bearings in this new and strange field of research and to interest others in it. One day a young man who had passed through a technical training college introduced himself with a manuscript which showed very unusual comprehension. We persuaded him to go through the *Gymnasium* [Secondary School] and the University and to devote himself to the non-medical side of psycho-analysis. The little society acquired in him a zealous and dependable secretary and I gained in Otto Rank a most loyal helper and co-worker. . . .'[1]

Freud makes no mention here of the first doctor to practice psychoanalysis after him. It was Rudolf Reitler who, with Max Kahane, had for a long time attended his lectures at the University. The colleague to whose initiative

[1] *Std Edn* XIV, p. 25.

he attributed the formation of the first group is Wilhelm Stekel, a doctor who suffered from serious neurotic disturbances and who, about 1901 or 1902, had come to him for treatment. Max Kahane left the Society in 1907. Strictly speaking he had never been a psychoanalyst since he did not use the psychoanalytic method. Some years later Adler's departure provoked the first split within the movement; Stekel's withdrawal, less damaging in its "ideological' consequences, also caused a serious dispute.

At the start the newcomers met every Wednesday evening in Freud's waiting room and for this reason gave their group the modest name of the 'Psychological Wednesday Society'. Most of the members not yet having published anything—apart from Stekel, who had written a book about coitus in childhood—the main topics of discussion were Freud's work and purely theoretical problems. Stekel, who was a regular contributor to the *Neues Wiener Tagblatt*, reported its discussions every week. In 1908 the Vienna Psychological Society changed its name to the 'Vienna Psycho-Analytical Society'. For two more years the Society held its meetings at 19 Berggasse, but afterwards this accommodation proved too cramped and the meetings moved to a room in the College of Physicians.

During its early years the existence of the Society, which slowly increased in size, did not make any great change to Freud's daily life, which was geared primarily to the demands of work and was therefore highly organized. Fully occupied with carrying on his practice and writing his numerous books, Freud led the simplest of lives in the bosom of his family and within the narrow circle of his old friends, who were mostly doctors he had known in his youth. His relaxations were few, but he was keen on them and never gave them up completely, even when he had to defend his private life from the importunate demands of fame. They were a daily walk, of which he took advantage to renew his stock of cigars; a game of cards every Saturday night with his friends Professor Königstein and Dr Rie, then, later, with his own children when they were old enough to be his partners; from time to time he went to the opera or the theatre, though this was rare; above all he went searching for antiquities which he had begun to collect some years earlier and which, more than any other hobby, held a large place in his life.

This passion for archaeology showed that Freud had a taste for the past which was not limited to the childhood of the spirit but, as he said himself, extended to 'every human form of prehistory'. We have seen how he liked to compare himself to those explorers of the past who brought to light buried worlds and civilizations. He found in their lives and work more than one profound resemblance to his own. Thus his letters to Fliess show him to be full of interest and sympathy for Burckhardt's *Cultural History of Greece* and for Schliemann's *Ilias,* in which the author traces back his discovery of buried Troy to a childhood dream which never ceased to inspire him. 'This man,' he said, 'found happiness in discoverng Priam's treasure, which goes to prove that the realization of a childish wish is alone capable of engendering happiness.' He often returned to this theme and to this law of happiness which explains his predilection for archaeology, just as it dominates his research:

'Happiness is the deferred fulfilment of a prehistoric wish. That is why wealth brings so little happiness; money is not an infantile wish. . . .'[1]

And again:

'The repetition of experiences of the prehistoric period is a wish-fulfilment in itself. . . .'[1]

A love of travel was an equally strong passion with Freud, although it had long been frustrated by lack of money and the inhibition which self-analysis finally allowed him to overcome. In the early years of the century travel became for him a need that was all the more natural, as it was his only means of escape from an excessively sedentary life, his only means, too, of escaping from Vienna, which he hated.

The climate of Vienna justified long summer holidays. Freud's family generally spent three months in the country, either a long way from the capital or close to it according to their financial situation at the time. Freud joined them towards the end of July but, more often than not, left again on the long tours which took him all over —to Germany, to the South Tyrol and above all to Italy, where he went nearly every summer. His travel programmes were so full and carried out at such dizzy speed

[1] Letters to Fliess, *Origins,* pp. 244 and 246.

that in the end his wife, who tired easily, stopped going with him. He was then accompanied by his sister-in-law Minna, Fliess (in the days of their 'congresses'), his brother Alexander and, much later, his youngest daughter, Anna, who was to continue his work and whom, in his old age, he gratefully called his Antigone. He also spent many traveling holidays with Sandor Ferenczi, the only one of his followers who became a real friend.

One of these journeys at the beginning of the century deserves our attention because, for many years, it set Freud a little puzzle, of which the solution is to be found in a famous letter to Romain Rolland, published under the title of *A Disturbance of Memory on the Acropolis.* This was in 1936, more than thirty years after the apparently insignificant episode which was the subject of the analysis. Romain Rolland was seventy, Freud eighty:

'My dear Friend, I have been urgently pressed to make some written contribution to the celebration of your seventieth birthday and I have made long efforts to find something that might in any way be worthy of you and might give expression to my admiration for your love of the truth, for your courage in your beliefs and for your affection and good will towards humanity; or, again, something that might bear witness to my gratitude to you as a writer who has afforded me so many moments of exaltation and pleasure. But it was in vain. I am ten years older than you and my powers of production are at an end. All that I can find to offer you is the gift of an impoverished creature, who has "seen better days".

'You know that the aim of my scientific work was to throw light upon unusual, abnormal or pathological manifestations of the mind—that is to say, to trace them back to the psychical forces operating behind them and to indicate the mechanisms at work. I began by attempting this upon myself and then went on to apply it to other people and finally, by a bold extension, to the human race as a whole. During the last few years, a phenomenon of this sort, which I myself had experienced a generation ago, in 1904, and which I had never understood, has kept on recurring to my mind. I did not at first see why; but at last I determined to analyse the incident—and I now present you with the results of that enquiry. In the process, I shall have, of course, to ask you to give more attention to some events in my private life than they would otherwise deserve.'

Freud then relates the circumstances of the incident which constantly recurred and troubled him. He was travelling in Italy with his brother Alexander, who was ten years his junior and therefore the same age as Romain Rolland, as he does not fail to point out. From Trieste the two men planned to go to Corfu and rest for a few days; but a friend dissuaded them and advised them to go instead to Athens. After thinking up a lot of objections to this new plan which, without their knowing why, put them in a bad temper, Freud and his brother nevertheless bought their tickets and found themselves in Athens, in a way without really having decided to go there:

'When, finally, on the afternoon after our arrival, I stood on the Acropolis and cast my eyes around upon the landscape, a surprising thought suddenly entered my mind: "So all this really *does* exist, just as we learnt at school!" To describe the situation more accurately, the person who gave expression to the remark was divided, far more sharply than was usually noticeable, from another person who took cognizance of the remark; and both were astonished, though not by the same thing. The first behaved as though he were obliged, under the impact of an unequivocal observation, to believe in something the reality of which had hitherto seemed doubtful. If I may make a slight exaggeration, it was as if someone, walking beside Loch Ness, suddenly caught sight of the form of the famous Monster stranded upon the shore and found himself driven to the admission: "So it really *does* exist—the sea-serpent we've never believed in!" The second person, on the other hand, was justifiably astonished, because he had been unaware that the real existence of Athens, the Acropolis, and the landscape around it had ever been objects of doubt. What he had been expecting was rather some expression of delight or admiration.'

According to the principle which he applied to the little pathology of everyday life—unwonted moods, forgetting, blunders, mistakes etc.—Freud analyzes his memory disturbance as he would a dream. He finds in it the tendentious distortion common to all psychical products of this kind, the apparently innocent falsification of which the cause, as always, must be sought in the most distant past. The true and the false are mixed up in this ephemeral feeling of depersonalization thanks to which Freud, on the Acropolis, believes he remembers that in his youth he had actually had doubts about the reality of Athens. Once again a childhood memory re-establishes the truth:

'It is not true that in my schooldays I ever doubted the real existence of Athens. I only doubted whether I should ever see Athens. It seemed to me beyond the realms of possibility that I should travel so far—that I should "go such a long way". This was linked up with the limitations and poverty of our conditions of life in my youth. My longing to travel was no doubt also the expression of a wish to escape from that pressure, like the force which drives so many adolescent children to run away from home. I had long seen clearly that a great part of the pleasure of travel lies in the fulfilment of these early wishes—that it is rooted, that is, in dissatisfaction with home and family. When first one catches sight of the sea, crosses the ocean and experiences as realities cities and lands which for so long had been distant, unattainable things of desire—one feels oneself like a hero who has performed deeds of improbable greatness. I might that day on the Acropolis have said to my brother: "Do you still remember how, when we were young, we used day after day to walk along the same streets on our way to school, and how every Sunday we used to go to the Prater or on some excursion we knew so well? And now, here we are in Athens, and standing on the Acropolis! We really *have* gone a long way!" So too, if I may compare such a small event with a greater one, Napoleon, during his coronation as Emperor in Notre Dame, turned to one of his brothers—it must no doubt have been the eldest one, Joseph—and remarked: "What would *Monsieur notre Père* have said to this, if he could have been here to-day?"

'But here we come upon the solution of the little problem of why it was that already at Trieste we interfered with our enjoyment of the voyage to Athens. It must be that a sense of guilt was attached to the satisfaction in having gone such a long way: there was something about it that was wrong, that from earliest times had been forbidden. It was something to do with a child's criticism of his father, with the undervaluation which took the place of the overvaluation of earlier childhood. It seems as though the essence of success was to have got further than one's father, and as though to excel one's father was still something forbidden.

'As an addition to this generally valid motive there was a special factor present in our particular case. The very theme of Athens and the Acropolis in itself contained evidence of the son's superiority. Our father had been in business, he had had no secondary education, and Athens could not have meant much to him. Thus what interfered with our enjoyment of the journey to Athens was a feeling of *filial piety*. And now you will no longer wonder that the recollection of this incident on the Acropolis should have troubled me so often since I myself have grown old and stand in need of forbearance and can travel no more.' [1]

In this letter, in which he portrays himself better than his biographers ever will, Freud speaks of the year 1904 as a time when he felt sure of success. In fact fame was still far off. The four years which had just passed had not made much difference to his position in the scientific world; but here and there, even abroad, people read his *Interpretation of Dreams* and the Psychological Wednesday Society, although still weak and incongruous, was actually beginning to extend his influence. Each year saw the number of his pupils increase—Viennese from nearly every walk of life, doctors and laymen, some motivated by scientific curiosity, others by inner difficulties, by personal suffering which, in some way, gave authenticity to their vocation. From the beginning of 1908 the Vienna Psycho-Analytical Society had thirty-two members and after 1907—an important date for the movement—it welcomed a number of foreign visitors, Swiss, English, Americans, Germans, who were to form the first nucleus of the International Psycho-Analytical Association. The somewhat chancy growth of the movement; the completely unsystematic recruiting of its members who, let us not forget, did not have a dogma or even a finished doctrine to serve as a basis for agreement, but a man on his own who was sustained only by a few definite ideas and his intuitive genius; and finally the peculiar character of the science, which possessed neither a tradition nor a past and which could only be constructed by first sending the researcher back to his own subjectivity: all these things were bound to have a

[1] *Std Edn* XXII, pp. 239–48.

definite effect on the subsequent fate of psychoanalysis, sometimes to the extent of endangering its success. To avoid the dissensions which he doubtless foresaw and which did in fact materialize, Freud at the beginning had devised a procedure which allowed anybody who wanted to leave the group to do so without causing any fuss or embarrassment. Ernest Jones quotes a 1907 circular in which Freud explained his proposal:

'Allow me to give the reason for this action which may well seem to you to be superfluous. We are only taking into account the natural changes in human relationships if we assume that to one or another member in our group membership no longer signifies what it did years earlier —whether because his interest in the subject is exhausted, or his leisure time and mode of life are no longer compatible with attendance, or that personal associations threaten to keep him away. Presumably he would still remain a member, fearing lest his resignation be regarded as an unfriendly action. For all these cases the dissolving and reorganizing of the Society has the purpose of re-establishing the personal freedom of each individual and of making it possible for him to stay apart from the Society without in any way disturbing his relations with the rest of us. We have further to bear in mind that in the course of years we have undertaken (financial) obligations such as appointing a secretary, of which there was no question at the beginning.

'If you agree after this explanation with the expediency of reconstituting the Society in this way, you will probably approve of its being repeated at regular intervals—say every three years. . . .'[1]

This procedure was hardly practicable in the long run and after 1910 it was abandoned altogether. Ernest Jones is undoubtedly right in seeing in it a proof of Freud's tact, for Freud always tried not to intervene in the Society's difficulties, although he was not always able to escape his role as arbitrator. It can also be interpreted as a half-confessed wish to change the composition of the group which in many repsects left much to be desired. Freud did not feel any great liking for some of his first adherents, as we know from Ludwig Binswanger, the Swiss psychiatrist who

[1] Ernest Jones, II, pp. 9–10.

went to Vienna in 1907 and to whom Freud said after one meeting: 'You've seen this collection!' A passage in the *History of the Psycho-Analytic Movement* expresses the same sort of disillusionment less brutally:

'The small circle soon expanded, and in the course of the next few years often changed its composition. On the whole I could tell myself that it was hardly inferior, in wealth and variety of talent, to the staff of any clinical teacher one could think of. It included from the beginning the men who were later to play such a considerable, if not always a welcome, part in the history of the psycho-analytic movement. At that time, however, one could not yet guess at these developments. I had every reason to be satisfied, and I think I did everything possible to impart my own knowledge and experience to the others. There were only two inauspicious circumstances which at last estranged me inwardly from the group. I could not succeed in establishing among its members the friendly relations that ought to obtain between men who are all engaged upon the same difficult work; nor was I able to stifle the disputes about priority for which there were so many opportunities under these conditions of work in common. The difficulties in the way of giving instruction in the practice of psycho-analysis, which are quite particularly great and are responsible for much in the present dissensions, were evident already in this private Vienna Psycho-Analytical Society. I myself did not venture to put forward a still unfinished technique and a theory still in the making with an authority which would probably have enabled the others to avoid some wrong turnings and ultimate disasters. The self-reliance of intellectual workers, their early independence of their teacher, is always gratifying from a psychological point of view; but it is only of advantage to science if those workers fulfil certain personal conditions which are none too common. For psycho-analysis in particular a long and severe discipline and training in self-discipline would have been required. In view of the courage displayed by their devotion to a subject so much frowned upon and so poor in prospects, I was disposed to tolerate much among the members to which I should otherwise have made objection. . . .'[1]

[1] *Std Edn* XIV, pp. 25–6.

These grave dissensions which ended in the departure of Adler, then Jung, then Otto Rank and estranged from Freud even the follower he loved like a son, Sandor Ferenczi, will be described in due course. These quarrels, debated loudly and heatedly in public, gave the outside world a rather damaging picture of the movement and they were certainly not calculated to silence sarcastic comment. All the same, it would be a mistake to compare them with the internal disputes of a political party, for the various Psychoanalytical Societies had no fixed body of doctrine, subscribing only to two or three central ideas; the development of these could not be foreseen and, whatever one might think, they were still closely bound up with their creator. Freud himself always opposed the idea of a psychoanalytical orthodoxy. What he wanted to defend in psychoanalysis was not a complete ideological structure but a minimum number of conceptions without which work in common seemed to him not to be possible. Thus he wrote in Marcuse's *Manual of Psychoanalysis*, published in 1926:

'Psychoanalysis is not like a philosophical system which starts from a few strictly defined fundamental principles, uses them to embrace the totality of the world and, once perfected, has no room for new discoveries or improvements. On the contrary, it remains linked with the facts which are produced in its field of activity, it tries to solve the immediate problems of observation, tentatively continues its experience, it is always incomplete, always ready to correct or modify its theories. Like physics or chemistry it allows that its fundamental concepts are vague and its assumptions provisional, it does not expect a more rigorous definition than future work . . . .'[1]

Thus psychoanalysis is and must remain an empirical science. It cannot, therefore, give birth to a 'school', but it can be practised by all who unreservedly accept what Freud, again in the *Manual*, lays down as its main foundations:

'The existence of unconscious psychical processes; the theory of resistance or repression; the appreciation of the role of sexuality and of the Oedipus complex are the main contents of psychoanalysis and the foundation of its

[1] Quoted by Heinrich Meng: 'Aus meiner psychoanalytischen Anfangszeit,' in *Psychoanalyse*, S. Karger, Basle, 1962, 351–60.

theory. Whoever does not accept them should not reckon himself to be a psychoanalyst.'

Exactly the same idea is to be found in a letter he wrote in 1917 to Georg Groddeck, a Berlin doctor and writer who, unlike so many others, refused to join the ranks of his followers. In his wonderful *Buch vom Es,* written with as much profundity as literary skill, Groddeck first launched the idea of psychosomatic medicine. At the same time he gave the Freudian unconscious a new name and unforeseen richness.

'I note that you urge me to confirm to you officially that you are not a psychoanalyst, that you don't belong to the flock of disciples, but that you may be allowed to consider yourself as something apart and independent. I evidently would be doing you a great favour by rejecting you and relegating you to the place where Adler, Jung and others stand. But this I cannot do: I must lay claim to you, must insist that you are an analyst of the first order who has grasped the essence of the matter once for all. The man who has recognised that transference and resistance are the hubs of treatment belongs irrevocably to the "Wild Hunt". . . .'[1]

The internecine struggles in the psychoanalytical movement revolved round a few points—theory of the unconscious, resistance and repression; the importance of sexuality and the Oedipus complex—which Freud insisted be accepted without question by whoever used his name. Each secession was, in fact, motivated by the partial or total abandoning of these conceptions, or else by the deviations or extensions which stripped them of their original meaning. In some cases, as with Adler, the psychology of the conscious recovered its old primacy, neurosis was no longer bound up with infantile sexuality but with simple organic defects and known data of social life; or, as with Jung, the individual unconscious existed, but de-sexualized, drowned in a comforting collective unconscious where metaphysics re-entered by a back door; in yet other cases, Rank's for example, the 'trauma of birth' explained all human ill by life's very beginning, thus dispensing with the Oedipean drama. For more than thirty years all these 'heresies', whatever truth they might contain, seem to have

[1] To Georg Groddeck, June 5, 1917, *Letters,* p. 316.

had as their aim only the re-establishment of an earlier state of psychology. In other words they set out to annul the scandal of Freudian thought in an ingenious way. And contrary to what one is often inclined to think, Freud was not always the first to sense this coming.

We still need to know why these divergences gave rise to such sensational dissensions instead of being settled by a calm discussion of ideas. The fact is that in this case, but more obviously than in many other spheres, the ideas were not the only, not even perhaps the real cause of the conflict. It cannot be denied that the so-called tyranny of which Freud has so often been accused counted for less in these lamentable affairs than his moral and intellectual authority, which put his most gifted pupils in a very difficult position. The fact is that Freud, who kept losing the friendship of so many people to whom he was deeply attached, remained connected all his life with men of very different background, scientific interests and ways of thinking. To quote only two cases, Ludwig Binswanger and Oskar Pfister (one a psychiatrist, the other a clergyman) remained unshakably loyal to him throughout all the vicissitudes of the movement without giving up their scientific or religious convictions. Freud undoubtedly preferred this attitude, which they stated with tact and something akin to graciousness for more than a quarter of a century, to that adopted by certain of his followers who aped him and whose devotion was sometimes not far removed from hatred. If one reads the correspondence he kept up with these two men until the end of his life one can see how touched he was by their attitude and that it was not his fault if he did not meet it more often.

Ludwig Binswanger had set himself the task of building a bridge between psychoanalysis and psychiatry, or more exactly to create a solid basis of common work between the two disciplines which were still alienated from one another. After the storm and stress of his break with Jung, Freud had thought for a moment of making him the 'heir' of the movement but, anxious about his career and his psychiatric research, Binswanger had different ideas. Freud's disappointment did not affect the warmth of his friendship for the young scientist and, a very long time after, he told him so:

'We have remained loyal to one another through a quarter

of a century, but this seemed perfectly natural and we did not make a fuss about it. . . .'[1]

As for Oskar Pfister, who always defended his ideas with vigour and great spirit, Freud called him his 'dear man of God', a 'real servant of God', the very idea and existence of whom had 'always appeared most improbable.' Pfister, a doctor of philosophy and theology, was the first to apply psychoanalysis to teaching. He was able to practise psychoanalysis without sacrificing the demands of his ministry, which he carried on in Zurich until he retired; and if he accepted Freud's sometimes very critical remarks, especially on the question of sexuality, he could also stand up for himself and say what he thought. When Freud published *The Future of an Illusion,* in which religion is treated as a collective neurosis, Pfister hit back by writing *The Illusion of a Future,* but the polemic between the two men never took on a churlish note, to which Freud was much more sensitive than he was to criticism. One day Freud slyly asked Pfister why psychoanalysis had not been invented by some godly man instead of by a completely irreligious Jew, and Pfister retorted:

'. . . Finally you ask why psycho-analysis was not discovered by any of the pious, but by an atheist Jew. The answer obviously is that piety is not the same as genius for discovery and that most of the pious did not have it in them to make such discoveries. Moreover, in the first place you are no Jew, which to me, in view of my unbounded admiration for Amos, Isaiah, Jeremiah, and the author of Job and Ecclesiastes, is a matter of profound regret, and in the second place you are not godless, for he who lives the truth lives in God, and he who strives for the freeing of love "dwelleth in God" (First Epistle of John, iv, 16). If you raised to your consciousness and fully felt your place in the great design, which to me is as necessary as the synthesis of the notes is to a Beethoven symphony, I should say of you: A better Christian there never was. . . .'[2]

[1] Ludwig Binswanger: *Erinnerungen an Sigmund Freud,* Francke Verlag, Bern, 1956, p. 109.

[2] Letter from Pfister, October 29, 1918, *Psychoanalysis & Faith,* p. 63.

14

THE PSYCHOPATHOLOGY OF EVERYDAY LIFE

The Interpretation of Dreams marked the beginning of an extremely productive period in Freud's life in which the books he wrote were as varied and original as they were numerous. In fact all the works he published in the following years sprang from his theory of dreams, either directly as in the *Fragment of an Analysis of a Case of Hysteria* in which the dream of a patient (who has since become famous under the name of 'Dora') explains in a masterly way a very obscure case; or indirectly as in *The Psychopathology of Everyday Life* and *Jokes and Their Relation to the Unconscious,* in which Freud uncovered profound analogies between the mechanisms of dream processes and those governing certain activities of the waking state. Even the *Three Essays on the Theory of Sexuality,* which exist in their own right, owe their first and decisive inspiration to *The Interpretation of Dreams.*

The publication dates of these different works give a mistaken idea of their origin. In point of fact they were conceived and written simultaneously, between 1897 and 1900, as is proved by Freud's letters to Fliess in which they are already outlined. From 1897 Freud interested himself in jokes and collected Jewish stories and anecdotes, at first because he liked them and then in order to understand the motives which made him tell them and introduce them into his writings. In 1898, struck by the fact that he had for no apparent reason forgotten the name of a poet that he knew perfectly well, he set about solving this little puzzle, which suddenly became important in the context of his self-analysis. It was the beginning of his research into the benign anomalies of everyday behaviour, the inexplicable forgetting of names and facts, faulty actions, blunders, mistakes in writing and remembering, all things which, like dreams, had until then been dismissed as so much rubbish devoid of all value for scientific investigation.

During this whole period Freud had such a powerful

sense of the profound unity of all his work that he was writing the *Three Essays on the Theory of Sexuality* and the *Jokes* both at the same time, the manuscripts lying on adjoining tables. This unity was in fact assured not only by the continuity of his scientific preoccupations which for many years revolved almost exclusively round dreams and sexuality, but even more by the work he had undertaken, which remained one of his life's tasks.

Freud first raised the question of *The Psychopathology of Everyday Life* in a letter to Fliess in which he briefly related the analysis of the forgetting of the name of a poet, Julius Mosen. Treating this unimportant lapse of memory as a nuerotic symptom, Freud discovered that he had repressed Mosen's name for very definite personal reasons; that the repression had been determined by infantile reasons; and finally that the substitute names which had come into his mind represented a compromise between the repressing force and the repressed ideas, like the hybrid formations produced in dreams. Note that Freud reveals nothing about the contents of the analysis and that consequently he did not link the Mosen example with the other personal cases in his collection.[1]

Another example of the forgetting of a proper name, accompanied by a mistaken reminiscence, was dealt with at the same time in a letter to Fliess, in an article which Freud published in 1898 and in the first chapter of *The Psychopathology of Everyday Life,* where it is given as a model of all disturbances of the same kind. Ernest Jones believes it represented an important event in Freud's life —doubtless one of those which had prompted him to embark on his own analysis. As so often, Freud published only part of the results of his interpretation. He briefly summed them up in a letter to Fliess in which he also wondered if the public would find them convincing:

'I have explained another instance of name-forgetting even more easily. I could not remember the name of the great painter who painted the Last Judgement at Orvieto, the finest I have seen. Instead Botticelli and Boltraffio occurred to me, with the certainty that they were wrong. Eventually I found out the name, Signorelli, and the fact that I then at once remembered the Christian name, Luca, showed that repression was at work and not true forgetful-

[1] Letter to Fliess, August 26, 1898, *Origins,* p. 260.

ness. It is clear why "Botticelli" came up; only *Signor* was repressed; the "Bo" in both substitute-names is explained by the memory responsible for the repression, which concerned something that happened in *Bosnia,* and began with someone saying: *"Herr* [Sir, *Signor*], what can be done about it?" I forgot the name of Signorelli during a short trip into *Her*zegovina, which I made from Ragusa with a lawyer from Berlin (Freyhau), with whom I got into conversation about pictures. In the course of the conversation, which aroused memories which, as I say, evidently caused the repression, we talked about death and sexuality. "Trafio" is an echo of Trafoi, which I saw on an earlier journey! How can I make this seem credible to anyone?'[1]

Despite his fear that he would not be understood, Freud ventured to publish the Signorelli case in 1898, that is two years before *The Interpretation of Dreams.* And he doubtless did so because the forgetting of a name seemed to him the perfect way of bringing home the reality of repression. What is the explanation of the obstinate flight of a perfectly well-known name which can usually be recalled at will? Or rather, what is it that resists the correct reproduction of the name which is being sought, and what lies behind it?

'In the course of our efforts to recover the name that has dropped out, other ones—*substitute names*—enter our consciousness; we recognize them at once, indeed, as incorrect, but they keep on returning and force themselves on us with great persistence. The process that should lead to the reproduction of the missing name has been so to speak *displaced* and has therefore led to an incorrect substitute. My hypothesis is that this displacement is not left to arbitrary psychical choice but follows paths which can be predicted and which conform to laws. In other words, I suspect that the name or names which are substituted are connected in a discoverable way with the missing name: and I hope, if I am successful in demonstrating this connection, to proceed to throw light on the circumstances in which names are forgotten. . . .'[2]

In the case of Signorelli, the name was forgotten under ordinary conditions, as is usual in this sort of disturbance.

[1] Ibid., September 22, 1898, pp. 264–5.

[2] *The Psychopathology of Everyday Life, Std Edn* VI, pp. 1–2.

Freud was travelling, he met a Berlin lawyer whom he did not know very well and who, like himself, was returning from Ragusa in Herzegovina. In the course of conversation he asked his companion if he had been to Orvieto and if he had seen the magnificent frescoes of . . .

'(Light was only thrown on the forgetting of the name when I recalled the topic we had been discussing directly before, and it was revealed as a case in which a *topic that has just been raised is disturbed by the preceding topic.* Shortly before I put the question to my travelling companion whether he had ever been to Orvieto, we had been talking about the customs of the Turks living in *Bosnia* and Herzegovina. I had told him what I had heard from a colleague practising among those people—that they are accustomed to show great confidence in their doctor and great resignation to fate. If one has to inform them that nothing can be done for a sick person, their reply is: "*Herr* [Sir] what is there to be said? If he could be saved, I know you would have saved him." In these sentences we for the first time meet with the words and names *Bosnia, Herzegovina* and *Herr,* which can be inserted into an associative series between *Signorelli* and *Botticelli—Boltraffio.*)'

Since the repression was not directed at Signorelli's name or anything which might be associated with the painter, Freud looked for a possible motive in what they had been talking about earlier in the conversation:

'I assume that the series of thoughts about the customs of the Turks in Bosnia, etc., acquired the capacity to disturb the next succeeding thought from the fact that I had withdrawn my attention from that series before it was brought to an end. I recall in fact wanting to tell a second anecdote which lay close to the first in my memory. These Turks place a higher value on sexual enjoyment than on anything else, and in the event of sexual disorders they are plunged in a despair which contrasts strangely with their resignation towards the threat of death. One of my colleague's patients once said to him: "*Herr,* you must know that if *that* comes to an end then life is of no value." I suppressed my account of this characteristic trait, since I did not want to allude to the topic in a conversation with a stranger. But I did more: I also diverted my attention from pursuing thoughts which might have arisen in my mind from the topic of "death and sexuality". On this occasion I was still under the influence of a piece of news which had reached me a few weeks before while I was making a brief stay at *Trafoi*. A patient over whom I had taken a great deal of trouble had put an end to his life on account of an incurable sexual disorder. I know for certain that this melancholy event and everything related to it was not recalled to my conscious memory during my journey to Herzegovina. But the similarity between "Trafoi" and "Boltraffio" forces me to assume that this reminiscence, in spite of my attention being deliberately diverted from it, was brought into operation in me at the time [of the conversation].'[1]

It will be noticed that Freud searches for the psychical mechanisms which cause the forgetting in exactly the same way that he analyses a dream to discover its latent content. The fact is that although they happen in apparently very different spheres, the two phenomena have some essential features in common—primarily distortion of the facts by which their meaning is truly betrayed, that is to say is half expressed, half silenced.

'I am forced to recognize the influence of a *motive* in the process. It was a motive which caused me to interrupt myself while recounting what was in my mind (concerning the customs of the Turks, etc.), and it was a motive which further influenced me so that I debarred the thoughts connected with them, the thoughts which had led to the news at Trafoi, from becoming conscious in my mind. I wanted, therefore, to forget something; I had *repressed* something. What I wanted to forget was not, it is true, the name of the artist at Orvieto but something else—something, however, which contrived to place itself in an associative connection with his name, so that my act of will missed its target and I forgot *the one thing against my will,* while I wanted to forget *the other thing intentionally*. The disinclination to remember was aimed against one content; the inability to remember emerged in another. It would obviously be a simpler case if disinclination and inability to remember related to the same content. . . .'[2]

[1] Ibid., pp. 3–4.
[2] Ibid., p. 4.

The conclusions of this first study are still extremely cautious. Freud does not say that all forgetting of proper names can be explained in this way but that side by side with simple, classical cases described by psychologists there are others *in which forgetting is determined by repression.*

The composition of *The Psychopathology of Everyday Life* brings out with great clarity the steps by which Freud advanced in this new domain, which was opened up by a purely personal experience. Having firmly established in the course of his self-analysis definite facts about a precise group of phenomena—those in which the forgetting of a proper name is accompanied by a mistaken reminiscence —he tries to explain empirically other harmless forms of amnesia—the forgetting of nouns in foreign languages, of words and word sequences—and finally gives his attention to all the passing behaviour disturbances which have come to be called faulty actions. The very composition of the book makes it clear that Freud did not conceive it in an abstract and hastily generalized way. On the contrary, it sprang from his probing an apparently trivial fact in his own life. An ordinary case of forgetting, one of those mistakes which everyone makes without stopping to think about, revealed to him what he wanted to hide from himself—his very painful feelings about a patient's suicide. The certainty that there is a link between these two orders of things of such unequal value entitled him to apply his method to all similar disturbances.

To find the examples he needed Freud was also obliged to make use of the results of his self-analysis. He could not draw on the material provided by his patients since he was not studying the manifestations of neurosis but the more or less normal disturbances of the healthy individual. Consequently his pupils got into the habit of collecting for him examples of lapses, faulty actions and symptomatic errors of all kinds; but at first there were very few cases which he was able to observe directly. The one he relates at the beginning of Chapter 2 is as amusing as it is illustrative.

The incident took place in the summer. Freud, still on his travels, met a young Jew whom he knew and who was conversant with his books. The young man burst out into bitter complaints about the inferior status to which he was condemned because he was a Jew and concluded his diatribe with the line from Vergil in which Dido appeals to posterity to avenge her for the outrage she has suffered from Aeneas:

'"*Exoriare . . .*" Or rather, he *wanted* to end it in this way, for he could not get hold of the quotation and tried to conceal an obvious gap in what he remembered by changing the order of the words: "*Exoriar (e) ex nostris ossibus ultor.*" At last he said irritably: "Please don't look so scornful: you seem as if you were gloating over my embarrassment. Why not help me? There's something missing in the line; how does the whole thing really go?"

"I'll help you with pleasure," I replied, and gave the quotation in its correct form: "*Exoriar (e) ALIQUIS nostris ex ossibus ultor.*"

'"How stupid to forget a word like that! By the way, you claim that one never forgets a thing without some reason. I should be very curious to learn how I came to forget the indefinite pronoun '*aliquis*' in this case."

'I took up this challenge most readily, for I was hoping for a contribution to my collection. So I said: "That should not take us long. I must only ask you to tell me, *candidly* and *uncritically,* whatever comes into your mind if you direct your attention to the forgotten word without any definite aim."

'"Good. There springs to my mind, then, the ridiculous notion of dividing up the word like this: *a* and *liquis.*"

'"What does that mean?" "I don't know." "And what occurs to you next?" "What comes next is *Reliquien* [relics], *liquefying, fluidity, fluid.* Have you discovered anything so far?"

'"No. Not by any means yet. But go on."

"'I am thinking," he went on with a scornful laugh, "of *Simon of Trent,* whose relics I saw two years ago in a church at Trent. I am thinking of the accusation of ritual blood-sacrifice which is being brought against the Jews again just now, and of *Kleinpaul's* book [1892] in which he regards all these supposed victims as incarnations, one might say new editions, of the Saviour."

'"The notion is not entirely unrelated to the subject we were discussing before the Latin word slipped your memory."

'"True. My next thoughts are about an article that I read lately in an Italian newspaper. Its title, I think, was 'What St *Augustine* says about Women'. What do you make of that?"

‘ “I am waiting.”

‘ “And now comes something that is quite clearly unconnected with our subject.”

‘ “Please refrain from any criticism and——”

‘ “Yes, I understand. I am thinking of a fine old gentleman I met on my travels last week. He was a real *original,* with all the appearance of a huge bird of prey. His name was *Benedict,* if it's of interest to you.”

‘ “Anyhow, here are a row of saints and Fathers of the Church: St *Simon,* St *Augustine,* St *Benedict.* There was, I think, a Church Father called *Origen.* Moreover, three of these names are also first names, like *Paul* in *Kleinpaul.*”

‘ “Now it's St *Januarius* and the miracle of his blood that comes into my mind—my thoughts seem to me to be running on mechanically.”

‘ “Just a moment: St *Januarius* and St *Augustine* both have to do with the calendar. But won't you remind me about the miracle of his blood?”

‘ “Surely you must have heard of that? They keep the blood of St Januarius in a phial inside a church at Naples, and on a particular holy day it miraculously *liquefies.* The people attach great importance to this miracle and get very excited if it's delayed, as happened once at a time when the French were occupying the town. So the general in command—or have I got it wrong? was it Garibaldi?—took the reverend gentleman aside and gave him to understand, with an unmistakable gesture towards the soldiers posted outside, that he *hoped* the miracle would take place very soon. And in fact it did take place. . . .”

‘ “Well, go on. Why do you pause?”

‘ “Well, something *has* come into my mind . . . but it's too intimate to pass on. . . . Besides, I don't see any connection, or any necessity for saying it.”

‘ “You can leave the connection to me. Of course I can't force you to talk about something that you find distasteful; but then you mustn't insist on learning from me how you came to forget your *aliquis.*”

‘ “Really? Is that what you think? Well then, I've suddenly thought of a lady from whom I might easily hear a piece of news that would be very awkward for both of us.”

‘ “That her periods have stopped?”

‘ “How could you guess that?”

‘ “That's not difficult any longer; you're prepared the

way sufficiently. Think of *the calendar saints, the blood that starts to flow on a particular day, the disturbance when the event fails to take place, the open threats that the miracle must be vouchsafed, or else. . . .* In fact you've made use of the miracle of St Januarius to manufacture a brilliant allusion to women's periods."

'"Without being aware of it. And you really mean to say that it was this anxious expectation that made me unable to produce an unimportant word like *aliquis?*"

'"It seems to me undeniable. You need only recall the division you made into *a-liquis,* and your associations: *relics, liquefying, fluid.* St Simon was *sacrificed as a child*—shall I go on and show how he comes in? You were led on to him by the subject of relics."

'"No, I'd rather you didn't. I hope you don't take these thoughts of mine too seriously, if indeed I really had them. In return I will confess to you that the lady is Italian and that I went to Naples with her. But mayn't all this just be a matter of chance?"

'"I must leave it to your own judgement to decide whether you can explain all these connections by the assumption that they are matters of chance. I can however tell you that every case like this that you care to analyze will lead you to 'matters of chance' that are just as striking."'[1]

The analysis of the 'Aliquis' case throws light on the true cause of the forgetting. The young man was a prey to contradictory emotions and, torn between his wish for children who would avenge him and his refusal to assume the burdens of parenthood, he could not fully express either of these thoughts. Freud shows that it is the same with all faulty actions, that they affect the memory and speech and lead to unusual sorts of behaviour. Lapses, mistakes in writing and reading, forgetting impressions and plans, oversights, blunders, clumsy movements, faulty recognition—all result from two intentions interfering with one another, one of which is manifest, the other repressed and therefore causing disorder.

Thus the condition necessary for any mistake is the repression of a statement which the interlocutor himself might consider indecent, wounding or incongruous. Being in this way suppressed in conversation, the repressed tendency manifests itself in spite of the person who is speak-

[1] Ibid., pp. 9–11.

ing, either by modifying the avowed tendency, by merging with it, or quite simply by taking its place. Thanks to the resultant slip the repressed tendency satisfies the censorship while finding a way towards a first form of expression.

Like dreams faulty actions are therefore a compromise between two antagonistic intentions which wish to express themselves together and can only do so at the cost of a sort of mutual concession, causing a distortion, a fault or an apparent inaccuracy of thought. Like dreams, they surreptitiously resist analysis, in such a way that the person involved generally denies that they are important while the victim or any witness never has much difficulty in perceiving their significance.

There is no need to dwell on the numerous examples of lapses and other mistakes cited by Freud as they are so well known. They are the ones which have done most to popularize the elementary ideas of psychoanalysis, and if it is now no longer possible to excuse a blunder as forgetfulness or inattention this is because of *The Psychopathology of Everyday Life,* even for people who have not read it. The little daily failings, the inoffensive aberrations which make the most normal person look like a sort of temporary liar are described and studied with such insight that, on this point at least, the reader who is most doubtful about the psychoanalytic explanation seems to give up all resistance. Of course something more than amusement at a few slips is needed before the whole body of Freud's thought can be accepted in its entirety; all the same it doesn't stop the popularity of this unique book from marking a considerable change in people's minds and on this ground alone it remains a historic event.

As far as Freud was concerned *The Psychopathology of Everyday Life* was to create a link between the pathology and the psychology of the normal man, until then two strictly separated spheres of which, for the first time, he revealed the common roots and the uncertain boundaries. It was like a witty and more comprehensible variation of *The Interpretation of Dreams,* on the obscure frontiers of everyday life and unreality.

However strange it may seem to the reader today, this gay and cheerful book which sweeps along with all the joy of discovery was for Freud rather in the nature of an intimate diary in which he tried once more to come to terms with himself. In it confession speaks with a note of serene impersonality which masks its dramatic character. But if one pauses to think of the standards Freud set himself and of the sternness of what might be called his 'scientific Super-Ego', one realizes what it must have cost him to point out, one by one, the mistakes in names, dates, references and quotations which he had allowed to pass in *The Interpretation of Dreams*. And his aim was not to apologize, but to show the reasons for his disturbance and, in so doing to confess it.[1] Apart from *The Interpretation of Dreams,* there is hardly any other scientific work in existence in which strict observation of fact and moving personal confession have been blended with such truth.

The unseen person who, at the time of *The Psychopathology of Everyday Life* disturbed Freud's actions and thought and was responsible for a crop of mistakes even in his books was, there can be no doubt, Wilhelm Fliess, who, by 1901, had already become very much less friendly. Shall we say that Freud wrote his book so that he should be understood by his friend, to complain that he felt he was being forsaken and to vindicate himself, as other people do by writing a novel or a poem? The letter to Fliess which accompanied the envoy to the book would almost entitle one to think so:

'There is no concealing the fact that we have drawn somewhat apart from each other. By this and that I can see how much. . . . In this you came to the limit of your penetration, you take sides against me and tell me that "the thought-reader merely reads his own thoughts into other people", which deprives my work of all its value.

'If I am such a one, throw my Every-day Life unread into the waste-paper basket. It is full of references to you: obvious ones, where you supplied the material, and concealed ones, where the motivation derives from you. Also you supplied the motto. Apart from any permanent value that its content may have, you can take it as a testimonial to the role you have hitherto played in my life. Having said this, I can send it to you as soon as it comes in without adding anything else. . . .'[2]

[1] Ibid., ch. 10. Most of the errors pointed out by Freud are mentioned in letters to Fliess.

[2] Letter to Fliess, August 7, 1901, *Origins,* p. 334.

15

THE THEORY OF SEXUALITY

The almost favourable reception given to *The Psychopathology of Everyday Life* seemed to open up a new era of peaceful penetration for psychoanalysis, but this first step in the direction of reconciliation had no sequel, for *Three Essays on the Theory of Sexuality* appeared in the following year and compromised Freud's relations with the public for a very long time. *The Interpretation of Dreams* had been greeted as a tissue of chimeras or ridiculous old wives' tales, but the *Three Essays* became an open scandal and Freud, who had been looked on as a pseudo-scientist, was henceforth considered to be an obscene and dangerous spirit. Certainly no other book of his brought down on him so much stupid abuse and hatred.

The titles of the *Three Essays*—Sexual Aberrations; Infantile Sexuality; The Changes of Puberty—are in themselves enough to explain the reason for the general indignation which otherwise seems difficult to understand. However hypocritical the age might be on the matter—and it certainly was extremely hypocritical—sexuality could not be entirely banned from the domain of science. Whether one liked it or not, sexology did exist. Works such us Krafft-Ebing's *Psychopathia Sexualis* had proved this without creating too much of an uproar. And as it was not strictly speaking the subject which aroused indignation so much as the fact that Freud, disagreeing with the catalogues of perversions and aberrations, abolished every line of demarcation between normal and perverted and particularly between adult sexuality and the alleged innocence of childhood. In so far as it described and classified anomalies, sexology was in no way upsetting since the normal reader found in it proof of his own healthiness. But Freud's *Three Essays* showed man a revolting image which he refused to recognize as his own.

Against the conventional idea that sexuality appeared fully developed and complete with norms at a given moment in human life—puberty—Freud put forward the idea of an original sexual instinct striving to find satisfaction from infancy onwards and passing through many intermediate phases before fulfilling the purpose of reproduction. This conception assumed a considerable broadening of the very idea of sexuality, which, partly freed from its close dependence on the genital organs, became a bodily function embracing the whole being and, like it, capable of a complicated evolution. This conception also allowed for the inclusion of sexual facts which had previously been considered abnormal or non-existent and concerned children and so-called 'perverts'. It also meant that aberrant phenomena were no longer to be classified according to the more or less shocking way in which they depart from the norm but as a stage in the evolution of the libido, in each case marking the point at which this stops.

Freud's intention in the *Three Essays* is not to define sexuality but to show by the study of perversions and neuroses that the usual definition covers the reality only if the innumerable aberrant cases are ignored. To say that the aim of sexuality is the physical union of two people of opposite sex, which was the current definition, is to exclude from the study all the deviations which prove precisely that the sexual instinct is not by nature necessarily connected either with an objective or a definite love object as norm. On the contrary, Freud proposes to study normal sexuality by starting from the frequent variations in which the instinct frees itself so remarkably from what is alleged to be its purpose.

After classifying the deviations into two groups according to whether they are concerned with the partner, described as a love object, as in the case of homosexuality, or objective, as is the case with fetishism, exhibitionism and voyeurism, sadism and masochism, etc., Freud established that they all exist to some extent in the normal person's activity. Homosexuality, he says, hardly deserves to be called perversion; it springs from the bisexual constitution common to everybody and there is hardly a neurotic who, in analysis, fails to show some element of inversion in his choice of sexual object. As for those perversions which seem most unnatural and commonly arouse disgust, Freud says:

'Perhaps, it is precisely that we must recognize the most prolific psychic participation for the transformation of the sexual instinct. In these cases a piece of psychic work has been accomplished in which, in spite of its gruesome success, the value of an idealization of the instinct cannot be disputed. The omnipotence of love nowhere perhaps shows itself stronger than in this one of her aberrations. The highest and lowest in sexuality are everywhere most intimately connected. ("From heaven through the world to hell.")'[1]

The analysis of neurotics regularly brings to light perverse tendencies in relation to either the sexual objective or the choice of the love object. The only difference between the pervert and the neurotic is that the former satisfies his desires in the world of reality whereas the latter, dominated by a sense of shame, disgust and an unconscious feeling of guilt, represses them in such a way that he can fulfil them only in imagination. This is what justifies Freud's famous formula that perversion is the negative of neurosis. The individual's sexual destiny, which makes him a pervert, a neurotic or a normal person, and in most cases makes him a mixed personality in which these three psychological types co-exist, is determined by a constitutional disposition acting in conjunction with the more or less historic circumstances which attended the development of his psyche at a very early age.

The problem of infantile sexuality takes up the whole of the second chapter, which is far and away the most original in the book. Freud seeks first to understand why this problem, even when its existence is not simply denied, generally passes unnoticed. The reason is that the vast majority of people have completely forgotten their infancy and the violent emotions they then felt, which are so decisive for the formation of their personality. This general amnesia explains why the sexual activity of children, which can however easily be observed, has been ignored by teachers and parents.

From the very beginning of life children are capable of experiencing sensual feelings and sensations. Their sexual instincts develop progressively up to the age of about four, then, until puberty, this development comes to a halt and there is a period of calm extending from the age of five to eleven. This is what Freud, adopting a term proposed by Fliess, calls the 'latency period'. This interruption is more

[1] *Three Essays on the Theory of Sexuality* (Brill translation). See *Std Edn VII*, pp. 161–2.

or less total, depending on the individual, and seems to be the distinctive privilege of the little human animal. It lies at the root of the remarkable process called 'sublimation', by which the unemployed sexual instincts can be deflected from their purpose and made to serve all sorts of creative activities of benefit to society. Along with normal sexual fulfilment, perversion and neurosis, sublimation is one of the great outlets possible in the evolution of the libido, which is subjected by nature to a number of risks and dramatically complicated.

The connection between perversions and infantile sexuality is established by a conception of the instincts, often called 'impulses' or 'drives' to render the German word *Trieb,* which can only be translated imperfectly. What differentiates these impulses from one another and gives them a specific character is their source and their aim. The source is always some stimulus evoked by a part of the body. The aim is the satisfaction of this stimulus. The body is made up of 'erogenous zones'—so called by analogy with the 'hysterogenic zones'—which can be the seat of erotic sensations. In babies these erogenous zones to some extent cover the whole body. But some are always more sensitive than others, for example the alimentary orifices and the genital organs.

As children's genital organs are not fully developed they play only a relatively minor role in the precocious manifestations of infantile sexuality. There is the root of the misunderstanding between Freud and his critics who attached to the word 'sexuality' the meaning that Freud proposes to reserve for the last phase of its development, that of fully developed genitality. Before being at the service of reproduction the libido finds ways of expressing and fulfilling itself with the help of organic functions which are non-sexual but are essential to the maintenance of life. Thus babies derive pleasure from imbibing their food which, on the one hand, relieves the painful tension of hunger and, on the other, is accompanied by sucking which in itself is pleasurable. In line with other writers, Freud sees sucking as the child's first sexual pleasure:

'We would say that the child's lips behaved like an *erogenous zone* and that the stimulus from the warm stream of milk was really the cause of the pleasurable sensation. To be sure, the gratification of the erogenous zone was at first united with the gratification of the need for nourishment.

The sexual activity leans first on one of the self-preservative functions and only later makes itself independent of it. He who sees a satiated child sink back from the mother's breast and fall asleep with reddened cheeks and blissful smile, will have to admit that this picture remains as typical of the expression of sexual gratification in later life. But the desire for repetition of sexual gratification is then separated from the desire for taking nourishment; a separation which becomes unavoidable with the appearance of teeth when the nourishment is no longer sucked but chewed. The child does not make use of a strange object for sucking but prefers his own skin, because it is more convenient, because it thus makes him independent of the outer world, which he cannot control, and because in this way he creates for himself, as it were, a second, even if an inferior erogenous zone. This inferiority of this second region urges him later to seek the same parts, the lips of another person. ("It is a pity that I cannot kiss myself," might be attributed to him.) . . .'[1]

This phase of organization, called 'oral' because of the preponderant part played in it by the mucous membranes of the lips and mouth, is followed, without however being completely terminated, by a second phase in which the essential erogenous zone is another alimentary orifice—the anus. This second phase, called 'sadistic-anal' because it is connected with aggressive behaviour on the part of the child, exhibits exactly the same characteristics as the first: it is based on an essential physiological function, its objective is determined by the activity of an erogenous zone and it is auto-erotic since it has no sexual object. Anal eroticism, connected mainly with the retention of faeces which causes increased stimulation of the mucous membrane, is destined to play a decisive role in the subsequent development of the character.

In view of the lack of maturity of the corresponding organs, the young child's strictly genital activity can only have free expression in the form of infantile onanism, the appearance and disappearance of which correspond to distinct phases. The first phase occurs at the time of suckling, the second during the brief period when the child develops sexually, towards the fourth year, and finally the third, the only one of which has always held the attention of observ-

[1] Ibid., see pp. 181–2.

ers, at the time of puberty. But between the age of two and five children not infrequently feel an erotic attraction for one definite person among those in their immediate circle. This is what makes this period, despite the uncertain character of the choice of object, one of the most important of those preceding final sexual formation.

Thus, during the first years of his life, the child finds the source of his pleasure in himself and his demand for gratification knows no law or restraint. He is utterly without shame, he likes to exhibit himself and to discover other people's bodies; he can take pleasure both in the suffering he inflicts and in the suffering he endures; he is, as has often been said, naturally cruel and pitiless. In a word, he behaves just as though he had an innate disposition to perversion, and in those forms which most outrage good taste and morality. The only difference between a child and an adult pervert is that the former is free to indulge in all the available satisfactions which offer themselves while the latter is by choice fixed to a given deviation. This is what Freud meant when he called a child a 'polymorphous pervert'.

None of Freud's ideas has caused an outcry or roused so many indignant protests as this definition, which was obviously innocent of any moral judgement.[1] Freud was accused of defiling the sacred purity of childhood and slandering man by repudiating the idea of the blessed innocence of man's early years and putting in its place a dark tale of unimaginable horrors. People forgot that long before him sincere and courageous writers such as Schopenhauer and Rousseau had also discovered strange things in the childhood paradise which is so necessary to bourgeois morality and poetic convention. Nor did they see—doubtless because they did not wish to—that an idea ad-

[1] This is the origin of all the misunderstandings about the Freudian ethic and philosophy included in psychoanalysis. Freud did not deny morality or man's spiritual aspirations; he simply wanted to say nothing about them, thinking that others had made this their business and would do so again after him. His rule, educationally sound, was to suspend all moral judgement and to refuse to advance premature syntheses, and many even among his followers found this difficult. Ludwig Binswanger (op. cit. p. 98) relates how one day he was dumbfounded to hear Freud say: 'The spirit is everything . . .' and then add: 'Humanity has always known it has a soul, it fell to me to show it that it also has instincts . . . But men are never satisfied, they cannot wait, they always want things straightaway, whole and perfect . . .'

vanced as a sort of working instrument for laboratory use did not necessarily implicate its inventor's morality any more than it necessarily corresponded to his own desires and the delicacy of his feelings. Freud, who later gave an account of the analysis of a five year old boy—the famous little Hans—with a love, a tenderness and a respect which one wishes his critics could have shown, had to give up any hope of being understood and resign himself to being regarded as a monster.

Going back over the controversies of the period one is amazed that so many people were roused to fury and that so few appreciated Freud's description of the epic struggle for maturity and health in which the child is inescapably engaged from the dawn of life. Weaker and more defenceless than the little animal he still resembles, the child has to face up to a number of trials in which, because of the imperfection of his organization and the feebleness of his weapons, he is in constant danger of failing or only partially succeeding. Almost as soon as he is born life imposes crushing tasks on him, asks of him accomplishments and sacrifices for which he is not properly equipped either by his physical development or his mental organization.

Thus each time he as to adapt himself to a new state he has to renounce the old one and the difficulty of this wrench is increased by the fact that his happiness was complete and his pleaure bound up with a feeling of absolute security. After being weaned, sometimes at the cost of great suffering, he must become clean; that is, he must renounce the intense satisfaction he found in the products of his own body and instead of pleasure he must feel disgust, shame and embarrassment. A little later his relationship with his parents is completely upset by the Oedipus complex which gives him his first experience of love and hatred. His life's happiness depends largely on the way he resolves this primitive conflict in which he has to fight alone. And just as he can mature only by gradually freeing himself from the objects he has loved, so he can reach his full intellectual development only by separating his curiosity from the sexuality which first aroused it and transferring it to the multiple objects in the world. Puberty is only the last of these stages, in which development goes by fits and starts and at the cost of painful sacrifices. For a time it throws the adolescent back into the erotic world of his childhood which he is, however, compelled to abandon because of the ban on incest. Like the fairy-tale hero who wanders alone through an enchanted forest he can overcome the perils which beset him only if he can leave his father's house without leaving his heart behind or looking back.

Thinking about this slow evolution, which is in danger of being diverted by so many obstacles, one is inclined to be amazed that individuals can successfully negotiate all its stages without too many accidents and become balanced people capable of loving and freely realizing their potentialities of action and thought. The psychoanalyst considers that such people are rare. They are the ones who have succeeded in fusing the indestructible tendencies of infantile sexuality so that these can serve their affective life. The rest, whose development has been arrested or forced to regress by constitutional propensities, family troubles and all kinds of complex causes, are more or less serious pathological cases—unless they are gifted enough to be able to transform their difficulties into works of art, action or creative thought.

The *Three Essays on the Theory of Sexuality* is only the first stone of the edifice on which Freud worked all his life. The 1905 edition has constantly been enlarged over the years and Freud followed up its ideas in subsequent works, for example in his first Lectures [1] and in his autobiography. Certain problems raised in the *Three Essays* were not solved until much later. Ideas which Freud had thrown in without going into at all deeply were the starting point for many studies by his pupils. But the book has remained what it was from the first—the unshakable foundation of the theory. Not only has it stood the test of time, but the accuracy of its view has been confirmed in the minutest detail.

For more than fifty years, in fact, innumerable observations carried out directly on children, particularly babies, have regularly confirmed the surprising conclusions to which Freud had been led simply by analysing his adult patients. What was considered in 1905 to be the product of an unhealthy imagination is now admitted by specialists and even by a large section of the public to be an indisputable scientific truth. The *Three Essays* which were so virulently attacked are one of the direct causes of the irrevocable change which has taken place in the education of

[1] *Introductory Lectures on Psychoanalysis, Std Edn* XV.

young children and in teaching methods in the last fifty years. Freud's detractors could not have received a more fitting answer.

Child analysis began about 1908, the Swiss clergyman Oskar Pfister being the first person to carry it out. He conceived of a pedagogy based on Freud's theories, called it 'pedanalysis' and devoted himself to it with enthusiasm and faith throughout his life. We have already spoken about Freud's friendship for this man, whom he called his 'dear man of God', although he by no means shared all his ideas. Pfister was a theologian and a philosopher; his religious faith was always ardent and genuine and never clashed with his Freudian convictions, which later brought him into serious trouble with his ecclesiastical superiors. Freud had an unbounded admiration for his love of life, his gaiety and his vigour. From the first he showed the keenest interest in Pfister's educational work although, at the time, he was rather sceptical about the practical application of his theory. In 1908 Pfister had published an article on 'Delusion and Student Suicide' and Freud's first letter to him was concerned with this:

'I must also express my satisfaction that our psychiatric work has been taken up by a minister of religion who has access to the minds of so many young and healthy individuals. Half in jest, but really quite seriously, we often complain that psychoanalysis requires a state of normality for its application and that the organized abnormalities of mental life impose a limitation on it, with the result that the optimum conditions for it exist where it is not needed—i.e., among the healthy. Now it seems to me that this optimum exists in the conditions in which you work. . . .'[1]

Freud sometimes reproached Pfister with being pusillanimous, at least in speech, in matters concerning sexuality. Pfister took serious note of what he said but for his part accused Freud of underestimating sublimation, which, he maintained, could make psychoanalytic treatment of great educational value. By temperament perhaps or, as he said, because of his disappointing experiences with his own patients, Freud remained rather pessimistic about this:

'The permanent success of psycho-analysis certainly de-

[1] Letter to Pfister, January 18, 1909, *Psychoanalysis & Faith*, p. 15.

pends on the coincidence of two issues: the obtaining of satisfaction by the release of tension, and sublimation of the sheer instinctual drive. If we generally succeed only with the former, that is to be attributed to a great extent to the human raw material—human beings who have been suffering severely for a long time and expect no moral elevation from the physician, and are often inferior material. In your case they are young persons faced with conflicts of recent date, who are personally drawn towards you and are ready for sublimation, and to sublimation in its most comfortable form, namely the religious. They do not suspect that success with them comes about in your case primarily by the same route as it does with us, by way of erotic transference to yourself. But you are in the fortunate position of being able to lead them to God and bringing about what in this one respect was the happy state of earlier times when religious faith stifled the neuroses. For us this way of disposing of the matter does not exist. Our public, no matter of what racial origin, is irreligious, we are generally thoroughly irreligious ourselves and, as the other ways of sublimation which *we* substitute for religion are too difficult for most patients, our treatment generally results in the seeking out of satisfaction. On top of this there is the fact that we are unable to see anything forbidden or sinful in sexual satisfaction, but regard it as a valuable part of human experience. You are aware that for us the term "sex" includes what you in your pastoral work call love, and is certainly not restricted to the crude pleasure of the senses. Thus our patients have to find in humanity what we are unable to promise them from above and are unable to supply them with ourselves. Things are therefore much more difficult for us, and in the resolution of the transference many of our successes come to grief. . . .'[1]

Freud's pessimism about the possibilities of elevating his patients is also reflected in his scepticism about education. The remark attributed to him on the subject may not be authentic, but it undoubtedly contains a great deal of truth. When one mother asked what she ought to do to bring her children up rationally in accordance with the ideas of psychoanalysis, Freud's reply is said to have been: 'Please yourself. Whatever you do will be bad.' However,

[1] Letter to Pfister, February 9, 1909, *Psychoanalysis & Faith,* pp. 16–17.

in an article in 1907 he sharply defended the necessity of an enlightened sexual education adjusted to the child's curiosity and intelligence. This was the occasion on which he mentioned little Hans (in the article he was called Herbert) whose case history he published a little later. At the age of three little Hans, a very intelligent boy, had by himself fathomed the secret of his sister's birth, thus confirming Freud's ideas on sexual curiosity in children.

Little Hans was the first child to be treated, and cured, by means of psychoanalysis. When he was five he was affected by a serious phobia mainly to do with horses and in the end he would never go out of the house. The child's parents had been among the first to support Freud, who had treated the young wife before her marriage. The father regularly attended Freud's lectures and it was he, not Freud, who conducted the analysis. Freud had only one conversation with little Hans but he had many with his father, who agreed to the case history being published. It was the famous *Analysis of a Phobia in a Five-year-old Boy,* one of the five case histories which form the purely clinical part of Freud's writings. Freud had followed the father's intelligent but necessarily very unorthodox work with ardent attention. To his great surprise, the analysis was completely successful and fourteen years later he had one of the greatest pleasures it was possible for him to experience when little Hans, who had grown into a strong, good-looking young man who was about to be married, paid him a visit. A remarkable fact was that Hans remembered Freud but did not remember a thing about the analysis.

The success of this first child analysis did not lessen Freud's doubts about the technical possibilities of the method. He said so in the first part of his account:

'No one else [than the father], in my opinion, could possibly have prevailed on the child to make any such avowals; the special knowledge by means of which he was able to interpret the remarks made by his five-year-old son was indispensable, and without it the technical difficulties in the way of conducting a psycho-analysis upon so young a child would have been insuperable. It was only because the authority of a father and of a physician were united in a single person, and because in him both affectionate care and scientific interest were combined, that it was possible in this one instance to apply the method to a use to which it would not otherwise have lent itself. . . .'[1]

The extraordinary development of child analysis and all the psychotherapeutic techniques inspired by it has shown that, for once at least, Freud's perspicacity was at fault on an important matter. Must we think that after carrying the exploration of child psychism further than it had ever been taken before, for inner reasons, remnants of scruples or inhibitions he refused to go any further himself? The fact is that in this field of research, in which remarkable women such as Hermine Hug-Hellmuth and Melanie Klein have become famous, Freud showed a singular reserve throughout his life. Whether it was prudence or misgiving about the study of the most obscure phenomena of early psychical processes, Freud never altogether abandoned his sceptical attitude, which was also due to his classical demand for certitude and clarity. Even his daughter Anna's brilliant career hardly made any difference to his views.

[1] *Analysis of a Phobia in a Five-year-old Boy, Std Edn* X, p. 5.

16

TWO WORKS OF 1905

Fresh fuel was added to the fire of scandal which raged round the *Three Essays on the Theory of Sexuality* by the clinical report which Freud published in the same year under the title *Fragment of an Analysis of a Case of Hysteria.* Besides the usual reasons for indignation, the 'Dora' analysis provoked criticisms which seemed to be more soundly based, since Freud, abandoning the doctor's necessary discretion, now disclosed the most intimate details about his patient, a girl of eighteen whose case history he published without asking her permission. This attitude appeared to most people to be especially unjustifiable as the analysis, based mainly on the interpretation of two revealing dreams, brought to light perverse tendencies which propriety and the morality of the day refused to attribute to a young girl. The furore was so great that it threw the critics into confusion. In spite of the clear evidence in the report, one of them remained convinced that Dora was only fourteen.

Freud had hesitated a long time before deciding to publish this work, which was meant to confirm at one and the same time both his theory of dreams and the principles already enunciated in the *Studies on Hysteria.* He kept the manuscript to himself for six years, waiting for the girl's life to change and for her to be less sensitive to the memory of that period of her life. Dora lived in a small provincial village and was completely unknown in Vienna. She learned of the existence of the account only in 1923 through a psychoanalyst to whom she spoke about Freud's treatment, and naturally he had no difficulty in identifying her.

Freud was particularly upset by the charge of indiscretion because he was generally very careful to avoid it, as he himself said in a passage in the 'Non Vixit' dream analysis. To get round the difficulty he had tried to think of a name which would guarantee the girl complete anonymity without offending the susceptibilities of anyone he knew.

In *The Psychopathology of Everyday Life* he explains why he felt that the only Christian name he could choose from the infinite number of possible ones was 'Dora':

'With a view to preparing the case history of one of my women patients for publication [1] I considered what first name I should give her in my account. There appeared to be a very wide choice; some names, it is true, were ruled out from the start—the real name in the first place, then the names of members of my own family, to which I should object, and perhaps some other women's names with an especially peculiar sound. But otherwise there was no need for me to be at a loss for a name. It might have been expected—and I myself expected—that a whole host of women's names would be at my disposal. Instead, one name and only one occurred to me—the name "Dora".

'I asked myself how it was determined. Who else was there called Dora? I should have liked to discuss with incredulity the next thought to occur to me—that it was the name of my sister's nursemaid; but I have so much self-discipline or so much practice in analysing that I held firmly to the idea and let my thoughts run on from it. At once there came to my mind a trivial incident from the previous evening which provided the determinant I was looking for. I had seen a letter on my sister's dining-room table addressed to "Fräulein Rosa W.". I asked in surprise who there was of that name, and was told that the girl I knew as Dora was really called Rosa, but had had to give up her real name when she took up employment in the house, since my sister could take the name "Rosa" as applying to herself as well. "Poor people," I remarked in pity, "they cannot even keep their own names!" After that, I now recall, I fell silent for a moment and began to think of a variety of serious matters which drifted into obscurity, but which I was now easily able to make conscious. When the next day I was looking for a name for someone *who could not keep her own,* "Dora" was the only one to occur to me. The complete absence of alternatives was here based on a solid association connected with the subject-matter that I was dealing with: for it was a person employed in someone else's house, a governess, who exercised a decisive influence on my patient's story, and on the course of the treatment as well. . . .' [2]

[1] 'Dora' analysis.

[2] *The Psychopathology of Everyday Life, Std Edn* VI, pp. 240–1.

The Dora analysis was the first in which Freud, putting scientific interest above the principles of medical ethics, took it on himself to tell everything without even toning down the crudity of the words actually used. Contrary to what his colleagues imagined, such a decision caused him considerable pain; and for years he retained a feeling of embarrassment which one day found expression in a symptomatic action:

'Years later this little incident had an unexpected sequel. Once, when I was discussing in a lecture the long since published case history of the girl now called Dora, it occurred to me that one of the two ladies in my audience had the same name Dora that I should have to utter so often in a whole variety of connections. I turned to my young colleague, whom I also knew personally, with the excuse that I had not in fact remembered that that was her name too, and added that I was very willing to replace it in my lecture by another name. I was now faced with the task of rapidly choosing another one, and I reflected that I must at all costs avoid selecting the first name of the other lady in the audience and so setting a bad example to my other colleagues, who were already well grounded in psycho-analysis. I was therefore very much pleased when the name "Erna" occurred to me as a substitute for Dora, and I used it in the lecture. After the lecture I asked myself where the name Erna could possibly have come from, and I could not help laughing when I noticed that the possibility I had been afraid of when I was choosing the substitute name had nevertheless come about, at least to some extent. The other lady's family name was Lucerna, of which Erna is a part.' [1]

In his foreward to the Dora case Freud explains the reasons which made him disregard considerations of discretion not only in his analytic work but in what he published. It is not surprising that this explanation failed to satisfy the public, since it never completely convinced some of his followers:

'The presentation of my case histories remains a problem which is hard for me to solve. The difficulties are partly of a technical kind, but are partly due to the nature of the

1 *Std Edn* VI, pp. 241–2.

circumstances themselves. If it is true that the causes of hysterical disorders are to be found in the intimacies of the patients' psycho-sexual life, and that hysterical symptoms are the expression of their most secret and repressed wishes, then the complete elucidation of a case of hysteria is bound to involve the revelation of those intimacies and the betrayal of those secrets. It is certain that the patients would never have spoken if it had occurred to them that their admissions might possibly be put to scientific uses; and it is equally certain that to ask them themselves for leave to publish their case would be quite unavailing. In such circumstances persons of delicacy, as well as those who were merely timid, would give first place to the duty of medical discretion and would declare with regret that the matter was one upon which they could offer science no enlightenment. But in my opinion the physician has taken upon himself duties not only towards the individual patient but towards science as well; and his duties towards science mean ultimately nothing else than his duties towards the many other patients who are suffering or will some day suffer from the same disorder. Thus it becomes the physician's duty to publish what he believes he knows of the causes and structure of hysteria, and it becomes a disgraceful piece of cowardice on his part to neglect doing so, as long as he can avoid causing direct personal injury to the single patient concerned. I think I have taken every precaution to prevent my patient from suffering any such injury. . . .'[1]

After recalling that only one of his colleagues, probably Wilhelm Fliess, had known about his treatment of Dora and that he had delayed publication for several years, Freud concluded his preamble on a note which was firm yet also somewhat arrogant and sad because he found it humilating to have to justify himself:

'I am aware that—in this city, at least—there are many physicians who (revolting though it may seem) choose to read a case history of this kind not as a contribution to the psycho-pathology of the neuroses, but as a *roman à clef* designed for their private delectation. I can assure readers of this species that every case history which I may have

[1] 'Fragment of an Analysis of a Case of Hysteria,' *Std Edn* VII, pp. 7–8.

occasion to publish in the future will be secured against their perspicacity by similar guarantees of secrecy, even though this resolution is bound to put quite extraordinary restrictions upon my choice of material.

'Now in this case history—the only one which I have hitherto succeeded in forcing through the limitations imposed by medical discretion and unfavourable circumstances—sexual questions will be discussed with all possible frankness, the organs and functions of sexual life will be called by their proper names, and the pure-minded reader can convince himself from my description that I have not hesitated to converse upon such subjects in such language even with a young woman. Am I, then, to defend myself upon this score as well? I will simply claim for myself the rights of the gynaecologist—or rather, much more modest ones—and add that it would be the mark of a singular and perverse prurience to suppose that conversations of this kind are a good means of exciting or of gratifying sexual desires.'

And Freud ended with a quotation from Richard Schmidt's book, *Essays on Indian Eroticism:*

'It is deplorable to have to make room for protestations of this sort in a scientific work; but let no one reproach me on this account but rather accuse the spirit of the age, owing to which we have reached a state of things in which no serious book can any longer be sure of survival. . . .'[1]

Freud was wrong in thinking that no patient would agree to the publication of his own case history. The other observations which, together with the President Schreber analysis, comprise his clinical writings were published with the express permission of the people concerned—little Hans's father, the Wolf Man and the Rat Man, who had spontaneously put themselves at the service of the cause in this way. And it is remarkable that in its early days, psychoanalysis found more support and understanding among patients than it did among doctors and psychiatrists. Some famous patients, such as the Wolf Man, could even have claimed they had contributed to its advance.

It is not only in the outside world that the problem connected with the patient's intimate life and Freud's deliber-

[1] Ibid., p. 9.

ate indiscretion for the sake of science caused an outcry. Freud could see for himself that some of his followers were also disturbed and that the Swiss in particular found it difficult completely to disregard propriety and defy public opinion. Even in 1909, which was well before his break with Freud, Jung confessed to Ernest Jones that he thought it did no good to let patients dwell on disgusting details. It made it very unpleasant to meet them afterwards in society. It was better merely to touch on such matters; the patients would understand without the doctor having to speak crudely about them.[1] Likewise, Pastor Pfister, in spite of the courage with which he stood up to the anger of his superiors, could not always bring himself to report his clinical cases in plain language. Freud reproached him over this in a letter in which he again insisted on the importance of his own rule:

'Well, then, I think your *Analysis* suffers from the hereditary vice of—virtue; it is the work of too decent a man, who feels himself bound to discretion. Now, these psycho-analytical matters are intelligible only if presented in pretty full and complete detail, just as an analysis really gets going only when the patient descends to minute details from the abstractions which are their surrogate. Thus discretion is incompatible with a satisfactory discription of an analysis; to provide the latter one would have to be unscrupulous, give away, betray, behave like an artist who buys paints with his wife's house-keeping money or uses the furniture as firewood to warm the studio for his model. Without a trace of that kind of unscrupulousness the job cannot be done.' [2]

Besides the reasons dictated by moral scruples and professional ethics, Freud could have had another motive for not releasing the Dora case history. In the first place, the report of the analysis was very fragmentary since it was limited to the detailed interpretation of two dreams and might well be considered inconclusive: then the girl's treatment, which had been broken off after three months, was by no means a success, was even a rather bad example of a failure which Freud knew very well could be used against

1 Ernest Jones, Vol. II.

2 Letter to Pfister, June 5, 1916, *Psychoanalysis & Faith*, p. 38.

him. The girl, who suffered from a 'little hysteria', with a nervous cough, aphonia, migraine and depression, had gone away free of symptoms but not cured, and in 1905 Freud knew enough about her state not to harbour any illusions about the efficacy of the treatment. In any case, a real cure would not have been possible after only three months' treatment: but Freud had unwittingly compromised the treatment by technical mistakes due to the inevitable inadequacy of his theory.

It was with the definite intention of drawing a lesson from these mistakes that he decided, after much hesitation, to publish details of the case, one of the first in which his aim was not only to cure the patient's symptoms but, by allowing her total freedom of association, to make her understand the causes and structure of her illness. The differences between the cases described in *Studies on Hysteria* and the Dora observation do not explain this change of method which, in an unexpected way, displaced the centre of the treatment. Until then treatment concentrated on the symptoms to be suppressed. The treatment of Dora compelled Freud to deepen his conception of transference, a phenomenon which he had long known to exist without fully realizing that it played such a decisive part. The comparative failure of the treatment was largely due to this ignorance, and when Freud became aware of all the consequences it was too late.

'What are transferences? They are new editions of facsimiles of the impulses and phantasies which are aroused and made conscious during the progress of the analysis; but they have this peculiarity, which is characteristic for their species, that they replace some earlier person by the person of the physician. To put it another way: a whole series of psychological experiences are revived, not as belonging to the past, but as applying to the person of the physician at the present moment. Some of these transferences have a content which differs from that of their model in no respect whatever except for the substitution. These then—to keep to the same metaphor—are merely new impressions or reprints. Others are more ingeniously constructed; their content has been subjected to a moderating influence—to *sublimation,* as I call it—and they may even become conscious, by cleverly taking advantage of some real peculiarity in the physician's person or circumstances and attaching themselves to that. These, then, will no longer be new impressions, but revised editions.' [1]

Later work by psychoanalysts shows that transference is a general phenomenon which occurs to a greater or lesser extent in most human relationships. For the moment Freud only established that it always exists in the patient-doctor relationship and that it is responsible as much for the failure as for the success of many treatments.

'Psycho-analytic treatment does not *create* transferences, it merely brings them to light, like so many other hidden psychical factors. The only difference is this—that spontaneously a patient will only call up affectionate and friendly transferences to help towards his recovery; if they cannot be called up, he feels the physician is "antipathetic" to him, and breaks away from him as fast as possible and without having been influenced by him. In psycho-analysis, on the other hand, since the play of motives is different, all the patient's tendencies, including hostile ones, are aroused; they are then turned to account for the purposes of the analysis by being made conscious, and in this way the transference is constantly being destroyed. Transference, which seems ordained to be the greatest obstacle to psycho-analysis, becomes its most powerful ally, if its presence can be detected each time and explained to the patient.' [2]

The Dora case history contains a lesson which was very useful for psychoanalytic practice as well as for the development of psychoanalytic theory. This is that the slightest error of judgement, the slightest misunderstanding or negligence in utilizing transference entails a more or less immediate sanction which in extreme cases is, quite simply, the patient's flight. Left in the dark about her deepest feelings, Dora had taken revenge on her doctor in the way many neurotics do—by refusing to be cured and so proving to him personally that he is very bad at his job and, in fact, powerless.

While the *Fragment of an Analysis of a Case of Hysteria* had created a furore, Freud's book published almost

[1] 'Fragment of an Analysis of a Case of Hysteria,' *Std Edn* VII, p. 116.

[2] Ibid., p. 117.

immediately afterwards on *Jokes and Their Relation to the Unconscious* roused few passions. The work, which deals with language and aesthetics, makes hard reading. It is the least understood and even today the least read of Freud's books. As a large number of the 'jokes' quoted as examples are difficult to translate into other languages, it is also the book which is translated least often.

This study, which has nothing to do with psychopathology, seems to have originated in a remark by Fliess who was astonished to find so many funny stories, puns and bad jokes in Freud's letters. Freud apologized, saying that these spontaneous verbal productions frequently cropped up in his patients' free associations and when they were describing their dreams. But Freud began to wonder why creations of this kind appeared so often in unconscious material and whether there was not a connection, so far unsuspected, between the latter and ordinary jokes. In 1897 he told Fliess that he had found the solution, but at that period he was too busy writing *The Interpretation of Dreams* and gave up the project.

In 1898 he was so stimulated by reading Theodor's Lipps's book *The Comic and Humour* that he resumed his study. It was the beginning of a long period of extensive research and thought on a subject which at first sight seemed to be of only indirect value to psychoanalysis. In his Introduction, Freud justifies the hard work which this apparently very adventitious research, so remote from his usual preoccupations, had cost him:

'Is the subject of jokes worth so much trouble? There can, I think, be no doubt of it. Leaving on one side the personal motives which make me wish to gain an insight into the problems of jokes and which will come to light in the course of these studies, I can appeal to the fact that there is an intimate connection between all mental happenings —a fact which guarantees that a psychological discovery even in a remote field will be of an unpredictable value in other fields. We may also bear in mind the peculiar and even fascinating charm exercised by jokes in our society. A new joke acts almost like an event of universal interest; it is passed from one person to another like the news of the latest victory. Even men of eminence who have thought it worth while to tell the story of their origins, of the cities and countries they have visited, and of the important people with whom they have associated, are not ashamed in their autobiographies to report their having heard some excellent joke.'[1]

In fact there is not such a big gulf as one would imagine between *Jokes and Their Relation to the Unconscious* and, for instance, the *Three Essays on the Theory of Sexuality,* on which Freud was working at exactly the same time. For all their apparent differences the two books have a common theme—pleasure, the Freudian theme par excellence which was soon to be raised to the status of a principle. The psychological value of jokes lies in the pleasure they give and, like all pleasure, this takes the sadly reasonable adult back to his childhood play:

'During the period in which a child is learning how to handle the vocabulary of his mother-tongue, it gives him obvious pleasure to "experiment with it in play", to use Groos's words. And he puts words together without regard to the condition that they should make sense, in order to obtain from them the pleasurable effect of rhythm or rhyme. Little by little he is forbidden this enjoyment, till all that remains permitted to him are significant combinations of words. But when he is older attempts still emerge at disregarding the restrictions that have been learnt on the use of words. Words are disfigured by particular little additions being made to them, their forms are altered by certain manipulations (e.g. by reduplications or '*Zittersprache*'), or a private language may even be constructed for use among playmates. These attempts are found again among certain categories of mental patients.

'Whatever the motive may have been which led the child to begin these games, I believe that in his later development he gives himself up to them with the consciousness that they are nonsensical, and that he finds enjoyment in the attraction of what is forbidden by reason. He now uses games in order to withdraw from the pressure of critical reason. But there is far more potency in the restrictions which must establish themselves in the course of a child's education in logical thinking and in distinguishing between what is true and false in reality; and for this reason the rebellion against the compulsion of logic and reality is deep-going and long-lasting. Even the phenomena of imag-

[1] *Jokes and Their Relation to the Unconscious, Std Edn* VIII, p. 15.

inative activity must be included in this [rebellious] category. The power of criticism has increased so greatly in the later part of childhood and in the period of learning which extends over puberty that the pleasure in "liberated nonsense" only seldom dares to show itself directly. One does not venture to say anything absurd. But the characteristic tendency of boys to do absurd or silly things seems to me to be directly derived from the pleasure in nonsense. In pathological cases we often see this tendency so far intensified that once more it dominates the schoolboy's talk and answers. I have been able to convince myself in the case of a few boys of secondary school age who had developed neuroses that the unconscious workings of their pleasure in the nonsense they produced played no less a part in their inefficiency than did their real ignorance. . . ." [1]

If *Jokes* is related to *The Theory of Sexuality* by the emphasis given to the notion of pleasure in the second book, it stems even more directly from *The Interpretation of Dreams,* which during this whole period remained the principal source of Freudian discoveries. The connection can already be seen in the composition of the book which, like *The Interpretation of Dreams,* deals with two distinct types of material, the secondary literature on the subject and the examples meant to illustrate each category of phenomena. The examples given in the book are many and varied and they give it a grace which contrasts strongly with the serious sections and the sometimes rather pedantic analysis. Freud took his examples either from other collections or from the repartee of famous people such as the Austrian Minister, Dr. Unger, to whom he is indebted for his best jokes, or else from the treasure-house of witty writers like Heine and Lichtenberg whose special technique would need a whole book to itself. But his main source was clearly the Jewish tradition to which he was bound by the indestructible ties of his childhood and of his own circumstances.[2]

Freud obviously takes great pleasure in piling up his examples which, moreover, are selected with remarkable skill. He rather spoils it for the reader by over-condensing

[1] Ibid., pp. 125–6.

[2] He had begun to collect Jewish anecdotes as early as 1898 (cf. letters to Fliess).

the philosophical ideas expressed on the subject and this sometimes confuses the exposition of his theory. He had undoubtedly forced himself to undertake this meticulous work as he had in *The Interpretation of Dreams* to comply in spite of everything with the rules governing scientific publications. Here, then, once more we find a trace of his personal scruples in matters of intellectual ownership and priority. And what is remarkable, he feels these scruples not in his own special field but in those of his books which encroach on other branches of knowledge and thereby lay themselves open to specialist criticism.

The books he used were helpful in that they allowed Freud to reduce to essentials the usual definitions of laughter, humour and wit. What is there in common between all these forms of verbal productions, the mechanisms of which are so difficult to grasp? The answer, said Freud, is that they all obey the same principle of pleasure, and to produce it they use a certain technique which is by no means confined to them alone but governs many other psychic activities. On more than one point this technique is astonishingly like the elaboration and the work done by dreams. Jokes are nothing other than the elaboration of infantile unconscious material which, if he does not want to offend propriety, the adult cannot express in plain, straightforward language. To translate its profound tendencies—pleasure in nonsense and the gratuituous play of words. aggressiveness forbidden by social good manners—wit employs the same technical procedures which allow dreams to fulfill an untimely or illicit wish. Like dreams, it transforms ideas into images, condenses and displaces its elements, and in this way both veils and betrays its thought; finally, like dreams, it finds a meaning even in its absurdity. This common technique brings close together the two phenomena which, otherwise, have nothing like the same social importance, for dreams are always dreamed alone, while jokes always need a public:

'A dream is a completely asocial mental product; it has nothing to communicate to anyone else; it arises within the subject as a compromise between the mental forces struggling in him, it remains unintelligible to the subject himself and is for that reason totally uninteresting to other people. Not only does it not need to set any store by intelligibility, it must actually avoid being understood, for otherwise it would be destroyed; it can only exist in masquerade. For that reason it can without hindrance make use of the mechanism that dominates unconscious mental processes, to the point of a distortion which can no longer be set straight. A joke, on the other hand, is the most social of all the mental functions that aim at a yield of pleasure. It often calls for three persons and its completion requires the participation of someone else in the mental process it starts. The condition of intelligibility is, therefore, binding on it; it may only make use of possible distortion in the unconscious through condensation and displacement up to the point at which it can be set straight by the third person's understanding. Moreover, jokes and dreams have grown up in quite different regions of mental life and must be allotted to points in the psychological system far remote from each other. A dream still remains a wish, even though one that has been made unrecognizable; a joke is developed play. Dreams, in spite of all their practical nonentity, retain their connection with the major interests of life; they seek to fulfil needs by the regressive détour of hallucination, and they are permitted to occur for the sake of the one need that is active during the night—the need to sleep. Jokes, on the other hand, seek to gain a small yield of pleasure from the mere activity, untrammelled by needs, of our mental apparatus. Later they try to catch hold of that pleasure as a by-product during the activity of that apparatus and thus arrive *secondarily* at not unimportant functions directed to the external world. Dreams serve predominantly for the avoidance of unpleasure, jokes for the attainment of pleasure; but all our mental activities converge in these two aims.'[1]

[1] *Jokes and Their Relation to the Unconscious, Std Edn* VIII, pp. 179–80.

17

THE END OF ISOLATION

1906 was an important date in Freud's life for in that year psychoanalysis ceased to be the personal affair in which he had fought almost alone to get his ideas accepted. It began to be known and discussed outside Vienna and gradually became what he soon called *die Sache,* the 'cause'. By a coincidence (Freud himself perhaps gave it a different name) that year saw both the beginning of his friendship with Jung and his final break with Wilhelm Fliess which had dragged on for six years.

Freud was then fifty and for the first time his birthday was celebrated by his little group of Viennese adherents. On that occasion, which later gave rise to ceremonies and world-wide expressions of sympathy, his followers had hit upon the idea of presenting him with a medallion showing Freud's profile on one side and on the other Oedipus answering the Sphinx, and round it a line from Sophocles: 'Who divined the famed riddle and was a man most mighty.'

Ernest Jones relates a disturbing episode in this connection:

'At the presentation of the medallion there was a curious incident. When Freud read the inscription he became pale and agitated and in a strangled voice demanded to know who had thought of it. He behaved as if he had encountered a *revenant,* and so he had. After Federn told him it was he who had chosen the inscription, Freud disclosed that as a young student at the University of Vienna he used to stroll around the great arcaded court inspecting the busts of former famous professors of the institution. He then had the phantasy not merely of seeing his own bust there in the future, which would not have been anything remarkable in an ambitious student, but of its actually being inscribed with the *identical* words he now saw on the medallion.

'Not long ago I was able to fulfil his youthful wish by presenting to the University of Vienna, for erection in the court, the bust of Freud made by the sculptor Königsberger in 1921, and the line from Sophocles was added. It was unveiled at a ceremony on February 4, 1955. It is a very rare example of such a daydream of adolescence coming true in every detail, even if it took eighty years to do so. . . .'[1]

For Freud, however, the outstanding event in the year was the beginning of a correspondence with Jung, one of the first foreign psychiatrists who had thought seriously about his theory and had even begun to apply it. As assistant of Professor Bleuler, at Burghölzli, the famous psychiatric establishment which attracted students from all over Europe, Jung was obviously an invaluable recruit for the young psychoanalytic movement, which did not include many eminent men and which, as we have seen, inspired very mixed feelings in its founder. Freud was dazzled by this unexpected support, which opened for him the doors of one of the high places of science and, therefore, of Europe. The young foreign scientist who came to see him of his own accord and also gained for him the sympathy of his famous chief, impressed him at once by his powerful intellect, his extensive culture and, above all, by his courage, for at that time courage was certainly needed to risk one's reputation by openly making use of his ideas. Grateful and charmed, Freud saw in Jung the ideal champion of the cause, even the man who would be his second-in-command or take over from him completely in his fight. And from their first exchange of letters he let Jung understand, perhaps unwisely, how badly he needed his support.[2]

Jung had read *The Interpretation of Dreams* very soon after its publication and had even mentioned it several times in his book on occultism. In 1904 Freud had received from Bleuler himself the impressive news that the Zürich professor had been interested in psychoanalysis for years and at the instigation of Jung, his chief assistant, was investigating possible applications of the new method in the obscure field of schizophrenia. Bleuler, who was pursuing and extending the work of the great German psychiatrist Kraepelin on dementia praecox, was a recognized world authority whose adherence, in itself flattering, added considerable scientific weight to the movement. Freud was

[1] Ernest Jones, II, p. 13.
[2] Letters to Jung in 1907 and 1908.

deeply touched and transferred all his gratitude to Jung, who had been the energetic intermediary.

A word or two must be said about Burghölzli, where psychoanalysis suddenly found such precious allies. Naturally the Swiss predominated, but Burghölzli also accepted many foreign students and doctors who sometimes spent several years there. In spite of its cosmopolitanism this famous psychiatric clinic was a rather special place, acquiring an almost mystical character from the Swiss, grouped round their masters Forel and Bleuler. As well as having the same scientific interests, they shared the same religious convictions and philosophy of life. Most of them were vegetarians and abstainers, which raised something of a barrier between them and their foreign colleagues. This sectarian attitude, obviously quite alien to the habits of Freud and his Viennese followers, was not exactly compatible with their enthusiasm for the new psychology. Certain doctors who worked under Bleuler and Jung had an uneasy feeling that the Burghölzli mysticism would make a real rapprochement between Zürich and Vienna rather problematic. Thus Karl Abraham, who had spent three years with Bleuler and knew the place very well, tried from the first to open Freud's eyes to these incompatibilities which seemed to him to augur badly for the future. But Freud had set such hopes on Jung, and was so charmed by the man he was already thinking of making his successor that for a long time he was impervious to all warnings.

Freud's evident elation over the Swiss might seem like blind infatuation to his Viennese followers who, from clear-sightedness or jealousy, looked on the favour shown to the newcomers with a certain amount of apprehension. Although the future proved the sceptics right, Freud's emotional and intellectual enthusiasm sprang from profound and anything but purely selfish motives. Freud, as has been stressed many times, had remained Brücke's disciple and, like his master, believed the basis of science was primarily observation and the measurement of facts. But in the nature of things he had not been able to give his work the experimental basis which would have purified it of its adventurous character and would alone have fully satisfied him. And contrary to what he perhaps hoped, his first pupils did not seem particularly anxious to establish psychoanalysis on more solid foundations. What is more, they simply did not have the means to do so and we saw in the *History of the Psycho-Analytic Movement* how greatly he suffered from their comparatively low scientific standards.

The school of Bleuler made up this deficiency in the form of laboratory experiments for which Freud longed at heart in spite of his conviction that he was right. Jung and his pupils had in fact devised an experimental method for studying associations. Derived from Wundt's psychology and applied to the symptom of dementia praecox, it demonstrated brilliantly Freud's ideas on the reproduction of memories and thereby an essential point of the theory of the unconscious. The demonstration was all the more valuable as Jung had modified his tests in accordance with the data of a rigorous experiment, taking into account not the norms which he had set up for himself but innumerable mistakes which, to the observer's astonishment, constantly falsified the results.

These tests, called 'association experiments', must not be confused with the method of free association invented by Freud, whose starting point and objective were both quite different. The association experiments have a purely diagnostic value, while free associations are the very substance of Freudian treatment. Jung later abandoned his method, which is now only of didactic interest. Freud never really used it.

The association experiments are not unlike psychological projection tests such as the Rorschach, the Thematic Apperception Test, the Szondy etc. Jung described them many times in his books. Here is an explanation from one of his lectures:

'The experimenter has a list of words, called *stimulus words,* which he has selected at random and which must be unrelated in meaning—a condition essential for an experiment in pure association. Here is an example: 'water', 'round', 'chair', 'grass', 'blue', 'knife', 'help', 'weight', 'ready'. When these words are called out one after another to a subject they prompt no suggestion (which is always the case as soon as several words constitute any sort of theme). *The experimenter invites his subject to react to each stimulus word as quickly as possible by saying only the first word which comes into his mind.* At the word 'water', thrown at the subject, so to speak, by the experimenter, the subject will respond as quickly as possible with the very first word to cross his mind, for example 'wet' or 'green' or 'H_2O' or 'wash', etc. The experimenter measures the reaction time with a stop watch which shows fiftieths of a second. The stop watch is started each time the last syllable of the stimulus word is called out and it is stopped as soon as the subject utters the first syllable of his association word. The time that has elapsed, called the reaction time, is noted. I proceed to get some fifty or more reactions. To take too many is, however, bad because of the fatigue that sets in.' [1]

In another passage Jung explains how this experiment, devised in the first place for the study of normal association processes, forced him to take into account not what he was seeking to discover but the innumerable mistakes which disturbed the processes. From being concerned originally with the average speed of reaction, the interest of the experiment finally came to concentrate entirely on the reaction mistakes:

'In the course of the experiments it is noticeable that the reaction times vary greatly, being sometimes short, sometimes long: it is also noticeable that certain responses are disturbed. The subject forgets the original instruction to answer with a single word and comes out instead with a whole phrase; or he pays no attention to the meaning of the stimulus word and reacts with a tonal association, which is also a slight violation of the instructions. Other irregularities also occur. The experimenter says the word "water" and the subject reacts with "water—no—green", which is a repetition of the stimulus word; or he says "green. Oh! I meant to say blue", i.e., the subject has made a mistake. Or he starts laughing and gives an unsatisfactory answer, saying "yes" or "no", for example, before giving the required reaction. Or the subject misunderstands or imperfectly understands the clearly enunciated stimulus word, or he reacts with a stereotyped word, i.e. with the same word each time, whatever the stimulus word may be. Some subjects, for instance, frequently react by repeating the word "beautiful". These disturbances, like the prolonged reaction times or the absence of any reaction, are called *complex indices*. It has been proved, in fact, that stimulus words which cause any disturbance at all are those which encounter in the subject an *emotional content* in some way

[1] C. G. Jung: *L'Homme à la découverte de son âme,* pp. 136 f. Seminar report, edited by R. Cahen-Salabelle, Geneva, 1950.

affecting a personal sphere of taboo. When a stimulus word only interests the surface of the consciousness, the reaction is normal and nothing unusual occurs; but when, on the contrary, it breaches and crosses the defences protecting the inner life and penetrates to the intimate regions of the ego, it provokes an external reaction disturbance by releasing within the subject an automatic action for which he was not prepared and which captures his attention, subjugates him in some way and prevents him from carrying out the instructions he was given.'[1]

Jung's exposition allows one to form an idea of the word 'complex' which has gained such wide currency and which through generalization and approximation has gradually lost all precise meaning. Incidentally, it should be noted that the word was not invented either by Jung or Freud but by a German psychiatrist, Ziehen, who was also one of the most rabid opponents of psychoanalysis. In the sense in which Jung understands it, the complex is a strictly experimental concept designating an affectively toned psychical content which can be in varying degrees either conscious or unconscious and by which the words selected for the experiment are magnetized. Jung later completed his association experiments by the use of a galvanometer which registered the changes in the functioning of the vegetative organs and a pneumograph which measured the rhythm and amplitude of the subject's breathing. The correlated results of these different tests enabled him to assert that complexes are affective entities, in other words emotional phenomena which can be measured exactly. Naturally the experimental situation does not create them, but it alone can make them appear with a more or less numerical value and make them verifiable for any witness. According to Jung the complex, produced by laboratory work, can be defined scientifically:

'What, scientifically speaking, is an "affective complex"? It is the long-lived emotional image of an arrested psychical situation, an image incompatible, moreover, with the usual conscious attitude and atmosphere: it possesses a strong internal cohesion, a sort of totality of its own and a relatively high degree of autonomy: its submission to the consciousness is only fleeting and consequently it behaves like a *corpus alienum* endowed with a life of its own. At the cost of an act of will a complex can usually be repressed or held in

[1] Ibid.

check; but no such act of will can ever destroy it and at the first favourable opportunity it reappears with all its original force. Experimental research seems to indicate that its curve of activity or intensity is undulatory, with a wave-length that can vary from a few hours or days to a few weeks. This very complicated matter has not yet been elucidated.'[1]

Jung differentiated as many complexes as there are traumatic situations, disturbances, and possible embarrassments for the individual. Influenced by him, people spoke of a father, mother, sister, brother, etc. complex, and although he would have denied that the affective content thus defined was morbid in itself, he readily admitted that people 'had' complexes, which suggested that they were caught like an illness. In any case Jung usually treated complexes as parasitic phenomena which the healthy man must get rid of. And when he accused Freud—which he often did—of having a badly resolved father complex, he himself countenanced the popular conception of his idea.

This is the place to ask if there is more than a verbal connection between the Jungian theory of 'complexes' and the 'Oedipus complex' which, as Freud said in the *Three Essays on the Theory of Sexuality,* is the 'shibboleth' of his psychology. Without even speaking of the subsequent extensions of the Jungian complex, which took on the sense of an independent personality or of a soul made up of a number of small, separate parts, it seems that from the first the word covered very different psychical realities. In Jung's view people 'have' complexes and the 'complexes' possess them; it is really a matter of a sort of momentary, accidental possession which may have recent or long-standing causes which are connected with events, crises, traumas, or some difficulty or other of life. They are entities of the human psychism, but one can 'have' them or 'not have' them, they come and go, appear and disappear as they fancy and Jung compares them to evil geniuses or to the hobgoblins of popular imagination who interfere with men's actions by their tricks. Playing the role of separate little persons inside the soul it is they who also cause the hallucinations and visions of the insane.

It is at once clear that the 'Oedipus complex'—with castration the only Freudian concept to which the word 'com-

[1] Ibid.

plex' is still attached—has not much in common with these little demons for which Freud, moreover, found another psychological explanation. The Oedipean situation, in fact, is defined as an *infantile* conflict which all men go through without exception and must somehow overcome. It is not therefore a question of 'having' it, one has to live it: what counts is not getting rid of it, but unravelling it in such a way that it contributes to happiness and to the fullness of life. No laboratory experiment can measure the size and value of this infantile situation from which spring not only conflicts but also, when it is happily resolved, the balance and the joys of the adult.

It is not easy to discover just when the word 'complex' appeared in Freud's work. In the course of successive editions each book was altered and added to and the dates of these changes are not always known. But it seems that the 'Oedipus complex' does not exist by name in the first edition of *The Interpretation of Dreams* and the *Three Essays*, but only in subsequent editions, so that its earliest appearance dates from 1905, that is when Freud was corresponding with Bleuler and knew the work of the Swiss. Whether he borrowed it directly from Jung or invented it himself he adopted it because, as he explained, he thought it a convenient word to use; but having little taste for terminological precision he did not define it.

The history of this word which has become part of popular speech, in which it represents almost the only thing people actually know about Freud, illustrates in an illuminating way how ideas propagate themselves, move off their original course, combine with others, triumph and vanish. Originating in the laboratory, the word 'complex' first designated those untimely and displaced emotions which, in a more or less critical situation, betray the individual and thwart his action. The father, mother, brother, sister, etc. complexes then become a convenient explanation for all the personality and behaviour disturbances which, from the strictly Freudian point of view, revert to the category of neuroses. After which, the word lost the rather magic nuance it had taken on in Jung's psychology and gradually came to be applied to anything to do with feelings of inferiority. This idea was as alien to Jung as to Freud, the latter seeing it only as a weakening of the 'castration complex'. But the idea was essential to the psychology founded by Adler. Nowadays to have complexes no longer means being 'possessed' but feeling inferior because of some organic or intellectual inadequacy, imagined or real, and in any case a source of social embarrassment. Inferiority complex, or just complex, the word undoubtedly sends us back implicitly to Freud. But it only 'succeeded' at the price of losing, one after another, all its ties with the psychology of the unconscious and consequently with the principles of Freudian thought.

Freud, as had been said, hardly used association experiments. He did not consider them to be of any value except in rebellious cases, principally in psychotic states such as dementia praecox. He did nothing to guard against the confusion which the Jungian 'complexes' were likely to introduce into his own system. He sometimes used the word himself although, as a letter to Pfister dated 1910 shows, he always distrusted it:

'With the complexes one must be very careful; indispensable as the idea (of the complexes) is in various performances, when one is theorizing one should always try to find out what lies behind the complex, not make a frontal attack, which is too vague and inadequate.'[1]

We see that even in 1910, when things were imperceptibly beginning to go wrong between Vienna and Zürich, Freud did not worry unduly about the deviations which Jung's cast of mind or the work he was doing at the time could impose on his theory. However, a less trusting person would have been able to foresee that there would not be all that much difference between the complex as defined by Jung, which was almost detached from its infantile origins and so to speak 'psychologized', and the archetypes which, later, replaced the flesh and blood father and mother by purely symbolic figures. But Freud liked Jung and was convinced that there existed no stouter defender of his work or worthier successor to carry it on. And even if he saw clearly what his jealous or clear-sighted followers interpreted as ill omens he knew that a clergyman's son, brought up in a solid moral and religious tradition and still very dependent on his milieu, showed more merit than anyone else in overcoming his prejudices and joining his 'wild army'. That was the argument he used with one of his closest adherents, Karl Abraham, who made little at-

[1] Letter to Pfister, January 10, 1910, *Psychoanalysis & Faith,* p. 31.

tempt to conceal his instinctive dislike of Jung and had clashed with him very early on.

This happened in 1908, in Salzburg, during the first International Psycho-Analytical Congress which, at Jung's suggestion, bore the modest name of 'Meeting for Freudian Psychology'. Unlike those which followed, this Congress lasted only one day. There was no president, or secretary, or committee, not even an agenda. The only thing which clouded this historic day was the dispute which erupted between Abraham and Jung over dementia praecox, the main work done at Burghölzli. Jung presented the views of his master, Bleuler, who held that dementia praecox is due to an organic state of the brain determined by a hypothetical psycho-toxin. Abraham, for his part, upheld Freud's ideas about the illness, namely that dementia could not be ascribed to a destruction of mental capacities but to a massive blockage of the affective processes. On top of this, he forgot to mention the work done by Bleuler and Jung, to which he did not attach much value, and Jung took this omission, which had a truly Freudian significance, very badly. To induce him to adopt a conciliatory attitude, Freud wrote Abraham a letter in which he explained his policy but which was more well meant than it was diplomatic:

'*Lieber und geehrter Herr College,*

'I am glad to hear that you regard Salzburg as a gratifying event. I myself cannot judge, since I stand in the midst of it all, but my inclination is also to consider this first gathering to be a promising test.

'In connection with it I would make a request to you on the fulfillment of which all sorts of things may depend. I recollect that your paper led to some conflict between you and Jung, or so at least I gathered from a few words you said to me afterwards. Now I consider some competition between you unavoidable and within certain limits quite harmless. In the matter at issue itself I unhesitatingly thought you were in the right and I attributed Jung's sensitiveness to his own vacillation. But I shouldn't like any bad feeling to come between you. We are still so few that disharmony, especially because of any personal complexes, should be out of the question among us. It is also important for us that Jung should find his way back to the views he has just forsaken, of which you have been such a consistent advocate. I believe there is some prospect of that, and Jung himself writes to me that Bleuler is showing himself amenable and almost inclined to abandon again the conception of the organic nature of dementia praecox. So you would do me a personal favor if you would communicate with Jung before publishing your paper and ask him to discuss his objections with you so that you can take them into account. A friendly gesture of that kind will assuredly put an end to the nascent disagreement between you. It would greatly please me and would show that all of us are able to gain from psychoanalysis practical advantages for the conduct of our own life. Don't make the little victory over yourself too difficult.

'Be tolerant and don't forget that really it is easier for you to follow my thoughts than for Jung, since to begin with you are completely independent, and then racial relationship brings you closer to my intellectual constitution, whereas he, being a Christian and the son of a pastor, can only find his way to me against great inner resistances. His adherence is therefore all the more valuable. I was almost going to say it was only his emergence on the scene that has removed from psychoanalysis the danger of becoming a Jewish national affair. . . .'[1]

Abraham gave way and wrote a conciliatory letter to Jung, but without much success. He already foresaw that Jung would not stay long in the movement, but Freud answered his doubts by saying: 'We Jews have an easier time, having no mystical strain.' Then in his next letter:

'I will do all I can to put matters right when I go to Zürich in September. Do not misunderstand me: I have nothing to reproach you for. I surmise that the repressed anti-Semitism of the Swiss, from which I am to be spared, has been directed against you in increased force. But my opinion is that we Jews, if we want to co-operate with other people, have to develop a little masochism and be prepared to endure a certain amount of injustice. There is no other way of working together. You may be sure that if my name were Oberhuber my new ideas would, despite all the other factors, have met with far less resistance. . . .'[2]

[1] Letter to Abraham, May 1908, Ernest Jones, II, p. 48.

[2] Ernest Jones, II, pp. 49–50.

The seven years during which Jung and Freud tried to work together for the 'cause' were by no means free of quarrels, which sprang from jealousy, ideological divergences and temperamental differences. As early as 1909, during their American trip, Jung had inwardly grown a long way from the man who, three years before, had been, to quote his own words, 'the most important event in my life'. Freud, however, still looked on him as the Joshua destined to enter the promised land of psychiatry which he, like Moses, was condemned to contemplate from afar. And to the very end he did not or would not see the profound incompatibilities which foreshadowed the break.

18

AMERICAN JOURNEY

Freud is one of those men who are difficult to picture as young because with them the natural effect of the years does not appear to be age so much as dignity, a sort of inherent nobility which gives their countenance a rather anonymous wisdom. Freud was over fifty when he became one of the most famous figures of his day. It is not easy to discover the legendary old man's face, at once penetrating and serene, through the photographs and literature which try to make him known to us. Stefan Zweig had seen it himself and gave his description in *Mental Healers*:

'Over the years caricaturists have been driven to despair by his features, for there is nothing in the perfectly regular oval face which lends itself to exaggeration, no dominant, vulnerable line on which to seize. It is useless to compare the portraits of him as a young man in the hope of discovering some salient feature, some revealing indication of his character. The features of the man at the age of thirty, then at forty or fifty are as inscrutable as his public life. They merely show us a good-looking man of virile appearance and with features that are almost too regular. The grave, concentrated look undoubtedly denotes the man of thought, but scarcely anything else. At a loss, one closely examines the photographs without ever discovering anything except a typical doctor's face framed by a well-trimmed, ideally masculine beard, such as Lenbach and Makart liked to paint; a gentle, sombre, grave face but not really very revealing. The door which shuts his life from view also conceals his face and, going from photograph to photograph, one is compelled to give up all efforts to read the character of the face which is so well protected by its symmetry. But, suddenly, the last portraits tell us something. Illness and old age have clearly carved a countenance out of the simple material of the features. Since his hair began turning grey and his beard no longer completely covers the firm jaw and casts a lighter shadow over the strongly marked mouth, something hard, something definitely aggressive emerges—the inflexible, almost fierce will which characterizes his nature. And the gaze, which before seemed only contemplative, takes on a profounder, more penetrating quality, a crease of bitter distrust cuts the high, furrowed forehead like the clean line of a wound. The thin, stern lips are pressed together as though to say "No" or "That is not true." For the first time one feels Freud's vehemence and vigour and then one thinks: this is no benevolent, white-haired old man who has grown gentle and sociable with age, but a pitiless examiner who cannot be deceived by anything and who scorns to practise any deception himself. A man to whom one would be afraid to tell a lie.'

The portrait which Ernest Jones draws differs appreciably from that imposing, patriarchal figure. Of course, Freud was twenty years younger and Jones, who had no literary pretensions whatever, was able to observe him from close quarters with the naturalness and perspicacity which comes from knowing a person intimately:

'At the age of fifty-two Freud was only beginning to show slight signs of grayness. He had a strikingly well-shaped head, adorned with thick, dark, well-groomed hair, a handsome moustache, and a full pointed beard. He was about five feet eight inches tall, somewhat rotund—though probably his waist did not exceed his chest measurement—and he bore the marks of a sedentary profession. Since I am mentioning figures I may add that the circumference of his head was fifty-five and a half centimeters, the diameters measuring eighteen and fifteen and a half centimeters respectively. So with a cephalic index of eighty-six he was decidedly dolichocephalic. He had a lively and perhaps somewhat restless or even anxious manner with quick darting eyes that gave a serious and penetrating effect. I dimly sensed some slightly feminine aspect in his manner and movements, which was perhaps why I developed something of a helping or even protective attitude toward him rather than the more characteristic filial one of many analysts. He spoke with an absolutely clear enunciation—a feature appreciated by a grateful foreigner—in a friendly tone of voice, more pleasing when low than on the rare occasions when he raised it. He was clever at elucidating my English mispronunciation of German words, but seemed sensitive to mistakes in gender; I can recall, for instance, his impatience when I spoke of *"die Schnee".*' [1]

With Freud's marked paternal features went a certain feminine streak, as Jones notes with considerable acumen, and this explains why, for all his extraordinary tenacity and the courage to defy the whole world if need be, he was also capable of giving up and often tried to get someone stronger than himself to take over practical responsibilities connected with the movement. This man who was so naturally cut out for the role of father and master could be uniquely grateful for advice and help. His correspondence proves this, notably his letter to Oskar Pfister expressing his unbounded joy at having been understood and helped:

'The Matterhorn now crowns the pile of unanswered letters on my desk. I gladly accept the small fragment of Switzerland in the symbolic sense you suggest, as homage from the only country in which I feel a man of property, knowing that the hearts and minds of good men there are well disposed towards me. I have no intention of defending myself. I have deliberately set myself up only as an example, but never as a model, let alone an object of veneration.

'The Matterhorn can easily be given another and more modest meaning. The proportion of one to 50,000 may be roughly that in which fate fulfills our wishes and we ourselves fulfill our intentions. Incidentally it has struck me how little figures mean to our imagination; I have the greatest difficulty in believing that one would have to put only 50,000 of these small objects on top of one another to reach the height of a huge mountain. I should have guessed that more than a million would have been required.

'I propose to endow the Matterhorn with yet a third meaning. It reminds me of a remarkable man who came to see me one day, a true servant of God, a man in the very idea of whom I should have had difficulty in believing, in that he feels the need to do spiritual good to everyone he meets. You did good in this way even to me. After your exhortation I asked myself why I did not feel really happy, and I soon found the answer. I renounced the impracticable proposition of getting rich honourably, decided

[1] Ernest Jones, II, p. 43.

after the loss of a patient not to accept a replacement for him, and since then I have felt well and happy and admit that you were right; and subsequently I have adhered to this principle on no fewer than three occasions. But for your visit and your influence I should never have managed it. . . .'[1]

People might find it surprising that Freud should feel incapacitated and a little weary and anxious about his achievement and always uncertain how to organize his own life just at the time when the first signs of success were coming from abroad. This phenomenon, which has become a common-place for psychoanalysts and which he himself later described as the illness of 'those who are wrecked by success', was the same as the one that had for so long prevented him from going to Rome and made him doubt the reality of Athens, and the same as the one which seemed to take from him the right to make his way in the world. In 1909, after accepting an invitation to go to America to give a course of lectures, he became exhausted from a sort of apathy, and this man whose imagination was generally inexhaustible when it came to travel seemed disillusioned in advance and did not even make any preparations for his journey. The letter he wrote to Oskar Pfister just before leaving strangely insists on this state of depression:

'I am still completely unproductive. This year has taken more out of me than previous years. I do not feel like preparing anything for America. Perhaps contact with Jung and Ferenczi (he too is one of the best) will stimulate something. Fortunately I am no longer so necessary and can gradually shrink into an ornament; perhaps there is a bit of providence in that.'[2]

Freud could not really have been under any misapprehension about the importance of this invitation which, coming from a great American university, was to mark the entry of psychoanalysis into the world. It is probable that his apathy merely concealed his anxiety before facing a test of which the outcome seemed to him to be doubtful. One imagines that he did not say anything about this to Jung

[1] Letter to Oskar Pfister, May 10, 1910, *Psychoanalysis & Faith*, p. 24. The 'Matterhorn' was a silver model of the mountain which Pfister had given to Freud.

[2] Ibid., August 16, 1909, pp. 28–9.

or Ferenczi, who were going with him. But although he claimed he attached no importance to his lectures and even refused to prepare them, he confided to his closest friends afterwards that he had had to resort to a subterfuge to master his agitation. He said he had persuaded himself that he was going to America mainly to see a wild porcupine and only incidentally to lecture! He did in fact see some of these creatures and returned home with the feeling that he had fulfilled his difficult task. Freud had been invited by Stanley Hall, the President of Clark University, Worcester, Massachusetts, on the occasion of the twentieth anniversary of the foundation. Stanley Hall was an authority on experimental psychology and his official support was obviously a considerable help to American psychoanalysis, which was only just coming into being and which could boast of only one notable figure, A. A. Brill. However, Freud was in no hurry to accept. He did not want to go in August as that would have meant losing three weeks' practice, although, he said, "America ought to bring me in, not cost me money." In the end the ceremony was postponed until the first week in September and Freud no longer had a reason for refusing to go. Almost all the cost of his journey was paid so that he could take Ferenczi with him as well, and as Jung had also been invited the three of them decided to travel together.

They met in Bremen, where they spent the day. Freud invited his companions to lunch and while he was acting as their host there occurred a symptomatic incident which was to affect him for some time, although he analysed it immediately. Backed up by Ferenczi, he urged Jung to drink a little wine, and Jung, a fanatical believer in the anti-alcoholic principles of Burghölzli, succumbed. Freud had hardly won this little victory when, to his friends' consternation, he fainted. Three years later, in Munich, the same thing happened during a more serious clash with Jung when Freud had a similar attack after routing Jung. The Bremen lunch had other unforeseen consequences. It contributed to Jung's dispute with his chief, Bleuler, who later seriously accused Freud of driving his assistant to drink!

The arrival of the three men in New York created little stir. Freud looked round the city, but the thing which particularly attracted him was the Metropolitan Museum and its Greek antiquities. On September 4th he left New York for Worcester, where he was due to begin his lectures next day. Jones, who had joined them in New York, recalls that first contact with the American public:

'New England was by no means unprepared to listen to Freud's new doctrines. In the autumn of 1908, while staying with Morton Prince in Boston, I had held two or three colloquiums at which sixteen people were present: among others, J. J. Putnam, the Professor of Neurology at Harvard University; E. W. Taylor, later Putnam's successor; Werner Munsterberg, the Professor of Psychology there; Boris Sidis; and G. W. Waterman. The only one with whom I had any real success was Putnam. Then in May of the following year, not long before Freud's visit, there was an important Congress in New Haven at which Putnam and I read papers that provoked much discussion. So Freud's arrival was awaited with a good deal of eagerness.

'Freud had no idea what to talk about, or at least so he said, and at first was inclined to accept Jung's suggestion that he devote his lectures to the subject of dreams; but when he asked my opinion I advised him to choose a wider one and on reflection he agreed that Americans might regard the subject of dreams as not "practical" enough, if not actually frivolous. So he decided to give a more general account of psychoanalysis. Each lecture he composed in half an hour's walk beforehand in Ferenczi's company—an illustration of how harmoniously flowing his thoughts must have been.

'Freud delivered his five lectures in German, without any notes, in a serious conversational tone that made a deep impression. A lady in the audience was very eager to hear him talk on sexual subjects, and begged me to ask him to do so. When I passed on her request, he replied: *"In Bezug auf die Sexualität lasse ich mich weder ab- noch zubringen."* That goes better in German, but it means he was not to be driven *to* the subject any more than *away* from it. . . .'[1]

Freud's American lectures show the same care for clarity as all his expositions meant for the public. After recalling Breuer's share in the invention of psychoanalytic method and his own work on hysteria, he spoke about dreams, faulty actions, infantile sexuality and the profound nature of those illnesses in which the individual paradoxically

[1] Ernest Jones, II, p. 57.

finds his profit. In his conclusion, which was clearly calculated for America, he dealt with the problem of the repression of the instincts and their excesses, which are just as serious a danger to the health of the individual as to the health of a civilization:

'We ought not to exalt ourselves so high as completely to neglect what was originally animal in our nature. Nor should we forget that the satisfaction of the individual's happiness cannot be erased from among the aims of our civilization. The plasticity of the components of sexuality, shown by their capacity for sublimation, may indeed offer a great temptation to strive for still greater cultural achievements by still further sublimation. But, just as we do not count on our machines converting more than a certain fraction of the heat consumed into useful mechanical work, we ought not to seek to alienate the whole amount of the energy of the sexual instinct from its proper ends. We cannot succeed in doing so; and if the restriction upon sexuality were to be carried too far it would inevitably bring with it all the evils of soil-exhaustion.

'It may be that you for your part will regard the warning with which I close as an exaggeration. I shall only venture on an indirect picture of my conviction by telling you an old story and leaving you to make what use you like of it. German literature is familiar with a little town called Schilda, to whose inhabitants clever tricks of every possible sort are attributed. The citizens of Schilda, so we are told, possessed a horse with whose feats of strength they were highly pleased and against which they had only one objection—that it consumed such a large quantity of expensive oats. They determined to break it of this bad habit very gently by reducing its ration by a few stalks every day, till they had accustomed it to complete abstinence. For a time things went excellently: the horse was weaned to the point of eating only one stalk a day, and on the succeeding day it was at length to work without any oats at all. On the morning of that day the spiteful animal was found dead; and the citizens of Schilda could not make out what it had died of. . . .'[1]

We can imagine Freud's emotion when, at the end of the ceremonies, a Doctorate was conferred on him. His speech

[1] Fifth lecture in *Five Lectures on Psychoanalysis, Std Edn* XI, pp. 54–5.

of thanks began with these words: 'This is the first official recognition of our endeavours. . . .' In his autobiography he described the men to whom he owed this honour and his feeling of suddenly living an incredible diurnal dream:

'Hall was justly esteemed as a psychologist and educationalist, and had introduced psychoanalysis into his courses several years earlier; there was a touch of the "king-maker" about him, a pleasure in setting up authorities and in then deposing them. We also met James J. Putnam there, the Harvard neurologist, who in spite of his age was an enthusiastic supporter of psychoanalysis and threw the whole weight of a personality that was universally respected into the defence of the cultural value of analysis and the purity of its aims. He was an estimable man, in whom, as a reaction against a predisposition to obsessional neurosis, an ethical bias predominated; and the only thing in him that we could regret was his inclination to attach psychoanalysis to a particular philosophical system and to make it the servant of moral aims. Another event of this time which made a lasting impression upon me was a meeting with William James the philosopher. I shall never forget one little scene that occurred as we were on a walk together. He stopped suddenly, handed me a bag he was carrying and asked me to walk on, saying that he would catch me up as soon as he had got through an attack of angina pectoris which was just coming on. He died of that disease a year later; and I have always wished that I might be as fearless as he was in the face of approaching death. . . .'[1]

The American journey proved to Freud that psychoanalysis was not the product of a fevered imagination but part of a reality which eminent men were pleased to consider valuable. All the same he was amazed and half incredulous, and as soon as he got back home he wrote to Oskar Pfister:

'One of the most agreeable phantasies is that without our knowing it decent people are finding their way to our ideas and aspirations and then suddenly popping up all over the place. That is what happened in the case of Stanley Hall. Who would have imagined that over in America, an hour's train journey from Boston, a worthy old gentle-

[1] *An Autobiographical Study, Std Edn* XX, pp. 51–2.

man was sitting and waiting impatiently for the Year Book, reading and understanding everything, and then, as he himself put it, ringing the bell for us?'[1]

In spite of the personal satisfaction and the political benefit that he derived from his journey, Freud did not bring back a good impression of America. Neither the cities nor the natural sights seem to have interested him, except Niagara Falls; but even this was spoiled for him by a guide who remarked while he was pointing out the features: 'Let the old gentleman go first!' In a general way everything in America irritated him. He said to Ernest Jones that it was 'a mistake; a gigantic mistake, it is true, but none the less a mistake.' And Freud who, as a rule, always tried to be fair, never entirely lost this prejudice, even when America was completely conquered by his ideas.

The reason for this aversion was not preconceived social or political ideas so much as poor health, which partly spoiled his stay. For years he attributed all the ills which came his way to the detested American food. He had undoubtedly felt out of his element in America and had not been able to complain to his family. Furthermore Freud had a profound need to be understood and to make himself understood; but he misunderstood the Americans, literally and morally, for their language, their way of life and their idea of scientific work baffled him and failed to rouse any sympathy in him. More than fifty years after his trip one wonders whether, in spite of the tremendous success he enjoyed, America understood him any better than he understood America.

Freud naturally followed the progress of the psychoanalytical movement on the new continent with the greatest interest. He was on excellent terms with Putnam, who contributed to the *Jahrbuch* which Jung edited. Then, when Jung had joined the ranks of the dissidents, and his review disappeared, Putnam wrote for the *Internationale Zeitschrift für ärztliche Psychoanalyse* (International Review of Medical Psychoanalysis), the official organ of the International Association. Stanley Hall continued for some time to sound the call to arms, then he went over to Adler, whose ideas had their greatest success in the United States. Later, Freud had many American pupils and patients who

[1] Letter to Pfister, October 4, 1909, *Psychoanalysis & Faith,* pp. 29–30.

were sent to him by his correspondents, especially Ernest Jones when he had settled in Canada. During the period of famine and dire poverty in Vienna at the end of the First World War this influx of American patients was Freud's salvation.

Freud's attitude to America was probably rooted in an old mistrust of the country's traditional puritanism, which made America at once receptive to Freudian ideas and dangerous for the few truths on which Freud absolutely insisted. Logically, psychoanalysis was to achieve its major successes in places where sexual morality was excessively rigid and hypocritical; but, looked at from another point of view, it was in such places that psychoanalysis also ran the greatest risk of being distorted. Years after his trip Freud was perfectly aware that there was something wrong about the vogue for psychoanalytical ideas in America. In 1925, for example, he wrote in his autobiography:

'It has not lost ground in America since our visit; it is extremely popular among the lay public and is recognized by a number of official psychiatrists as an important element in medical training. Unfortunately, however, it has suffered a great deal from being watered down. Moreover, many abuses which have no relation to it find a cover under its name, and there are few opportunities for any thorough training in technique or theory. In America, too, it has come in conflict with Behaviourism, a theory which is naïve enough to boast that it has put the whole problem of psychology completely out of court.'[1]

This leads one to think that Freud was not very happy about the development of American psychoanalysis which, even when it claims to be faithful to his theory, serves ends of which he would have disapproved, seeing how extremely individual his thought was. Freud and European psychoanalysis believed that psychoanalytic therapy has always preserved precise clinical indications, and the idea that it can somehow be applied in the mass and concern itself less with making an individual an integrated person than making him conform to social standards, thereby bringing him down to a common level, is undoubtedly something which would have disheartened Freud as much as the various deviations which his teaching had under-

[1] *An Autobiographical Study, Std Edn* XX, p. 52.

gone disturbed him when he was alive. That is why, in spite of the honours that came his way in his old age, his fame never gave him an unmixed joy. What he said in a letter to Pfister in 1920 was probably what he thought until the end of his life:

'It is true that things are moving everywhere, but you seem to over-estimate my pleasure in that. What personal pleasure is to be derived from analysis I obtained during the time when I was alone, and since others have joined me it has given me more pain than pleasure. The way people accept and distort it has not changed the opinion I formed of them when they non-understandingly rejected it. An incurable breach must have come into existence at that time between me and other men.'[1]

Whatever Freud's disappointment in America may have been, the fact remains that his journey there marks an important stage in the diffusion of his ideas. The year 1909 saw a sort of awakening almost everywhere—for instance in Canada, under Ernest Jones, and even in Australia, where a Presbyterian Church minister in Sydney started a little group and gave lectures on psychoanalysis to various societies. He was, however, less lucky or less prepared than Oskar Pfister and he had to resign on account of his 'Freudian opinions'. Towards the end of the same year a French doctor, Professor Morichau-Beauchant of Poitiers, wrote Freud a letter which constitutes France's first contribution to the psychoanalytical movement. But this was a completely isolated contribution and some years went by before there were any others. Freud was particularly sensitive to this abstention, or rather this resistance on the part of France, because his conception of the country was still bound up with the image of his master, Charcot, and the very idea of intellectual freedom.

The absence of Freud and Jung had made it impossible to hold an international congress in 1909, but the Second Congress took place the following year, this time in Nuremberg, with members from the main European countries and an American delegate taking part. For some time Freud had been thinking of bringing analysts together into one association. He got Ferenczi to raise the question at the Congress, giving him a programme of work and a pre-

[1] Letter to Pfister, December 25, 1920, *Psychoanalysis & Faith*, p. 79.

cise plan for such an organization. Ferenczi's programme, which proposed that Zürich should be the seat of the future association and Jung its president, drew violent protests from the Viennese psychoanalysts and the speaker had to take them seriously to task. His proposals also included granting the president discretionary powers with the right to check all communications and articles written by the psychoanalysts of all countries. Nobody was disposed to accept such a dictatorship. Ernest Jones described the atmosphere and the outcome of the stormy discussions that ensued:

'It was this attitude of Ferenczi's that was later to cause such trouble between European and American analysts which it took me, in particular, years to compose. The discussion that arose after Ferenczi's paper was so acrimonious that it had to be postponed to the next day. There was, of course, no question of accepting his more extreme suggestions, but the Viennese, especially Adler and Stekel, also angrily opposed the nomination of Swiss analysts to the positions of President and Secretary, their own long and faithful services being ignored. Freud himself perceived the advantage of establishing a broader basis for the work than could be provided by his Viennese colleagues, who were all Jewish, and that it was necessary to convince the Viennese of this. Hearing that several of them were holding a protest meeting in Stekel's hotel room, he went up to join them and made an impassioned appeal for their adherence. He laid stress on the virulent hostility that surrounded them and the need for outside support to counter it. Then, dramatically throwing back his coat, he declared: "My enemies would be willing to see me starve; they would tear my very coat off my back."'[1]

Finally things somehow sorted themselves out, though not for long. The International Association was created with Jung as President. To compensate the Viennese, Freud agreed to publish a new review alongside Jung's *Jahrbuch* under the editorship of Adler and Stekel, the two principal leaders of the revolt. In the end Freud thought the best way to assure peace was for him to step aside and to act only as a contributor or a scientific adviser to the Viennese Society. The idea that he ought to retire into the back-

[1] Ernest Jones, II, pp. 69–70.

ground seems to have preoccupied him during those years in which, after standing alone, he had to face the partisan enthusiasms of his followers. This comes out most clearly in a letter he wrote to Ferenczi commenting on the Congress or, as he called it, the 'Reichstag' of Nuremberg which ended the childhood of the movement:

'There is no doubt that it was a great success. And yet we two had the least luck. Evidently my address met with a poor response; I don't know why. It contained much that should have aroused interest. Perhaps I showed how tired I was. Your spirited plea had the misfortune to evoke so much contradiction that they forgot to thank you for the important suggestions you laid before them. Every society is ungrateful: that doesn't matter. But we were both somewhat to blame in not reckoning with the effect they would have on the Viennese. It would have been easy for you to have entirely omitted the critical remarks and to have assured them of their scientific freedom; then we should have deprived their protest of much of its strength. I believe that my long pent up aversion for the Viennese combined with your brother complex to make us shortsighted.

'That, however, is not the essential thing. What is more important is that we have accomplished an important piece of work which will have a profound influence in shaping the future. I was happy to see that you and I were in full agreement, and I want to thank you warmly for your support which after all was successful.

'Events will now move. I have seen that now is the moment to carry out a decision I have long had in mind. I shall give up the leadership of the Vienna group and cease exercising any official influence. I will transfer the leadership to Adler, not because I like to do so or feel satisfied, but because after all he is the only personality there and because possibly in that position he will feel an obligation to defend our common ground. I have already told him of this and will inform the others next Wednesday. I don't believe they will even be very sorry. I had almost got into the painful role of the dissatisfied and unwanted old man. That I certainly don't want, so I prefer to go before I need, but voluntarily. The leaders will all be of the same age and rank; they can then develop freely and come to terms with one another. . . .' [1]

[1] Letter to Ferenczi, April 3, 1910, Ernest Jones, II, p. 71.

19

DISSENSIONS

Contrary to Freud's hopes the Second International Congress at Nuremberg at which the foundation of the International Psycho-Analytical Association had been decided on did not inaugurate an era of peace but a minor war which lasted almost without interruption for four years. All that Freud gained by handing over power to Adler in the Vienna Society was to unleash the more or less latent jealousies in the group. Relations began to deteriorate between Adler and Stekel, the joint editors of the *Zentralblatt für Psychoanalyse,* the review which had been founded at the Congress. Adler gave up the position and proclaimed with ever increasing vehemence his wish to break free. He finally did so at the Weimar Congress in 1911 and started a new group under the name of 'Society for Free Psychoanalysis'. The following year it was Stekel's turn to leave and then in 1913 at the Munich Congress Jung and his followers did the same. In his *History of the Psycho-Analytic Movement,* written in 1914, Freud commented at length on these events which had on two occasions threatened the unity of his work and cast a shadow over his life at the very moment when he could see a real prospect of success:

'The disappointment that they caused me might have been averted if I had paid more attention to the reactions of patients under analytic treatment. I knew very well of course that anyone may take to flight at his first approach to the unwelcome truths of analysis; I had always myself maintained that everyone's understanding of it is limited by his own repressions (or rather, by the resistances which sustain them) so that he cannot go beyond a particular point in his relation to analysis. But I had not expected that anyone who had reached a certain depth in his understanding of analysis could renounce that understanding and lose it. And yet daily experience with patients had shown that total rejection of analytic knowledge may result whenever a specially strong resistance arises at any depth in the mind; one may have succeeded in laboriously bringing a patient to grasp some parts of analytic knowledge and to handle them like possessions of his own, and yet one may see him, under the domination of the very next resistance, throw all he has learnt to the winds and stand on the defensive as he did in the days when he was a carefree beginner. I had to learn that the very same thing can happen with psycho-analysts as with patients in analysis. . . .'[1]

Freud suggests, then, that the unconscious resistances of the first analysts explain the stormy history of those four years which were to leave the movement weakened, or at least partly deprived of the benefits of success. To tell the whole truth Freud should have added that most of his first adherents had only a purely intellectual experience of analysis and that when they had been analysed their treatment had been too short and too superficial to produce any lasting result. Stekel, who suffered from a typical and marked neurosis, had been analysed by Freud for some weeks, but under unfavourable conditions since the two men knew one another too well to be able to keep the strict distance between doctor and patient which is indispensable for successful analysis. Later, when the ideas of resistance, transference and counter-transference were technically specified, it became evident that the training of every analyst, whether he considered himself neurotic or not, should include an analysis of his own self in every way identical to the analysis of a patient. Every Institute then made a didactic analysis compulsory for trainees and today this is an absolute rule. At the beginning, however, such a measure was inconceivable. Freud could not impose any condition on strangers who had the courage to go to him and naturally went as doctors, not patients; even when, from the psychoanalytical standpoint, their psychical balance did not appear to be absolutely sound. It seems that at first Freud analysed those of his young colleagues who asked him to or showed that they needed analysis. The others did like all students and got their knowledge from books, in other words from Freud's writings, which at that time were the only material they could study.

There were also other reasons which made it difficult to insist on a compulsory didactic analysis. The first candi-

[1] *Std Edn* XIV, pp. 48–9.

dates for psychoanalytical training were not young people. The majority were already doctors, others came from various professions and for them to undergo a didactic analysis like those which are now carried out would have involved a great sacrifice of time, energy and money—an important consideration for people every one of whom was poor. Freud himself never made a fortune. In the days when he had to train pupils he more often than not had to confine his teaching to improvised conversations during long walks when the candidate was analysed and instructed in the theory at the same time. Those 'Socratic' dialogues were for a long time the only training that future analysts received. However keen they might be, those conversations hardly made it easier to break off 'transference', that is the detachment from the person of the therapist without which no analysis is ever really complete.

As there was no systematic analysis available which would guarantee a therapeutic cure, Freud's early supporters carried on a sort of diffuse psychoanalytic activity which had nothing but happy results in their everyday life. Naturally enough they all felt like analysing one another rather than themselves, and they did so with far greater insight. The outcome was mutual reproach and criticism, with analytical truth replacing the usual social code, which in no way prevented them from hurting each other's feelings. In the guise of analytical understanding many jealousies which in other circumstances would have assumed a politer, more hypocritical form were frankly expressed. Finally, the powerful feelings which both cemented and divided the primitively closed community were turned against the man who was its leader and master and who, as the fount of all knowledge and help, was forced to play his paternal role in the open.

To his followers Freud represented something more than a scientist who had become famous in his own special field. He was its creator. Having no predecessors or rivals, he embodied both the past and the future of a new science and those who went to him expected to get from him not just more, but every scrap of the knowledge they were seeking. This had material as well as moral consequences, since the first psychoanalysts depended for their practice entirely on the master sending them patients. The more ambitious of them might also have been afraid they would find their way barred for ever by the man to whom they owed everything and who, naturally, completely overshadowed them.

Freud did not dwell on this point in his *History of the Psycho-Analytic Movement.* However, he did mention a revealing remark by Adler which others, later, might equally well have made:

'I may even speak publicly of the personal motive for his work, since he himself announced it in the presence of a small circle of members of the Vienna group:—"Do you think it gives me such great pleasure to stand in your shadow my whole life long?" To be sure, I see nothing reprehensible in a younger man freely admitting his ambition, which one would in any case guess was among the incentives for his work. But even though a man is dominated by a motive of this kind he should know how to avoid being what the English, with their fine social tact, call "unfair"—which in German can only be expressed by a much cruder word. How little Adler has succeeded in this is shown by the profusion of petty outbursts of malice which disfigure his writings and by the indications they contain of an uncontrolled craving for priority. At the Vienna Psycho-Analytical Society we once actually heard him claim priority for the conception of the "unity of the neuroses" and for the "dynamic view" of them. This came as a great surprise to me, for I had always believed that these two principles were stated by me before I ever made Adler's acquaintance.' [1]

Freud's crushing authority was not the only thing to cause conflict and uneasiness. There was also his love which he dispensed unequally among his followers. There, again, it was too much like paternal love. Thus while greatly respecting Adler's intellectual qualities, he thought him unpleasant and a bore and did not feel in the least attracted by him. On the other hand he made no secret of his great liking for Jung and for many years he displayed towards Rank and Ferenczi, for instance, an affection and a solicitude, even a tenderness which contrasted strongly with the harshness which he could show to no less gifted and sometimes more loyal pupils. Otto Rank who, on Freud's advice, had begun to study comparatively late, never practised psychoanalysis in Vienna and as he was extremely

[1] Ibid., p. 51.

poor nobody ever really knew what he lived on. It is probable that Freud, unknown to anyone, often helped him out. Ernest Jones even suspected that he once offered to pay for him to go to Greece. Ferenczi, the only one to become a friend of the family and who regularly went on holidays abroad with him, he treated like a sort of adopted son and even confessed to him one day that he had hoped to see him marry his eldest daughter. On the strength of all this Ferenczi demanded of Freud total love, trust and sincerity the whole time. This unreasonable demand clearly revealed his infantile character. It often spoiled the holidays the two men spent together and provoked many little quarrels which Freud afterwards had to patch up. In 1910 after a journey to Sicily during which Ferenczi had been very miserable, Freud wrote to him a moving letter which throws light on the least known aspect of his relations with his followers:

'Dear Friend, Your letter reminded me that I am the same person who picked papyrus in Syracuse, had a scuffle with the railway staff in Naples, and bought antiques in Rome. The identity has been re-established. It is strange how easily one gives in to the tendency to isolate parts of one's personality.

'You will believe me when I say I look back upon your company during the journey with nothing but warm and affectionate feelings, although I frequently felt sorry for you because of your disappointment, and in some respect I would have liked you to be different. You were disappointed because you probably expected to swim in constant intellectual stimulation, whereas I hate nothing more than striking up attitudes and out of contrariness frequently let myself go. As a result I was probably most of the time a quite ordinary elderly gentleman, and you in astonishment kept measuring the distance between me and your phantasy ideal. On the other hand I often wished that you would pull yourself out of the infantile role and place yourself beside me as a companion on an equal footing, something you were unable to do, and in a practical respect I would like you to have carried out your share of the responsibility, orientation in space and time, a little more reliably. But you were inhibited and dreamy.'[1]

Ferenczi, who felt for Freud the same consuming passion

[1] To Ferenczi, October 2, 1910, *Letters,* p. 283.

which he felt for his father and which, twenty years later, led him to make unfortunate changes in psychoanalytical technique, was not appeased by this kindly explanation. In a second letter Freud decided to speak more frankly:

'It is remarkable how much more clearly you can express yourself in writing than in speaking. Naturally I knew very much or most of what you write and now need to give you only a few explanations. Why I didn't give you a scolding and so opened the way to a mutual understanding? Quite true, it was weak of me. I am not the psychoanalytical superman that you construed in your imagination, nor have I overcome the counter-transference.[1] I couldn't treat you in that way, any more than I could have my three sons because I am too fond of them and should feel sorry for them.

'You not only noticed, but also understood, that I *no longer* have any need to uncover my personality completely, and you correctly traced this back to the traumatic reason for it. Since Fliess's case, with the overcoming of which you recently saw me occupied, that need has been extinguished. A part of homosexual cathexis has been withdrawn and made use of to enlarge my own ego. I have succeeded where the paranoiac fails.

'Moreover, you should know that I was less well, and suffered more from my intestinal trouble, than I was willing to admit. I often said to myself that whoever is not master of his Konrad [2] should not set out on travels. That is where the frankness should have begun, but you did not seem to me stable enough to avoid becoming overanxious about me.

'As for the unpleasantness you caused me, including a certain passive resistance, it will undergo the same change

[1] 'Counter-transference' is the whole body of affective reactions, unconscious until analysed, of the psychoanalyst towards his patient, within the analytic situation. Like the patient's 'transference', 'counter-transference' is a reliving of infantile and therefore irrational feelings and its analysis is a very important part of the therapist's task.

[2] A frequent expression in Freud's letters. He borrowed it from the novel *Imago* by the Swiss author, Carl Spitteler, where it personifies the bowel and its functions. The famous review *Imago* takes its name from this novel in which the main themes are astonishingly similar to the Oedipean themes described by psychoanalysts. Hanns Sachs, editor of the review with Otto Rank and himself a writer, was a great admirer of Carl Spitteler.

as memories of travels in general: one refines them, the small disturbances vanish and what was beautiful remains for one's intellectual pleasure.

'That you surmised I had great secrets, and were very curious about them, was plain to see and also easy to recognize as infantile. Just as I told you *everything* on scientific matters I concealed very little of a personal nature. . . . My dreams at that time were concerned, as I hinted to you, entirely with the Fliess affair, which in the nature of things would be hard to arouse your sympathy.

'So when you look at it more closely you will find that we haven't so much to settle between us as perhaps you thought at first.

'I would rather turn your attention to the present. . . .'[1]

It is a great shame that Freud's correspondence with his closest supporters has not been published in full. It alone would explain the obscure crises which shook the psychoanalytical movement throughout almost the whole of its history and still clouded Freud's old age, when he was racked by illness. It undoubtedly needed real strength of character to remain at once loving and free in the presence of this imposing man whose make-up included so many contradictory elements. Some people, such as Ernest Jones and Karl Abraham, managed to pursue a line of their own and at the same time maintain a harmonious and healthy relationship with him. Others exchanged their independence for blind subservience to his views. A few loudly proclaimed their freedom and eventually left him. Others again tried to live with him the daily drama of love and revolt at the risk of getting worse and going under completely.

With these people the solution depended on their individual psychical and intellectual organization, even on their social position. It was probably most difficult of all for the Jews, who were sensitive to any constraint and traditionally very dependent on family ties; the English, with the 'fine social tact' Freud spoke of, were generally able to find a neat solution; the Swiss who did not follow Jung remained devoted to Freud, showing a balance of common sense and detachment. In any case Freud could hardly influence their choice by his actions or decisions. He was

[1] Letter to Ferenczi, October 6, 1910, Ernest Jones, II, p. 84.

destined to provoke and to try on his own person all the compromise solutions, good or bad, healthy or morbid, by which *sons* have always tried to break away.

No one should be surprised that the first generation of psychoanalysts included so many who were unbalanced, socially maladjusted or even suffering from serious psychical disturbances. Who but men with a personal experience of suffering could have felt the urgency and foreseen the extent of the Freudian revolution? If the popular belief that all psychiatrists are mad is untrue, they do at least have a special link with the illness which largely justifies their vocation. Psychoanalysis offered at once an outlet and intellectual sustenance to gifted minds who, through ignorance or lack of opportunity, had not been able to use their talents, or to highly strung, unstable people who saw a chance of escaping their fate. They have left a tragic mark on its history not only by the crises which, to an outsider, may seem puerile, but also by suicide and madness.

From his youth onwards Freud had lived in an atmosphere of tragedy marked by mental disorder and disease, especially tuberculosis. His friend Paneth had died in his prime, he had witnessed Ernst von Fleischl's slow torture, one of his hospital friends had committed suicide almost before his very eyes:[1] all those experiences had profoundly upset him, quickening in him the idea of death which was ever with him and finally found a central place in his doctrine. Later on several of his followers killed themselves: the Swiss psychoanalyst Honegger; Otto Gross, a young man from Graz whose work revealed an extremely brilliant mind. Viktor Tausk, whose death was one of the greatest losses suffered by psychoanalysis. Lastly, he had to watch Otto Rank's slow descent into madness; then, a few years later, the tragic collapse of Ferenczi, the only friend he really made among his pupils. Otto Rank was apparently unable to endure the ordeal of the First World War, like Gross and Tausk who committed suicide at the end of hostilities. Rank's last works, in particular *The Trauma of Birth* which deviated consider-

[1] Cf. letter to Martha Bernays, September 16, 1883, which shows how greatly Freud was upset by the suicide of Nathan Weiss, his colleague and friend. This letter is interesting for its detailed account of the young man's family history and affective situation, which Freud describes in a way which vaguely anticipates some of his future ideas.

ably from the Freudian line and led to the break between the two men, reveal a vigorous and by no means disordered mind. And Ferenczi died before his bold and exciting speculations could lead to a similar split.

It would be quite unjust to ascribe the dissensions within the psychoanalytical movement to purely psychological and largely unconscious causes. Freud himself did not go as far as that and although he secretly felt that the greatest theoretical distortions were aimed at him he did not deny their value as a basis for debate. Psychoanalysis had, in fact, brought together men of such different and sometimes even opposite taste, temperament and background that it should have been clear at once that they were bound to disagree. Adler and Jung, for instance, had absolutely nothing in common. Adler came from an intellectual milieu whose main interests were political. His wife, of Russian origin, was an intimate friend of Trotsky and the émigré revolutionary leaders. He himself inspired a small group of socialist psychoanalysts all of whom left the Vienna Society when he did. It is certain that his 'individual psychology', based on the primacy of the Ego and the conscious, directly reflected his political convictions, like Nietzsche's theory of the will to power which he eventually incorporated in his system.

Jung, on the other hand, was utterly unconcerned about social questions. His interest had always lain in esoteric, occult and religious phenomena, and the general problem of symbolism. It is probable that he had always thought of psychoanalysis not as an end but a means to be used in the service of vaster syntheses. His later theory of the 'collective unconscious' and 'archetypes' shows that he remained faithful to himself in this respect.

After meeting briefly under the Freudian flag, the two dissident leaders followed their own paths, which had in fact never crossed. Freud would not perhaps have been so grieved if both had not presented their dissent as an advance for psychoanalysis and, what was painful in view of his susceptibilities about age, as a victory for their youth. It was largely to protest against this claim that, in 1914, he wrote the *History of the Psycho-Analytic Movement* in which he weighed the claims made by the two doctrines against their actual contributions:

'These two retrograde movements away from psycho-analysis, which I must now compare with each other, show another point in common: for they both court a favourable opinion by putting forward certain lofty ideas, which view things, as it were, *sub specie aeternitatis*. With Adler, this part is played by the relativity of all knowledge and the right of the personality to put an artificial construction on the data of knowledge according to individual taste; with Jung, the appeal is made to the historic right of youth to throw off the fetters in which tyrannical age with its hide-bound views seeks to bind it. A few words must be devoted to exposing the fallacy of these ideas.

'The relativity of our knowledge is a consideration which may be advanced against every other science just as well as against psycho-analysis. It is derived from familiar reactionary currents of present-day feeling which are hostile to science, and it lays claim to an appearance of superiority to which no one is entitled. None of us can guess what the ultimate judgement of mankind about our theoretical efforts will be. There are instances in which rejection by the first three generations has been corrected by the succeeding one and changed into recognition. After a man has listened carefully to the voice of criticism in himself and has paid some attention to the criticisms of his opponents, there is nothing for him to do but with all his strength to maintain his own convictions which are based on experience. One should be content to conduct one's case honestly, and should not assume the office of judge, which is reserved for the remote future. . . .'[1]

After noting that Adler's ideas on the relativity of scientific truths were not really taken seriously by Adler himself or his followers, who hailed him as the Messiah, Freud examines Jung's argument that it was a liberating revolt of youth:

'Jung's argument *ad captandam benevolentiam* rests on the too optimistic assumption that the progress of the human race, of civilization and knowledge, has always pursued an unbroken line; as if there had been no periods of decadence, no reactions and restorations after every revolution, no generations who have taken a backward step and abandoned the gains of their predecessors. His approach to the standpoint of the masses, his abandonment of an innovation which proved unwelcome, make it *a priori* improb-

[1] *Std Edn* XIV, pp. 58–9.

able that Jung's corrected version of psychoanalysis can justly claim to be a youthful act of liberation. After all, it is not the age of the doer that decides this but the character of the deed. . . .'[1]

Examining the two dissident theories to see if they had retained any authentic psychoanalytic elements, Freud finds that Adler's is based entirely on the instinct of aggression and believes that, in its exclusion of love, it should repel not attract the public. That such a bleak and depressing conception of the world should find supporters is a further proof that humanity, weighed down by its own sexual needs, will agree to any system which allows it to subdue them. However, Adler's doctrine should be given more credit than Jung's modification, which is like Lichtenberg's knife which has lost its blade and its handle. Jung gave it a new blade and a new handle but kept the trade mark and claims it is still the same knife:

'Of the two movements under discussion Adler's is indubitably the more important; while radically false, it is marked by consistency and coherence. It is, moreover, in spite of everything, founded upon a theory of the instincts. Jung's modification, on the other hand, loosens the connection of the phenomena with instinctual life; and further, as its critics (e.g. Abraham, Ferenczi and Jones) have pointed out, it is so obscure, unintelligible and confused as to make it difficult to take up any position upon it. Wherever one lays hold of anything, one must be prepared to hear that one has misunderstood it, and one cannot see how to arrive at a correct understanding of it. It is put forward in a peculiarly vacillating manner, one moment as "quite a mild deviation, which does not justify the outcry that has been raised about it" (Jung), and the next moment as a new message of salvation which is to begin a new epoch for psycho-analysis, and, indeed, a new *Weltanschauung* for everyone. . . .

'It must be admitted, however, that the exponents of the new theory find themselves in a difficult position. They are now disputing things which they themselves formerly upheld, and they are doing so, moreover, not on the ground of fresh observations which might have taught them something further, but in consequence of fresh interpretations

[1] Ibid., pp. 59–60.

which make the things they see look different to them now from what they did before. For this reason they are unwilling to give up their connection with psycho-analysis, as whose representatives they became known to the world, and prefer to give it out that psycho-analysis has changed. . . . Just as Adler's investigation brought something new to psycho-analysis—a contribution to the psychology of the ego—and then expected us to pay too high a price for this gift by throwing over all the fundamental theories of analysis, so in the same way Jung and his followers paved the way for their fight against psycho-analysis by presenting it with a new acquisition. They traced in detail (as Pfister did before them) the way in which the material of sexual ideas belonging to the family-complex and incestuous object-choice is made use of in representing the highest ethical and religious interests of man—that is, they have illuminated an important instance of the sublimation of the erotic instinctual forces and of their transformation into trends which can no longer be called erotic. This was in complete harmony with all the expectations of psycho-analysis, and would have agreed very well with the view that in dreams and neurosis a regressive dissolution of this sublimation, as of all others, becomes visible. But the world would have risen in indignation and protested that ethics and religion were being sexualized. Now I cannot refrain from thinking teleologically [1] for once and concluding that these discoverers were not equal to meeting such a storm of indignation. Perhaps it even began to rage in their own bosoms. The theological prehistory of so many of the Swiss throws no less light on their attitude to psycho-analysis than does Adler's socialist prehistory on the development of his psychology. One is reminded of Mark Twain's famous story of all the things that happened to his watch and of his concluding words: "And he used to wonder what became of all the unsuccessful tinkers, and gunsmiths, and shoemakers, and blacksmiths; but nobody could ever tell him." ' [2]

All the way through this important book one gets the feel-

[1] This was a point of disagreement between Freud and Jung's school, which criticized him for reasoning too exclusively in a 'causal' way and neglecting the 'ends' to which human behaviour naturally tends. For the Swiss school the neurosis itself had a finality which the therapist had to take into account.

[2] Ibid., pp. 60–1.

ing that Freud himself was very angry at having to descend to polemics. Although he forced himself to be calm and fair, he did not always succeed in hiding his bitterness. The fact is that Jung's defection, even more than Adler's, came as such a blow that in 1914 he did not know whether psychoanalysis would ever recover completely. He nevertheless concluded on an optimistic note, less, it would seem, to express his own certainty than to maintain law and order in his own ranks:

'Some people may be inclined to fear that this secession is bound to have more momentous consequences for analysis than would another, owing to its having been started by men who have played so great a part in the movement and have done so much to advance it. I do not share this apprehension.

'Men are strong so long as they represent a strong idea; they become powerless when they oppose it. Psycho-analysis will survive this loss and gain new adherents in place of these. In conclusion, I can only express a wish that fortune may grant an agreeable upward journey to all those who have found their stay in the underworld of psycho-analysis too uncomfortable for their taste. The rest of us, I hope, will be permitted without hindrance to carry through to their conclusion our labours in the depths.'[1]

[1] Ibid., p. 66.

20

THE CLINICAL WORKS

In *Leonardo da Vinci and a Memory of his Childhood* Freud explains the painter's strange destiny as a conflict, largely unconscious, between art and science from which art emerged not victorious but to some extent denied and destroyed. One naturally tends to think this was an allusion to his own case, since Freud often analyses himself through the great figures he takes as his subject and could, in fact, see a parallel conflict at the very root of his own work.

In the case of Freud, who was and had always wanted to be a scientist, the conflict had naturally been much weaker. He did not have two equally clear and declared vocations. On the one hand he pursued a scientific ideal of strict truth which he had set himself in his youth; on the other he felt a need to express himself aesthetically, to give free rein to the imagination which his background, training and probably powerful inner inhibitions had led him to repress very early in his life. Freud naturally put science first, feeling that he had a real vocation for it.

He declared, perhaps more frequently than he realized, that he had no skill in the prestige domain of artistic creation, into which he was drawn only by the necessities of research. But his insistent denials on this point, his obvious longing for the novelist's or poet's gifts are good enough reasons for thinking that art was something to which he always remained sensitive,[1] rather like an old sorrow. Sentiments of this kind find expression in a veiled form in all his books and an echo of them is to be heard in a letter to Arthur Schnitzler, the Viennese author whose work created a scandal rather like Freud's and who later became a personal friend:

'For many years I have been conscious of the far-reaching conformity existing between your opinions and mine on

[1] Cf. letters to Fliess on *The Interpretation of Dreams*, chap. 9.

many psychological and erotic problems; and recently I even found the courage expressly to emphasize this conformity (*Fragment of an Analysis of a Case of Hysteria,* 1905). I have often asked myself in astonishment how you came by this or that piece of secret knowledge which I had acquired by a painstaking investigation of the subject, and I finally came to the point of envying the author whom hitherto I had admired.

'Now you may imagine how pleased and elated I felt on reading that you too have derived inspiration from my writings. I am almost sorry to think that I had to reach the age of 50 before hearing something so flattering.' [1]

We shall return later to this unavowed conflict, which Freud perhaps thought he should not admit and which he resolved by an original compromise between literature and science, allying the truth demanded by his work with the imaginative and stylistic gifts he knew he possessed but which he never dared to claim completely. His judgement on his own writing depended largely on how far this compromise was possible. In view of the nature of his work it could not always be equally successful and so he often felt dissatisfied. In a general way his preferences were for the books in which the literary qualities were easy to appreciate, even by a public unfamiliar with his ideas. Thus he thought his book on Jensen's novel *Gradiva* was graceful; and, probably because he felt them to be very successful from a literary point of view, he liked his studies of Leonardo da Vinci and Michelangelo's Moses although, out of a feeling of timidity which his detractors would never have believed of him, he did not at first have the courage to publish *Moses* under his own name. On the other hand, as we have seen, he severely criticized the heaviness and clumsiness of certain passages in *The Interpretation of Dreams* in which the synthesis of his two main requirements seemed to him to have failed.

Freud probably experienced less of the sheer joy of writing in his purely theoretical work than in his clinical studies and in that very large section of his output which he jokingly said did not belong to the psychoanalytical metropolis but to its distant colonies. His finest work is, in fact, what he wrote about Leonardo da Vinci, Goethe and Shakespeare, Michelangelo's Moses and, at the very end of

[1] May 8, 1906, *Letters,* p. 251.

his life, about the Biblical Moses. In them he is truly the writer whom the most famous men of his day were happy to honour by awarding him the Goethe Prize, a high literary distinction which was to compensate for the injustice shown by scientific circles. And it justifies what Einstein, another great scientist who was also an artist, wrote about his whole work in a letter to Freud:

'I thank you warmly for sending me your new work, which has naturally interested me greatly. I had already read your two essays in *Imago*, which Dr Klopstock, a physician friend, had brought me. Your idea that Moses was a distinguished Egyptian and a member of the priestly caste has much to be said for it, also what you say about the ritual of circumcision.

'I quite specially admire your achievement, as I do with all your writings, from a literary point of view. I do not know any contemporary who has presented his subject in the German language in such a masterly fashion. I have always regretted that for a non-expert, who has no experience with patients, it is hardly possible to form a judgement about the finality of the conclusions in your writings. But after all this is so with all scientific achievements. One must be glad when one is able to grasp the structure of the thoughts expressed. . . .'[1]

While Freud was highly flattered, he was perhaps angered even more by Einstein's praise, for however keen he was to write well, literary success was not his main aim and could not console him for not being understood. The fact remains that the quality of his writing gained him a large following among educated people who otherwise would have discovered his ideas only with great difficulty or more slowly.

Freud's skill as a writer, offering the reader what he calls in his psychology a 'pleasure premium', shows best in those works where theoretical considerations are worked into a story round a central figure whose features are gradually disclosed by analysis. This applies to the case histories which Freud transcribed from his experience after the *Studies on Hysteria*, some of them forming the first textbook for students in all psychoanalytical institutes. The heroes of these histories—Dora, little Hans, the Rat

[1] Ernest Jones, III, p. 243.

Man, Schreber, the Wolf Man—are known and commonly cited along with the most famous characters of romantic literature. And rightly so, for Freud portrayed them with the human warmth and understanding which mark the true novelist and which appear all too infrequently in psychiatric treatises. If literature and psychoanalysis have anything in common it is undoubtedly this intense power of identification, thanks to which Freud's patients have become profoundly moving people, who are still living and true.

Not all the five people concerned were Freud's patients. Little Hans had been psychoanalysed by his own father. President Schreber had had nothing to do with psychoanalysis and Freud only knew him through the astonishing book he had written about his illness seven years earlier. The only one who had undergone a long analysis was the Wolf Man, so named because of his famous dream about the seven wolves which enabled Freud to study a serious infantile neurosis after the event. The Wolf Man excited such interest in psychoanalytical circles that he became inordinately arrogant: in the course of a relapse he claimed to be Freud's favourite son, his heir and the only one of Freud's patients to have had his case history published.

Apart from their clinical value, *Schreber* and *The Wolf Man* are of special interest as they reflect the evolution of Freud's thought at a time when the conflicts we have mentioned obliged him both to extend the field of his interests and maintain the unity of his movement. In 1910 Jung had introduced him to Schreber's autobiography, published under the title of *Memoirs of a Neuropath.* It was therefore under his pupil's influence that Freud first entered the domain of psychiatry proper by tackling the insurmountable problems raised by psychoses, schizophrenia and paranoia. But Jung had his own ideas about Schreber's case which Freud's analysis failed to corroborate. Jung even let something of this disagreement appear in *Symbols of the Libido,* which was published at almost the same time. Although still half hidden, that was the first serious difference to arise between the two men, at least over their scientific ideas.

Schreber, however, was not polemical in character. In 1911 Freud believed it was still possible to iron out the difficulties which arose with the Swiss psychiatrists from time to time on various points of doctrine. This is not true of *The Wolf Man* which was planned and written in 1914–15, that is, after the two main rebels had left the movement, and which Freud could use as an argument against the two rival and henceforward independent schools. Having, thanks to the famous dream about the wolves, had the chance to re-create the infantile neurosis from which the adult patient had suffered, Freud thought he would be able to annihilate the violent attacks made by Jung and Adler against his etiology of neuroses. The main burden of his proof rested on the all-important fact that the patient had not dreamed his dream during his treatment but at the age of four, after his grandfather had told him the story of the Wolf and the Tailor, one of the many Grimms' tales in which a wolf appears.

This memory, which the patient illustrated with a drawing, appeared especially convincing as it fitted in with other biographical facts. A few years later, however, Otto Rank questioned its accuracy, suggesting that Freud, by taking the wolf dream for a childhood dream when it had undoubtedly been dreamed during the patient's analysis, had been either dishonest or credulous. Thus the case of the Wolf Man, written with a polemical intention, itself became the subject of later disputes and was involved in a new split.

To study the Schreber case Freud had only the *Memoirs* which the patient had published himself, omitting almost all personal antecedents or detailed biographical data. In 1885 Schreber had left Professor Flechsig's psychiatric clinic in Leipzig completely cured, and full of gratitude and affection for his doctor. His trouble, apparently neurotic, had been described as hypochondria.

Nine years later, shortly after being appointed President of the Dresden Court of Appeal, Schreber fell ill again, this time much more seriously. He received six months' treatment and recovered his health, except for one or two fixed delusions to which he still clung. In spite of the pressures put on him he had insisted on publishing his *Memoirs*, putting forward reasons which Freud accepted to justify his own publication:

'It is possible that Dr Schreber may still be living to-day and that he may have dissociated himself so far from the delusional system which he put forward in 1903 as to be pained by these notes upon his book. In so far, however, as he still retains his identity with his former personality, I can rely upon the arguments with which he himself—"a man of superior mental gifts and endowed with an unusual keenness alike of intellect and of observation." [1]—countered the efforts that were made to restrain him from publishing his memoirs: "I have been at no pains", he writes, "to close my eyes to the difficulties that would appear to lie in the path of publication, and in particular to the problem of paying due regard to the susceptibilities of certain persons still living. On the other hand, I am of opinion that it might well be to the advantage both of science and of the recognition of religious truths if, during my life-time, qualified authorities were enabled to undertake some examination of my body and to hold some enquiry into my personal experiences. To this consideration all feelings of a personal character must yield." . . . "I trust", he says, "that even in the case of Prof. Dr Flechsig any personal susceptibilities that he may feel will be outweighed by a scientific interest in the subject-matter of my memoirs." . . .' [2]

Schreber was a paranoiac and what excited the psychiatrists in his case was the number of his delusions of persecution and grandeur and the rare penetration with which he traced their history. Here again, Freud found that the psychiatrists' astonishment was not the real starting-point for understanding the case. Convinced that the mind's strangest and most absurd manifestations originate in the natural processes of psychic life, Freud undertook to find out why and how Schreber, who was otherwise a man of sound mind and perfectly capable of performing his high office, had undergone such an astounding transformation.

Freud had given a great deal of attention to paranoia fifteen years before, and he said its secret had been revealed to him by Fliess at the time of their friendship. This secret, now a piece of standard psychoanalytic knowledge, is that paranoia is intimately bound up with repressed homosexuality. Schreber, whose delusion revolved mainly round the idea of his transformation into a woman and his rape by his persecutor, Professor Flechsig, was obviously the best possible subject to furnish proof of this.

Schreber's illness, which had recurred soon after his appointment as President of the Dresden Court of Appeal,

[1] This self-portrait of Schreber, which is extremely accurate, appears on page 35 of his book.

[2] 'The Case of Schreber', *Std Edn,* XII, p. 10.

had two distinct phases. In the first, he imagined himself to be the victim of horrible homosexual assaults by Flechsig, who soon had God Himself for an accomplice; in the second, he accepted his fate with blissful resignation, while God took the place of Flechsig and the delusion was organized round a profusion of religious ideas and a complicated cosmogony. Finally, Schreber believed himself to be the female saviour of the world, destined to renew the world by begetting a new race of superior human beings.

In connection with the formation of the symptoms of delusion, Freud shows the most striking feature to be the phenomenon of *projection*. Projection consists in the subject's feeling a previously repressed inner perception in which the content has undergone a certain distortion to be a perception coming from outside. Feeling is reversed: what should be felt internally as love is perceived externally as hatred. In fact, experience shows that in paranoiac delusion, the persecutor is always a person to whom the patient was previously much attached. Flechsig's alleged hatred of Schreber was merely the reversal of Schreber's unconscious love for his doctor and, through him, for Dr Schreber, his own father.

Love is the central point of this dangerous illness and appears outwardly in the form of jealousy and hatred. Directed towards a person of the same sex, it is scandalous and unacceptable. The four forms of delusion to which it gives rise are only rather formal ways of denying it or at the very least of contradicting its main proposition.

Freud set out these transformations of the paranoiac libido which engender the most surprising fantasies in a famous formula.[1] Everything happens, he said, as though the known forms of paranoia were all led back in different ways to contradict a single proposition: 'I, a man, love him, a man.' The delusion of persecution loudly proclaims: 'I do not love him. I hate him'; then, by projection: 'He hates me and persecutes me, which justifies the hatred I feel for him.' The delusion of the erotomaniac who believes himself to be loved and pursued by the other person's love attacks another element of the outrageous proposition. It says: 'It is not he that I love, it is *she* that I love—*because she loves me.*' Another form of contradiction is provided by the delusion of jealousy, which says: 'It is not I who love the man, it is *she* who loves him.'

[1] Ibid., pp. 60 ff.

Finally, the delusion of grandeur finds an even more radical form of contradiction: it says: 'I do not love anything or anybody.' But since the libido must be directed to some object, the proposition becomes: 'I only love myself.' This explains the fantastic sexual overestimation of the Ego which is at the root of megalomania.

Lack of biographical data prevented Freud from going deeply into President Schreber's relations with his father, who was obviously originally the coveted and hated love object. All that is known is that Dr Schreber was a physician, which allowed him, like Flechsig, to play his role of God as both saviour and murderer. In this connection Freud draws attention to a striking feature of paranoia which, he says, *divides* whereas hysteria *condenses*. In hysteria, each symptom is the result of a condensation of feelings about various people loved by the subject. In paranoia, every feeling is susceptible of embodiment in many different forms, each one appearing as a distinct delusion. For Schreber the persecutor is divided into Flechsig and God, then Flechsig himself is divided into a higher and lower Flechsig, just as God is divided into God on earth and God in Heaven. All these figures are the doubles of an important and identical relationship, like those to be found in myths, legends and polytheistic religions, in which the gods embody the multiple feelings and wishes of the faithful in various forms. Schreber's delusion, which mixes together a mythology, a cosmogony, an apocalypse and a prophecy in an inextricable confusion, functions in exactly the same way as the mind's highest products.

The case of *The Wolf Man* is just as remarkable as President Schreber's, although its difficulties and gravity are of another kind. When this patient came to consult Freud he was a young Russian aged twenty-two, the son of a lawyer who owned land in Odessa and left his son an immense fortune. An extremely serious neurosis rendered him incapable of solving even the simplest problems of living. He had to have a doctor and a servant with him wherever he went as he was incapable of doing anything himself, even dressing. He had gone to Germany for treatment, had been in several private hospitals and consulted famous psychiatrists such as Ziehen and Kraepelin, but all to no avail. In despair, the young man had gone back to Russia, where another doctor inspired him with new courage. And while travelling to Switzerland to make another attempt to get better, he and his doctor stopped in Vienna where they chanced to hear about Freud and went to ask his help.

This case, which had defeated the most eminent specialists, was of exceptional difficulty. Freud did not relate it *in extenso* for two reasons. First, to give a complete account of an analysis extending over several years is an almost impossible task because of the richness and the inevitable chaos of the material; second, the patient was very well known in Vienna and although he insisted on his case being published complete Freud could not take the responsibility of revealing all the details of the treatment. On the other hand, he wanted to make use of the providential case to refute certain ideas advanced by Adler and Jung, who were inclined to replace the infantile sexual traumas responsible for the adult's neurosis by later pathogenic factors, for example those produced by the various cultural variations and influences. If the Wolf Man had really had his first neurotic troubles at the age of four, he made nonsense of the idea of a late etiology. Freud therefore concentrated on the study of the infantile neurosis and obtained unexpected material, which he personally considered to be staggering:

'A third peculiarity of the analysis which is to be described in these pages has only increased my difficulty in deciding to make a report upon it. On the whole its results have coincided in the most satisfactory manner with our previous knowledge or have been easily embodied into it. Many details, however, seemed to me myself to be so extraordinary and incredible that I felt some hesitation in asking other people to believe them. I requested the patient to make the strictest criticism of his recollections, but he found nothing improbable in his statements and adhered closely to them. Readers may at all events rest assured that I myself am only reporting what I came upon as an independent experience, uninfluenced by my expectation. So that there was nothing left for me but to remember the wise saying that there are more things in heaven and earth than are dreamed of in our philosophy. Anyone who could succeed in eliminating his pre-existing convictions even more thoroughly could no doubt discover even more such things. . . .' [1]

[1] 'History of an Infantile Neurosis', *Std Edn,* XVII, p. 12.

One gets the feeling that while writing this case history Freud could not dispel from his mind certain doubts about many vital points which were, however, confirmed later by many similar cases, Two letters mentioned by Ernest Jones reveal the strange way he interpreted this state of mind: he related it to the doubts which had assailed him as early as November 1914 about an Austrian victory and the outcome of the World War.

The first analysis of the Wolf Man—there were four in all, two with Freud and twelve years later two more with one of his pupils, Ruth Mack Brunswick—lasted four years and most of that time got nowhere. Not knowing how to overcome his patient's stubborn resistance, Freud decided on an exceptional technical measure, which brought almost immediate success.

'The patient . . . remained for a long time unassailably entrenched behind an attitude of obliging apathy. He listened, understood, and remained unapproachable. His unimpeachable intelligence was, as it were, cut off from the instinctual forces which governed his behaviour in the few relations of life that remained to him. It required a long education to induce him to take an independent share in the work; and when as a result of this exertion he began for the first time to feel relief, he immediately gave up working in order to avoid any further changes, and in order to remain comfortably in the situation which had been thus established. His shrinking from a self-sufficient existence was so great as to outweigh all the vexations of his illness. Only one way was to be found of overcoming it. I was obliged to wait until his attachment to myself had become strong enough to counterbalance this shrinking, and then played off this one factor against the other. I determined—but not until trustworthy signs had led me to judge that the right moment had come—that the treatment must be brought to an end at a particular fixed date, no matter how far it had advanced. I was resolved to keep to the date; and eventually the patient came to see that I was in earnest. Under the inexorable pressure of this fixed limit his resistance and his fixation to the illness gave way, and now in a disproportionately short time the analysis produced all the material which made it possible to clear up his inhibitions and remove his symptoms. All the information, too, which enabled me to understand his infantile neurosis is derived from this last period of the work, during which resistance temporarily disappeared and the patient gave an impression of lucidity which is usually attainable only in hypnosis. . . .'[1]

The major part of this material is the dream about the wolves which had inaugurated for the patient, at the age of four, a period of anxiety and phobia, the object being the wolves. Freud had already reported this dream elsewhere, in a paper on fairy-tale elements in dreams.[2] He told it again unchanged:

'I dreamt that it was night and that I was lying in my bed. (My bed stood with its foot towards the window; in front of the window there was a row of old walnut trees. I know it was winter when I had the dream, and night-time.) Suddenly the window opened of its own accord, and I was terrified to see that some white wolves were sitting on the big walnut tree in front of the window. There were six or seven of them. The wolves were quite white, and looked more like foxes or sheep-dogs, for they had big tails like foxes and they had their ears pricked like dogs when they pay attention to something. In great terror, evidently of being eaten up by the wolves, I screamed and woke up. My nurse hurried to my bed, to see what had happened to me. It took quite a long while before I was convinced that it had only been a dream; I had had such a clear and life-like picture of the window opening and the wolves sitting on the tree. At last I grew quieter, felt as though I had escaped from some danger, and went to sleep again.

'The only piece of action in the dream was the opening of the window; for the wolves sat quite still and without making any movement on the branches of the tree, to the right and left of the trunk, and looked at me. It seemed as though they had riveted their whole attention upon me.—I think this was my first anxiety-dream. I was three, four, or at most five years old at the time. From then until my eleventh or twelfth year I was always afraid of seeing something terrible in my dreams. . . .'[3]

The patient made a drawing of his dream, showing not six or seven, but five white wolves staring in front of them

[1] Ibid., p. 12.

[2] 'Fairy Tales in Dreams', *Std Edn,* XII, pp. 283.

[3] 'History of an Infantile Neurosis', *Std Edn,* XVII, p. 29.

and looking like dogs. The dream had been related at the very beginning of the treatment. It took Freud and his patient several years to unravel its meaning. In the end the patient understood it by comparing it to Little Red Riding Hood, the Wolf and the Seven Little Goats and the Grimms' fairy tale in which the tailor cuts off a wolf's tail, all stories he had read or heard in circumstances which he remembered in detail. In conformity with its usual rule, the dream had completely reversed the basic thought. The wolves' long tails signified the absence of tails, in other words castration; the fixed, attentive look came not from the wolves but from the little dreamer himself, and their terrifying immobility signified the strange movement which the child had chanced to see one winter's night, doubtless in the very distant past—a movement which had terrified him at the time and still terrified him. The analysis allowed of the reconstruction of the agonizing sight which the child had witnessed in his earliest childhood, when he was about eighteen months old, and which ever since has been called the 'primal scene' in psychoanalytic literature: this was the copulation of his parents, an act beyond his understanding at the time and the source of that archaic fear of the wolf or the ogre which is common to many fairy tales and myths. The 'primal scene' in this case was not an actual memory, but a reconstruction which the convergence of many details made extremely plausible. Remembering his recent mistake about the precocious seduction of hysterics, Freud wondered whether it concealed a genuine experience or was merely the patient's fantasy. He concluded that in either case the role played by the scene in the genesis of the neurosis would have been the same.

Just as Schreber had led Freud to compare paranoia to certain mythological creations (he had created a sun myth which was surprisingly like the one to be found in primitive religions), so the Wolf Man enabled him to discover profound analogies between dreams and the themes of universal folklore which nourish the child mind in all ages. At this time Freud also began to turn his attention to the history of religions and the problems of mythology (Otto Rank's special field) which, even in 1912, had raised insurmountable differences between him and Jung. This new line of research culminated in 1913 in the publication of *Totem and Taboo,* one of his most important and certainly one of his most provocative books in the second half of his work.

Since Freud, many other books have been written about Schreber's *Memoirs* and interest in them has still not been exhausted. As for the Wolf Man, the singularity and richness of his pathological history, the risks of his different treatments, Freud's gratitude to him for everything he had learned, and finally the tragedy of his personal life all made him a case apart in the annals of psychoanalysis, and he became almost an historical character. After his first course of treatment he had gone back to Russia completely recovered psychically and able to face up to the difficulties of life. He lost his vast fortune in the Bolshevik Revolution and was reduced to the direst poverty. In 1919 he managed to escape and returned to Vienna. Not only did Freud treat him for nothing, he also organized regular collections among his colleagues and pupils, enabling the Wolf Man and his wife, who was also ill, to subsist for six years in starving, post-war Vienna. In 1926 the patient, who had twice been saved by Freud's affection and generosity, suffered a grave relapse which necessitated renewed treatment. Whereas he was previously affected by an obsessional neurosis, he now suffered from a paranoiac psychosis, in which his homosexual attachment to his first analyst, which had not been 'liquidated' and had even been intensified by Freud's gifts and material help, found a new and dangerous outlet. He came under the care of one of Freud's pupils, Ruth Brunswick, who treated him several times and published a number of studies which enriched our knowledge of the case.[1] Her last paper appeared in 1940, when the Wolf Man seemed to be enjoying perfect health. After the last war other psychoanalysts had the opportunity to meet him and reported their interviews. Ernest Jones, who was still corresponding regularly with him in 1956, affirmed that his letters contained many things about Freud's technique and personality that were true and instructive, and unknown to his followers.

[1] R. Mack Brunswick: 'A Supplement to Freud's "History of an Infantile Neurosis",' *Int. J. Psycho-Anal.*, 9, p. 439.

21

FREUD AND LITERATURE

When one considers Freud's deep interest in literature, which is so obvious from the wealth of allusion and the quotations which crop up everywhere in his writings and even invade his letters and his dreams, one might expect him to have devoted a large number of books to this subject. But this is not the case. The type of literary analysis which he instituted and which, until very recently, enjoyed an extraordinary vogue in psychoanalytical circles, is represented in his complete works only by four fairly short studies, plus, it is true, a few vital pages on literary creation and the problems of language. The volume of his work along these lines is in no way commensurate with the importance and the originality of his ideas: it indicates perhaps one of those inner conflicts which Freud described in *The Interpretation of Dreams* and, in a sphere where he felt rather like an interloper, resolved by means of a compromise.

Unlike his most brilliant pupils, who took either the personality of an author, or a work as a whole, or vast domains like mythology and folklore as the object of analysis, Freud concerned himself only with works and writers who in some way revealed to him some aspect of himself at a given moment. While writers like Jung, Otto Rank, Theodor Reik, Karl Abraham or Ernest Jones applied to literature solid psychoanalytic knowledge which was usually deployed with much understanding and skill, Freud wrote his essays on literature as he had written *The Interpretation of Dreams* or *The Psychopathology of Everyday Life*—while carrying out his own analysis.

This explains why Freud did not write psychoanalytical monographs like the one Ernest Jones did on Hamlet, Marie Bonaparte on Edgar Allan Poe or René Laforgue on Baudelaire. Freud discusses only what fascinated him in the course of his reading and with which he identified himself closely enough to give him some right to make the analysis. Naturally, his choice was dictated by his personal preferences: it even happened, as in his study of *King Lear*, for example, that this was connected with an event in his own life.

Freud's first literary study deals with Wilhelm Jensen's *Gradiva*, a charming novel which, in his eyes, had at least two merits. First, it was constructed entirely on the hero's delusion and his dreams, in other words on oneirical data invented by the author. Freud found it tempting to interpret the artificial delusion and dreams as he would have analysed spontaneous nocturnal dreams. The results were surprising and naturally went to fill in the many gaps in the plot which the author had left to heighten the fantasy. Once again the Freudian dream key proved to be a master key which unlocked secret doors and hidden drawers.

The other merit of *Gradiva* concerned the hero's vocation. An archaeologist by profession, he of course shared Freud's passion for antiquities and bringing the past to light. Freud had long realized that his own love of antiquities was a kind of double of his psychological activity. Young Norbert, engrossed to the point of hallucination in the childhood of mankind just as he was the prisoner of his own childhood, provided Freud with graceful confirmation of his idea.

Dr Norbert Hanold had admired among a collection of Roman antiquities a bas-relief, which had made an extraordinary impression on him. A cast of this bas-relief, which is of a date and origin unknown to him, hangs prominently in his study and whenever he contemplates it he falls into a strange reverie.

'The sculpture represented a fully-grown girl stepping along, with her flowing dress a little pulled up so as to reveal her sandalled feet. One foot rested squarely on the ground; the other, lifted from the ground in the act of following after, touched it only with the tips of the toes, while the sole and heel rose almost perpendicularly. It was probably the unusual and peculiarly charming gait thus presented that attracted the sculptor's notice and that still, after so many centuries, riveted the eyes of its archaeological admirer. . . .'[1]

Norbert is fascinated by the walk of the stone girl, whom he calls Gradiva—the girl walking forward. And this man,

[1] *Delusions and Dreams in Jensen's 'Gradiva', Std Edn*, IX, p. 10.

who is not interested in women, is even unaware of their existence, goes out into the streets to examine their feet and assure himself that Gradiva's unusual step can be reproduced by living women. However, his observation does not settle the problem. Shortly afterwards he has a terrible dream in which he is transported to ancient Pompeii, in the year 79, that is to say when Vesuvius has erupted and is about to engulf the city. There he suddenly sees Gradiva standing before him and unaware of the imminent catastrophe. He then has the idea, which is decisive for his delusion, that Gradiva was a young woman of Pompeii, that she was living in her native city and, without knowing it, at the same time as he. Before he can do anything to warn her, Gradiva lies down on the portico of the temple and falls asleep until she is buried by a shower of ashes.

The young man's delusion is carried over into waking life and Gradiva appears before him really alive, amid the ruins of Pompeii, which he is visiting. Her appearance makes him believe that at noon, the hour when phantoms appear, ancient Pompeii begins to live again as it was before it was engulfed. He speaks to the girl, in Greek naturally, but Gradiva answers with a smile: 'If you want to talk to me you must speak German.'

Nevertheless, the young man remains a prisoner of his delusion. Gradiva then decides to cure him. First she enters his dream, then gradually leads him back to reality, using methods which bear a strong resemblance to those employed in an analytic treatment. Finally, Norbert recognizes in Gradiva a pretty neighbour, Zoe Bertgang, who was also his childhood playmate and from whose love he had been fleeing without knowing it. By demonstrating to him that his feelings for the stone woman were really his feelings for the living woman, the shrewd Gradiva has broken the circle of the delusion.

The themes in *Gradiva* seem to be conceived expressly to give brilliant confirmation of *The Interpretation of Dreams* and the theory of the unconscious. Freud elucidates them with the skill of a detective, but also with visible tact and amusement. He reconstructs Norbert's life, his infantile love for his playmate, then the repression which led him to become a fetishist (he is what psychiatrists call a 'foot fetishist') and finally sever his ties with the real world, mainly with women and love. The whole of Freud's analysis is done with a lightness of touch and clarity which has earned it a well-deserved fame. It concludes with a number of observations on a functional analogy between psychoanalysis and the novel:

'Our procedure consists in the conscious observation of abnormal mental processes in other people so as to be able to elicit and announce their laws. The author no doubt proceeds differently. He directs his attention to the unconscious in his own mind, he listens to its possible developments and lends them artistic expression instead of suppressing them by conscious criticism. Thus he experiences from himself what we learn from others—the laws which the activities of this unconscious must obey. But he need not state these laws, nor even be clearly aware of them; as a result of the tolerance of his intelligence, they are incorporated within his creations. We discover these laws by analysing his writings just as we find them from cases of real illness; but the conclusion seems inescapable that either both of us, the writer and the doctor, have misunderstood the unconscious in the same way, or we have both understood it correctly. This conclusion is of great value to us, and it is on its account that it has been worth while to investigate by the methods of medical psychoanalysis the way in which the formation and the cure of the delusions as well as the dreams are represented in Jensen's *Gradiva.*' [1]

Gradiva had appeared in 1903, Freud's study in 1906, which no doubt brought Wilhelm Jensen unexpected fame. Freud, desirous as always to verify his results by biographical data, wrote to the elderly poet with a request for precise details about his life. On May 15, 1907, Freud read his reply to the members of the Vienna Society and a few days later wrote a brief account for Jung's benefit:

'What Jensen himself has to say? He wrote very warmly about it. In his first letter he expressed his pleasure, etc., and declared that the analysis agreed in all important points with the purpose of the story. Of course he wasn't referring to our theory, since as an old gentleman he seems altogether incapable of entering into any other but his own poetic intentions. He suggested the agreement could be ascribed to poetic intuition, and partly perhaps to his early medical studies. Then in a second letter I became

[1] Ibid., p. 92.

indiscreet and asked for information about the subjective share of the work, where the material came from, where his own person is hidden, etc. I now learned from him that the antique relief actually exists, that he possesses a reproduction of it, but has never seen the original. It was he himself who invented the story of the relief representing a woman from Pompeii; it was he too who loved to day-dream in the noon heat of Pompeii, where he once experienced an almost visionary state. Otherwise he knows nothing about the origin of the subject-matter; the beginning suddenly occurred to him while he was working on something else, whereupon he dropped everything, started to write it down, never hesitated, found all the material as though it had been waiting for him, and finished it in one spurt. All of which suggests that a continued analysis would lead through his childhood to his own most intimate erotic experiences. So the whole thing is once again an egocentric phantasy.'[1]

Some time later Jung came across three other novels by Jensen and an analysis of these enabled him to advance more precise hypotheses. Jung was sure that, as a child, Jensen must have been devoted to a little girl, perhaps his sister, who had disappointed and grieved him. This child had perhaps been afflicted by a physical infirmity which the writer had probably recalled and at the same time denied by inventing Gradiva's graceful walk. Questioned by Freud on this point, Jensen, who did not answer the query about the physical defect, said he had not had a sister but, as a child, had been passionately in love with a little girl who was brought up with him and who died of tuberculosis at the age of eighteen. A long time afterwards he had fallen in love with a girl who reminded him of the other one and who died suddenly in the full bloom of youth.

Gradiva led Freud to study more thoroughly the analogies he had always seen to exist between dreams and literary creation and which, several years before, had suggested the analysis of Conrad Ferdinand Meyer's *Die Richterin* as well as the famous passages in *The Interpretation of Dreams* in which he dealt with *Hamlet* and *Oedipus Rex*. In 1907 he wrote a short essay entitled *Creative Writers and Day Dreaming*,[2] and he talked about these ideas to a

[1] To Jung, May 26, 1907, *Letters*, pp. 252-3.

[2] *Creative Writers and Day Dreaming, Std Edn* IX, pp. 143 ff.

group of writers at his publisher's. Unlike his other lectures, this improvisation was warmly received and he took this to be a good augury for the future relations between psychoanalysis and his new 'colony'. It is true that in that essay he confined himself to generalities, not yet tackling the intimate analyses of the authors and the works which were soon to draw down on him once again the charge of sacrilege. Bourgeois opinion and academic circles might, understandably, be alarmed by his method, but writers, at least the more sincere and clear-sighted of them, had really very little reason to be shocked.

In point of fact the essay brings out very clearly Freud's extraordinary respect for art and artists. By virtue of an excessive, rather naïve regard for literature, which he shared with the bourgeoisie of his day, Freud looked on the creator in this realm as a mysterious, almost divine being, endowed with superhuman power, wonderful and incomprehensible, however hard one tried to penetrate his secret. In all his writing about literature he keeps saying that analysis leaves off where art begins and that while it can contribute much towards a profound knowledge of the human soul by throwing light on its finest achievements, it has absolutely nothing to say about inspiration, which remains the unique and inexplicable sign of the artist.

One can well imagine that in laying hands on Goethe and Shakespeare—albeit lightly and reverently—he felt rather sacrilegious but found that his very fervour gave him the strength he needed to overcome his scruples. His study on *The Theme of the Three Caskets* [1] in Shakespeare is hardly psychoanalytical. It is imbued with a delicacy and melancholy which must satisfy even the most fanatical devotees of the bard. And he thought about *A Childhood Recollection from 'Dichtung und Wahrheit'* [2] for several years before he published it, in 1917, as he was anxious not to assert anything which was not confirmed by the clinical facts. His conclusion only adds to the Olympian's glory.

Shakespeare gives the theme of the three caskets a comic treatment in *The Merchant of Venice* and a tragic treatment in *King Lear*. Freud discovers a relationship with the many folk and mythological stories in which the hero is faced with a choice between three women, three

[1] *The Theme of the Three Caskets, Std Edn,* XII, pp. 291 ff.

[2] *A Childhood Recollection from 'Dichtung und Wahrheit', Std Edn,* XVII.

embodiments of love, the primitive meaning being the Moirai, the goddesses of Death. After studying this reversal of meaning by giving numerous examples, Freud comes back to King Lear:

'So far we have been following out the myth and its transformation, and it is to be hoped that we have correctly indicated the hidden causes of the transformation. We may now turn our interest to the way in which the dramatist has made use of the theme. We get an impression that a reduction of the theme to the original myth is being carried out in his work, so that we once more have a sense of the moving significance which had been weakened by the distortion. It is by means of this reduction of the distortion, this partial return to the original, that the dramatist achieves his more profound effect upon us. . . .

'Lear is an old man. It is for this reason, as we have already said, that the three sisters appear as his daughters. The relationship of a father to his children, which might be a fruitful source of many dramatic situations, is not turned to further account in the play. But Lear is not only an old man: he is a dying man. In this way the extraordinary premise of the division of his inheritance loses all its strangeness. But the doomed man is not willing to renounce the love of women; he insists on hearing how much he is loved. Let us now recall the moving final scene, one of the culminating points of tragedy in modern drama. Lear carries Cordelia's dead body on to the stage. Cordelia is Death. If we reverse the situation it becomes intelligible and familiar to us. She is the Death-goddess who, like the Valkyrie in German mythology, carries away the dead hero from the battlefield. Eternal wisdom, clothed in the primaeval myth, bids the old man renounce love, choose death and make friends with the necessity of dying.

'The dramatist brings us nearer to the ancient theme by representing the man who makes the choice between the three sisters as aged and dying. The regressive revision which he has thus applied to the myth, distorted as it was by wishful transformation, allows us enough glimpses of its original meaning to enable us perhaps to reach as well a superficial allegorical interpretation of the three female figures in the theme. We might argue that what is represented here are the three inevitable relations that a man has with a woman—the woman who bears him, the woman who is his mate and the woman who destroys him; or that they are the three forms taken by the figure of the mother in the course of a man's life—the mother herself, the beloved one who is chosen after her pattern, and lastly the Mother Earth who receives him once more. But it is in vain that an old man yearns for the love of woman as he had it first from his mother; the third of the Fates alone, the silent Goddess of Death, will take him into her arms.'[1] This splendid passage is—without appearing to be—a confession in which Freud, although still only fifty-seven, identifies himself with the old and dying King.[2] Like Lear, he is haunted by the thought of death; like him he has three daughters, one about to marry, between whom he has already chosen; his Cordelia, whom he also called his Antigone, is Anna, his youngest daughter who was to look after him devotedly every moment for sixteen years and whose love did, in fact, help him to die.

A Childhood Recollection from 'Dichtung und Wahrheit'[3] has very little connection with literature. It is a purely psychoanalytical study, based on an episode in *Dichtung und Wahrheit* in which Goethe remembers himself, as a young child, throwing his parents' china out of the window. By comparing the birth dates of Goethe's brothers and sisters, Freud was able to interpret this apparently meaningless gesture as an aggressive reaction to the birth of a brother, a reaction he had already encountered in the case of little Hans and, it will be remembered, in his own analysis. Nevertheless, the hypothesis seemed doubtful to him for a long time, and it was only after his pupils sent him many similar examples that he decided to publish the study.

Freud's last literary study is devoted to Dostoevsky or, to be more precise, to the subject of parricide as treated by the Russian novelist in *The Brothers Karamazov* and in many other of his books. In itself, such an analysis was not of particular interest and in this case, where parricide is paraded and described with disconcerting frankness, there was not much to reveal. Freud, however, drew some

[1] *The Theme of the Three Caskets, Std Edn,* XII, pp. 300-1.

[2] Letter to Ferenczi, July 7, 1913: 'My closest companion will be my little daughter, who is developing very well at the moment (you will long ago have guessed the subjective condition for the theme "Three Caskets").'

[3] *A Childhood Recollection from 'Dichtung und Wahrheit,' Std Edn,* XVII, pp. 145 ff.

interesting deductions about the novelist's personality, his passion for gambling and above all, his epilepsy, which Freud suggests is more a form of hysteria. The most remarkable part is where he describes the different forms of moral sense, Dostoevsky providing the example. Freud is clearly shocked that a writer of genius whom he ranks with the very greatest, could have degraded himself by sinking to servile conformism and dully reactionary ideas. The temper of the whole work is in sharp contrast to his usual neutrality and one senses that his admiration is disturbed by something deep of which he cannot speak.[1] He wrote about this to Theodor Reik who, in a long criticism on the essay, had noted this state of mind:

'You are right in supposing that really I don't like Dostoevsky in spite of all my admiration for his intensity and superiority. That is because my patience with pathological natures is drained away in actual analyses. In art and in life I am intolerant of them. That is a personal characteristic of my own, which needn't hold good with other people.'[2]

These occasional works of literary criticism represent only one aspect of Freud's connection with literature. To do the subject justice we should have to speak again about the books he loved,[3] his contacts with writers and the way literature itself repaid his interest.

We should also need to evoke the unique movement which he started and which, grouped round the review

[1] 'Dostoevsky and Parricide,' *Std Edn* XXI, pp. 187–8.

[2] Theodor Reik: *Freud als Kulturkritiker,* 1930, Ernest Jones, III, pp. 426–7.

[3] Freud read and admired the classics in particular (Goethe was his great man). He frequently expressed his dislike and incomprehension of *avant-garde* literature and art. Thus he wrote to Pfister, June 21, 1930: 'I began reading your little book about Expressionism with as much interest as aversion, and finished it at a sitting . . . And I kept saying to myself: What a decent chap this Pfister is, benevolent and incapable of the slightest injustice; you cannot compare with him, but how pleasant that you can give your approval to everything he discovers in his own way. For I think you ought to know that in actual life I am terribly intolerant of cranks, that I see only their harmful side and that as far as these "artists" are concerned, I am definitely one of the philistines you go for . . .' The same attitude is found in Freud's letter to Stefan Zweig, July 20, 1938, where he describes the surrealists as 'absolute cranks' (let us say 95 per cent, like alcohol)'.

Imago, has produced a mass of books, some exciting, others of doubtful value, from which literary criticism has profited more or less unwittingly. By creating a new genre in which literature was for the first time subjected to scientific treatment, Freud was undoubtedly basing it on universal examples of intense human interest. He achieved much more and if our ideas about literature, the writer's position and task have undergone such radical changes, he is one of those who have done most to bring this about.

Less spectacular but of great importance for research is Freud's work in the neighbouring sector of linguistics, which has only recently been followed up. For the inventor of a therapeutic method in which speech is the only instrument that can be used, the study of language was obviously a matter of fundamental interest and Freud was well aware of this. But he lacked any specialist knowledge, and not having the time to acquire it he dared not venture too deeply into such a remote domain. Inspired by his inexhaustible reflections about dreams and rather haphazard reading, his linguistic work could be no more than sketchy or, more exactly, an incentive to research. Apart from a few remarks on the sacred tetragram of the Hebrews (*Significance of Sequences of Vowels*[1]), it is concentrated almost entirely in a few pages, the idea having been suggested to him by a work by Karl Abel on primitive languages. This is Freud's little essay entitled *The Antithetical Meaning of Primal Words*[2] which a whole group of French psychoanalysts have for several years used as a basis for research.

Abel taught Freud that what he had observed so many times in dreams—namely that in oneirical language one thing can mean both itself and its opposite—was a feature common to the languages of the most ancient cultures which, like dreams, saw nothing absurd about that. This coincidence came at a very opportune moment to corroborate his views. It constitutes the central theme of the article, which abounds in quotations from Abel's treatise:

'I did not succeed in understanding the dream-work's singular tendency to disregard negation and to employ the same means of representation for expressing contraries until I happened by chance to read a work by the philologist

[1] *Std Edn*, XII, p. 341.

[2] *Std Edn*, XI, pp. 155 ff.

Karl Abel, which was published in 1884 as a separate pamphlet and included in the following year in the author's *Sprachwissenschaftliche Abhandlungen* [Philological Essays]. The subject is of sufficient interest to justify my quoting here the full text of the crucial passages in Abel's paper (omitting, however, most of the examples). We obtain from them the astonishing information that the behaviour of the dream-work which I have just described is identical with the peculiarity in the oldest languages known to us.

'After stressing the antiquity of the Egyptian language which must have been developed a very long time before the first hieroglyphic inscriptions, Abel goes on (1884, 4):

' "Now in the Egyptian language, this sole relic of a primitive world, there are a fair number of words with two meanings, one of which is the exact opposite of the other. Let us suppose, if such an obvious piece of nonsense can be imagined, that in German the word 'strong' meant both 'strong' and 'weak'; that in Berlin the noun 'light' was used to mean both 'light' and 'darkness'; that one Munich citizen called beer 'beer', while another used the same word to speak of water: this is what the astonishing practice amounts to which the ancient Egyptians regularly followed in their language. How could anyone be blamed for shaking his head in disbelief? . . ." '[1]

In view of the high level of Egyptian culture, Abel easily dismisses the idea that this absurdity is due to inferior intellectual development. It seems much rather to be deliberate, as is proved by other bizarre forms in which it appears:

'Of all the eccentricities of the Egyptian vocabulary perhaps the most extraordinary feature is that, quite apart from the words that combine antithetical meanings, it possesses other compound words in which two vocables of antithetical meanings are united so as to form a compound which bears the meaning of only one of its two constituents. Thus in this extraordinary language there are not only words meaning equally "strong" or "weak", and "command" or "obey"; but there are also compounds like "old-young", "far-near", "bind-sever", "outside-inside" . . . which, in spite of combining the extremes of

[1] *Std Edn,* XI, pp. 155–6.

difference, mean only "young", "near", "bind" and "inside" respectively . . . So that in these compound words contradictory concepts have been quite intentionally combined, not in order to produce a third concept, as occasionally happens in Chinese, but only in order to use the compound to express the meaning of one of its contradictory parts—a part which would have had the same meaning by itself . . .'[1]

Abel then wonders whether this characteristic of the Egyptian language was not also shared by the Semitic and Indo-European languages. From the latter Freud picks out examples which allow him to think that this is the case:

'In Latin "*altus*" means "high" and "deep", "*sacer*" "sacred" and "accursed"; here accordingly we have the complete antithesis in meaning without any modification of the sound of the word. Phonetic alteration to distinguish contraries is illustrated by examples like "*clamare*" ("to cry") —"*clam*" ("softly", secretly") "*siccus*" ("dry"—"*succus*" ("juice"). In German "*Boden*" ["garret" or "ground"] still means the highest as well as the lowest thing in the house. Our "*bös*" ("bad") is matched by a word "*bass*" ("good"); in Old Saxon "*bat*" ("good") corresponds to the English "bad", and the English "to lock" to the German "*Lücke*", "*Loch*" ["hole"]. We can compare the German "*kleben*" ["to stick"] with the English "to cleave" ([in the sense of] "to split"); the German words "*stumm*" ["dumb"] and "*Stimme*" ["voice"], and so on. In this way perhaps even the much derided derivation *lucus a non lucendo* would have some sense in it.

'In his essay on "The Origin of Language" Abel (1885, 305) calls attention to further traces of ancient difficulties in thinking. Even to-day the Englishman in order to express "*ohne*" says "without" ("*mitohne*" ["with-without"] in German), and the East Prussian does the same. The word "with" itself, which to-day corresponds to the German "*mit*", originally meant "without" as well as "with", as can be recognized from "withdraw" and "withhold". The same transformation can be seen in the German "*wider*" ("against") and "*wieder*" ("together with").

'For comparison with the dream-work there is another extremely strange characteristic of the ancient Egyptian

[1] Ibid., p. 157.

language which is significant. "In Egyptian, words can—apparently, we will say to begin with—*reverse their sound as well as their sense.* Let us suppose that the German word "*gut*" ["good"] was Egyptian; it could then mean 'bad' as well as 'good', and be pronounced 'tug' as well as 'gut'. Numerous examples of such reversals of sound, which are too frequent to be explained as chance occurrences, can be produced from the Aryan and Semitic languages as well. Confining ourselves in the first instance to Germanic languages we may note: *Topf* [pot]—pot; boat—tub; wait—*täuwen* [tarry]; hurry—*Ruhe* [rest]; care—reck; *Balken* [beam]—*Klobe* [log], club. If we take the other Indo-Germanic languages into consideration, the number of relevant instances grows accordingly; for example, *capere* [Latin for 'take']—*packen* [German for 'seize']; *ren* [Latin for 'kidney']—*Niere* [German for 'kidney']; leaf—*folium* [Latin for 'leaf]; *dum-a* [Russian for 'thought,], *θυμός* [Greek for 'spirit', 'courage']—*mêdh, mûdha* (Sanscrit for 'mind'], *Mut* [German for 'courage']; *rauchen* [German for 'to smoke']—*Kur-it* [Russian for 'to smoke']; *kreischen* [German for 'to shriek']—to shriek, etc."

'Abel tries to explain the phenomenon of reversal of sound as a doubling or reduplication of the root. Here we should find some difficulty in following the philologist. We remember in this connection how fond children are of playing at reversing the sound of words and how frequently the dream-work makes use of a reversal of the representational material for various purposes. (Here it is no longer letters but images whose order is reversed.) We should therefore be more inclined to derive reversal of sound from a factor of deeper origin.'[1]

We shall see that Freud assumed, with infinite modesty, the role of pioneer forced on him by the very logic of his work. Very few of his pupils showed his caution and his sense of proportion and very few fully understood the classical cast of his mind. Seen from outside, his incursions into the territory of other scientific disciplines often seemed misplaced and attracted much criticism. We shall later have an opportunity to see that he did everything possible to give them a pattern, at the risk of appearing too timorous for the liking of some of his followers and too fanciful for the liking of the public.

[1] Ibid., pp. 159–61.

22

FREUD AND ART

We have said that Freud's literary studies were partly inspired by the need for self-knowledge that also lies at the root of *The Interpretation of Dreams* and gives the crucial passages in Freud's books all the significance of a discreet personal confession. What attracted Freud in Jensen's *Gradiva* was, of course, the oneirical theme, and, more secretly, the opportunity it offered him to analyse his intense love for archaeology and the past. If he chose the incident of the smashing of the china from Goethe's autobiography it was because of the existence of profound analogies between his own and Goethe's childhood. He, too, had wished for the death of a new-born brother and that, too, had been granted in such a way that he had always been his mother's favourite. And if he was more taken by the theme of the three caskets than by any other of the countless subjects for thought to be found in Shakespeare it was less for theoretical reasons than because he had discovered in the theme singular affinities with his own intimate feelings. In every case Freud started from the extreme subjectivity which is the first step in psychoanalytic knowledge and which, by very reason of its radicalism, gives research something of the power of poetry.

It is the same with his writing on art, which reflects not only the theoretical interest of the psychologist, but also the passion of a man perpetually beset by questions and capable of living intensely the torment of his own spirit through other people. When he is writing about Leonardo da Vinci Freud is still speaking, in a whisper, about himself. He confesses to the reader the insatiable intellectual curiosity which he had in common with the painter and of which he felt it his duty, as the founder of a new science, to rediscover the deep underlying causes. In the same way the thing that fascinates him in the legendary figure of Michelangelo's Moses is the debate, which he himself knows so well, between the violent emotions and their opposite and the way the hero, fiery and dominating like himself, subdues the storms that rage within himself.

But for the personal experience which he regarded as giving him some right to speak, Freud would undoubtedly have been incapable of rising above the level of dilettantism in the highly complex matter of art. There is evidence that he felt scruples of this kind about his *Moses of Michelangelo* since he agreed to put his name to the essay only because of his pupils' repeated insistence and then only after a lapse of several years. The plastic arts did not, in fact, offer him even the neighbourly intercourse which literature, through the medium of language anyway, normally maintained with psychoanalysis. They formed a strictly defined cultural domain which was jealously guarded, to exclude amateurs of all kinds, among whom he was bound to count himself. His acquaintance with the works of art he was going to discuss was only that of an average amateur who was extremely sensitive to their beauty but who had a very limited knowledge and lacked the special equipment that would have made his task easier. It was sheer madness to venture into such a territory, as he perceived from the storm of indignant protest which greeted his *Leonardo* and even from the alarm shown by some of his followers.

Once again it is necessary to refer back to his time to understand this almost universal reaction to the Freudian conception of man. For the vast majority, who felt and thought in accordance with the ready-made standards inherited from the previous century, one thing stood inviolable amidst the social, political and philosophical vicissitudes of the age: that was what is called a scale of values, with a clear, distinct top and bottom, the two separated by the great gulf which history and culture set between the body and the soul as well as between the social classes. Spiritual and moral creations of all kinds, the beautiful, the good, the sublime formed the top. The body and its appetites, hunger, love, bare necessity made up the bottom. This part could aspire to rise, provided it first denied or destroyed itself. The top was completely isolated: it created and judged but, by its very nature, was ignorant of what was happening in the lowest reaches.

About 1910 this schema, which was the upper classes' exclusive source of inspiration, at least for writing and speech, had long since ceased to be a norm or a true measure. The great demolition work of the preceding century had really destroyed nothing: it had only shown up the true state of the edifice, of which the apparently well-preserved and highly ornate super-structure was in fact already crumbling. Marx, Darwin, Nietzsche, Stirner, Kropotkin, to name only the most powerful wreckers, had shaken the ideological façade so severely that the top and the bottom were in danger of reversing their roles and thereby mutually denying one another. Humiliated by the discovery of its origins, taxed with illegality or impotence, accused of theft or lying, the top saved itself temporarily by taking refuge in those regions in which it had been least compromised—in art, beauty and in the sublimity of aesthetics.

The Freudian revolution dealt the final blow to this conception of values to which the general public clung all the more tenaciously as it was utterly doomed. Yet this revolution helped to bring about the reversal by making a contribution of its own. It did not say that the noble products of religion, ethics, art and philosophy have no right to the worship accorded them: it confined itself to asserting, but in a categorical way, that the top and the bottom spring from the same source, that they are impelled by exactly the same energy and that however imposing it may be, the top is never anything other than the sublimation of the lowest instincts. This filiation, which explained the precarious, adventurous and moving character of all human civilization, could have been understood as a new attestation of nobility. It was not. The people of Germany and Central Europe, who were, however, soon to be summoned to plunge into a very different sort of abyss, were horrified, as though they were the victims of a diabolical slander.

This was quite stupid and most unjust, as Freud (a point that had been made repeatedly, even at the risk of over-stressing it) in many ways remained a petit-bourgeois, distinguished only by his heroic thirst for knowledge and his integrity of mind. For him, as for all who identified him with the devil, art was unquestionably the last depositary of the sacred, perhaps one of the few things which a reasonable man might still worship. But even the sacred could not impose silence on him. Man magnified by his own creation, he still saw as man; and he had to go back over all man's tracks in order slowly to re-create the road along which man had advanced. When he was sure of the accuracy of his re-creation, he had the feeling that however trivial and disillusioning it might appear to minds infatuated with the idea of nobility, his truth was still a genuine homage to genius.

Actually it is impossible to imagine anything more delicate, more respectful, more sensitive to human endeavour than *Leonardo da Vinci and a Memory of his Childhood*[1] which, in 1910, stirred up such bitter controversy, even in certain psychoanalytical circles, and is today rightly considered to be a German literary classic. In it Freud tackled the problem of the origins of the thirst for knowledge, a thirst which, according to him, explains the Master's strange attitude towards his own achievements and the fate that befell his work. Proceeding step by step, with a meticulousness and a logic which take every possible objection into account, he retraces the artist's progress towards science which, originally, was meant merely to serve his art:

'. . . He directed his efforts to the properties and laws of light, colours, shadows and perspective in order to ensure mastery in the imitation of nature and to point the same way to others. It is probable that at that time he already overrated the value to the artist of these branches of knowledge. Still constantly following the lead given by the requirements of his painting he was then driven to investigate the painter's subjects, animals and plants, and the proportions of the human body, and passing from their exterior, to proceed to gain a knowledge of their internal structure and their vital functions, which indeed also find expression in their appearance and have a claim to be depicted in art. And finally the instinct, which had become overwhelming, swept him away until the connection with the demands of his art was severed, so that he discovered the general laws of mechanics and divined the history of the stratification and fossilization in the Arno valley, and until he could enter in large letters in his book the discovery: *Il sole non si muove*. His investigations extended to practically every branch of natural science, and in every single one he was a discoverer or at least a prophet and pioneer. Yet his urge for knowledge was always directed to the external world; something kept him far away from the investigation of the human mind. In the "Academia

[1] *Leonardo da Vinci and a Memory of his Childhood, Std Edn*, XI, pp. 63 ff.

Vinciana", for which he drew some cleverly intertwined emblems, there was little room for psychology.'[1]

This last remark reminds us that Freud, who was also passionately interested in natural science, had not sacrificed the study of nature for the study of man without a struggle. Meditating over his own case undoubtedly enabled him to discover at the heart of the painter's scientific activity the fundamental question regarding the source from which all intellectual knowledge springs.

The obsession for investigation, which in Leonardo to a considerable extent obstructed the full flowering of his art, is explained by the facts of infantile sexuality on which Freud based his theory in the *Three Essays*. It originated in a predominant tendency to curiosity which, in the painter's early childhood, was directed exclusively to the mysteries of sexuality and was afterwards put at the service of the intellect, while still retaining the restless, insatiable and excessive form characteristic of its origin. This curiosity, diverted from its object by premature repression, is susceptible of developments which vary with the individual concerned. In Leonardo's case, Freud perceives three such developments, which exhaust all the possible courses open to him.

In fact it either shares the fate of repressed sexuality, with the result that the intelligence cannot range freely, but is fettered for the rest of life; or else sexual curiosity is stifled but is powerful enough to sexualize thought, with the result that mental activity then becomes a source of pleasure or anxiety, just like sexuality itself. In that case intellectual speculation develops an obsessive character, for it is like the speculations of the child mind, which is by nature inconclusive and never-ending. The third case is the rarest and the purest. In this instance there is neither inhibition nor obsession, but a precocious sublimation of the libido which, escaping from repression, immediately reinforces the already powerful instinct for research. There are no signs of neurosis and the intellect, detached from the primitive data of infantile investigation, can freely devote itself to its interests and develop all its faculties—except on one point, that of the sexuality which was proscribed by the very conditions of its development.

'If we reflect on the concurrence in Leonardo of his over-

[1] Ibid., pp. 76–7.

powerful instinct for research and the atrophy of his sexual life (which was restricted to what is called ideal [sublimated] homosexuality) we shall be disposed to claim him as a model instance for our third type. The core of his nature, and the secret of it, would appear to be that after his curiosity had been activated in infancy in the service of sexual interests he succeeded in sublimating the greater part of his libido into an urge for research. But it is not easy, to be sure, to prove that this view is right. To do so we should need some picture of his mental development in the first years of his childhood, and it seems foolish to hope for material of that sort when the accounts of his life are so meagre and so unreliable, and when moreover it is a question of information about circumstances that escape the attention of observers even in relation to people of our own generation. . . .'[1]

Freud, however, discovered a definite fact about Leonardo's childhood in one of his scientific works. The painter is writing about the flight of the vulture and breaks off to evoke a childhood memory which is, in an odd way, connected with his subject:

'It seems that I was always destined to be so deeply concerned with vultures; for I recall as one of my very earliest memories that while I was in my cradle a vulture came down to me, and opened my mouth with its tail, and struck me many times with its tail against my lips.'[2]

From this one fantasy—which is easily translated into erotic terms, the word 'tail' being the equivalent of *membrum virile* in Italian as in all languages—Freud reconstitutes one by one all the elements in the precocious drama and its painful consequences which the adult painter both suffered and exploited. With the help of these few lines, which were disdained by Leonardo's biographers and unknown to the art critics, he throws dazzling light on all the unusual features of the Master's life, on his interest in bird flight and his dream of human flight as well as on his relations with his pupils, his excessive liking for toys and the enigmatic smile which he gave to so many of his figures.

Freud's proof, which fits in with the known biographical

[1] Ibid., pp. 80–1.
[2] Ibid., p. 82.

facts, is based on this fantasy about the vulture, which Freud also found in many superstitious or mythological beliefs. In Egyptian mythology the vulture is a maternal divinity possessing a male attribute, and is consequently the prototype of what psychoanalysts call a 'phallic mother'. For the Fathers of the Church it serves as a natural proof of the dogma of the Immaculate Conception, for it is believed to be able to fertilize itself. Freud discovers it to be the image of the painter's mother, that young peasant girl whose passionate and excessive caresses had sealed the child's fate.

An illegitimate, abandoned child who was then taken back by his father; removed at a very tender age from a young mother who, after being his whole world of love, vanished completely from his life, giving way to a step-mother who was full of tenderness and love, the more so for being herself childless, Leonardo painted motherhood as he had known it in his earliest childhood, with the ambiguity and, literally, the double face whose haunting memory Freud discovered in the disturbing composition of 'Saint Anne'.

'Leonardo's childhood was remarkable in precisely the same way as this picture. He had had two mothers: first, his true mother Caterina, from whom he was torn away when he was between three and five, and then a young and tender step-mother, his father's wife, Donna Albiera. By his combining this fact about his childhood with the one mentioned above (the presence of his mother and grandmother) and by his condensing them into a composite unity, the design of "St Anne with Two Others" took shape for him. The maternal figure that is further away from the boy—the grandmother—corresponds to the earlier and true mother, Caterina, in its appearance and in its special relation to the boy. The artist seems to have used the blissful smile of St Anne to disavow and to cloak the envy which the unfortunate woman felt when she was forced to give up her son to her better-born rival, as she had once given up his father as well. . . .' [1]

That explains the peculiar defect in composition which has so often perplexed the critics. Anne and the Virgin are not, in fact, clearly distinguished: they are almost com-

[1] Ibid., pp. 113–4.

pletely fused, like two dream figures whose condensation is imperfect. The fact is that the painter merged into one single person the two mothers of his childhood, but gave to the real one the smile which she perhaps actually had and which, belonging to both the adolescents and the women in his pictures, is rightly considered to be indefinable.

'We thus find a confirmation in another of Leonardo's works of our suspicion that the smile of Mona Lisa del Giocondo had awakened in him as a grown man the memory of the mother of his earliest childhood. From that time onward, madonnas and aristocratic ladies were depicted in Italian painting humbly bowing their heads and smiling the strange, blissful smile of Caterina, the poor peasant girl who had brought into the world the splendid son who was destined to paint, to search and to suffer. . . . For his mother's tenderness was fateful for him; it determined his destiny and the privations that were in store for him. The violence of the caresses, to which his phantasy of the vulture points, was only too natural. In her love for her child the poor forsaken mother had to give vent to all her memories of the caresses she had enjoyed as well as her longing for new ones; and she was forced to do so not only to compensate herself for having no husband, but also to compensate her child for having no father to fondle him. So, like all unsatisfied mothers, she took her little son in place of her husband, and by the too early maturing of his erotism robbed him of a part of his masculinity. . . .'[1]

Here Freud comes to the point in his analysis which caused the greatest outcry—the painter's latent homosexuality, which Freud's contemporaries took, probably mistakenly, for a declared inversion. As a result of an exclusive infantile attachment, Leonardo had proscribed all women, then identified himself with the androgynous figure who dominated his earliest fantasies, so that his amorous choice fell on the very object his mother had loved and caressed—the young boy, a fascinating image in which he rediscovered both his own features and the traces of maternal love. However, an absolute fidelity to the original image ensured that this tendency remained purely ideal. Therefore the painter's inversion materialized only in his art, through

[1] Ibid., pp. 114–7.

the inexplicable smile he places on the lips of his adolescents:

'When, in the prime of life, Leonardo once more encountered the smile of bliss and rapture which had once played on his mother's lips as she fondled him, he had for long been under the dominance of an inhibition which forbade him ever again to desire such caresses from the lips of women. But he had become a painter, and therefore he strove to reproduce the smile with his brush, giving it to all his pictures (whether he in fact executed them himself or had them done by his pupils under his direction). These pictures breathe a mystical air into whose secret one dares not penetrate; at the very most one can attempt to establish their connection with Leonardo's earlier creations. The figures are still androgynous, but no longer in the sense of the vulture-phantasy. They are beautiful youths of feminine delicacy and with effeminate forms; they do not cast their eyes down, but gaze into mysterious triumph, as if they knew of a great achievement of happiness, about which silence must be kept. The familiar smile of fascination leads one to guess that it is a secret of love. It is possible that in these figures Leonardo has denied the unhappiness of his erotic life and has triumphed over it in his art, by representing the wishes of the boy, infatuated with his mother, as fulfilled in this blissful union of the male and female natures. . . .'[1]

The conclusion of this admirable essay, in which feeling and thought fire one another without the argument losing any of its coherence, brings the discussion on to the problem of psychical determinism, about which Freud had long made up his mind. Is there any ground, he asks, for indignation that so much influence on man's fate should be attributed to the sheer chance of parental constellation, by making Leonardo's fate, for example, dependent on his illegitimate birth and his step-mother's sterility?

'I think one has no right to do so. If one considers chance to be unworthy of determining our fate, it is simply a relapse into the pious view of the Universe which Leonardo himself was on the way to overcoming when he wrote that the sun does not move. We naturally feel hurt that a just God and a kindly providence do not protect us

[1] Ibid., pp. 117–8.

better from such influences during the most defenceless period of our lives. At the same time we are all too ready to forget that in fact everything to do with our life is chance, from our origin out of the meeting of spermatozoon and ovum onwards—chance which nevertheless has a share in the law and necessity of nature, and which merely lacks any connection with our wishes and illusions. The apportioning of the determining factors of our life between the "necessities" of our constitution and the "chances" of our childhood may still be uncertain in detail; but in general it is no longer possible to doubt the importance precisely of the first years of our childhood. We all still show too little respect for Nature which (in the obscure words of Leonardo which recall Hamlet's lines) "is full of countless causes [*'ragioni'*] that never enter experience".

'Every one of us human beings corresponds to one of the countless experiments in which these *ragioni* of nature force their way into experience.' [1]

Freud's study of Leonardo is, in its way, an act of piety and love to the Mother who, like Nature, to which Freud finally dedicated his work, both saves and destroys her favourite sons. In this respect it forms a perfect contrast to his study of Michelangelo's Moses,[2] which deals exclusively with the father, to the extent that the person of the artist disappears, to the almost total benefit of his subject. The true hero of this essay which, strictly speaking, does not belong to psychoanalytical literature, is not Michelangelo but Moses, the awe-inspiring Biblical Moses who brought men and law and, with it, the terrible promise and threat of manly achievement. While waiting to vie with the giant whose Law he endeavours to re-write, Freud contemplates him with admiration and fear, no longer as an analyst clothed with authority, but with all the curiosity, love and secret envy of a son.

As mentioned earlier, Freud for a long time refused to put his name to these pages which, seeing that they had very little connection with psychoanalysis, were, however, far less compromising than others and too cautious to annoy the specialists. He explained this reserve by his incompetence in matters of art, but his Leonardo study, written four years earlier, is good enough proof that this

[1] Ibid., p. 137.

[2] *The Moses of Michelangelo, Std Edn,* XIII.

scruple was not insurmountable. One wonders, therefore, whether there were not more profound reasons and whether, for example, he did not find it repugnant to show publicly this reversal of the situation which put him in the place of the son, but this time without the excuse that it was a theoretical necessity. Was it not by way of dropping a hint that he wrote to Ernest Jones: 'Why should I wrong Moses by coupling my name with his?' [1] What is more, there is nothing psychoanalytical about the work. It arises out of a detail in a sculpture which Freud compares with the whole work in order to infer the psychological meaning. And before venturing on a systematic analysis of the prophet, he waited until almost the very end of his life.

There can be no doubt that the overwhelming figure of Moses occupied an immense place in the mind of Freud, who knew the Bible very well and could not fail to feel the prophet as a grand embodiment of paternal law, perhaps the most striking and the most absolute embodiment of paternal law in history. This omnipotent and eternal image explains the strange power of attraction exerted on him by Michelangelo's sculpture, which he went to see on his first visit to Rome, in 1901, and saw again with the same exaltation every time he returned to the city. In his essay he describes the intense feelings which the sight of the statue inspired in him:

'It always delights me to read an appreciative sentence about this statue, such as that it is "the crown of modern sculpture" (Grimm [1900, 189]). For no one piece of statuary has ever made a stronger impression on me than this. How often have I mounted the steep steps from the unlovely Corso Cavour to the lonely piazza where the deserted church stands, and have essayed to support the angry scorn of the hero's glance! Sometimes I have crept cautiously out of the half-gloom of the interior as though I myself belonged to the mob upon whom his eye is turned—the mob which can hold fast no conviction, which has neither faith nor patience, and which rejoices when it has regained its illusory idols.' [2]

And a little farther on, seeking to find out if Moses, as

[1] Ernest Jones, Vol. II.

[2] *The Moses of Michelangelo*, *Std Edn*, XIII, p. 213.

some critics insist, is sculpted just as he is about to leap and smash the Tables, Freud recalls his hope or his imaginary fear of seeing the stone come to life:

'And indeed, I can recollect my own disillusionment when, during my first visits to San Pietro in Vincoli, I used to sit down in front of the statue in the expectation that I should now see how it would start up on its raised foot, dash the Tables of the Law to the ground and let fly its wrath. Nothing of the kind happened. Instead, the stone image became more and more transfixed, an almost oppressively solemn calm emanated from it, and I was obliged to realize that something was represented here that could stay without change; that this Moses would remain sitting like this in his wrath for ever. . . .'[1]

Was it to liberate himself from this eternity that Freud tried to rediscover the hero's hypothetical movement at the very moment when he was transmuted into stone? In any case a powerful motive must have been at work for him to devote two years to an essay only a few pages long. When he was in Rome in 1912 he went to see Moses every day. Then he plunged into the task of reading everything that had been written on the subject. Ernest Jones tells of the alternating moods of faith and doubt which he experienced and which even drove him to give up work on his essay for several months:

'At that time I sent him photographs from Florence of two statues in the Duomo there, one of which, by Donatello, was supposed to have provided Michelangelo with the stimulus for his great work. This shook Freud badly, since it opened the possibility of the reason for the pose being a purely artistic one without any special ideational significance. I then sent him two photographs from Rome, and at his request had some also specially taken of the lower edge of the Tables.

'Nothing further happened for nearly a year, probably because of his doubts about the correctness of his interpretation. . . .'[2]

It is in order to elucidate the reasons for his own fascina-

[1] Ibid., pp. 220–1.

[2] Ernest Jones, II, p. 365.

tion that Freud concentrates on the study of the statue. What is so enigmatic about the figure? First, what does it represent? Apart from a few unambiguous features, writers are not agreed on its significance and Freud carefully points out their surprising differences of opinion. As always he finds the gist of his argument in refuting the observations of others, comparing all the facts and details supposedly acquired with the real thing. Thus it is generally said that Moses' hand is plunged in or playing in his long, flowing beard and that, with his right arm, he is holding the Tables which are beginning to slip from him. Freud, on the contrary, proves that the Titan is pressing into his beard with his index finger only and that the Tables, which actually overturned a moment before, are now solidly fixed together. By co-ordinating the relationships between the right arm, the beard and the Tables, he reconstructs the history of an inner impulse which culminated not in the explosion of wrath described in the Bible story but in a formidable, super-human act of self-mastery. Once again, the patient detection of a half-hidden reality reveals to Freud not some future event, but the past.

'For the Moses we have reconstructed will neither leap up nor cast the Tables from him. What we see before us is not the inception of a violent action but the remains of a movement that has already taken place. In his first transport of fury, Moses desired to act, to spring up and take vengeance and forget the Tables; but he has overcome the temptation, and he will now remain seated and still, in his frozen wrath and in his pain mingled with contempt. Nor will he throw away the Tables so that they will break on the stones, for it is on their especial account that he has controlled his anger; it was to preserve them that he kept his passion in check. In giving way to his rage and indignation, he had to neglect the Tables, and the hand which upheld them was withdrawn. They began to slide down and were in danger of being broken. This brought him to himself. He remembered his mission and for its sake renounced an indulgence of his feelings. His hand returned and saved the unsupported Tables before they had actually fallen to the ground. In this attitude he remained immobilized, and in this attitude Michelangelo has portrayed him as the guardian of the tomb. . . . In this way he has added something new and more than human to the figure of Moses; so that the giant frame with its tremendous physical power becomes only a concrete expression of the highest mental achievement that is possible in a man, that of struggling successfully against an inward passion for the sake of a cause to which he has devoted himself. . . .'[1]

The Moses of Michelangelo appeared in February 1914 in the review *Imago* with the following amusing editorial note: 'The editors did not refuse to accept this article, which does not strictly come within their province, because the author, who is known to them, is in close touch with psychoanalytical circles and because his way of thinking shows a certain analogy with the methods of psychoanalysis.'

Freud only gave up his anonymity ten years later, in 1924, that is, when the first edition of his complete works was published. Meanwhile, he, too, had been disowned by a part of his 'people' and, as he wrote to Ferenczi, he had been afraid that in those violent crises in which his 'law' was in danger of being destroyed, he had sometimes been more like the intractable Biblical hero than Michelangelo's superman.[2] Be that as it may, it was another quarter of a century before he had done with Moses.

[1] *The Moses of Michelangelo, Std Edn,* XIII, pp. 229–30.

[2] Letter to Ferenczi, October 17, 1912, Ernest Jones, II, p, 367. At the moment the situation in Vienna (the break with Stekel) makes me feel more like the historical Moses than the Michelangelo one . . .'

23

TOTEM AND TABOO

There is no sphere in which Freud risked his scientific reputation more than that of religious psychology, into which he ventured on several occasions, drawn by intellectual curiosity as well as by the logic of his research. *Totem and Taboo*,[1] *The Future of an Illusion*[2] and *Moses and Monotheism*[3] were the three main moments in this compromising adventure which, considered inadmissible even by those it concerned—believers, theologians and anthropologists—lost him a body of supporters and is still a thorny problem for a certain group of psychoanalysts.

Freud was a confirmed atheist and, as mentioned earlier, his adolescent convictions were sometimes expressed in rather theatrical ways, being clearly a reaction against the religious education he received in his youth. Jakob Freud, his father, was not a religious man as understood by strict, practising Jews, but he still cared for the Bible and it was from him that Freud had acquired the intimate knowledge of the book which has left so many traces on his work. His toleration and humanist ideas may also have enabled his son to become an unbeliever without going through the agonies of serious inner crises and helped him to convert faith into an intellectual interest in religious questions.

It seems likely that Freud's knowledge of Jewish ritualism partly suggested the ideas he expressed as early as 1907 in *Obsessive Actions and Religious Practices*,[4] in which he compares certain individual and collective actions in religious ceremonies with what is called the 'ceremonial of the obsessed'. Whether it originates in an obsessional neurosis or legitimate religious customs, the ritual

1 *Std Edn*, XIII.

2 *Std Edn*, XXI.

3 *Std Edn*, XXIII.

4 *The Future of an Illusion:* Obsessive Actions and Religious Practices, *Std Edn*, XXI.

act springs from an inner constraint, a *compulsion* which is tinged with fear of a misfortune or punishment following the omission or the incorrect execution of the rite. The idea of an imperative urge which must be satisfied on pain of automatic punishment is the same in both cases: but for the obsessed person it remains strictly individual and is only performed by himself, whereas the believer shares it with the whole body of the faithful. Common to both actions is a strong, unconscious feeling of guilt. They differ, however, in that in one case it is mainly the sexual tendencies which are repressed and in the other the egoistic and aggressive tendencies dangerous to society. Freud sums up the difference by saying that if the obsessional neurotic seems to make something like a religion just for his own personal use, religion can be described as an obsessional neurosis affecting the general mass of people.

This article by no means exhausted the question. Freud did not pursue the idea as might have been expected, by investigating, for example, the psychogenesis of the great historic religions or of the mythologies of antiquity, fields in which he was not without knowledge. For many different reasons, one perhaps concerned with Jung's virtuosity in the analysis of myths and religious symbols, he sought to find connections in the most obscure and most fascinating sector of anthropology—totemism.

Freud's taste for this subject, which was then all the rage and something quite new in psychoanalytic literature, found much to satisfy it in Frazer's monumental work, *Totemism and Exogamy,* which was published in four large volumes in 1910 and created a sensation in learned circles. Freud immediately found something he knew about in the mass of facts which Frazer reported about totemic cults and the strange links these implied or created between man and animal. He had met parallels in infantile phobias connected with the motiveless fear of an animal, as in the case of little Hans, for instance, who in many respects treated the horse as primitive man treated his totem. Was the animal phobia, which, in cases reported by Abraham and Ferenczi, was sometimes linked with a tree or some inanimate object, the psychical model of this astounding conception of the world in which anthropology then saw the origin of all existing human cultures? The question was obviously worth asking in connection with the genesis and psychogenesis of religions.

As was his habit, Freud plunged impatiently into reading the specialized works on the subject. Ernest Jones, who was knowledgeable in anthropological matters, seems to have been his technical adviser. He sent Freud the important books but his list was not exhaustive and Freud consulted writers working along similar lines, quite oblivious to the fact that the very notion of totemism, so severely attacked since, was already being questioned. Also, his indispensable preparatory work both excited and exasperated him. As at the time of *The Interpretation of Dreams,* he grew impatient at having to absorb so much indigestible literature before expounding his own ideas. Two months after he began compiling his material, in 1911, he wrote to Ferenczi:

'I am not pleased with anything here, and am in that bodily and mental state to which I am accustomed during intensive inner work—or, rather, the preparation for such. It is a kind of misery; I am rarely productive when I feel well. I read and read and it ferments. Whether it will come to anything I don't know.'[1]

A letter written to Ernest Jones the same day expresses the same impatience:

'There are a great many things boiling in my head, but they are very slow to come out, and I always find it hard to conform completely to another's thoughts. I cannot do everything myself, and the contributions of others, say Jung for example, are of the highest importance. . . . I am working hard on the psychogenesis of religion, finding myself on the same track with Jung's "Wandlungen". . . .'[2]

In January 1912 he finished the first section on the 'Horror of Incest' among primitive peoples. The following month he informed Jones of the general plan of the essay: 'My contribution "Inzestscheu" is by no means famous, but the next two articles may prove much better. The second is entitled "Tabu and Ambivalenz" and will I hope show up the essence of that marvellous "taboo"; it is half written and all finished in thought. The third is not yet shaped in a definite form; it will bear the name: Die

[1] Letter to Ferenczi, November 5, 1911, Ernest Jones, II, p. 352.
[2] Ernest Jones, ibid., pp. 351–2.

Magie und die Allmacht der Gedanken. These three papers I conceive as forerunners of another more important one which intends to proclaim "Die infantile Wiederkehr des Totemismus". I have got all the books you indicated to me: Crawley, Bourke, (Scatalogical Rites), Hartland, (Paternity), Pearson, (Grammar of Science), so I need not trouble you for sending me one of these from Toronto. I am now even in possession of the Encyclopedia Britannica. . . .'[1]

In April 1913 he began the fourth section, 'The Infantile Return of Totemism', in which he explained the origin of religion and society by the murder of the primitive father; and this, for various reasons, united the great majority of specialists against him. In his search for the interrelations between the psychical life of primitive people and that of neurotics—that is the sub-title of the work—he reached a conclusion of which he himself seemed somewhat scared:

'I am now slowly composing the fourth of the Ubereinstimmungen, that on Totemism, which is close to the nerves. It is the most daring enterprise I have ever ventured. On Religion, Ethics and quibusdem aliis. God help me!'[2]

Freud never suspected that his *Totem and Taboo* would become a polemical issue and precipitate the crisis which had already been brewing for some time between him and Jung. At first he believed he was following in his pupil's footsteps, but as his work proceeded he realized that the original killing of the father, as he reconstructed it on the basis of a suggestion of Darwin's, would prevent any attempt at conciliation even if it did not actually cause the break. His letters to Ernest Jones, Abraham and Ferenczi show him as being convinced of the value of his work, than as suddenly beset by obscure scruples. At first he was sure of what he had done:

'Everything went well during the writing itself. "I am writing Totem at present with the feeling that it is my greatest, best, perhaps my last good work. Inner confidence tells me that I am right. Unfortunately I have very little time for the work, so I have continually to force myself into the

1 Ernest Jones, II, p. 352.
2 Ibid, p. 353.

mood afresh and that injures the style." A few days later: "I am working on the last section of the Totem which comes at the right moment to deepen the gap by fathoms; reading and polishing will take me all my time before the 15th of June." '[1]

The same feelings come out in a letter dated May 13, 1913, the day the work was finally finished:

'Since *The Interpretation of Dreams* I have not worked at anything with such certainty and elation. The reception will be the same: a storm of indignation except among those near to me. In the dispute with Zurich it comes at the right time to divide us as an acid does a salt. . . .'[2]

As so often with Freud, this elation was followed by a period of depression and doubt, which completely modified his opinion. He was so troubled that he sent the first proofs of the book to three of his followers, asking for their suggestions about the difficult last section. Ernest Jones relates how he and Ferenczi managed to reassure him:

'Ferenczi and I read the proofs together in Budapest and wrote to Freud in a similar strain. We suggested he had in his imagination lived through the experiences he described in the book, that his elation represented the excitement of killing and eating the father, and that his doubts were only the reaction. When I saw him a few days later on a visit to Vienna and asked him why the man who wrote *The Interpretation of Dreams* could now have such doubts he wisely replied: "Then I described the wish to kill one's father, and now I have been describing the actual killing; after all it is a big step from a wish to a deed." . . . On June 30, 1913, we celebrated the occasion by giving Freud a dinner, which we called a totemic festival, on the Konstantinhügel in the Prater. Loe Kann presented him with an Egyptian figurine which he adopted as his totem. . . .'[3]

Freud not unreasonably compared *Totem and Taboo* with

[1] Ibid., p. 354.

[2] Letter to Ferenczi, Ernest Jones, II, p. 354.

[3] Ibid., pp. 354–5.

The Interpretation of Dreams, the book whose ideas and thinking impregnate the whole of his work and which he had made his own guide. The two books are, indeed, of the same order. Both bear the double stamp of concrete experience and imagination which Freud so admired in poets; both reveal a restless mind which refused even to allow itself the relaxation which age can legitimately expect. Aged fifty-seven, at last famous after endless struggle and sacrifice, Freud threw everything into the melting pot and embarked on a complete review of his whole position, which frightened him, as if the primordial murder of which he had the vision were really his own fault. This intense participation in the original drama which he imagines is what gives the book its value.

As already mentioned, the essay comprises four unequally developed sections, the longest being 'Taboo and the Ambivalence of Feelings' and 'The Infantile Return of Totemism', which had so far been the most generally disputed. In the first chapter Freud deals with the prohibition of incest, the only human prohibition which is absolutely universal and which, among primitive tribes, is so compelling that it determines the whole organization of society and creates a complex network of interdicts which covers even the most trivial actions. If incest is forestalled and forbidden by such a complicated and rigid system it is, he notes, because the temptation is stronger in primitive tribes than in developed cultures. In this respect primitive man can be compared with the neurotic who, to safeguard himself from violent temptations, invents phobias and other symptoms which have all the force of taboos.

In 'Taboo and the Ambivalence of Feelings' Freud stresses the ambivalence attaching to the word 'taboo', a word which no longer has an equivalent in our languages, but corresponds fairly closely to the Roman *sacer,* for example, or the Hebrew *kadosh*. The taboo is autonomous. It has no rational motivation, or any moral or social justification; it represents something like our 'categorical imperative'—the only law, Freud said, of which we have direct and immediate knowledge—and its violation releases rigorously automatic sanctions, so that the outraged taboo is spontaneously and almost immediately avenged.

These characteristics of primitive taboos are exactly like the symptoms of obsessional neurotics, which also lack conscious motivation, arise from an imperious inner need, have a tendency to be displaced and infect other people, and, finally, find expression in the performance of certain rites designed to ward off the misfortune feared.

But the closest parallel between neurotics and primitive people lies in their ambivalence of feeling, in other words, in an unconscious hostility towards those who are loved or especially respected. By raising insurmountable ritual barriers between himself and his leaders, his priests, his lords, and his ancestors, primitive man gives free play to this affective ambivalence, which is also found operating in all neurosis; for in isolating those people in high positions on the pretext of protecting them primitive man protects himself, as if he considered them dangerous, and, by adoration and respect, revenges himself on them by making their existence untenable. The same mixed feelings of fear, hatred and love explain primitive people's attitude to death, funerary rites and the worship of the dead.

The third section of *Totem and Taboo* sticks closely to the ideas about animism and magic which were current at the time and which have been abandoned by most modern ethnologists. Freud admits that animism and magic thought is at the origin of all subsequent religious conceptions and that it obeys the mechanism called by one of his patients [1] the 'omnipotence' of thoughts. In neurotics as in primitive people, this omnipotence, which is really belief in the power of wishes, springs from an exaggerated belief in purely psychical acts and is therefore related to the narcissistic stage of development of the libido in which the subject loves not an object, but himself, his body and his own thought. Primitive thought offers Freud the opportunity to define more precisely the idea of 'narcissism' (or 'narcism' as he called it), which he introduced more or less officially into the theory in 1914:

'We would say that among primitive people thinking is still highly sexualized and that this accounts for the belief in the omnipotence of thought, the unshaken confidence in the capacity to dominate the world and the inaccessibility to the obvious facts which could enlighten man as to his real place in the world. In the case of neurotics a considerable part of this primitive attitude had remained as a constitutional factor, while on the other hand the sexual repression occurring in them has brought about a new sexualization of the processes of thought. In both cases, whether we deal with an original libidinous investment of

[1] 'The Rat Man,' *Std Edn,* X, p. 311.

thought or whether the same process has been accomplished regressively, the psychic results are the same, namely, intellectual narcism and omnipotence of thought.

'If we may take the now established omnipotence of thought among primitive races as a proof of their narcism, we may venture to compare the various evolutionary stages of man's conception of the universe with the stages of the libidinous evolution of the individual. We find that the animistic phase corresponds in time as well as in content with narcism, the religious phase corresponds to that stage of object finding, which is characterized by dependence on the parents, while the scientific stage has its full counterpart in the individual's state of maturity where, having renounced the pleasure principle and having adapted himself to reality, he seeks his object in the outer world.

'Only in one field has the omnipotence of thought been retained in our own civilization, namely in art. In art alone it still happens that man, consumed by his wishes, produces something similar to the gratification of these wishes, and this playing, thanks to artistic illusion, calls forth effects as if it were something real. We rightly speak of the magic of art and compare the artist with a magician. But this comparison is perhaps more important than it claims to be. Art, which certainly did not begin as art for art's sake, originally served tendencies which today have for the greater part ceased to exist: Among these we may suspect various magic intentions.' [1]

'The Infantile Return of Totemism' is generally regarded by specialists as an ingenious and fascinating fiction of no scientific value. Here Freud leaves the clinical territory which was still the basis of the first section and plunges into a rash hypothesis, logically developing it and all its consequences without, however, being able to prove its premises. He found himself in this position through trying to solve the crucial and still unsolved problem of anthropology: Why and how did the universal prohibition of incest, which has ever since weighed heavily on mankind, come about in the first place?

Freud first summarizes the definitions of totemism which he found mainly in the works of Frazer, Salomon Reinach and in Wundt's *Völkerpsychologie*. However, he

[1] *Totem and Taboo* (Brill translation). See *Std Edn*, XIII, pp. 89–90.

confines his consideration to animal totemism, whereas the totem can be almost anything, a plant, an element, an inanimate object or some natural phenomenon. In fact he adopts Frazer's view and Wundt's formulation that 'totems were originally only animals and were considered to be the ancestors of the tribes'. He also admits that the main prohibition applied to the murder and the eating of the animal ancestor with, as a corollary, the interdiction against marriage between members sharing the same totem, that is, exogamy.

Ideas about totemism were, and still are, very confused. Freud did not bother unduly about them as his plan was not to put forward a new theory but to throw light on the psychological facts about the phenomena, taking the analyst's clinical experience as a basis. By its identification of man with the animal and the sort of sacred terror which the totem inspired, totemism reminded the psychoanalyst of the strange phobias he sometimes met in his practice. After recalling the case of little Hans, Freud quotes that of Arpád, called the Little Cock-Man,[1] reported by Ferenczi:

'When little Arpád was two and a half years old he once tried, while at a summer resort, to urinate into the chicken coop, and on this occasion a chicken bit his penis or snapped at it. When he returned to the same place a year later he became a chicken himself, was interested only in the chicken coop and in everything that occurred there, and gave up human speech for cackling and crowing. During the period of observation, at the age of five, he spoke again, but his speech was exclusively about chickens and other fowl. He played with no other toy and sang only songs in which there was something about poultry. His behaviour towards his totem animal was subtly ambivalent, expressing itself in immoderate hating and loving. He loved best to play killing chickens. "The slaughtering of poultry was quite a festival for him. He could dance around the animals' bodies for hours at a time in a state of intense excitement." But then he kissed and stroked the slaughtered animal, and cleaned and caressed the chicken effigies which he himself had ill-used.

'Arpád himself saw to it that the meaning of his curious

[1] Sandor Ferenczi: 'Ein kleiner Hahnemann', *International Psychoanalytical Review,* 11, 1913, 1, No. 3.

activity could not remain hidden. At times he translated his wishes from the totemic method of expression back into that of everyday life. "Now I am small, now I am a chicken. When I get bigger I shall be a fowl. When I am bigger still, I shall be a cock." On another occasion he suddenly expressed the wish to eat a "potted mother" (by analogy, potted fowl). . . .'[1]

The Little Cock-Man who wanted to marry his mother as well as eat her and who killed his father symbolically by sacrificing cocks opened up new perspectives to psychoanalytic research by re-establishing the link missing between the two major commandments of totemism:

'If the totem animal is the father, then the two main commandments of totemism, the two taboo rules which constitute its nucleus—not to kill the totem animal and not to use a woman belonging to the same totem for sexual purposes—agree in content with the two crimes of Oedipus, who slew his father and took his mother to wife, and also with the child's two primal wishes whose insufficient repression or whose re-awakening forms the nucleus of perhaps all neuroses. If this similarity is more than a deceptive play of accident it would perforce make it possible for us to shed light upon the origin of totemism in prehistoric times. In other words, we should succeed in making it probable that the totemic system resulted from the conditions underlying the Oedipus complex, just as the animal phobia of "little Hans" and the poultry perversion of "little Arpád" resulted from it. . . .'[2]

Freud continues his argument, basing it partly on the idea of sacrifice as expounded by Robertson Smith in his *Lectures on the Religion of the Semites* and partly on a hypothesis of Darwin's about the habits and customs of the primitive human horde. According to Robertson Smith, the ancient sacrifice was accompanied by a ritual feast in which the members of the clan partook of the animal's flesh, the animal being a companion of the god or the god itself. The eating of the animal gave rise to manifestations and solemn ceremonies during which the taboos were ritually transgressed. Smith sees this as a developed

[1] *Totem and Taboo,* ibid., see *Std Edn,* XIII, pp. 130–1.
[2] Ibid., see p. 132.

form of the totemic feast in which, originally, the animal that was sacrificed and eaten was considered to be a member of the clan.

Darwin's hypothesis is quite unrelated to the problem of totemism. It simply presupposes the existence of a primitive human horde similar to those of the great anthropoid apes, in which the jealousy of the oldest and strongest male prevented all sexual promiscuity. In the state of nature this horde was imagined to be modelled on the gorilla bands:

'We may indeed conclude from what we know of the jealousy of all male quadrupeds, armed, as many of them are, with special weapons for battling with their rivals, that promiscuous intercourse in a state of nature is extremely improbable. . . . If we therefore look back far enough into the stream of time and judging from the social habits of man as he now exists, the most probable view is that he originally lived in small communities, each with a single wife, or if powerful, with several, whom he jealously defended against all other men. Or he may not have been a social animal and yet have lived with several wives, like the gorilla; for all the natives agree that only the adult male is seen in a band; when the young male grows up a contest takes place for mastery, and the strongest, by killing and driving out the others, establishes himself as the head of the community. The younger males being thus driven out and wandering about would also, when at last successful in finding a partner, prevent too close breeding within the limits of the same family. . . .'[1]

Freud believed that by combining Smith's theory about sacrifice with Darwin's and Atkinson's theory about the original human horde he was correctly reconstructing the decisive event—not psychological this time, but historical—to which later civilizations owed their beliefs, their laws and their social organization. He was not blind to the fanciful nature of such a hypothesis but he persisted in advocating it because it re-established continuity between a number of known but so far unrelated phenomena:

'The most primitive organization we know, which today is still in force with certain tribes, is *associations of men* con-

[1] Ibid., p. 903.

sisting of members with equal rights, subject to the restrictions of the totemic system, and founded on matriarchy, or descent through the mother. Can the one have resulted from the other, and how was this possible?

'By basing our argument upon the celebration of the totem we are in a position to give an answer: "One day the expelled brothers joined forces, slew and ate the father, and thus put an end to the father horde. Together they dared and accomplished what would have remained impossible for them singly. Perhaps some advance in culture, like the use of a new weapon, had given them the feeling of superiority. Of course these cannibalistic savages ate their victim. This violent primal father had surely been the envied and feared model for each of the brothers. Now they accomplished their identification with him by devouring him and each acquired a part of his strength. The totem feast, which is perhaps mankind's first celebration, would be the repetition and commemoration of this memorable, criminal act with which so many things began, social organization, moral restrictions and religion."

'In order to find these results acceptable, quite aside from our supposition, we need only assume that the group of brothers banded together were dominated by the same contradictory feelings towards the father which we can demonstrate as the content of ambivalence of the father complex in all our children and in neurotics. They hated the father who stood so powerfully in the way of their sexual demands and their desire for power, but they also loved and admired him. After they had satisfied their hate by his removal and had carried out their wish for identification with him, the suppressed tender impulses had to assert themselves. This took place in the form of remorse, a sense of guilt was formed which coincided here with the remorse generally felt. The dead now became stronger than the living had been, even as we observe it today in the destinies of men. What the father's presence had formerly prevented they themselves now prohibited in the psychic situation of "subsequent obedience" which we know so well from psychoanalysis. They undid their deed by declaring that the killing of the father substitute, the totem, was not allowed, and renounced the fruits of their deed by denying themselves the liberated women. Thus they created two fundamental taboos of totemism out of the *sense of guilt of the son,* and for this very reason these had to correspond with the two repressed wishes of the Oedipus complex. Whoever disobeyed became guilty of the only two crimes which troubled primitive society. . . .'[1]

In one sense the murder of the father was a fraud because the brothers, in order to settle the quarrels which arose among themselves, had to give up the very thing which had motivated their revolt. Looked at from another point of view, the sons' remorse gave rise to an institution of a higher order, designed to prevent a repetition of similar crimes and to keep alive a perpetual wish for reconciliation with the father who had been sacrificed. Guilt, renunciation, nostalgia—totemism was born of this inextricable mixture of feelings which Freud believed forms the very essence of religion:

'In this connection some features were formed which henceforth determined the character of every religion. The totem religion had issued from the sense of guilt of the sons as an attempt to palliate this feeling and to conciliate the injured father through subsequent obedience. All later religions prove to be attempts to solve the same problem, varying only in accordance with the stage of culture in which they are attempted and according to the paths which they take; they are all, however, reactions aiming at the same great event with which culture began and which ever since has not let mankind come to rest. . . .'[2]

Totem and Taboo was received as Freud had foreseen, although this time not all the critics were unfair or systematically hostile. The work was unacceptable to anthropologists, for one reason because of its unscientific method and its many inaccuracies, for another because it moved arbitrarily from psychology to history which, in view of our total ignorance of the real facts, meant that Freud could avoid having either to prove or disprove anything. However, the experts themselves disagreed. Some even changed their views appreciably as time passed: for instance, Kroeber condemned the work in 1919[3] for being inaccurate and unscientific and then, twenty years later, considerably

[1] Ibid., see pp. 141–3.

[2] Ibid., p. 918.

[3] A. L. Kroeber: 'Totem and Taboo: An Ethnological Psychoanalysis' (1920), in *The Nature of Culture*, Chicago, 1952.

revised his judgement.[1] Today it is generally agreed that the drama of the primordial parricide was not the historical event that Freud suggested (without ever pressing the point), but a myth, one of those dreams which psychoanalysis rightly discovered to be true and important for a profound understanding of man. As Claude Lévi-Strauss said in *Elementary Structures of Kinship, Totem and Taboo* is fiction, but fiction which is in a sense truer than a mere historical fact would be:

'It has been said repeatedly that what makes *Totem and Taboo* unacceptable as an interpretation of the prohibition of incest and its origins is the unwarranted hypothesis of the male horde and the original murder, producing a vicious circle of argument which deduces the social order from premises which presuppose it. But, like all myths, the myth presented with such dramatic power in *Totem and Taboo* admits of two interpretations. The desire for the mother or the sister, the slaying of the father and the remorse of the sons certainly do not correspond to any historical fact or body of facts. But they do perhaps represent an old and enduring dream in symbolic form. And the prestige of this dream, its power to mould men's thoughts without their knowing it, spring precisely from the fact that the acts it describes have never been committed, because they have been condemned by all cultures, in all ages and in all places. The symbolic satisfactions in which, according to Freud, the incestuous desires find an outlet do not commemorate an actual event. They are something altogether different. They are the permanent expression of a wish for disorder, or rather for counter-order. The ceremonies enact social life contrariwise, not because it ever was like that, but because it never was like that, and will never be otherwise. The nature of the past is valuable as an explanation only in so far as it coincides with that of the future and the present.'

[1] A. L. Kroeber: 'Totem and Taboo in Retrospect', (1939), ibid.

24

THE WAR YEARS

The little war which had been brewing within the psychoanalytical movement since 1900 broke out just before the Great War, the main schism occurring in 1914, first in April, when Jung resigned his position as President of the International Association, then in August, when he definitely left the organization, taking most of his compatriots with him. Long nourished by racial and national antipathies, the enmities in this remote region of science were a sort of announcement or small-scale rehearsal for the hostilities which, a few days later, set Europe ablaze.

Freud had resigned himself to losing Jung as a friend, but he was anxious to keep him as an ally in a common fight for the 'cause'. It was 1913 before he realized this was an illusion, when he perceived that his work was taking him farther and farther from what he called in a letter the 'psychology of the Aryans'. From that moment he gave up his efforts to spare his opponent and instead of playing down their incompatibilities he resolved to highlight them.

This need to clear away everything which was beginning to clutter up his path made Freud think again about some debatable theoretical points which, in view of the inexactitude which was, in a way, natural to psychoanalytic terminology, were really open to various interpretations. It is to define them precisely that he wrote his *History of the Psycho-Analytic Movement,* which clinched Jung's defection, then, at the beginning of 1914, *On Narcissism: an Introduction* [1] which struck his followers with the force of a minor revolution.

Everything hinged on the concept of the 'libido'. Freud wanted to keep its strict meaning of sexual energy, while Adler regarded it as a force at the service of social life and Jung so widened the meaning that it became synonymous with energy itself, something like the driving force

[1] *Std Edn* XIV, pp. 73 ff.

of all life. The 'libido' was thus in grave danger of melting away, especially as Jung maintained that Freud himself had used the word in a much broader sense in the Schreber case history. Freud had to say whether the word was to be restricted to its narrow meaning, or whether he agreed to an extension of meaning which would have reconciled to the concept of the libido many people who were in revolt against his ideas.

Freud stuck to his original conception of the libido, but at the cost of an important theoretical revision which brought constant trouble. Jung, in effect, had concluded from his work that, in the affections, the libido which withdraws as a whole from all external objects is no longer distinguishable from the total psychical energy, so that it loses all specific value. This might seem to be true if one clung to the fundamental opposition between the Ego or self-preservation instincts and the sexual instincts moved by an energy of their own and directed towards their own special ends, which are alien or even hostile to the Ego. The conflict which, in the so-called 'transference' neuroses broke out between these two categories of instincts could not exist in the psychoses where, on the contrary, the sick Ego drove the libido it withdrew from the external world back on itself. It was therefore necessary either to admit, with Jung, that the libido was nothing more than an undifferentiated psychical energy or to conceive of the Ego itself as possessing a sexual energy and characteristics which did away with the duality of the instincts.

Freud avoided these two extremes by introducing into his theory the concept of *narcissism* which he had already brought into other works, in particular the Schreber case, where the homosexual tendency ends in reversal: 'I love nothing and nobody. I only love myself,' and in *Totem and Taboo,* where the fantastic over-estimation of the Ego which is common to all primitive peoples explains the omnipotence of thought and therefore of magic. As it is described in the 1914 essay, narcissism does not change in meaning but takes an unexpected place in his theory.

The word 'narcissism' is borrowed from the psychiatric clinic. According to Freud it was coined by Näcke, according to Jones by Havelock Ellis, who applied it to a perversion rather like that of Narcissus in the Greek fable, who died of extreme self-love. However, narcissism is not a morbid tendency only: it is highly developed in children, people who are seriously ill and old people, as well as being found in the megalomania of the insane or in the hypochondriac's concern for his own body. It is present even in normal love relationships, so that Freud, tracing its different forms in health and sickness, is able to make it the beginning and so to speak the model of all love.

And so a new conflict takes shape, not this time between the Ego and sexuality but within the libido itself, which is called 'narcissistic' when it remains fixed or is directed on the subject's Ego, or called 'objectal' when it flows outwards and attaches itself to an object, in other words to some other person. Nevertheless this new distinction does not suppress the first one, for although Freud asserts the existence of a libidinal Ego inconceivable in the earlier theory, he insists on sex and the Ego keeping their contradictory character. The theoretical paradox is clear, but he does not seriously try to resolve it: he is content to push it aside temporarily by invoking the vast mass of clinical proof which is provided just as much by normal psychology as by pathology.

This seriously worried Freud's followers, for the new polarity introduced by narcissism seemed to require a complete revision of the theory. This misgiving can still be felt in the exposition which Jones gave more than twenty years after the publication of the book:

'Now the reason why I called Freud's essay on narcissism a disturbing one was that it gave a disagreeable jolt to the theory of instincts on which psycho-analysis had hitherto worked. The observations on which the new conception of narcissism was founded were so unmistakable and easily confirmed that we had to accept it unreservedly, but it was at once plain that something would have to be done about the theory to which we were accustomed. For if the ego itself was libidinally invested, then it looked as if we should have to reckon its most prominent feature, the self-preservative instinct, as a narcissistic part of the sexual instinct. Adverse critics of psychoanalysis had always overlooked one half of the unconscious conflicts to which Freud had called so much attention and had charged him, *tout court*, with "reducing everything to sex", with "seeing nothing in the mind but sex". They were, it is true, supported by the fact that at that time most of Freud's discoveries had been in the field of repressed sexual impulses and very little in the other half of the mind. But he could easily rejoin that his main point was the fact of a conflict between sexual and non-sexual impulses, a "fifty-fifty" view of the mind. Now, however, that the ego itself was to be regarded as libidinal, were not the critics right from the start when they denounced Freud's tendency to "reduce everything to sex"? And what had become of his famous conflict? It is true that the psychoneuroses, his proper field of study, could still be described in terms of conflict: namely, that between narcissistic and object-libido. But did this mean that the only conflict was that between one form of sexual instinct and another form, that there was no other source of conflict in the mind? These and similar questions were thronging our minds just as the great war broke out, and Freud was not able to give any answer to them until after its termination.'[1]

The real answer is to be found in one of the lectures which Freud gave in Vienna during the war years and which were not published until 1919, as an introduction to psychoanalysis and the main points of his theory.[2] In the lecture entitled 'The Libido Theory and Narcissism', Freud cuts discussion short by admitting that narcissism is the libidinal complement of the egoism natural to the instinct of self-preservation, or more exactly, that the Ego is made up of two tendencies, one narcissistic and therefore sexual, the other egoistical and self-preserving, their objects coinciding or conflicting according to individual cases. The narcissistic tendency is the source of the Ego Ideal, a completely inner exemplary image which the Ego tries to live up to so as to re-establish the self-satisfaction and feeling of perfection which it previously derived from its infantile narcissism and which is so cruelly disappointed by adult life.

It has often been noted that Freud's thought is fundamentally dualistic, to the point of shunning anything which might contribute to a conception of unity. His concepts always go in pairs of opposites which generate conflicts: the conscious and the unconscious, the Ego instincts and the sexual instincts, the pleasure principle and the reality principle, later the Ego and the Id, and, finally, the life instinct and the death instinct, an antithetical pair in which all conflicts are summed up and which, one last time, upset the theory. Was it a coincidence or a reflection

1 Ernest Jones, II, pp. 302–3.

2 *Introductory Lectures on Psychoanalysis, Std Edn* XV.

of psychical determinism to which logical thought is itself subject? The doctrine of the libido went through three stages which for Freud were also three essential phases of life: the first, in which the idea of sexuality is dominant, forced itself on him when he was in his prime; the second, in which narcissism has the fundamental role, at the moment of that falling back on oneself which heralds old age; finally, the third, in which death triumphs over life, coincided with a period of grievous bereavements, of physical pain due to a cruel illness and, for the lonely old scientist, a feeling of his own decline.

The essay on narcissism also undoubtedly represents one of those periods of loneliness which recurred continually throughout Freud's life and culminated in spectacular breaks, or in sudden changes in thinking, or in unforeseeable calamities such as war and illness. Loneliness was a strange disaster to befall this man who hated it and partly brought it on himself and who, in spite of the love of his family, the fanatical devotion of his followers and even fame, finally had to resign himself to it. Coming after the breaks with Breuer and Fliess, Jung's defection affected him more than he dared show: not only did it threaten the unity and the future of the movement, it also threw him back into the solitary circle he had had so much difficulty in breaking out of fifteen years before.

It was to forestall this danger that Ernest Jones, realizing that there was going to be trouble with Jung, and that in future Freud would undoubtedly be exposed to trials of the same kind, thought even as early as 1913 of a secret Committee comprising a small group of trustworthy analysts united by their close solidarity and faith in what they were doing. This Committee would form a sort of 'Old Guard' round Freud and comfort him in the event of new dissensions, reply to critics in his stead since he hated doing that, and would help him in many ways to carry out his work. There would be only one stipulation in this strange contract:

'There would be only one definite obligation undertaken among us: namely, that if anyone wished to depart from any of the fundamental tenets of psycho-analytical theory, infantile sexuality, etc., he would promise not to do so publicly before first discussing his views with the rest. The whole idea of such a group had of course its prehistory in my mind, stories of Charlemagne's paladins from boyhood, and many secret societies from literature.

'Ferenczi heartily concurred in my suggestion and we next put the matter before Otto Rank; I also wrote to Freud about it. Rank, of course, agreed, but in the talk a curious episode occurred which stayed in my mind. Ferenczi, in his usual candid fashion, asked Rank if he thought he would remain loyal to psycho-analysis. I thought myself it was an offensive question to put to someone so devoted as Rank then was, and he was somewhat embarrassed to find a suitable reply. I mention it now because of the odd coincidence that those two were in years to come the only ones who did not stay faithful to our undertaking of mutual consultation.' [1]

Freud enthusiastically agreed and answered Jones' letter by return of post:

'What took hold of my imagination immediately is your idea of a secret council composed of the best and most trustworthy among our men to take care of the further development of psycho-analysis and defend the cause against personalities and accidents when I am no more. . . . I know there is a boyish and perhaps romantic element too in this conception, but perhaps it could be adapted to meet the necessities of reality. I will give my fancy free play and leave to you the part of censor.

'I daresay it would make living and dying easier for me if I knew of such an association existing to watch over my creation.

'First of all: This committee would have to be *strictly secret* in its existence and in its actions. It could be composed of you, Ferenczi and *Rank* among whom the idea was generated. *Sachs,* in whom my confidence is unlimited in spite of the shortness of our acquaintance—and *Abraham* could be called next, but only under the condition of all of you consenting. I had better be left outside of your conditions and pledges: to be sure I will keep the utmost secrecy and be thankful for all you communicate to me. I will not drop any utterance about the matter before you have answered me, not even to Ferenczi. Whatever the next time may bring, the future foreman of the psycho-analytical movement might come out of this small but select

[1] Ernest Jones, II, p. 152.

circle of men, in whom I am still ready to confide in spite of my last disappointments with men.'[1]

The Committee, which owed its existence to practical needs as much as to the nostalgic reveries of its members, met for the first time on May 25, 1913, and to celebrate the solemn occasion Freud presented each one of the five with an antique Greek intaglio from his personal collection. The members had them mounted in gold rings, like all who subsequently received the precious gift. With Freud's own ring and the one Max Eitingon received when he became the seventh member in 1919, there were in all seven rings, like those reproduced in Hanns Sachs's book *Freud, Master and Friend.* In point of fact other people seem to have enjoyed the same favour without belonging to the Committee, for instance Anna Freud, who continued her father's work and to whom Ernest Jones dedicated his biography of Freud, and the German writer Arnold Zweig who, it appears, still wears his ring.

The Committee began to function before war was declared but it hardly had time to prove its value since its members were scattered all over Europe after 1914 and its activities interrupted. Ernest Jones was English, Ferenczi Hungarian, Abraham German; only Otto Rank and Hanns Sachs were Viennese and, before being mobilized, they were able to stay some time with Freud who would otherwise have been completely isolated. The war took all of them by surprise except Jones, who had foreseen it and predicted that it would go on for years. Although he had become an 'enemy', Jones tried to keep in touch with Freud who, except for a few holiday journeys, lived in Vienna for the whole of the war. This was due to the efforts of Dutch psychoanalysts and 'the old American gentleman', James Putnam, until the United States entered the war.

Freud did not react to the outbreak of war with the feeling of horror that one might have expected from such an independent thinker who was naturally distrustful of collective enthusiasms, sceptical about the real motives behind human action and had given a life-long devotion to intelligence as the only safeguard against the anarchy of the passions. It certainly seems inconceivable today that he was not one of those rare spirits—they were indeed rare

[1] Ernest Jones, II, pp. 153–4.

—who at the very opening of hostilities publicly protested against the slaughter. The fact is, however, that in spite of the inferior status assigned him by Austria's official racial policy, in spite of his pacifist temperament and his horror of brutality, Freud's first reaction to the declaration of war was not sorrow or uneasiness, but an almost joyous upsurge of patriotic feeling. Like millions of men all over Europe, he did not believe the war would last long and felt his own fate was bound up with his country's. He therefore approved of Germany's various declarations of war and, if Ernest Jones is to be believed, asserted that he had 'given all his libido to Austria-Hungary'.[1]

Feelings like these were not unusual among German and Central European Jews who, cut off from any form of national life because of their special status, clung all the more tenaciously to the German language and culture as their only ties and the only things which could in any way give them a sense of belonging to a nation. In the struggle between the minorities and the double monarchy, they instinctively sided with the Central Powers who, in spite of their incompetence and stupidity, represented the most highly developed culture in existence and even a certain form of liberalism. Moreover, the very minorities which were fighting for their independence were themselves animated by a fierce anti-Semitism compared with which German and Austrian anti-Semitism seemed almost reassuring. In 1914 German, Austrian and Hungarian Jews went to fight in the naïve belief that they would rediscover or gain a fatherland. It was this belief which moved Freud to say that, for the first time in thirty years, he really felt himself to be an Austrian. Freud, it is true, soon came to his senses again but a large number of his fellow Jews retained this patriotic belief in their country until the end of the war. We know what happened thirty-five years later to those who lived that long.

Freud's eldest son, Martin, volunteered in the second week of the war; the other two, Oliver and Ernst, joined up a few days later, like one of their cousins, who was killed in 1917. The only colleague left with Freud was Hanns Sachs, who was discharged, and Otto Rank, who was called up a little later and sent to Cracow, where he stayed until the end of hostilities. Abraham had gone back to Germany; Ferenczi, who had gone to Vienna for a

[1] Ibid.

training analysis with Freud, was also called to the colours and posted to a Hungarian hussar regiment where he served as a doctor with the rank of major. This enabled him to send Freud and his family food at the army's expense when starvation began to threaten Vienna.

There is no doubt that, emotionally, Freud had linked his fate with that of Austria-Hungary. The first disasters that befell the Empire depressed him, Germany's victories both reassured and disquieted him. At the end of the autumn his letters no longer bore any trace of the confidence he had felt in the summer. One, addressed to a friend, the writer Lou Andreas-Salomé, even betrayed the extreme pessimism which he did not yet openly express but which, after the war, injected the idea of death and destruction into the heart of his work:

'I don't doubt but that humanity will recover from the war, but I am sure that neither I nor my contemporaries will find a happier world. Everything is too horrible. And the saddest part about it is that psychoanalysis, with its knowledge of man and his behaviour, should have been able to foresee and prevent it. That is why I can never join in your happy optimism. This is my personal opinion: that if we are to look upon our civilization—the highest developed of all—merely as a gigantic hypocrisy, it must follow that organically we are not made for it, and the Great Unknown or the Great Boss hidden behind our destiny will replace this experiment with a different race. . . .'[1]

Against that sombre apocalyptic vision, Freud began to work again and his last letter of the year, which he wrote to Jones without knowing whether it would ever reach him, shows him to be preoccupied with the only thing for which he felt himself responsible—the future of the 'cause':

'I have no illusions about the fact that the flowering time of our science has been violently disrupted, that there is a bad time ahead of us, and that the only thing we can do is to keep a glow of fire going on a few hearths until a more favourable wind will allow it to blaze up again. What Jung and Adler have left of the movement is being ruined by the strife of nations. Our Association can as little be kept

[1] Lou Andreas-Salomé: *Lebensrückblick,* 1951, p. 368.

together as anything else that calls itself International. Our periodicals look like coming to an end; perhaps we may manage to keep the *Jahrbuch* going. Everything that we tried to cultivate and care for we have now to let run wild. Naturally I am not anxious about the ultimate future of the cause to which you show such a touching devotion, but the near future, in which alone I can be interested, seems to me to be hopelessly clouded over. . . .'[1]

Naturally Freud's patients were also dispersed and he at last had leisure to devote himself to his writing. 'That,' he said, 'is what fulfilled wishes look like.' This freedom, which he wanted but at the same time disliked, made the year 1915 one of the most productive in the second phase of his work, which was almost over in 1919. Believing he had only a few more years to live—superstitious calculations constantly revised since the Fliess period led him to believe he would die in 1918—Freud began to do something which he had long contemplated but which, for some unknown reason, he had always put off. This was to make a general synthesis of his psychological conceptions or, as he said, of his 'metapsychology'. He conceived this work in the form of twelve essays which would be published in one volume after the war and which, if he died, would in a way be the *Summa* of his ideas. Unfortunately for those who came after him, this *Summa* was never finished. It was reduced to five studies [2]: 'Instincts and Their Vicissitudes'; 'Repression'; 'The Unconscious'; 'A Metapsychological Supplement to the Theory of Dreams' and 'Mourning and Melancholia'. The general range of these studies is such that the missing essays are a great loss. We do not know if the other seven were ever written, if Freud gave up the idea of publishing them, or if he lost or deliberately destroyed them. Jones inclines to the last theory, on the grounds that new ideas had made the essays out of date, even before they were completed. But, surprisingly, although the members of the Committee would have known about Freud's plan, after the war none of them thought of asking him what had happened to the essays.

The military disasters of the following years cast ever darker shadows over Freud's life. In addition to his growing material difficulties and his perpetual anxiety about his

1 Ernest Jones, II, p. 179.

2 *Papers on Metapsychology*.

sons, Freud was cut off from his immediate fellow-workers and could make no active preparations for the rebirth of the movement after the end of the general upheaval. Psychoanalysis existed only through its reviews, and even these were seriously threatened. The *Jahrbuch,* formerly Jung's commitment, soon ceased to appear. *Imago* continued, thanks to the desperate efforts of Sachs and Rank, but when the latter was called up the review had to be produced in Cracow, and there were always great difficulties to be overcome. The *International Journal* was now international in name only and as a result of a proposal by Ferenczi nearly lost this last link with its past. Jones, however, was against changing the title of the periodical and the word 'international' was kept on the cover with the names of the two 'enemy' joint editors.

In 1916 food rationing and the closing of the frontiers completely isolated Freud, who could leave Vienna only for the traditional holiday weeks. It was these material worries which made him long to be awarded the Nobel Prize for which he had been proposed in 1915, and which he did not receive either the next year or later. The general situation began to be worrying and Freud's activity was affected. He wrote nothing new, but prepared the lectures he intended to give in the winter of 1916–1917 and which appeared under the title of *Introductory Lectures on Psychoanalysis.* Written in a familiar style, these very clear, very complete lectures put the principal aspects of psychoanalysis within the reach of the general public. They certainly contributed greatly to the unexpected lease of life which the movement experienced after 1918.

1917 was a terrible year. There was no food, undernourishment and the complete lack of heating made any work impossible. Freud suffered so badly from the cold that he could not even hold a pen. But, strangely enough, he said he felt very well in spite of everything and was in no way depressed by his physical suffering. His main grumble was at having to go without tobacco which, he said, with touching hypocrisy, aggravated the swelling in the roof of his mouth. This swelling was highly suspect. It probably heralded the cancer which appeared in his jaw six years later.

In the midst of every kind of disappointment and the disintegration of Austria, Freud had the pleasure of gaining three important new recruits, one of whom, Professor Pötzl, defended psychoanalysis in an official course of lectures at the University. The other two were Georg Groddeck, a brilliant doctor whose personality and talent as a writer earned him a place in psychoanalytical literature, and Anton von Freund, a wealthy Budapest brewer who went to Vienna to be treated by Freud and became the first patron of psychoanalysis.

The last months of the war only made material conditions and the state of morale in Vienna worse. Political uncertainty, the privations which became more severe every day, the fate of his eldest son, of whom he had no news, all so drained Freud of hope and courage to struggle on that he waited for death with a feeling of resignation and would even have welcomed it but for the thought of the grief it would have brought his mother, who was then eighty-three. But two things suddenly changed this sad and gloomy atmosphere. The first was a munificent donation by Anton von Freund to the Psycho-Analytical Association, enabling it to set up its own publishing house and fulfilling an old dream of Freud's who was weary of his publisher's tyrannical ways. Then came the unexpected chance of organizing an International Congress without having to wait for the armistice. This Congress, the fifth, took place on September 28 and 29, 1918, in Budapest, a city which seemed destined to replace Vienna as the future centre of psychoanalytic activity.

The Fifth Congress, which was international in a symbolic way only since the war was not yet over, was unusual in that for the first time it was attended by official representatives of the German, Austrian and Hungarian governments, something quite unheard of in the annals of psychoanalysis and unexpected at this troubled juncture. The explanation for this devotion was the extreme importance which the military authorities were beginning to attach to 'war neurosis', a morbid phenomenon which baffled the doctors and which psychoanalysis had elucidated with great success. The results obtained by Abraham, Ferenczi and Eitingon so impressed the military doctors that they proposed setting up psychoanalytical clinics at various centres. The first of these clinics was to be opened in Budapest, but, of course, the whole project collapsed in the ruin of general defeat.

Freud really gained new life from the success of the Congress, the enthusiasm of those taking part, the lavish reception by the Budapest City Council, the warm interest of the students, a thousand of whom sent the University

Rector a petition asking him to invite Ferenczi to give a course of lectures on psychoanalysis. This sudden vogue of the accursed science was obviously encouraging and although the collapse of the Austro-Hungarian monarchy put an end to it as far as practical results were concerned, it went deep enough to give the movement a new lease of life.

Meanwhile, Freud lost his half-brother Emmanuel, then his nephew, his favourite sister's only son. He also learned of the death of James Putnam, for whom he felt great affection, and saw his friends come back from the war, some ill, like Hanns Sachs, who contracted tuberculosis, others, like Rank and Ferenczi, whose mental health was seriously threatened. When the Austro-Hungarian Empire collapsed the anxieties he felt about the future were perhaps tinged with a sadness which he dared not admit to himself. During those four years his usual clear-sightedness failed him, he was as mistaken in his forecasts as in his feelings, and he was too honest not to acknowledge this. He admitted it without, however, rejoicing in the Allied victory:

'Dear Jones, I concede that all your predictions about the war and its consequences have come true, but I should be sorry if we could not meet before June. . . .

'I have had no news from America these two years and I feel the loss of dear old Putnam grievously. He was a pillar of psycho-analysis in his country and behaved most truly and gallantly towards me in opposition to the whimsical, unreliable Stanley Hall. I had no notion what had become of the movement there beyond the pond, whether psycho-analysis had not been dethroned by Adlerism or some other invention, so I found some consolation in your favourable report.

'These last months are becoming the worst we have had to endure while this war lasted. My eldest son is still a prisoner in Italy. We are all of us slowly failing in health and bulk, not alone so in this town I assure you. Prospects are dark. I am ready to confess that fate has not shown injustice and that a German victory might have proved a harder blow to the interests of mankind in general. But it is no relief to have one's sympathy on the winning side when one's well-being is staked on the losing one. . . .'[1]

[1] Letter to Ernest Jones, January 15, 1919, Ernest Jones, II, p. 205.

25

EROS AND DEATH

The days that followed the war brought Vienna such a surfeit of misfortune and catastrophe that Freud, who had stoically endured four years' ordeal and anxiety about his sons, thought them almost worse than the war itself, which had at least held out hope of peace. Everywhere there was hunger, cold and poverty, and soon the crowning misery of inflation, the worst calamity of those disastrous days. Freud, whose three sons had returned from the front unscathed but with no prospects for the future, saw what few savings he had been able to put by during a lifetime of work melt away in no time. And so, at the age of sixty-three, he found himself face to face with what he feared most—the old spectre of poverty.

On top of that and as a result of the political upheavals arising out of the war, Austria was condemned to a massive territorial amputation and to an isolation which cut her off from the western world just as much as from Germany and Hungary, the two countries in which the rebirth of psychoanalysis was immediately possible. Many people at the time foresaw that the new Austria would not be viable, and so the neutral or formerly Allied psychoanalysts thought of assuring the future of Freud and his family by helping them to settle elsewhere: in England, which Jones wanted, or in Switzerland, where Pfister offered him a refuge. But Freud rejected these suggestions, giving them the same answer that he gave his friends twenty years later when the Nazis marched into Vienna. He told them he would not leave his post as long as he could reasonably hold it. And until 1938 he did in fact share the fate of the city which he loved as much as he hated. Even then it was not he who abandoned Vienna so much as Vienna which abandoned him.

Not that Freud had many illusions about the chances for the scientific and social development of his movement in Vienna. But he was ignorant of what was happening in the Anglo-Saxon countries and, what is more, he did not want to lose touch with Berlin and Budapest, as this last city in particular seemed to him destined to become some day the true centre of European psychoanalysis. The great hopes he set on Ferenczi, sealed by the success of the Budapest Congress; the material support he found unexpectedly in the person of Anton von Freund, the patient who had so quickly become his friend and patron; and, finally, the sudden popularity of his ideas in Hungary led him to look in that direction rather than to London or New York. which must have seemed very far away. But once again events were to thwart his plans and raise new obstacles to hinder the reunification of the movement which then, as in 1914, was still his first concern.

Most serious of all was the Hungarian revolution which, in 1919, cut all communications with Austria, with the result that for several months Freud was without any news of Ferenczi, which prevented him from taking any action. But the affair had a good side to it, for Béla Kun's government was more sympathetic to psychoanalysis than any previous regime. It created a Chair at the University and Ferenczi became its first occupant, and a Chair of Anthropology which was given to Géza Róheim, the only psychoanalyst who was also a professional anthropologist. Coming from a hated government whose fall was awaited by the whole world, this first official blessing given to the 'cause' was in fact rather compromising and dangerous. Béla Kun's successors, who were reactionary and violent anti-Semites, managed to equate Jew and revolutionary, a trick which would subsequently prove highly successful. Ferenczi had to hide away for weeks to escape their police. And when calm was finally restored they repaid his short-lived professorship by making every sort of trouble.

This change was made so much the worse by the fact that the large sum of money which Anton von Freund had given to provide the International Psychoanalytical Association with its own publishing house, among other things, had been deposited in Hungary and could only be transferred to Vienna as a result of very complicated administrative arrangements. The fund amounted to about five hundred thousand dollars, but hardly a quarter of it could be sent to Vienna; the rest was blocked in Budapest, and after innumerable arguments and negotiations the Hungarian authorities more or less appropriated it. And so the only large donation which had ever been given to psychoanalysis was diverted from its real object. The International Psychoanalytical Association had its publishing house, but burdened from the start with serious financial difficulties, the enterprise became a further source of trouble for all the people concerned with it.

Freud was very keen on this publishing firm which was to assure complete independence for psychoanalytical literature, by giving its various publications the stamp of authority and distinguishing them from many other publications masquerading under the name. Although he manifestly lacked any organizing or commercial ability, he did not allow himself to be disheartened by the difficulty naturally inherent in an embryonic international organism in which national and sometimes contradictory requirements clashed.

The Directors were Freud, Ferenczi, Anton von Freund and Rank, who took over the commercial side. When the Hungarian patron seemed doomed, Jones took his place and managed the English branch which, in principle, had the same programme as the Vienna house. But trouble very soon broke out between the Anglo-Saxons and the Austrians, who naturally tended to give precedence to publications in the German language. With two managements, several heads and no money, the enterprise always led a precarious existence and Jones, remembering the enormous sacrifices it meant in time, money and energy, wondered if Freud was wise to battle on instead of handing it over to professionals. Without any doubt he would have been spared an extra burden at a time when his many different obligations were already too heavy for him to bear: but his calculations were not as bad as all that, for during the twenty years that it lasted, the Internationaler Psychoanalytischer Verlag regrouped and directed psychoanalytical literature as no commercial firm could have done without danger to the science. In any case the five reviews and some hundred and fifty books—including Freud's *Complete Works* in eleven volumes—which were published under its name were in the end enough to justify it.

We must return to the generous donor to whom the Verlag owed its existence, for in the difficult post-war period he brought Freud much sorrow as well as much joy. Anton von Freund was, with Max Eitingon, the only wealthy man in the psychoanalytic movement, most members being generally very poor and seriously affected by any economic troubles. The owner of a brewery in Budapest, von Freund had gone to Vienna to be treated by Freud for a serious neurosis which was connected with a tumour from which he was suffering. The treatment lasted from 1918 to 1919 and resulted in a complete cure. But in March 1919 suspicious signs reappeared and this time cancer was feared. Freud tried to reassure him by diagnosing a floating kidney, but a surgical operation left no doubt about the malignant nature of the disease. Von Freund, aware of his condition, returned the ring which Freud had given him as a future member of the secret Committee, then found replacements for all the positions he was getting ready to take. His death took place on January 20th. It was a brutal blow, the first of a number that were to strike Freud in that terrible year.

Three days later, on the very evening of his friend's funeral, Freud learned that his second daughter, Sophie, had gone down with influenza, which that year was ravaging the whole of Europe. The young woman lived in Hamburg with her husband and two young sons and her parents could not get to her because there were no trains running between Hamburg and Vienna. She was dead within a matter of days, swept away, Freud said, 'as though she had never existed'.

'We had been worried about her for two days, but were still hopeful. From a distance it is so difficult to judge. The distance still remains. We could not, as we wished to, go to her at once when the first alarming news came, because there were no trains, not even a children's train. The undisguised brutality of our time weighs heavily on us. Our poor Sunday child is to be cremated to-morrow. Not till the day after to-morrow will our daughter Mathilde and her husband, thanks to an unexpected concatenation of circumstances, be able to set off for Hamburg in an Entente train. At least our son-in-law was not alone. Two of our sons who were in Berlin are already with him, and our friend Eitingon has gone with them.

'Sophie leaves behind two boys, one aged six and the other thirteen months, and an inconsolable husband who will have to pay dearly for the happiness of these seven years. The happiness was only between them, not in external circumstances, which were war and war service, being wounded and losing their money, but they remained brave and cheerful.

'I do as much work as I can, and am grateful for the

distraction. The loss of a child seems to be a grave blow to one's narcissism; as for mourning, that will no doubt come later.

'However, as soon as the condolences have been coped with, Pfister junior shall come and see us. It is not the lad's fault, after all.'[1]

After these two grievous blows within the space of a few days Freud wrote to Ferenczi: '*La séance continue.* But it was a little too much for one week.' And as his friend was deeply concerned about the effect these repeated shocks might have on him, Freud reassured him with these moving lines:

'Do not be concerned about me. I am just the same but for a little more tiredness. The fatal event, however painful, has not been able to overthrow my attitude toward life. For years I was prepared for the loss of my sons; now comes that of my daughter. Since I am profoundly irreligious there is no one I can accuse, and I know there is nowhere to which any complaint could be addressed. "The unvarying circle of a soldier's duties" and the "sweet habit of existence" will see to it that things go on as before. Quite deep down I can trace the feeling of a deep narcissistic hurt that is not to be healed. My wife and Annerl are terribly shaken in a more human way. . . .'[2]

In his old age, which was shot through with bereavements and other ordeals, it was not Sophie but her youngest son who brought Freud his deepest suffering. Little Heinz was thirteen months old when his mother died and he had been taken to Vienna by his aunt Mathilde. Freud conceived an immense love for the tiny, wonderfully gifted child, a love which, he said, was stronger than all his other human affections. The little boy was not his only grandson, but charmed by his grace and outstanding intelligence, Freud adored him as though he stood to him for all his children and grandchildren. Freud's joy was shortlived. Very soon after the first of his thirty-three operations for cancer, little Heinz contracted an illness which the doctors could not at first diagnose. It was military tu-

[1] Letter to Pfister, January 27, 1920, *Psychoanalysis & Faith*, pp. 74–5.

[2] Letter to Ferenczi, Ernest Jones, III, p. 20.

berculosis, one of those infantile diseases for which there was then no cure. Freud, who probably knew what his own trouble was, watched with horror the death of the little boy who, it seems, was then his strongest tie with life. Afterwards he often said that the little boy's death had not only made him suffer but had killed something in him for ever. That was the secret of what the world called his courage in the face of suffering and of his indifference to his own pain.

When, in 1920, he published the essay which unexpectedly upset his established theory by introducing a death and destructive instinct alongside the libido, Freud fully expected that people would imagine there was a connection between his radical change of view and the loss he had suffered a few months before. His daughter had died in January 1920; *Beyond the Pleasure Principle*,[1] in which the death instinct is declared to be an entity, appeared in May of the same year, so it did not need much intelligence to suspect that the two events were closely connected. Fearing perhaps that such an interpretation would weaken the force of his ideas, Freud took a strange precaution. He asked the faithful Eitingon for a sort of certificate swearing that he had read the complete manuscript before January 1920, at a period when they both knew Sophie was still in perfect health. This denial was naturally useless. Freud had taught that there is no such thing as coincidence or chance in man's psychical life, and many psychoanalysts refused to admit that he was an exception to his own law. How greatly this rankled can be seen in a letter he wrote to Fritz Wittels three years later to correct the mistakes he had found in Wittels' biography[2]:

'That seems to me most interesting, and I regard it as a warning. Beyond question, if I had myself been analysing another person in such circumstances, I should have presumed the existence of a connection between my daughter's death and the train of thought presented by *Beyond the Pleasure Principle*. But the inference that such a sequence exists would have been false. The book was written in 1919, when my daughter was still in excellent health. She died in January 1920. In September 1919, I had sent

[1] *Std Edn* XVIII.

[2] Fritz Wittels: *Sigmund Freud, der Mann, die Lehre, die Schule*, Leipzig, 1924.

the manuscript of the little book to be read by some friends in Berlin [Eitingon and Abraham]. It was finished, except for the discussion concerning the mortality or immortality of the protozoa. What seems true is not always the truth.'[1]

However logical it might appear to the psychoanalysts, this strictly biographical explanation was inadequate if one accepts the fact that between 1919 and 1920 there were good reasons why the ideas of death and destruction would impose themselves on and even dominate people's minds. Surveying the terrible and still almost incalculable devastation, as well as the material, moral and intellectual collapse of mankind which, it was by then clear, neither victors nor vanquished had escaped, what thinker would not have wondered what was the reason for the chaos and what meaning lay behind the brutal fall of man and his civilization?

At the beginning of the war Freud, as has been said, had lost his usual clear-sightedness; but for four years, while he was writing his *Introduction to Psychoanalysis* and his *Metapsychology* his thoughts turned more and more to these last questions which, in view of the point from which his work had started, he had so far not considered to be urgent. The study of the psychoneuroses had led him to proclaim the universal rule of the libido, to assert that despite the never-ending conflicts of which it is both the cause and the victim, love moves the world, even by the means of hatred and destruction. But after 1915 some of his writings bear, even in their titles, the stamp of contemporary events. There are, for example, *On Transitoriness*[2], a paper written at the request of the Goethe Society for a publication it brought out the following year, and *Thoughts for the Times on War and Death,*[3] the second part of which, entitled Our Attitude to Death, was the text of a lecture given to the B'nai B'rith Society. The lecture itself contains nothing which actually limits the omnipotence of the libido, but the conclusion, in which Freud varies the well-known adage on peace and war by saying: 'If you want life, prepare for death,' was

1 To Wittels, December 18, 1923, *Std Edn* XIX, p. 287.
2 *Über die Vergänglichkeit.*
3 *Std Edn* XIV.

already the beginning of a revolution as far as the theory of the libido was concerned.

If the introduction of the idea of narcissism in 1914 had disturbed many minds, the introduction of the death instinct created a real uneasiness which time gradually diminished but never entirely dispelled. To isolate a special instinct responsible for all the negative tendencies of the psyche, to counterbalance the libido, which Freud now definitely identified with the Platonic Eros,[1] by a destructive force working by virtue of a general law against all living things was clearly serious, since psychoanalytic technique even more than psychoanalytic theory stakes everything on the resources of love. Psychoanalysts were right to be worried, especially as Freud had previously always rejected all speculation on this subject.

Actually these speculations were perfectly natural as psychoanalysis had from the start highlighted the strange phenomenon of ambivalence, in which love is closely linked with hatred. Adler had very soon derived from it his theory of aggression which, according to Freud, resulted in the depressing picture of a world without love and should be condemned on that score alone. Although Freud himself does not use it, the word 'Thanatos', which is currently employed to designate the death wish, had been suggested as early as 1909 by Stekel to describe the death wishes for which dreams are so ready to be the spokesman. And in 1912, Sabina Spielrein had published an article in the *Jahrbuch* entitled 'Destruction as Cause of Becoming',[2] in which the conception of the death instinct was anticipated almost in detail. Every time these ideas had appeared Freud had stubbornly opposed them and if

[1] People have pointed out the similarities between Freud's doctrine and Plato's. Freud himself stressed them in 'Group Psychology and the Analysis of the Ego' where he said: 'The philosopher Plato's Eros is exactly the same in its origin, function and connection with sexuality as the erotic energy or "libido" of psychoanalysis.' And again in the Preface to the fourth edition of *Three Essays on the Theory of Sexuality:* 'I beg all those who look down on psychoanalysis to remember how close the broadened concept of sexuality of psychoanalysis is to the divine Plato's "Eros".' Cf. Max Nachmansohn: 'Freud's Libidotheorie verglichen mit der Lehre Platons', *Zentralblatt,* 1915.

[2] Sabina Spielrein: 'Die Destruktion als Ursache des Werdens', *Jahrbuch* IV, 1912, 2nd Vol., pp. 465–503.

he suddenly adopted them in 1920—on trial, as he said himself—they became a certainty only in his later works. In 1930, in an important passage in *Civilization and Its Discontents*,[1] he went back on this long objection which, now, seemed to him incomprehensible:

'The assumption of the existence of an instinct of death or destruction has met with resistance even in analytic circles; I am aware that there is a frequent inclination rather to ascribe whatever is dangerous and hostile in love to an original bipolarity in its own nature. To begin with it was only tentatively that I put forward the views I have developed here, but in the course of time they have gained such a hold upon me that I can no longer think in any other way. To my mind, they are far more serviceable from a theoretical standpoint than any other possible ones; they provide that simplification, without either ignoring or doing violence to the facts, for which we strive in scientific work. I know that in sadism and masochism we have always seen before us manifestations of the destructive instinct (directed outwards and inwards), strongly alloyed with erotism; but I can no longer understand how we can have overlooked the ubiquity of non-erotic aggressivity and destructiveness and can have failed to give it its due place in our interpretation of life. (The desire for destruction when it is directed *inwards* mostly eludes our perception, of course, unless it is tinged with erotism.) I remember my own defensive attitude when the idea of an instinct of destruction first emerged in psycho-analytic literature, and how long it took before I became receptive to it. That others should have shown, and still show, the same attitude of rejection surprises me less. For "little children do not like it" when there is talk of the inborn human inclination to "badness", to aggressiveness and destructiveness, and so to cruelty as well. God has made them in the image of His own perfection. . . .'[2]

Beyond the Pleasure Principle—the echo of Nietzsche in the title is perhaps not mere chance—begins with a few remarks of limited clinical interest, then soars almost immediately into a realm of pure speculation. From the clinical point of view, the pleasure principle seemed to be

[1] *Std Edn* XXI.
[2] Ibid., pp. 119–20.

invalidated by certain phenomena such as the traumatic neuroses, in particular the war neuroses, in which the patient relives indefinitely the shock, the accident and the fear which he had suffered although those were the very things which the pleasure principle should logically have spared him. There seemed, therefore, to be at least one exception to the pleasure law, but Freud discovered another while observing a child's strange game.

The child was the brother of little Heinz, his daughter Sophie's eldest son. Eighteen months old at the time of observation, the little boy was very good and obedient, but everyone was baffled by his annoying habit of throwing everything within reach into a corner of the room or under a bed:

'As he did this he gave vent to a loud, long-drawn-out "vo-o-o-o", accompanied by an expression of interest and satisfaction. His mother and the writer of the present account were agreed in thinking that this was not a mere interjection but represented the German word *"fort"* ["gone"]. I eventually realized that it was a game and that the only use he made of any of his toys was to play "gone" with them. One day I made an observation which confirmed my view. The child had a wooden reel with a piece of string tied round it. It never occurred to him to pull it along the floor behind him, for instance, and play at its being a carriage. What he did was to hold the reel by the string and very skilfully throw it over the edge of his curtained cot, so that it disappeared into it, at the same time uttering his expressive "o-o-o-o". He then pulled the reel out of the cot again by the string and hailed its reappearance with a joyful *"da"* ["there"]. This, then, was the complete game—disappearance and return. As a rule one only witnessed its first act, which was repeated untiringly as a game in itself, though there is no doubt that the greater pleasure was attached to the second act.' [1]

Interpretation of the game left no doubt about its meaning. The disappearance and reappearance of the reel represented his mother's departure and her return, and as the game laid special emphasis on the disappearance, the obvious conclusion was that it deliberately chose to reproduce a painful event. Freud compared this with what

[1] *Beyond the Pleasure Principle, Std Edn* XVIII, pp. 14–15.

happens during a psychoanalytic treatment in which the neurotic makes no progress because he reproduces the same symptomatic situations, and he concluded that there exists in psychic life an irresistible tendency to *repetition,* an elementary and instinctive tendency which asserts itself outside or even at the expense of the pleasure principle, which, therefore, can no longer be considered a primitive tendency.

The pleasure principle was derived from the stability or constancy principle defined by Fechner, who postulated that the psychic apparatus always tends to maintain the stimuli coming from outside at as low a level as possible. To this Freud opposed the repetition principle which, in animal life, manifests itself by an instinct stereotype which is sometimes dangerous. From this automatism, which he calls 'demonic', Freud moved by a bold leap to the central idea of the essay, which is that all living things have a tendency to revert to a previous state, in other words death, since everywhere the non-living has preceded the living. Thus the goal of life is death and life itself is more or less one long detour in the universal journey to nothingness.

Such are the dominant themes of this grandiose vision in which Eros and Thanatos wage a confused struggle against one another and, at least as long as life persists, without any decisive outcome. Thanatos' sole aim is to lead all living matter back to the inorganic state: Eros works patiently to reassemble the groups which have become increasingly extended and to embrace life in its totality. Which of these two equally invincible forces will finally triumph? Freud does not venture to say in this essay, but in a later work, *The Ego and the Id,*[1] he indicates that he opts for the death instinct, against Eros which is, in the world, the eternal disturber of the peace.

It is noticeable that in describing the struggle between the two 'heavenly powers' Freud illustrates his theory of the 'eternal return of the same' by a return to his own past and to the origin of his research. *Beyond the Pleasure Principle,* in fact, brings back names which had long since disappeared from his books—Fechner, whose work was known to him through Breuer; Breuer himself, from the two 'heavenly powers' Freud illustrates his theory of free and bound energy; and Fliess, whose ideas on the inevitable periodicity of all living phenomena unmistakably

[1] *Std Edn* XIX.

inspired his demonic law of repetition. Was this return to the beginning a misdeed perpetrated by Thanatos or the opposite—a good deed on the part of the faithful Eros which suddenly would have revived his youthful passion?

One is inclined to believe it was the latter when one perceives that the whole essay, in spite of the abstruse character of its speculation, is essentially an attempt to bring psychoanalysis back to experimental biology, the only science which Freud accepted and ever wished to serve. This attempt failed and Freud asked of metaphysics what biology was unable to provide, but he never wearied of saying that even if it disappointed his expectation, it was the only thing which, until a new order arises, holds the final secrets.

It is not possible to go into the innumerable controversies that arose out of the idea of the death instinct both outside and inside the movement. Generally speaking debate centred and still centres on the opportuneness and the sound basis of the idea of the instinct[1] applied to life's regressive and destructive tendencies. Is it fair to put forward two diametrically opposite ideas to describe what, after all, is the same process? Instead of saying, as Freud seems to, that only what is going to die lives, could it not be said that only what is living dies? These questions are very embarrassing for psychoanalysts, who, whatever their personal convictions, cannot in any case use the death instinct therapeutically. The idea of an elementary tendency to destruction and self-destruction, of primary sadism and masochism, sends therapy very quickly back to a blind fate which it cannot acknowledge without immediately renouncing its claim to cure. Whatever its conception of the world, psychoanalysis can only act with Eros as its ally.

Those who believe in the death instinct are right to

[1] In a letter to Freud, Pfister said: 'I only see the death instinct as a diminution of vital energy, not as a real instinct, and even the death of the individual cannot stop the progress of the universal will.' To which Freud replied: 'If I doubt whether humanity is destined to advance towards greater perfection by way of culture, if I see in life a continual struggle between Eros and the death instinct, a struggle whose outcome seems to me to be impossible to predict, I do not think I am thereby expressing either my natural character or tendencies I have acquired. I am neither a self-tormentor nor a *Bosnickel* (a Viennese expression for a sadistic and brutal person), I should love to find something good for myself and others, and I should think it much finer and much more consoling to be able to count on a brilliant future.' *Psychoanalysis & Faith,* pp. 131–2. Freud's letter dated February 7, 1930.

answer that *Beyond the Pleasure Principle* is not a brief inspiration in Freud's work but undeniably the final position he adopted in his thinking. If it is disputed, *The Ego and the Id,* for example, must also be disputed, since this describes the psychic apparatus in terms of the dualism involved and has yet become the indispensable pillar of the theory. It is true that Freud never went back on the ideas in *Beyond the Pleasure Principle.* On the contrary, three years later he expressed them again with increased firmness:

'On the basis of theoretical considerations, supported by biology, we put forward the hypothesis of a death instinct, the task of which is to lead organic life back into the inanimate state; on the other hand, we supposed that Eros, by bringing about a more and more far-reaching combination of the particles into which living substance is dispersed, aims at complicating life and at the same time, of course, at preserving it. Acting in this way, both the instincts would be conservative in the strictest sense of the word, since both would be endeavouring to re-establish a state of things that was disturbed by the emergence of life. The emergence of life would thus be the cause of the continuance of life and also at the same time of the striving towards death; and life itself would be a conflict and compromise between these two trends. The problem of the origin of life would remain a cosmological one; and the problem of the goal and purpose of life would be answered dualistically. . . .'[1]

It will seem strange that the hypothesis of the death instinct should have lead Freud to deepen the psychology of the ego, which, until then, occupied only a modest place in his theory. To tell the truth, the theoretical ideas in the book were moving in the same direction as experience, which showed increasingly clearly that the ego was not completely assimilable into conscious life any more than it theoretically opposed the libido, as had first been asserted. Every day clinical experience of patients' unconscious resistance to treatment proved that the ego was partly unconscious, and as, on the other hand, it was not opposed to the libido, but to a world of contradictory instincts in which erotic impulses and death urges existed side by side,

[1] *The Ego and the Id, Std Edn* XIX, pp. 40–1.

it was the whole psychological apparatus which needed changing.

Freud then describes the structure, the dynamism and the scheme of the three psychic agencies which he calls *Ego, Id* and *Super-Ego,* whose interrelationship completely conditions health and sickness. These three agencies all have a common origin, stemming from that impersonal world which is very difficult to define and which Freud, following Nietzsche and Georg Groddeck,[1] henceforth calls the *Id:*

'It is the dark, inaccessible part of our personality; what little we know of it we have learnt from our study of the dream-work and of the construction of neurotic symptoms, and most of that is of a negative character and can be described only as a contrast to the ego. We approach the id with analogies: we call it a chaos, a cauldron full of seething excitations. We picture it as being open at its end to somatic influences, and as there taking up into itself instinctual needs which find their psychical expression in it, but we cannot say in what substratum. It is filled with energy reaching it from the instincts, but it has no organization, produces no collective will.' [2]

The id is unaware of negation, contradiction, feeling of duration or the idea of time. Nor, of course, has it any sense of values, of good and evil, or of morality. Everything it is not appertains to the other two components, the ego and the super-ego, which are responsible for the organization and maintenance of psychic life.

The ego is the most superficial part of the apparatus, a part of the id modified by the proximity of the external world, organized to perceive excitations and to resist them. The ego is what conceives time and space and has the ability to foresee and to form syntheses. In a word, it possesses a high degree of organization, which allows it to carry out precisely what the id cannot. If the latter is the kingdom of the untamed passions, the former is the kingdom of caution and reason.

The super-ego is born of the child's relationship with its parents by a complex process of identification, by which

[1] Georg Groddeck: *Das Buch vom Es.*

[2] *New Introductory Lectures on Psychoanalysis,* Third Lecture, *Std Edn* XXII, p. 73.

the external authority is transplanted inside the subject and plays the role normally attributed to the moral conscience. In spite of its apparently exalted position in the hierarchy, the super-ego, which is also partly unconscious, has more natural ties and affinities with the id than with the ego. It is more often than not a stern and inexorable judge. It is the super-ego which performs the act of repression, whether it acts by itself or orders the docile ego to execute its commands. Because of its archaic origin, it represents the past, tradition, the non-present. Its excessive tyranny is one of the great dangers which threaten the psyche.

Placed between three equally tyrannical and absolute masters—the external world, the id and the super-ego—the ego is in an unhappy position which makes its multiple tasks difficult of achievement. In the third lecture of the new series, entitled 'The Dissection of the Psychical Personality', Freud deliberately personifies the ego so as to heighten the agonizing drama in which it is caught up:

'When we follow the ego's efforts to satisfy them simultaneously—or rather, to obey them simultaneously—we cannot feel any regret at having personified this ego and having set it up as a separate organism. It feels hemmed in on three sides, threatened by three kinds of danger, to which, if it is hard pressed, it reacts by generating anxiety. Owing to its origin from the experiences of the perceptual system, it is earmarked for representing the demands of the external world, but it strives too to be a loyal servant of the id, to remain on good terms with it, to recommend itself to it as an object and to attract its libido to itself. In all attempts to mediate between the id and reality, it is often obliged to cloak the *Ucs.* commands of the id with its own *Pcs.* rationalizations, to conceal the id's conflicts with reality, to profess, with diplomatic disingenuousness, to be taking notice of reality even when the id has remained rigid and unyielding. On the other hand it is observed at every step it takes by the strict super-ego, which lays down definite standards for its conduct, without taking any account of its difficulties from the direction of the id and the external world, and which, if those standards are not obeyed, punishes it with tense feelings of inferiority and of guilt. Thus the ego, driven by the id, confined by the super-ego, repulsed by reality, struggles to master its economic task of bringing about harmony among the forces and influences working in and upon it. . . . If the ego is obliged to admit its weakness, it breaks out in anxiety—realistic anxiety regarding the external world, moral anxiety regarding the super-ego and neurotic anxiety regarding the strength of the passions in the id. . . .'[1]

It is clear that the sound functioning of the psychical apparatus depends largely on the strength and health of the ego, which must not be servile and anxious, but paramount and capable of harmonizing the relations between its three tyrants. That is why analytic treatment has a set way of proceeding, whatever case it has to handle. It must strengthen the ego, so as to put it in a position to impose its own order on the two obscure and rebellious powers. To discipline and control the chaos of the id, to reduce the demands of the super-ego to reasonable proportions is the whole task of analysis, a task, Freud said, which is no less costly than draining the Zuyder Zee or any other formidable undertaking facing human civilization.

1 Ibid., pp. 77–8.

26

NEW CRISES

Freud was apparently in good health when one day in February 1923 he noticed the first signs of the disease which, while it did not put an end to his scientific activity, made the last sixteen years of his life one long martyrdom. Anxious to spare his family and friends, and perhaps even more to stop news of such grave consequence to his patients from getting round, he did not seek medical advice and for more than two months said nothing about his condition.

In April Freud asked a doctor friend, Felix Deutsch, who had dropped in to see him, to examine what he described as 'something unpleasant' in his mouth.[1] Deutsch at once realized the malignant nature of the tumour but was alarmed by Freud's attitude. After pointing out how stricken his old mother would be should he die before her, Freud asked his friend to help him to 'disappear from this world with decency', if his pain and suffering became intolerable. Deutsch misunderstood Freud's meaning, taking his words to be a threat to commit suicide. He therefore decided to lie, while advising Freud to have an immediate operation to remove the tumour.

Freud thought it over for a few days, then, without a word to his family, went one morning to Professor Hajek, a well-known rhinologist whom he knew personally. Hajek's clinic was not a private one but a public hospital attached to the University. There Freud underwent the first of his thirty-three operations. It was performed in highly dramatic circumstances, and, as Ernest Jones relates in his biography, the fate which saved Freud's life appeared, ironically, in the form of an idiot:

'The family were surprised by getting a telephone message from the clinic requesting them to bring a few necessities for him to stay the night there. Wife and daughter hurried to the clinic to find Freud sitting on a kitchen chair in the

[1] Ernest Jones, III, p. 90.

out-patient department with blood all over his clothes. The operation had not gone as had been expected, and the loss of blood had been so considerable that it was not advisable for the patient to return home. There was no free room or even bed in the clinic, but a bed was rigged up in a small room already occupied by a cretinous dwarf who was under treatment. The ward sister sent the two ladies home at lunch-time, when visitors were not allowed, and assured them the patient would be all right. When they returned an hour or two later they learned that he had had an attack of profuse bleeding, and to get help had rung the bell, which was, however, out of order; he himself could neither speak nor call out. The friendly dwarf, however, had rushed for help, and after some difficulty the bleeding was stopped; perhaps his action saved Freud's life. Anna then refused to leave again and spent the night sitting by her father's side. He was weak from loss of blood, was half-drugged from the medicines, and was in great pain. During the night she and the nurse became alarmed at his condition and sent for the house-surgeon, who, however, refused to get out of bed. The next morning Hajek demonstrated the case to a crowd of students, and later in the day Freud was allowed to go home.'[1]

Although he was perfectly aware of the seriousness of the case, Dr. Hajek acted with amazing irresponsibility, neglecting certain measures which would have spared Freud many painful consequences. In particular he did nothing to prevent the scar from shrinking, which greatly reduced the opening of Freud's mouth and caused all manner of trouble. Professor Hajek, who was the brother-in-law of the writer Arthur Schnitzler, also achieved notoriety by the way he treated another famous patient, who was, it is true, unknown at the time. A year after the Freud disaster, Franz Kafka, suffering from tubercular laryngitis, was sent to hospital by Hajek in scandalous circumstances which horrified and angered the literary world. Franz Werfel, in particular, made such a fuss that Kafka, who was almost dying, was treated with more consideration and was at least given a separate room. Professor Hajek answered: 'A certain Werfel writes to me that I must do something for a certain Kafka. I know Kafka. He's patient number 12. But who is Werfel?'

[1] Ibid., pp. 90–1.

Freud, understandably, soon lost confidence in his surgeon, whose attitude was completely inconsistent. A few months after the operation he allowed him to go on holiday as usual, then asked him to send a report every fortnight, finally telling him he could stay in the south all the summer—just when Freud's cancer had reappeared. Still in the depths of despair over his grandson's recent death, Freud caused his family great anxiety. A second and very extensive operation was absolutely essential, but would Freud be willing to have it? Would he not, instead, choose to die?

Anna and Felix Deutsch, who even now did not tell Freud the truth, went to join the members of the Committee who were holding a holiday session nearby. Only Rank knew the real situation. It was the first the others learned of Freud's illness. Jones tells us that while they were discussing what to do and were mentioning Freud's name, Rank broke into a mad, hysterical laugh which, to everyone's horror, he was unable to control. None of them could understand the reason for this strange behaviour or realized the upheavals it augured.

The Committee wanted to convince Freud of the need for an operation, but how? Sachs suggested appealing to his love for Anna; Rank thought they should play on his consideration for his mother. Jones was against this whole approach:

'I protested that we had no right to take such a decision out of Freud's hands, and the other medical men present, Abraham, Eitingon and Ferenczi, supported me. Many years later, when Freud was living in London, I told him that we had discussed whether or not to inform him, and with blazing eyes he asked: "Mit welchem Recht?" ["With what right?"] But he told Ferenczi later that from the beginning he was sure the growth was cancerous. . . .'[1]

On September 26th, Hajek and a famous stomatologist, Professor Pichler, examined Freud and found a malignant tumour in his palate which extended to the neighbouring tissues, including the upper part of the jaw and the cheek. It was decided to operate at once. The operation was performed in two parts, on October 4th and 11th. The first was designed to remove the glands of the lower jaw, al-

[1] Ibid.

ready suspect because of their size. The second consisted of making a large aperture in lip and cheek and removing the whole of the upper jaw and part of the palate, an operation which eliminated the separation between mouth and nasal cavity. This terrible operation, carried out from beginning to end with only a local anaesthetic, left the patient incapable of speaking or eating for several days. But he recovered and at the end of the month was well enough to go back home.

So began sixteen years of continual torture, marked by numerous recurrences of the trouble and more operations either to remove the precancerous tissues or to improve the diabolical piece of equipment which Freud had to wear by way of prosthesis. This artificial jaw, designed to separate the mouth from the nasal cavity, was known as 'the monster', which it was indeed, for Freud, who could not open his mouth wide, was unable to put it in or take it out without someone else's help. As it had to fit the mouth closely to allow him to speak or eat, it constantly caused the most painful inflammation. But if it were taken out for more than a few hours the tissues shrank and the 'monster' would not go back.

From then onwards Freud could eat and speak only by making the most painful efforts. He took his meals alone and never spoke again in public. His daughter Anna, who looked after him every moment until his death, in accordance with a pact they had made, literally became his spokesman. It was she who read all his communications to the Congresses, and who, later, tried to fend off intruders who came from all over the world. Anna had promised to look after him with all the technical coldness of a surgeon, neither giving way to nor showing her feelings. And for thirteen years she kept her promise without fail.

The year 1923 brought another unnecessarily cruel blow, for it saw not only the beginning of Freud's torture but once more the disintegration of the Committee which had been created six years earlier to maintain peace and brotherly understanding round him. Actually, the two things were intimately connected, for the possibility of Freud's death had evoked in some of his followers complex feelings in which hatred went hand in hand with a panic fear of being left and an urgent need to break away. Of the six members of the secret Committee, Rank and Ferenczi, the most dedicated and the most vulnerable, were the ones who reacted most violently to Freud's possible death which, with the irrational logic of the unconscious, they felt to be a lack of love and a betrayal.

Naturally there was plenty of cause for disagreement among the rather heterogeneous group of people who were at once on intimate terms and separated by inevitable differences of language, origin and ways of thinking. Aggravated by four years of war, these differences were bound to come into the open when they dealt with the organization, expansion and general tactics of the movement. Thus Jones was working hard to get psychoanalysis going in England and America, while the Central Europeans, distrusting the Anglo-Saxons, whose work was indeed often mediocre, were fighting to ensure that the vast majority of the publications should remain German. And so quarrels broke out over the management and programme of the Verlag, the choice of contributors to the reviews, the election of the Presidents of the International Association and the cities where the annual Congresses were to be held. On top of this there were the internal politics of each Psychoanalytical Society, the publication of Freud's works in English and financial questions, which were always pressing. In all the discussions Jones's political skill and Abraham's common sense which, for all its incurable optimism was always acute enough to foresee disaster, regularly clashed with the passionate emotions of Rank and Ferenczi who, in 1923, finally united against their friends.

A constant feature of Freud's character is that, despite his unshakeable conviction and great energy, he could be strongly influenced by his immediate entourage and change his opinion in an unpredictable way up to the very moment when he made up his own mind. Jones was in London, Abraham in Berlin, only Rank and Ferenczi were in contant touch with him and as he knew how devoted they were to him, they were the first to get his support in the discussions. Irritated by the warnings from Abraham and Jones, who had always foreseen the defections in the past, he refused to take a tragic view of the two men's deviations, even when they had broken the pact made by the Committee.

Members of the Committee, it will be remembered, were under an obligation to consult one another before publishing anything which might provoke controversy in the movement or in public. Now at the end of 1923 Rank and Ferenczi published a book entitled *The Development of Psycho-Analysis,* which no member of the Committee except Freud had known about beforehand. The members of the Committee were particularly shocked as the conclusions which followed from the book's main idea seemed to be very doubtful. Freud, however, defended it.

The book dealt with the tendency of patients under analysis to act out their unconscious impulses, a tendency which Freud had already mentioned in a paper but to which the authors wanted to attach great therapeutic importance. From that they arrived, without explicitly saying so, at a conception of analytic technique in which all the emphasis is laid on current situations instead of on the infantile causes of neurosis. Jones and Berlin analysts reminded Freud that, exactly ten years earlier, Jung had rebelled and left the movement as a result of following the same course. Freud liked the book and refused to share their suspicions.

Gradually, however, Freud revised his opinion as he felt the authors were not being honest. Under its reassuring surface the book in fact concealed Rank's ideas on birth trauma and Ferenczi's ideas about a new technique which he called 'active therapy' and which was also designed to shorten an analysis. Shattered by a remark of Freud's on this point, Ferenczi protested vehemently that he would not dream of deviating for an instant from the orthodox doctrine. Freud replied:

'As for your endeavour to remain completely in agreement with me, I treasure it as an expression of your friendship, but find this aim neither necessary nor easily attainable. I know that I am not very accessible and find it hard to assimilate alien thoughts that do not quite lie in my path. It takes quite a time before I can form a judgement about them, so that in the interval I have to suspend judgement. If you were to wait so long each time there would be an end of your productivity. So that won't do at all. That you or Rank should in your independent flights ever leave the ground of psycho-analysis seems to me out of the question. Why shouldn't you therefore have the right to try if things won't work in another way from that I had thought? If you go astray in so doing you will find that out yourself some time or other, or I will take the liberty of pointing it out to you as soon as I am myself sure about it. . . .'[1]

[1] Ibid., pp. 57–8.

Freud adopted the same affectionate and tolerant attitude at first to *The Trauma of Birth,* which was published at almost the same time. There, however, the deviations were more glaring, for Rank, taking to its logical conclusion an idea already expressed by Freud, asserted that man's whole life is determined by the unique and painful experience of birth, during which the child is in danger of suffocating and experiences all the terrors of dying. The sole aim of man's subsequent actions and endeavours is to undo and overcome this deeply repressed trauma. He succeeds through coitus, which partly reproduces the original fusion with the mother's body, or through sublimation which allows him to live through artistic and religious creation the return to the mother's womb which is the fear and the wish of all life. The failure of these two attempts at adaptation is if not the only cause, at least the deepest cause in the etiology of the neuroses.

The disturbing feature about this was not so much the theory, for which Freud had after all provided the starting point, as the technical implications which stemmed directly from it and led in particular to a great reduction in the length of psychoanalytic treatment. If all the subsequent conflicts of life were merely screens concealing the original trauma and the absolutely primordial relationship with the mother, there was no longer any reason to spend much time analyzing the Oedipus complex or bringing childhood memories back to consciousness. In fact, Rank, and with him Ferenczi, whose theory of genitality is based on almost the same premises, came to advocate extremely short treatment in which the patient had not to *remember* but to relive the painful separation from his mother, in other words to *be born again* by finally overcoming his fear.

The Trauma of Birth left Freud greatly perplexed, as can be seen from the contradictory comments he made on it within a short space of time. At first the book came as a shock, for if Rank was right the whole of his life's work on the etiology of neurosis amounted to nothing. From another point of view his pupil's discovery seemed fundamental and he was delighted that Rank was now able to free himself from his long tutelage. But he did not see how to incorporate it into his theoretical system without the Oedipus complex losing its vital primacy. Perhaps he would not have taken up any definite stand if some analysts, especially those in Berlin, had not urged him to condemn the two authors and bring the theory back to its true centre of gravity. The orthodox analysts were greatly alarmed to see Rank and Ferenczi lay exclusive emphasis on the mother to the detriment of the father, who, in Freud's view, was the author of the ban on incest and consequently the incarnation of the law with and against which the individual is called to mould himself. As the crisis grew worse Freud thought he could allay it by sending a circular to all members of the Committee:

'Liebe Freunde, I have heard from various sides, not without some astonishment, that the recent publications of our Ferenczi and Rank—I refer to their joint work and that on birth trauma—have evoked considerable disagreeable and agitated discussion. One of our friends has begged me to ventilate among ourselves the as yet undetermined matter, in which he perceives a germ of dissension. When I accede to this request please do not think I am obtruding. I should myself prefer to keep as much as possible in the background and let each of you follow his own way.

'When Sachs was here recently I exchanged some comments on the Birth Trauma with him; hence perhaps the impression that I discern an antagonistic tendency in the publication of that work or that I absolutely disagree with its contents. I should have thought, however, that the very circumstance of my accepting the dedication should invalidate this idea.

"The fact of the matter is this: neither the harmony among us nor the respect you have often shown me should hinder any of you in the free employment of his productivity. I do not expect you to work in a direction to please me, but in whatever way accords with your observations and ideas. Complete agreement in all scientific details and on all fresh themes is quite impossible among half a dozen men with different temperaments, and is not even desirable. The sole condition for our working together fruitfully is that none of us abandons the common ground of psychoanalytical premises. Then there is another consideration with which you must be familiar and which makes me specially unfitted for the function of a despotic censor always on the watch. I do not find it easy to feel my way into alien modes of thought, and I have as a rule to wait until I have found some connection with my meandering ways. So if you wanted to wait with every new idea until I can endorse it you would run the risk of getting pretty old.'[1]

After paying tribute to the discoveries made by the two men who were now being accused, Freud launched into a frank examination of the points baffling him:

'Now comes the point where I find the difficulties begin. Obstacles, which evoke anxiety, the barriers against incest, are opposed to the phantastic return to the womb: now where do these come from? Their representative is evidently the father, reality, the authority which does not permit incest. Why have these set up the barrier against incest? My explanation was an historical and social one, phylogenetic. I derived the barrier against incest from the primordial history of the human family, and thus saw in the actual father the real obstacle, which erects the barrier against incest anew. Here Rank diverges from me. He refuses to consider the phylogenesis, and regards the anxiety opposing incest as simply a repetition of the anxiety at birth, so that the neurotic regression is inherently checked by the nature of the birth process. This birth anxiety is, it is true, transferred to the father, but according to Rank he is only a pretext for it. Basically the attitude towards the womb or female genital is supposed to be ambivalent from the start. Here is the contradiction. I find it very hard to decide here, nor do I see how experience can help us, since in analysis we always come across the father as the representative of the prohibition. But naturally that is not an argument. For the time being I must leave the matter open. . . .'[2]

This conciliatory and affectionate attitude completely failed to produce the desired effect, for in what Freud saw as a sincere and respectable piece of research, the Committee, haunted by the example of Jung and Adler, thought it recognized a heresy. Abraham answered Freud's circular with a letter in which he openly expressed his fears, and Freud, unwisely, reported the exchange to the two men concerned. The fat was in the fire and shortly afterwards Rank took the initiative and dissolved the Committee.

1 Ibid., circular of February 15, 1924, pp. 59–60.
2 Ibid., p. 62.

Freud was distressed. The letter he wrote to Ferenczi to assure him of his confidence is one of the few in which he complained without reservation:

'I do not doubt that the other members of the former Committee feel considerateness and good will towards me, and yet it has come to pass that I shall be left in the lurch just when I have become an invalid with diminished powers of working and in an enfeebled frame of mind which turns away from any increased burden and no longer feels equal to any carking care. I am not trying to move you by this complaint to take any step to retain the lost Committee. I know: gone is gone, and lost is lost. I have survived the Committee that was to have been my successor. Perhaps I shall survive the International Association. It is to be hoped that psycho-analysis will survive me. But it all gives a sombre end to one's life.' [1]

Freud made many attempts to keep the two 'sons' on whom he had set such hopes and these sometimes led him to be unjust to the others, particularly Jones and Abraham who irritated him by their rather narrow common sense and, in spite of their devotion to the 'cause', a certain lack of generosity. But while he succeeded in winning Ferenczi back, at least for a few years, he clearly saw he was bound to lose Rank, whose fate was already sealed by illness.

Just as with Jung a few years before, Rank openly rebelled on the occasion of a journey to America, during which he posed as the creator of a new theory and, what was much worse, of a revolutionary technique which greatly alarmed his American colleagues. The practice of excessively short treatments could easily lead to charlatanism, especially as Rank, who was not a doctor, preferred to address 'lay' analysts and thus opened the doors of the profession to all comers. The pupils who had always been dependent on the master had sought in a new country a material and spiritual emancipation which he knew to be impossible in Vienna and which Freud's fatal illness now made urgent. Three years later America, which unfailingly attracted the rebels, played the same role of tempter to Ferenczi.

Ferenczi had published a most remarkable book which, although it was full of almost mystical speculations on nature and its origins, coming after Rank's *The Trauma of*

[1] Ibid., pp. 65–6.

Birth gave the more balanced minds in the movement good cause for uneasiness. In his *Theory of Genitality*[1] Ferenczi in effect attempted nothing less than to establish the basis of a new science, *bio-analysis,* by applying the universal value of symbolism to biology. Having put forward the thesis that 'the symbolic or indirect modes of expression of psychism of the body, like the ancient hieroglyphs, contain a fragment of history submerged or inaccessible by other means,' Ferenczi decided to apply psychoanalysis, 'to the great mysteries of the evolution of the species', which, he was honest enough to recognize, amounted to promising his readers an exciting fairy tale.

In Ferenczi's case biology seemed to play much the same role as mythology in Rank's book, except that Ferenczi continued to base his thesis on certain biological theories, in particular those of Haeckel and Lamarck. This thesis, presented first in the form of a hypothesis but afterwards asserted as though it was proved, held that the intra-uterine existence of the higher mammals was only a repetition of the form of existence in the marine age and that birth was therefore no more than an 'individual recapitulation of that great catastrophe which, at the time the seas dried up, forced so many animal species and our animal ancestors to adapt themselves to life on terra firma.' Thus the eternal wish to return to the mother's womb no longer sprang, as with Rank, from the memory of the intra-uterine ecstasy which is lost and repressed by every man born, but from the nostalgia for the initial ocean from which all species issued. The human mother was merely the symbol or late substitute of Thalassa, the original sea and matrix of the world.

One would expect that these ideas, infinitely richer than can be shown in a short summary, would have alarmed Freud who still thought in a classical, balanced way. But on this particular point he was himself divided between two tendencies equally deeply rooted within himself. One was rational and made him stay close to experience; the other was romantic, and this he resisted all the more for knowing its strength. At certain times, as for example when he was friendly with Fliess and when he described the grandoise visions in *Beyond the Pleasure Principle,* romanticism triumphed over his aspiration for classical austerity, and the Father, the legitimate principle of psycho-

[1] Sandor Ferenczi: *Versuch einer Genitaltheorie,* Internationaler Psychoanalytischer Verlag, Vienna, 1924.

analytic thinking, lost some of his power to the Mother, to whom the repetition principle, the idea of eternal return and the obsession with death led back. Fascinated by the depths into which he dared not plunge and which on the other hand his love of clarity and order rendered suspect in his eyes, Freud was only too tempted by the hazardous adventure in which his most brilliant pupils were engaged. In the years of crisis now being described it was that as much as age and illness which was at the bottom of his indecisive attitude.

For some time, in fact, psychoanalysis had been changing before his eyes. Not only theoretical innovations but also clinical observations were displacing its centre of gravity. Interest was veering increasingly to the systematic study of the relation of the baby to its mother, a study which brilliantly confirmed Freud's ideas on the evolution of the child but which resulted in the cause of conflicts having to be put back to a much earlier stage. Direct observation of children, which is now current practice, led one of Ferenczi's pupils, Melanie Klein, to theoretical conceptions which subsequently brought her into conflict with Anna Freud, who was naturally the guardian of orthodoxy. Even psychosomatic medicine, developed under the inspiration of another of Ferenczi's pupils, Franz Alexander, led psychoanalysis into unexpected paths which perplexed even its creator.

Intimidated by these changes which were completely alien to his temperament and aims, Freud now intervened only hesitatingly in the theoretical quarrels. His last books disregard them altogether. To the fantastic Gorgon, the source of love and terror, endlessly devouring and devoured, who invades the thinking of some of his pupils, Freud continued to oppose the Mother-Wife whose role is fixed by the Oedipus complex, in contrast to the Father, who until the end remains for him the source of order, authority and culture—the first law on which both society and the fate of the individual depend. It was still of this law-giving Father, eternally hated and loved, eternal because death in no way diminishes his power, that he spoke just before he died by invoking the person whom he called, doubtless intentionally, 'the man Moses'.

If he did not try to influence the evolution of psychoanalytic theory, Freud at least determined to keep control over the technical innovations which threatened to bring an unpredictable anarchy into everyday practice. Ferenczi, having discovered the importance of experiences lived out during the treatment itself, had perfected an 'active therapy' designed to frustrate the patient by ordering him to restrain himself in everything, to eat and drink less, to urinate much less and to force himself to abstain from sexual intercourse, in other words to drive him beyond endurance. It was in a way a criticism of Freud's method. Freud —and he later bitterly reproached him for this—had neglected to analyse his 'negative transference' and had in a way so 'spoiled' him that he was unable to resolve their relations in a healthy way.

Freud unequivocally condemned these methods, seeing clearly that they were highly dangerous for ambitious beginners. A few years later Ferenczi again changed his method and switched from ascetic analysis to a radically different technique designed to give patients all the comfort, love and pleasure denied them by their families. Freud also opposed this new extreme and, in 1931, when Ferenczi had moved so far away from him that a rapprochement was no longer conceivable, he wrote him a long letter in which severity, perhaps bitterness, was tempered by irony:

'I see that the differences between us come to a head in a technical detail which is well worth discussing. You have not made a secret of the fact that you kiss your patients and let them kiss you; I had also heard that from a patient of my own. Now when you decide to give a full account of your technique and its results you will have to choose between two ways: either you relate this or you conceal it. The latter, as you may well think, is dishonourable. What one does in one's technique one has to defend openly. Besides, both ways soon come together. Even if you don't say so yourself it will soon get known, just as I knew it before you told me.

'Now I am assuredly not one of those who from prudishness or from consideration of bourgeois convention would condemn little erotic gratifications of this kind. And I am also aware that in the time of the Nibelungs a kiss was a harmless greeting granted to every guest. I am further of the opinion that analysis is possible even in Soviet Russia where so far as the State is concerned there is full sexual freedom. But that does not alter the facts that we are not living in Russia and that with us a kiss signifies a certain erotic intimacy. We have hitherto in our technique held to the conclusion that patients are to be refused erotic gratifications. You know too that where more extensive gratifications are not to be had milder caresses very easily take over their role, in love affairs, on the stage, etc.

'Now picture what will be the result of publishing your technique. There is no revolutionary who is not driven out of the field by a still more radical one. A number of independent thinkers in matters of technique will say to themselves: why stop at a kiss? Certainly one gets further when one adopts "pawing" as well, which after all doesn't make a baby. And then bolder ones will come along who will go further to peeping and showing—and soon we shall have accepted in the technique of analysis the whole repertoire of demiviergerie and petting-parties, resulting in an enormous increase of interest in psycho-analysis among both analysts and patients. The new adherent, however, will easily claim too much of this interest for himself, the younger of our colleagues will find it hard to stop at the point they originally intended, and God the Father Ferenczi gazing at the lively scene he has created will perhaps say to himself: maybe after all I should have halted in my technique by motherly affection *before* the kiss.'[1]

Ferenczi did not yield. He nursed a grudge against Freud, and the worst one imaginable in the circumstances—of having been badly analysed by the man he revered more than any other in the world. He persisted in lavishing mother love on his patients and, as the years went by, treated Freud with increasing coldness. However, the two men continued to correspond and if Ferenczi's letters became fewer and fewer, Freud's retained all their old warmth and concern. Affected by pernicious anaemia, Ferenczi saw his health slowly decline. In 1932 his physical illness developed side by side with the serious mental disorder which was undoubtedly the real cause of his trouble. This man, who was so remarkable in many ways and whose work is possibly among the most important in the Freudian period, died in 1933, a few days after the Reichstag was set on fire and Nazism was unleashed over Germany. And so, following the death of von Freund and Abraham, who died in 1926, Freud, in the evening of his life, lost one of the last and perhaps the dearest of his friends.

[1] Letter to Ferenczi, December 13, 1931, Ernest Jones, III, pp. 163–4.

27

FAME

Even before he was sixty Freud expressed the fear that his sources of inspiration would dry up and that he would have to resign himself to the worst trial he could imagine—the loss or diminution of his intellectual faculties. [1] When he stood on the threshold of old age each of his books seemed to be the last, and in 1925 he wrote his autobiography as though he had already completed his work and come to the end of his life. Declaring that he had 'opened many roads and started many things which will produce results in the future', he never dreamed, or dared not believe that a long period of activity still lay ahead.

How ill-founded these fears were is abundantly proved by the number and importance of the books he published in his last fifteen years. To be sure there were no more of the brilliant flashes which until then periodically rekindled the flame of genius which inspired *The Interpretation of Dreams,* but the same relentless curiosity, the same attention to the little as to the big things of life are evident. From the point of view of freshness and youthfulness of mind, the last three large volumes of his complete works are no whit inferior to the rest.

The final period added nothing really new to his theory, which if not completed was at least solidly established. However, Freud felt the need to modify considerably one of his most constant and least developed ideas, that of

[1] Letter to Pfister, March 6, 1910. 'I cannot imagine a life without work ever being completely happy. For me, to live by the imagination and to work are one and the same, nothing else gives me pleasure. That would be a recipe for happiness, but for the terrible thought that productivity is entirely dependent on a variable disposition. What does one do during a day or a period of time when ideas and words will not come? One never ceases to shake with fear at the thought of this possibility. That is why, while submitting to fate as an honest man should, I still say a secret prayer: "above all no illness, no physical suffering which might paralyse my creative faculties. . . ." As Macbeth says, let us die "with harness on our back". . . .'

neurotic anxiety which had been made topical again by Rank's *Trauma of Birth.*

It was hard thinking about Rank's ideas that moved Freud to write *Inhibitions, Symptoms and Anxiety,*[1] a very important work which corrected his theory. Freud had previously thought of anxiety as resulting from a transformation of the libido, but he had been unable to say what this transformation consisted of or how it occurred. Now, going back to a note in *The Interpretation of Dreams* which suggested that anxiety originates in the act of birth, 'the source and model of all anxiety states', he argued that anxiety is not the product of repression but that, on the contrary, it performs the act of repression, except where the neurosis is directly due to lack of sexual satisfaction. In this way he preserved the clinical entity of 'anxiety neuroses' or 'real neuroses' which many psychoanalysts had long considered to be of doubtful value. But although Freud always found it hard to give up an opinion, he admitted his mistakes as soon as he became convinced he was wrong. He did this seven years later when he abandoned the rest of his theory of anxiety. He was then seventy-seven.

The books published between 1925 and 1931 are a sort of general recapitulation of the important chapters in Freud's whole work.

Some deal with the theory of the libido. Apart from the essay just mentioned, these are papers on libidinal types, feminine sexuality and the psychic differences between the sexes. Others, including his autobiography, are designed to evaluate psychoanalysis as a science and practice. These are *Resistances to Psycho-Analysis*[2] and *The Question of Lay Analysis.*[3] In the latter Freud vigorously defended non-medical analysts against both the authorities and those analysts who, especially in England and the United States, wanted to prevent them from practising.

Before the 1914 war non-medical psychoanalysts were rare. There were perhaps only two, Pastor Pfister and Hermine Hug-Hellmuth, who worked exclusively with children. During the war Melanie Klein began her brilliant career as a child analyst in collaboration with Ferenczi at his Budapest clinic. Then Rank also decided to practise,

[1] *Std Edn* XX.
[2] *Std Edn* XIX.
[3] *Std Edn* XX.

at first confining himself to children in accordance with the widely held illusion that children posed less difficult problems than adults. Gradually, however, the number of non-medical analysts increased and, especially in Vienna, where the legal provisions were extremely strict, it was thought necessary to legalize their existence, a move which was made as much out of regard for the law as for the actual standing of the various Societies.

Freud, who might well have retained from the past a feeling of bitterness towards medicine, intervened in the debate on the occasion of an action brought by the Austrian authorities against Theodor Reik, one of the most prominent lay analysts in the Vienna Society. In 1926 one of Reik's patients accused him of harmful treatment, but the plaintiff was obviously mentally unbalanced and, thanks to Freud's approach to a senior official, Reik finally won the case. Of course the Viennese press made such capital out of the affair that Freud, angered and alarmed at what might become a precedent, hastily composed a reply to this new form of attack. Dragging analysts before the courts was, as he remarked in a letter to Eitingon, a more effective and no less perfidious weapon than slander had been in the past:

'The movement against lay analysis seems to be only an offshoot of the old resistance against analysis in general. Unfortunately many of our own members are so short-sighted, or so blinded by their professional interests, as to join in. I regard the whole movement as an expression of annoyance at the benevolent interest my seventieth birthday aroused in the outer world, and so feel partly responsible for it. . . .' [1]

The ideas Freud defended in these books [2] helped to intensify the opposition between the Europeans and the Anglo-Saxons, who at the time were demanding that their profession be recognized by law. The controversy is still going

[1] Ernest Jones, III, p. 293.

[2] Freud related them directly to his defence of psychoanalysis against the encroachments of religion. Cf. a letter to Pfister, November 25, 1928: 'I do not know if you have tumbled to the connection that exists between the *Lay Analysis* and the *Illusion*. In the first I want to protect analysis against the doctors, in the second I am defending it against the priests. I should like to send it to a corporation which does not yet exist, to a body of lay clergymen who would not have the right to be priests and no need to be doctors. . . .'

on, although, for all practical purposes, the matter has been decided by the legislation in force in the various countries concerned. In France, where psychoanalysis has no legal standing, the non-medical analysts are always exposed to action for illegal practice. It must be noted, however, that when a case of this nature came up in 1951 it was dismissed by the Paris courts.

And so Freud once again took up the fight with all his old ardour, even putting aside the remarkable reserve he had always maintained about the deep convictions of his age. His previous work was definitely violently critical of the moral and intellectual ideas as well as the aims of the contemporary world; but the criticism was made in an indirect way, by reducing all thought and behaviour to their remote, childhood origins, which were obscure for the individual and humiliating for society. Now, fortified by the deepest interest he roused almost everywhere in the world, Freud told his age what he thought of its illusions, its hopes and its childish consolations.

The Future of an Illusion,[1] written in 1927, returns to the subject of religion dealt with in *Totem and Taboo,* the difference being that in the new book Freud investigates not the psychology of religious fact but the objective value of religious faith and its relationship with truth. Naturally the little book contains, in the first place, a declaration of atheism, then a consideration of religious illusion, which is seen not as an error of judgement but, however sublime, as a form of compensation, a comforting thought like those inspired in a child by his infinite weakness. Against this illusion, which deludes the individual and lulls him into a false sense of security, Freud sets science, which is imperfect, largely powerless and liable to error but adult, capable of rectifying its own mistakes and, in spite of its groping, tentative advance, increasingly capable of progress. Finally, Freud answers the imaginary questioner he has brought into the discussion: 'No, our science is not an illusion. But it would be one to believe that we could draw from somewhere or other what it cannot give us.'[2]

Civilization and Its Discontents, published three years later, continues this reflection with a look at the future which, for the first time, tears Freud away from his pa-

[1] *Std Edn* XXI.

[2] Ibid.

tient exploration of the past. After an even harsher attack on the archaic and intellectually retrograde character of religious illusion, Freud wonders where the lofty civilization of which contemporary man is so proud, although it imposes enormous sacrifices on his search for happiness, is heading. To all appearances it is moving towards an increasingly severe repression of the instincts and Freud sees that as the cause of its discontent, since it is madness to force nature beyond a certain point and madness to think that the human libido is capable of indefinite sublimation. The abolition of private property as decreed by the young communist society might offer some hope as property is rooted in aggression and the destructive instincts which, periodically, imperil civilization. Civilization should, therefore, not have to drag in the myth of the good man who is naturally capable of self-denial and high ideals. In other words, it should refuse to countenance a new and dangerous illusion.

'The fateful question for the human species seems to me to be whether and to what extent their cultural development will succeed in mastering the disturbance of their communal life by the human instinct of aggression and self-destruction. It may be that in this respect precisely the present time deserves a special interest. Men have gained control over the forces of nature to such an extent that with their help they would have no difficulty in exterminating one another to the last man. They know this, and hence comes a large part of their current unrest, their unhappiness and their mood of anxiety. And now it is to be expected that the other of the two "Heavenly Powers", eternal Eros, will make an effort to assert himself in the struggle with his equally immortal adversary. . . .'[1]

During these years, when weakness and daily pain kept him to some extent out of the world and when the world, very belatedly, came to him, Freud did not give his mind merely to the great, ultimate questions, nor even to the more practical problems connected with the future of psychoanalysis. He also went back to his favourite subjects—the unconscious and dreams, which never ceased to interest him. In a little paper with the curious title of 'A Note

[1] *Civilization and Its Discontents, Std Edn* XXI, p. 145.

upon the "Mystic Writing-Pad" '[1] he made a further attempt to clarify the specific nature of the dark world he discovered by comparing the unconscious with those little writing pads where the writing is done with a dry point on a little pad made of two sheets superimposed on one another. The top one is celluloid, the underneath one wax-coated paper. If one wants to wipe out the day's jottings, one separates the two sheets and the writing disappears. But if the underneath sheet is carefully examined, it is seen to have retained an indelible trace of every single letter, like the unconscious on which everything is written and never erased.

It was a French writer, Maxime Leroy, who during these years afforded Freud a splendid opportunity to go back to the subject of dreams. In his book, *Descartes, le philosophe au masque,*[2] Maxime Leroy described one of Descartes' dreams which he invited Freud to interpret. Freud accepted, but impressed, perhaps even intimidated, by the stature of his subject, he tendered his results with considerable reserve, in an allusive form which was most unusual for him. Psychoanalysts could amuse themselves by writing down the analytic content of this dream which Freud, for once breaking his own rule of absolute frankness, rather clumsily concealed.

Here are Descartes's dreams as Maxime Leroy related them in Chapter VI of his book, *Dreams during a Night in Swabia*:

'Then, during the night, when all was fever, thunderstorms, panic, phantoms rose before the dreamer. He tried to get up in order to drive them away. But he fell back, ashamed of himself, feeling troubled by a great weakness in his right side. All at once, a window in the room opened. Terrified, he felt himself carried away by the gusts of a violent wind, which made him whirl round several times on his left foot.

'Dragging himself staggering along, he reached the buildings of the college in which he had been educated. He tried desperately to enter the chapel, to make his devotions. At that moment some people passed by. He wanted to stop in order to speak to them; he noticed that one of them was carrying a melon. But a violent wind drove him back towards the chapel.

[1] *Std Edn,* XIX, pp. 227–32.

[2] Rieder, Paris, 1929.

'He then woke up, with twinges of sharp pain in his left side. He did not know whether he was dreaming or awake. Half-awake, he told himself that an evil genius was trying to seduce him, and he murmured a prayer to exorcise it.

'He went to sleep again. A clap of thunder woke him again and filled his room with flashes. Once more he asked himself whether he was asleep or awake, whether it was a dream or a day-dream, opening and shutting his eyes so as to reach a certainty. Then, reassured, he dozed off, swept away by exhaustion.

'With his brain on fire, excited by these rumours and vague sufferings, Descartes opened a dictionary and then a collection of poems. The intrepid traveller dreamt of this line: *"Quod vitae sectabor iter?"* Another journey in the land of dreams? Then suddenly there appeared a man he did not know, intending to make him read a passage from Ausonius beginning with the words *"Est et non"*. But the man disappeared and another took his place. The book vanished in its turn, then re-appeared decorated with portraits in copper-plate. Finally, the night grew quiet.' [1]

This dream, or rather series of dreams, was analysed by Descartes himself. This is what Freud added in a letter written in French:

'On considering your letter asking me to examine some dreams of Descartes', my first feeling was an impression of dismay, since working on dreams without being able to obtain from the dreamer himself any indications on the relations which might link them to one another or attach them to the external world—and this is clearly the case when it is a question of the dreams of a historical figure—gives, as a general rule, only a meagre result. In the event my task turned out to be easier than I had anticipated; nevertheless, the fruit of my investigations will no doubt seem to you much less important than you had a right to expect.

'Our philosopher's dreams are what are known as "dreams from above" (*"Träume von oben"*). That is to say, they are formulations of ideas which could have been created just as well in a waking state as during the state of sleep, and which have derived their content only in certain parts from mental states at a comparatively deep level.

[1] 'Some Dreams of Descartes: A Letter to Maxime Leroy', *Std Edn* XXI, pp. 200–1.

That is why these dreams offer for the most part a content which has an abstract, poetic or symbolic form.

'The analysis of dreams of this kind usually leads us to the following position: we cannot understand the dream, but the dreamer—or the patient—can translate it immediately and without difficulty, given that the content of the dream is very close to his conscious thoughts. There then remain certain parts of the dream about which the dreamer does not know what to say: and these are precisely the parts which belong to the unconscious and which are in many respects the most interesting.

'In the most favourable cases we explain this unconscious [part] with the help of the ideas which the dreamer has added to it.

'This way of judging "dreams from above"—and this term must be understood in a psychological, not in a mystical, sense—is the one to be followed in the case of Descartes' dreams.

'The philosopher interprets them himself and, in accordance with all the rules for the interpretation of dreams, we must accept his explanation, but it should be added that we have no path open to us which will take us any further.

'In confirmation of his explanation we can say that the hindrances which prevented him from moving freely are perfectly well known to us: they are a representation by the dream of an internal conflict. The left side represents evil and sin, and the wind the "evil genius" (*animus*).

'The different figures who appear in the dream cannot of course be identified by us, although Descartes, if he were questioned, would not have failed to identify them. The bizarre elements, of which, incidentally, there are few, and which are almost absurd—such as "the melon from a foreign land", and the little portraits—remain unexplained.

'As regards the melon, the dreamer has had the—original—idea of seeing in it "the charms of solitude, but presented by purely human inducements". This is certainly not correct, but it might provide an association of ideas which would lead to a correct explanation. If it is correlated with his state of sin, this association might stand for a sexual picture which occupied the lonely young man's imagination.

'On the question of the portraits Descartes throws no light.'[1]

[1] Ibid., pp. 203–4.

Freud's extraordinary literary output during this period would be surprising in itself, quite apart from the tremendous number of activities which he could not or did not want to forgo in spite of his age and the almost unremitting pain he had to endure. After the war he had gradually stopped taking patients for treatment so that he could devote himself to the training of the young analysts who flocked to Vienna from abroad in ever growing numbers. And although he had to refuse many, these training analyses still took up much of his time.

There were also all kinds of problems to do with the intellectual and social life of the movement which Freud found it impossible to ignore as it was then approaching a decisive moment in its history. Psychoanalytical Societies were multiplying all over the world, Institutes were being set up almost everywhere, rather like private University Departments in which the teaching was carefully supervised and modelled on the Berlin Institute with its Polyclinic, which had been founded in 1922 thanks to a generous donaton given anonymously by Max Eitingon. Freud found it impossible not to help these undertakings any more than not to participate in the annual International Congresses, at which his papers, even if he was not there in person, were always the main attraction. Add to this the continual financial difficulties of the Verlag, by which he was personally affected, the proliferation of psychoanalytical reviews, which naturally demanded a great deal of extra work from everyone, and finally the enormous correspondence which the now famous old scientist kept up with the whole world, and one gets some idea of the really overwhelming task which he was called upon to perform and which he did almost without fail until the end.

The letters of this period, which have unfortunately been published only in part, reveal Freud as a man of unimpaired mind, perhaps with a touch of bitterness and a more marked tendency to scepticism than before, but as penetrating and as unyielding as ever where truth was involved. The honours which began to be showered on him hardly moved him, flattery annoyed him and marks of sympathy seemed to him to be due more to publicity and conventionality than to a genuine acceptance of his ideas. When the Vienna City Council, where the Social Democrats at last held a majority, bestowed the Freedom of the City on him in honour of his sixty-eighth birthday, he wrote to Abraham:

'The idea that my coming 68th birthday may be the last must have occurred to other people too, since the city of Vienna has hastened to bestow on me that honour of its *Bürgerrecht*, which usually waits for one's 70th birthday.' [1]

And to Ferenczi, who inquired what the title meant:

'There is little to be said about the Vienna *Bürgerrecht* you mention. It seems to be essentially a ritual performance: just enough for one Sabbath.' [2]

The same inflexibility emerges from a letter to Stekel, who had probably been very distressed by the rumours about Freud's health which were circulating in Vienna and had begged him to forget their old quarrels and accept his help against the enemies of the cause:

'I acknowledge receipt of your letter of 31.12.1923, and thank you for your good wishes regarding the improvement of my health. But I cannot refrain from contradicting you on a few important points.

'You are mistaken if you think that I hate or have hated you. The facts are that after an initial sympathy—perhaps you still remember how our relationship began—I had reason for many years to be annoyed with you while at the same time having to defend you against the aversion of everyone around me, and that I broke with you after you had deceived me on a certain occasion [3] in the most heinous manner. (You never mentioned this occasion—*Zentralblatt*—in your letters.) I lost confidence in you at that time and since then you have not provided me with any experience that could help me to regain it.

'I also contradict your often repeated assertion that you were rejected by me on account of scientific differences. This sounds quite good in public, but it doesn't correspond to the truth. It was exclusively your personal qualities—usually described as character and behaviour—which made collaboration with you impossible for my friends and myself. As you most certainly will not change—you don't

[1] Ernest Jones, III, p. 102.

[2] Ibid.

[3] After leaving the Psychoanalytical Association Stekel had refused to resign his editorship of the *Zentralblatt für Psychoanalyse*.

need to, for Nature has endowed you with an unusual degree of self-complacency—our relationship stands no chance of becoming any different from what it has been during the past twelve years. It will not annoy me to learn that your medical and literary activities have earned you success; I admit that you have remained loyal to psychoanalysis and have been of use to it; you have also done it great harm.'[1]

The controversy associated with his name hampered any reconciliation between Freud and his contemporaries who, apart from a few courageous ones, had been a little too slow in recognizing his genius. In America the sudden craze for Freud took the usual highly publicized form. The press and publicity interests joined in, even the film world became involved when Samuel Goldwyn asked Freud to make a 'psychoanalytical' film about the secrets of famous love stories. In principle he had no objections to the popularization of his ideas and he was not in the least shocked by this proposal as he thought his signature would be a guarantee of its seriousness. Moreover, the Verlag finances were once more very low and the contract was very tempting. He therefore accepted the offer but soon regretted his naïveté. The negotiations were broken off and the project was taken up by German psychoanalysts—but with no more success.

Europe behaved more seriously, but apart from England, which a little later bestowed on him the highest distinction he ever received—namely, Corresponding Member of the Royal Society—scientific circles in all countries remained as silent as in the past. In France, medicine in general always took its lead from the malevolent even dishonest criticism which Pierre Janet had made his speciality since the time of Charcot. And it was not medicine but literature which can take the credit for interesting a section of the cultured public in Freud. André Breton and his friends, and later André Gide, who declared in the *Nouvelle Revue Française* that Freud should be given a place of honour, championed the cause of psychoanalysis which scientists and University dons refused to recognize as being anything but a typical example of German extrava-

[1] To Stekel, January 13, 1924, *Letters*, pp. 347–8.

gance marred by 'bad taste' and irrationality, two things that were incompatible with 'French genius'.[1]

As early as 1926, however, the Paris Psycho-Analytical Society, founded through the efforts of Eugénie Sokolnicka, a pupil of Freud and Ferenczi, was responsible for a wider dissemination of Freud's ideas in psychiatric circles; and Edouard Pichon, hospital specialist, child psychiatrist and distinguished linguist, provided the Society with its indispensable tool by carefully working out the French psychoanalytical vocabulary.

The establishment of psychoanalysis in France was greatly helped by Princess Marie Bonaparte, who, as a friend and pupil of Freud, formed throughout these years the most solid link between Paris and Vienna. Besides writing her own books, of which some such as the one on Edgar Allan Poe have made her famous, Marie Bonaparte translated many of Freud's works. To her initiative, her moral and material help, was due the first French psychoanalytical Institute, to which she bequeathed her important library and still unpublished manuscripts. In 1938 her courage, intelligence and devotion made it possible for Freud to escape from the Nazis before it was too late.

The situation in Germany was somewhat different for there the controversies provoked by Freud were older and more bitter, and the partisanship more fanatical, often being for the anxious intellectuals of the inter-war years the equivalent of a political faith. In spite of a few sensational 'conversions' from the ranks of doctors and psychiatrists, the German medical world remained fundamentally hostile to analysis and, just as in France, the honour of intelligence was saved by writers and artists. During the political upheavals which preceded the advent of Nazism, all clear-thinking and talented people in Germany hailed Freud not only as one of the great men of the age but as an exemplary figure embodying the indomitable courage of the spirit.

[1] In 1932 Dr Génil-Perrin, head doctor of the Seine Asylums, wrote in *Maladies nerveuses et mentales* (Larousse, 1932): 'Freudianism deserves an honourable mention in the chapter on the causes of mental illness . . . Psychoanalysis presents itself as a religious revival, a mystical leap. On this score it can help people who suffer from having to give up mystical thought too soon.' And he quoted this definitive judgement by F. Achille-Delmas: 'Sigmund Freud is an ignorant psychiatrist and an incompetent clinician. In Freudian psychiatry there are things both good and new; but what is new is not good and what is good is not new.'

Some of the best known writers had long been his friends. He corresponded with Arthur Schnitzler, Stefan Zweig and Thomas Mann; and the latter, who occupied an exceptional position in German letters, had the rare generosity to put his own fame at Freud's service, as though to make up for his compatriots' stupidity and the scientists' injustice. After 1926 Freud's birthdays ceased to be a private affair shared by the little group of faithful friends, becoming instead a literary occasion which called forth public tributes with which the greatest names were happy to be associated. In 1930, Dr Alfons Paquet, Secretary of the Frankfurt Goethe Prize for Literature, proposed that the Prize should be awarded to Freud for his work as a whole, although it did not by its nature conform to the requirements for the Prize. This suggestion raised a fine storm, but Alfons Paquet, Alfred Döblin[1] and other people of importance stuck to their guns and in the end carried the day, so that Freud, who had given up so many legitimate honours, received the only distinction which he had doubtless never imagined would come his way. On July 26, 1930, he wrote to thank Alfons Paquet:

'I have not been spoiled by public honours, and have therefore accustomed myself to getting along without them. I cannot deny, however, that the Award of the Goethe Prize by the City of Frankfurt has given me great pleasure. There is something about it that particularly warms the imagination, and one of its conditions eliminates the humiliation normally associated with such distinctions.

'I owe you special thanks for your letter; it moved and surprised me. Quite apart from [my appreciation of] the trouble you have taken to study my work, [I must tell you that] I have never before found its secret personal intention recognized with so much clarity, and I would have liked to ask you how you happen to have divined it.

'I am sorry to learn from your letter to my daughter that I shall not be seeing you in the near future; delay at my time of life is somewhat risky. Of course I shall be very pleased to receive the gentleman (Dr Michel) announced by you.

'Unfortunately I cannot come to the celebration in Frankfurt; my health is not reliable enough for such an

[1] Alfred Döblin, novelist, famous author of *Berlin-Alexanderplatz*, was a doctor and worked at the Berlin psychoanalytic Polyclinic.

undertaking. The audience will lose nothing by my absence; my daughter is certainly more pleasant to the eye and ear than I am. She is going to read a few lines[1] dealing with Goethe in relation to psychoanalysis and defending the analysts against the reproach of having impugned the veneration due to the great man by their analytical investigations.'[2]

By now Freud was regarded as one of the three greatest living Jews, the other two being Bergson and Einstein, and his seventy-fifth birthday was the occasion for innumerable expressions of sympathy all over the world, so that Freud could see that everywhere, except in Vienna, times had really changed. The famous house in the Berggasse was flooded with telegrams, gifts and flowers, and from the depths of his sick room Freud received the homage of his most famous contemporaries, Romain Rolland, H. G. Wells, Einstein, Selma Lagerlöf, Theodore Dreiser and many others; but as he had just undergone a terrible operation and was exhausted by hunger and unable to speak, he could not see any of his friends. While the Sixth Congress of medical psychiatry, under the Presidency of the noted Kretschmer, was devoting its labours in Dresden to the psychology of dreams and two hundred famous people gathered in New York to celebrate the anniversary, a great Berlin newspaper carried the following tribute by Thomas Mann:

'I have always felt the most sincere admiration for this great explorer of the human mind and for his crusade for truth. He manifestly possesses many of the features of Dürer's Knight, the Knight between Death and the Devil to whom Nietzsche seems to allude when he speaks of Schopenhauer, that other spiritual kinsman of Freud: "A man, a knight with the steely look who has the courage to be himself, who can stand alone and waits neither for the orders of those who went before nor signs from on high." He has never taken any account of the fact that men heed only what flatters them. He has never spoken to the believer of the rewards of virtue, to Ixion of the clouds, to the people of liberty and equality. He has destroyed illu-

1 Speech of thanks accepting the Goethe Prize (August 28, 1930), *Std Edn* XXI, pp. 208–12.

2 To Alfons Paquet, July 26, 1930, *Letters*, p. 398.

sion, shocked humanity by suggesting to it knowledge of a radical naturalism which seemed to threaten its "dignity" and provoked resistance, the reasons for which were obvious to him. But all criticism of his work—I mean all criticism which does not intend to go beyond psychoanalysis, but only turn back—there is something vain and sterile about all criticism of his work, even where it is right, and it is difficult to understand that those who pour scorn on it do not realize the vanity of their efforts.

'I am happy to have had the opportunity to profess to him my faith, although it is too late to claim any credit for this. I am happy to do so because it has given the grand old man some joy. The gratitude he showed when, after saying "he believed he was a foreign body in this nation", I "gave him a place in German intellectual life" moved me deeply. I am very tempted to disclose many characteristic and revealing things in the magnificent letter he wrote to me then, but I cannot do so without his permission. I will, however, take the liberty of quoting one phrase in the belief that readers will prefer an unknown remark by Freud to a remark about him: "I have always admired—admired and envied the poets, especially when, like the ideal of my youth, Lessing, they subject their art to thought and put it at its service". . . .' [1]

In the year 1931, which saw economic collapse in Austria and the first assaults by Hitlerism in Germany, the publication of Freud's Complete Works was in the nature of a symbolic event. The extreme left-wing intellectuals, who were entering on the desperate phase of their futile struggle, felt that the psychoanalytic revolution was henceforth inseparable from the other revolution. The literary and political review *Die Weltbühne*, edited by Carl von Ossietzky, who was to be one of the first victims of the Nazis, published under the signature of the poet Kurt Tucholsky one of the finest and certainly one of the truest tributes which Freud could expect in his lifetime:

'Freud's Complete Works have been published. Eleven volumes which shook the world.

'One of the few people who see this man accurately appears to be Freud himself. He can adorn the rotten apples of his adversaries with the laurels of his fame and, if he is

[1] Letter to the editor of the *Vossische Zeitung*, May 6, 1931.

wise, he will contemplate the band of his pupils and draw his own conclusions. Let us forget the bad pupils and stick to the good ones and to him.

'According to Schopenhauer it is the fate of truth to appear at first paradoxical, then trivial. Freud is a good example of this. But his complete works reveal something else.

'The flesh and all that is fortuitous and commonplace about this work is dropping away, leaving the bare bone. We cannot know what will be left by 1995, nor even whether anything will be left in the form he gave it. But one can be sure that it will continue to be an active force.

'Parts of these eleven volumes, particularly in the early ones, are like thrilling detective stories. You can see how the theories slowly germinate, emerge from their broken covering, see the light of day and suddenly make their appearance with power and assurance. Freud's art is everywhere unvarying; in the fundamental works and in the short essays, as in the wonderful piece written in memory of Charcot—a clear mind, with a talent for order and method is at work everywhere.

"What is merely fashionable in his writings will pass. The childish joy which Americans and other nations warped by puritanism feel in at last being able to speak publicly of sex is not Freud's fault. The great renewer of old, buried truths—of the truth that the will of man is not free—will remain.

'Freud's limitations are obvious in his books. He is not God, but he has taught us to discern the part played by illness in the criticisms levelled against him. Let it be said for the benefit of semi-educated Catholics: his work is the Bible of the ungodly. Ignorance of his work means failure to understand the world. Sigmund Freud will be seventy-five on May 6th. We greet him in love and respect.' [1]

1 Kurt Tucholsky: 'Elf Bände die Welt erschütterten', *Die Weltbühne*, Berlin, May 1931.

28

MOSES AND EXILE

When he received the Goethe Prize, Freud must have felt that a melancholy phase of his career was beginning and that, with nothing new to say, he would simply have to wait for death while protecting himself as best he might against the distortions of his own legend. To outlive himself, to be erected in the midst of the present like a venerable and ancient monument was certainly a humiliating prospect for a man for whom thinking had been one long action and Freud never intended to accept it. His mother's death at the age of ninety-five after a slow decline at last afforded him the hope of escaping the fate which seemed to be in store for him. Behind this hope lay a strange line of argument which he had applied to himself many times before and which he now restated in a letter to Ferenczi:

'Above all my warm thanks for your beautiful words about the death of my mother. It has affected me in a peculiar way, this great event. No pain, no grief, which probably can be explained by the special circumstances—her great age, my pity for her helplessness towards the end; at the same time a feeling of liberation, of release, which I think I also understand. I was not free to die as long as she was alive, and now I am. The values of life will somehow have changed noticeably in the deeper layers. . . .

'The gruesome newspaper reports about my health will probably have reached you, too. I find them very interesting as a proof of the difficulty of forcing upon the general public something it doesn't like. For they are the reaction to the Goethe Prize and must warn us against the illusion that the resistance to psychoanalysis has subsided in a practical, tangible way. . . .

'I am glad you are working. What with the congratulations for the Prize, the letters of condolence concerning my own fatal illness and now the death of my mother, not to mention the discomforts of the continuous abstinence from smoking, I don't find time for anything.'[1]

As so often in the past Freud once more believed his inspiration had dried up for good; and his age and the physical misery he suffered after each of his operations seemed to justify his thinking like this. However, his literary activity was far from over; but it was no longer his main purpose in life, which was to counter the exaggerations that came with fame, from whatever quarter they emanated, by presenting to the world a true image of himself and his life. If he was hurt by the attacks or the insincerity of some panegyrics, he could no more stomach overzealous apologias which made him out to be a conventional person and thereby diminished his humanity. Much of his correspondence during his last ten years expresses this constant anxiety to correct all the inaccuracies and mistaken ideas of him which were circulating, whether they were due to ignorance, more or less camouflaged malevolence or his friends' rather uncritical admiration. For instance, this letter to an American writer who compared him to the two greatest contemporary representatives of Jewish genius:

'I cannot refrain from confessing to a certain disappointment. You do me great honour in the book; you mention my name among the greatest of our people (which goes far beyond my ambition) and so on; [but] in the essay ("Doctrine of Lapses") you express disbelief about just that part of psychoanalysis which has most readily found general recognition. How then are you going to judge our far less attractive discoveries? My feeling is that if your objections to my interpretation of lapses is justified, then I have very little claim to be mentioned with Bergson and Einstein among the intellectual giants. You realize what I am aiming at. I wish neither to be crowned with the Nobel Prize nor to be discussed in every newspaper; I hope to have gained a useful piece of new insight.

'I haven't yet read the paragraph about psychoanalysis in your book; I am afraid to find incorrect statements in it which I shall regret. In some of your assertions I recognise myself as little (for instance, no one has so far reproached me with "mystical leanings", and over the question of

[1] To Ferenczi, September 16, 1930, *Letters*, p. 401.

hypnosis I sided against Charcot, even if not entirely with Bernheim) as I do in the appalling picture of my physical appearance which you have included.

'It may interest you to hear that my father did indeed come from a Chassidic background. He was 41 when I was born and had been estranged from his native environment for almost 20 years. My education was so un-Jewish that today I cannot even read your dedication, which is evidently written in Hebrew. In later life I have often regretted this lack in my education.

'With the expression of that sympathy which your courageous defence of our people demands, I beg to remain, Yours sincerely, Freud.' [1]

The same love of truth, the same wish to be seen exactly as he was without the useless ornament of borrowed greatness finds expression in two letters written to Stefan Zweig about *Mental Healers,* in which Freud could see, doubtless with mixed feelings, a portrait of himself:

'That one doesn't like one's own portrait, or that one doesn't recognise oneself in it, is a general and well-known fact. I therefore hasten to express my satisfaction at your having recognized correctly the most important feature in my case. Namely, that in so far as achievement is concerned it was less the result of intellect than of character. This seems to be the core of your opinion, and one in which I myself believe. On the other hand I feel inclined to object to the emphasis you put on the element of *petit-bourgeois* correctness in my person.

'The fellow is actually somewhat more complicated; your description doesn't tally with the fact that I, too, have had my splitting headaches and attacks of fatigue like anyone else, that I was a passionate smoker (I wish I still were), that I ascribe to the cigar the greatest share of my self-control and tenacity in work, that despite my much vaunted frugality I have sacrificed a great deal for my collection of Greek, Roman and Egyptian antiquities, have actually read more archaeology than psychology, and that before the war and once after its end I felt compelled to spend every year at least several days or weeks in Rome, and so on. I realise from my experience with art in

[1] To A. A. Roback, February 20, 1930, about Roback's book, *Jewish Influence in Modern Thought, Letters,* pp. 394–5.

miniature that this medium compels the artist to simplify, but the result is often a distorted picture.' [1]

A year later Stefan Zweig received another correction, which Freud regarded as even more important. But this time it concerned the history of Freud's discoveries, not his personality:

'I re-read parts of your essay and discovered on page 272 an error of representaion which cannot be looked upon as unimportant and which, if you don't mind my saying so, actually belittles my merit. It declares that Breuer's patient under hypnosis made the confession of having experienced and suppressed certain "*sentimenti illeciti*" (i.e. of sexual nature) while sitting at her father's sick-bed. In reality she said nothing of the kind; rather she indicated that she was trying to conceal from her father her agitated condition, above all her tender concern. If things had been as your text maintains, then everything else would have taken a different turn. I would not have been surprised by the discovery of sexual etiology, Breuer would have found it more difficult to refute this theory, and if hypnosis could obtain such candid confessions, I probably would never have abandoned it.

'What really happened with Breuer's patent I was able to guess later on, long after the break in our relations, when I suddenly remembered something Breuer had once told me in another context before we had begun to collaborate and which he never repeated. On the evening of the day when all her symptoms had been disposed of, he was summoned to the patient again, found her confused and writhing in abdominal cramps. Asked what was wrong with her, she replied: "Now Dr B.'s child is coming!"

'At this moment he held in his hand the key that would have opened the "doors to the Mothers",[2] but he let it drop. With all his great intellectual gifts there was nothing Faustian in his nature.' [3]

This vigilant watch over the truth was not his sole preoccupation. He went on writing to raise money for the Verlag which was in considerable financial difficulty. In 1932

[1] To Stefan Zweig, February 7, 1931, *Letters*, pp. 402–3.

[2] An allusion to Faust's descent to the Mothers in Part II of Goethe's *Faust*.

[3] To Stefan Zweig, June 2, 1932, *Letters*, pp. 412–3.

he published *New Introductory Lectures on Psycho-analysis,*[1] a collection of fictitious lectures which form a sequel to his first lectures and give a complete account of his ideas. The same year he wrote, in collaboration with Einstein, Why War?[2], a pamphlet commissioned by the League of Nations in which he set against the pacificism of his illustrious colleague his own views on human nature, the essence of which he held to be always war and hated. This discussion, which he considered boring and sterile, led him to say that, as regards the perfection of his work, it would henceforth be like his prosthesis—both forced him to lower his old claims a lot.

But he was destined not to finish his work in peace and for a long time yet events bore out his pessimism. A few months after *Why War?* came the triumph of the Nazis in Germany, the beginning of the exodus of German psychoanalysts and the panic which drove many of them to Vienna. In April 1933 Ferenczi, who was rapidly going downhill and suffering from serious mental illness, begged Freud to flee before it was too late. In the last letter he wrote to him Freud refused, saying: 'If they kill me that would after all be as good a death as any other.' A month later Ferenczi's death left him apparently almost unmoved, although it is true that this man, the dearest of his followers, had long been a prey to terrible delusions in which his wonderful intelligence, like his passionate affection for his master, had gradually disintegrated.

At the same time Freud learned that his books had been burned in Berlin, but, quoting the words of a poet, he confessed he had 'ceased to understand the world', and he still believed the barbarous drama was merely a sinister symbol. He never suspected that it was the prelude to the actual extermination of his people and that, twelve years later, the four sisters he was to leave behind in Vienna would be numbered among the millions of martyrs.

Of course German psychoanalysis, being essentially Jewish, was the first of all German institutions to suffer. Eitingon, who was of Polish nationality, was forced to give up his post as director of the Berlin Institute and decided to emigrate. Settling in Palestine, he founded an Institute which still exists and where Israeli psychoanalysts continue to be trained. At the end of the year 1933, which

[1] *Std Edn* XXII.

[2] Ibid., pp. 199 ff.

for so many people marked the end of a world, one of the two original centres of European psychoanalysis, the most vital and the richest in promise, was competely destroyed.

In June 1933 the Deutsche Allgemeine Ärztliche Gesellschaft für Psychotherapie, that is, the German Society for Psychotheraphy, came under the control of the Nazi authorities. The President, Kretschmer, immediately resigned. He was replaced by Jung, who, as a Swiss national, was under no pressure whatsoever. Jung also edited the *Zentralblatt für Psychotherapie,* the Society's official organ in which Dr Göring, a cousin of the Nazi leader, was made a co-director in 1936. Jung's special task was to establish a 'scientific' dividing line between Aryan and Jewish psychology, in other words between the doctrine of the 'collective unconscious' and Freud's psychoanalysis, against which it was now easy for him to take revenge. Although he was violently attacked by his Swiss colleagues,[1] who considered he had violated their neutrality, Jung continued to collaborate with Göring until 1940: but the results of this period of his research never appeared in his subsequent work.

Dr Göring tried to prevent the complete dissolution of the Berlin Psychoanalytical Society, which continued to exist for some time thanks to the action of its Jewish members, who resigned of their own accord in the vain hope that a compromise might somehow help to save the 'cause'. But, as in many other cases, these sacrifices and compromises served no purpose. Ernest Jones described the unbelievable negotiations he had to undertake in an attempt to preserve even the semblance of life in the purged group:

'On July 19, 1936, I had a meeting in Basle with Göring, Boehm, and Müller-Braunschweig. Brill was also present. I found Göring a fairly amiable and amenable person, but it turned out later that he was not in a position to fulfil the promises he made me about the degree of freedom that was to be allowed the psycho-analytical group. No doubt in the meantime the Jewish origin of psycho-analysis had been fully explained to him. Training analyses were forbidden, but lectures still allowed. Göring, or his wife, how-

[1] Cf. G. Bally: 'Deutschstämmige Psychotherapie', *Neue Zürcher Zeitung,* No. 343, 1934 and, giving the other point of view, Ludwig Marcuse: 'Der Fall C. G. Jung', *Aufbau,* December 30, 1955 and April 27, 1956.

ever, made a point of attending the latter to ensure that no psychoanalytical technical terms were used, so the Oedipus complex had to figure under a synonym. In January 1937, Boehm managed to get once more to Vienna. At an interview Freud proposed that he describe the situation to a larger group, which he did on the following day. . . . Boehm talked for three hours until Freud's patience gave out. He broke into the exposition with the words: "Quite enough! The Jews have suffered for their convictions for centuries. Now the time has come for our Christian colleagues to suffer in their turn for theirs. I attach no importance to my name being mentioned in Germany so long as my work is presented correctly there". . . .'[1]

It is not surprising that these events induced Freud to meditate afresh on the people which he had always called his own and whose appalling fate now confronted the world. He thought about the Bible more than ever, he even turned to the inconceivable promised land to which he had never given the slightest thought and with which he suddenly felt one, without understanding what he owed to it or what could draw him to it. This idea, which anticipates his great book on Moses, is the subject of a letter to Arnold Zweig, who was back from Palestine and thinking of emigrating there.

'To think that this strip of our native earth is associated with no other [*sic*] progress, no discovery or invention—the Phoenicians are said to have invented glass and the alphabet (both doubtful!), the island of Crete is said to have given us Minoan art, Pergamon reminds us of parchment, Magnesia of the magnet, and so on *ad infinitum*—but Palestine has produced nothing but religions, sacred frenzies, presumptuous attempts to conquer the outer world of appearances by the inner world of wishful thinking. And *we* hail from there (although one of us considers himself a German also, the other doesn't), our ancestors lived there perhaps for half, perhaps a whole, millennium (but this also only perhaps), and it is impossible to say how much of the life in that country we carry as heritage in our blood and nerves (as is mistakenly said). Oh, life could be very interesting if only one knew and understood more about such things! But the only things we

[1] Ernest Jones, III, p. 187.

can be sure of are our feelings of the moment! Among them my warm feelings for you and your work!'[1]

While he tried to convince himself that Austria would be spared the Nazi plague or, if it did spread there, that his country's noble civilization or the Allies' vigilance would at least ensure that limitations would be imposed on it, Freud, moving back through time, joined company with the great Biblical figures who were responsible for the persecution of his people as much as for its mysterious indestructibility. Moses in particular haunted him, but he was also fascinated by the patriarchs, and Joseph, in whom he had always recognized himself. Thomas Mann's *Joseph and His Brethren,* which had just been published, revived his interest in the hero who appeared in so many significant guises in *The Interpretation of Dreams.* After Thomas Mann had delivered a brilliant lecture which owed much to psychoanalysis, Freud wrote to him:

'Not long ago I laid aside your new volume of the Joseph legend with the melancholy thought that this beautiful experience is now over and that I shall probably not be able to read the sequel.

'The effect of this story combined with the idea of the "lived vita" in your lecture and the mythological prototype has started within me a trend of thought which I am making the pretext of a talk with you as though you were sitting opposite me here in my study, but without wishing to provoke a polite reply, let alone a detailed appreciation. I myself do not take the experiment very seriously, but it does have for me a certain attraction, something like the cracking of a whip for an ex-coachman.

'I keep wondering if there isn't a figure in history for whom the life of Joseph was a mythical prototype, allowing us to detect the phantasy of Joseph as the secret daemonic motor behind the scenes of his complex life?

'I am thinking of Napoleon I.

'a) He was a Corsican, the second son of a large family of brothers and sisters. His eldest brother was called Joseph, and this fact, as chance and necessity are wont to combine in human life, was fateful for him. In a Corsican family the privilege of the eldest is guarded with a particularly sacred awe. (I think Alphonse Daudet once described

[1] To Arnold Zweig, May 8, 1932, *Letters,* pp. 411–2.

this in a novel. In *Le Nabob?* Or am I mistaken? Was it in some other book? In Balzac?) By this Corsican tradition a normal human relationship becomes exaggerated. The elder brother is the natural rival; the younger one feels for him an elementary, unfathomably deep hostility for which in later life the expressions death-wish and murderous intent may be found appropriate. To eliminate Joseph, to take his place, to become Joseph himself, must have been Napoleon's strongest emotion as a small child. It is strange, no doubt, and yet it has been correctly observed, that just these very excessive infantile impulses tend to turn into their opposite. The hated rival becomes the loved one. This was the case with Napoleon. We assume that he started out with an ardent hatred of Joseph, but we learn that later on he loved him more than any other human being and could hardly find a fault with this worthless, unreliable man. Thus the original hatred had been overcompensated, but the early aggression released was only waiting to be transferred to other objects. Hundreds of thousands of unknown individuals had to atone for the fact that this little tyrant had spared his first enemy.

'b) On another level the young Napoleon was tenderly tied to his mother and concerned to replace his prematurely deceased father by caring for his brothers and sisters. As soon as he became a General it was suggested that he marry a young widow, older than himself, who possessed both influence and rank. There were a number of things to be said against her, but what probably decided him was that her name was Josephine. Owing to this name he could transfer to her part of the tender attachment he felt for his elder brother. She did not love him, treated him badly, betrayed him, but he the despot, as a rule cynically cold towards women, clung to her passionately and forgave her everything; nothing she did could arouse his anger.

'c) The infatuation for Josephine B. was undoubtedly brought about by the name, but of course, it was not an identification with Joseph. This emerges most clearly in the famous expedition to Egypt. Where else could one go but to Egypt if one were Joseph and wanted to loom large in the brother's eyes? If we were to examine the political reasons for this enterprise of the young General, we would probably find that they were nothing but the wilful rationalisation of a fantastic idea. It was this campaign, by the way, that marked the beginning of Egypt's rediscovery.

'd) The intention which drove Napoleon to Egypt was to be realised in his later life in Europe. He took care of his brothers by making them kings and princes. The good-for-nothing Jerome was perhaps his Benjamin. And then he forsook his myth; he allowed himself to be swayed by practical considerations, to repudiate the beloved Josephine. With this act his decline began. The great destroyer now worked on his self-destruction. The rash, poorly-prepared campaign against Russia led to his downfall. It was like a self-punishment for his disloyalty to Josephine, for the regression from his love to his original hostility towards Joseph. And here too, although contrary to Napoleon's intention, Fate repeated another chapter in the Joseph legend. Joseph's dream—that the sun, the moon, and the stars should bow down to him—led to his being cast into the pit.'[1]

When he sent Thomas Mann this little psychoanalytical essay in which the heroes' fantasies are conceived of as the springs of history, Freud had already written, recast and abandoned the three essays which make up his *Moses and Monotheism*. Apart from Anna, his son Martin and one or two analysts nobody had read the manuscript and few people even knew of the existence of his plan. In 1934, in the midst of increasingly threatening political events, civil war in Vienna and his own intolerable pain, Freud suddenly attacked the great problem which had haunted him all his life—the problem of the origin of religions and of the degree of truth which they must be allowed, both as regards the psychology of the individual and the history of mankind.

The source of the religions which have made history must be sought in Jewish monotheism and the soul of its founder, the solitary figure of Moses whose great Law was flouted by those to whom it had been given and then revered and loved as a divine gift. Troubled by the problem of his own origins, obsessed by the cause of present-day persecution, which exceeded in horror all previous persecutions, Freud asked Moses if it was true that he had not only created the one God but the people which even today describes itself as 'the chosen'.

It was a strange thing to do at a time when pious Jews needed to set more store than ever by their prophet and

[1] To Thomas Mann, November 29, 1936, *Letters*, pp. 432–4.

the sacred letter of his Law. Freud clearly felt this. His letters during this period reveal him as intensely enthusiastic about his work but at the same time worried, intimidated, almost frightened by the result. Was the vast psychological fresco which he was planning an indirect tribute to his people, in spite of everything he believed? It might be thought so, but it was not for him to say it. The fact is that except for the thesis that Moses was an Egyptian, an idea which the orthodox consider blasphemous and archaeologists and historians think highly disputable, the book retraces a spiritual epic in which the figure of the law-giving prophet radiates power, intelligence and light. Misunderstood, derided and murdered by those whom he wanted to raise up to his own level, Moses, with only the help of his stupendous vision of man, transcended time and founded the moral civilization from which a whole world was born. The mysterious perenniality of the Jewish people is his achievement. It owes its origin solely to his destiny as a tragic hero and the power of his terrible will.

The three essays were finished in 1934, yet Freud decided to keep them secret, for reasons which he frequently explained in his letters; but the reasons are not very convincing and are still to some extent obscure. For instance, in a letter to Arnold Zweig which was written in September he said:

'Faced with the renewed persecutions, one asks oneself again how the Jew came to be what he is and why he has drawn upon himself this undying hatred. I soon found the formula: Moses created the Jew. And my essay received the title: *The Man Moses, a historical novel* (with more right than your novel about Nietzsche). The material is divided into three parts, the first reads like an interesting novel; the second is laborious and lengthy, the third substantial and exacting. The enterprise foundered on the third section, for it contains a theory of religion which, although nothing new to me after *Totem and Taboo,* is nevertheless bound to be something fundamentally new and shattering to the uninitiated. Concern for these uninitiated compels me to keep the completed essay secret. For we live here in an atmosphere of Catholic orthodoxy. It is said that the politics of our country are made by a Father Schmidt who lives in [the monastery] St Gabriel near Mödling and is a confidant of the Pope. Unfortunately he himself is an ethnologist and a religious scholar who in his books makes no secret of his horror of psychoanalysis and above all of my totem theory. The good Edoardo Weiss has founded a psychoanalytic group in Rome and has published several numbers of a *Rivista Italiana di Psicoanalisi.* All of a sudden this publication has been stopped, and although Weiss has direct access to Mussolini and received from him a favourable promise, the ban could not be lifted. The ban is said to come straight from the Vatican and Father Schmidt is said to be responsible. Now it stands to reason that a publication of mine would be bound to create a certain sensation and not escape the notice of the inimical priest. This would mean running the risk of having psychoanalysis banned in Vienna and the end of all our publications here. Were this danger confined to myself it would make little impression on me, but to deprive all our members in Vienna of their livelihood strikes me as too great a responsibility. And in addition to all this is the feeling that the essay doesn't seem too well substantiated, nor do I like it entirely. So all in all it isn't quite the proper occasion for martyrdom. . . .'[1]

Should these diplomatic explanations be taken too literally? Freud gave no others. They are the ones he included in his book to explain how it was written when, in 1938, having left Vienna for ever, he finally decided to give it to the world. The work is in three parts. The first two, 'Moses, an Egyptian' and 'If Moses was an Egyptian . . .' formed a book in themselves and were published in the review *Imago* in 1937, while the third, entitled 'Moses and His People', was revised many times before taking its final form. Freud said his long hesitation was due to the fascination the central theme of the chapter held for him and the paralysis which came over him as soon as he proposed to expound it to the public.

This time his theme is no longer the illusory and consoling nature of religion but the grandiose idea that religion contains a part of historical truth. *Moses and Monotheism* is, therefore, more directly related to *Totem and Taboo* than to *The Future of an Illusion,* except that the original crime from which order and civilization sprang is no longer placed in the darkness of pre-history but in the full light of historical reality. Moses, an Egyptian prince and a

[1] To Arnold Zweig, September 20, 1934, *Letters,* pp. 421–2.

believer in the monotheism[1] founded in the fourteenth century B.C. by the Pharaoh Amenhotep IV, who later took the name of Ikhnaton, was forced to flee from Egypt when the priests of the ancient cults rebelled and overthrew his master's religion. Determined to preserve and propagate his faith, he 'chose' one of the Hebrew tribes living in slavery in the border-lands of the Empire and imposed his law on them. But the primitive people, who were indeed 'chosen' since Moses chose them, were not mature enough to understand the sublimity of his thought. Incapable of enduring the intense frustration of the instincts which the monotheistic faith demanded, they constantly reverted to the worship of the 'golden calf', as the Bible recalls, and revolted against their spiritual leader. During one of these revolts the Israelites murdered Moses, but, like the brother murderers in *Totem and Taboo,* they never forgot their crime. It was their remorse which, in the course of centuries, gave Mosaic Law its ideal form and its imprescriptible content. It was the horror of their earlier deed, not mythical but real, which historically assured their astonishing power of survival.

In spite of the dramatic and criminal character he ascribed to the Biblical events, Freud was fascinated by what Moses achieved and he admired him, not only from the point of view of the psychologist, but also from that of the moralist and humanist in love with reason and truth. This comes out clearly in a letter written to an unknown correspondent, in which he says:

> 'I was astounded to find that already the first so to speak embryonic experience of the race, the influence of the man Moses and the exodus from Egypt, conditioned the entire further development up to the present day—like a regular trauma of early childhood in the case history of a neurotic individual. To begin with, there is the temporal conception of life and the conquest of magic thought, the rejection of mysticism, both of which can be traced back to Moses himself and, although not with all the historical certainty that could be desired, perhaps a little further.'[2]

[1] Karl Abraham had devoted an excellent psychoanalytical study ('Amenhotep IV', *Imago,* October 4, 1912) to the heretical young Pharaoh who is held to be the first historical character to proclaim a spiritual religion. In his account of Egyptian monotheism Freud seems not to have remembered him.

[2] To Anon., December 14, 1937, *Letters,* p. 439.

Would it be forcing his thought too much to number him among those 'few others' who, long after the time of Moses, continued his work by combating magic and mystical thought in the name of the highest claims of the intellect? His Moses, whose virile character he brought out with great power, resembled him in many ways but naturally he could only hint at the similarities. Like Moses he proclaimed a difficult law which swept away the old superstitious cults, but 'his people' rose up against him and, periodically, relapsed into apostasy. While they did not kill him they often forsook, betrayed or denied him. And now remorse and the feeling that an irreparable wrong had been committed against him drove them to excessive veneration of his person; but like Moses he did not know what would become of his work and, before he died, he had to undergo one final ordeal—exile.

Until 1938 Freud obstinately refused to leave Vienna, which he looked on as his 'post' which it was his duty to hold. At the beginning of the year he underwent another of the operations which had now become a matter of course, but this time the biopsy showed that his cancer had returned. Nevertheless, ten days later he began to see patients again and in March, when the Nazis invaded Austria, he still would not heed Jones's urgent appeal to him to take refuge in England. But he finally agreed to leave. It was now a matter of getting the indispensable exit visas which the Nazis seemed disposed to grant, or rather sell him for the highest sum they could extort.

His house was searched by a group of Brown Shirts, but perhaps taken aback by Martha, who politely asked them to sit down, they went away with a mere 840 dollars, leaving manuscripts and other papers. They returned a week later. This time they took Anna away with them and she was detained all day by the Gestapo. However, international opinion was roused. W. C. Bullitt, the United States Ambassador to France, telegraphed to Roosevelt, who was his personal friend, asking him to intervene at once. He also approached the German Ambassador to France and Edoardo Weiss asked Mussolini's help. This international vigilance probably saved Freud from being molested or harassed, but the Nazis would probably have let him leave in any case.

The Verlag was confiscated, Freud's complete works were burned, on March 13th the Vienna Psycho-Analytical Society disbanded itself and all the members decided to emigrate. It would have to be formed again wherever Freud could find a home. Freud accepted, saying:

'Immediately after the destruction of the Temple in Jerusalem by Titus, the Rabbi Jochanan ben Zakkai asked permission to open the first Torah school in Jabneth. We are taking the same course ourselves. After all we are used to persecution. . . .'[1]

Ernest Jones set about getting the many visas which were necessary not only for Freud but for his children and grandchildren, his servants, his personal physicians and also for those Viennese psychoanalysts who were going to try to settle in England. The famous physicist, Sir William Bragg, to whom he went for a letter of recommendation to the Home Secretary, Sir Samuel Hoare, naïvely asked: 'Do you really think the Germans are unkind to the Jews?' Fortunately Sir Samuel Hoare was better informed and granted the visas, so that Freud's residence in England was assured.

Then came a wait of three months, during which negotiations with the Nazis continued. To pass the time Freud translated Marie Bonaparte's book about her dog 'Topsy' and continued work on the third part of *Moses*. The Nazi authorities finally gave their consent to his departure, on a payment of a special emigration 'tax' which obviously had to be paid in cash. Freud had no money. Marie Bonaparte advanced him the four thousand eight hundred and twenty-four dollars he needed. While he was waiting to leave Freud wrote to his son Ernst, who was already in London:

'Two prospects keep me going in these grim times: to rejoin you all and die in freedom. I sometimes compare myself with the old Jacob, who, when a very old man, was taken by his children to Egypt, as Thomas Mann is to describe in his next novel. Let us hope that it won't also be followed by an exodus from Egypt. It is high time that Ahasuerus came to rest somewhere. . . .'[2]

On June 4, 1938, Freud left the city where he had lived for seventy-nine years. After a stop in Paris, where he

[1] The first sentence of this remark is identical to a passage in 'Moses and His People', *Std Edn* XXIII, p. 115.

[2] To Ernst Freud, May 12, 1938, *Letters*, pp. 442–3.

stayed with Marie Bonaparte, he arrived in the country in which he had so often dreamed of settling. London gave him a royal welcome and for the first time in his life he had a feeling of being famous, as not only the official authorities and leading public figures but also the anonymous crowds, the common people of England paid him their tribute. British doctors were proud that their country had given him refuge, while unknown admirers sent him little antiques to replace the famous collection which they believed he had lost. However, the very day he arrived, Freud wrote:

'The emotional climate of these days is hard to grasp, almost incredible. The feeling of triumph on being liberated is too strongly mixed with sorrow, for in spite of everything I still greatly loved the prison from which I have been released. . . .'[1]

Henceforth he tried to forget Vienna and even pretended not to remember his own name. Almost as soon as he had settled in he began to work again, just as though nothing had happened. During the year of life which was left to him he wrote and did four hours' analysis every day, almost to the very end.

Many distinguished visitors came to his first London home; Stefan Zweig, the anthropologist Malinowski, the Zionist leader Chaim Weizmann, whom Freud greatly admired, H. G. Wells, Dr Yahuda, the Jewish Professor of Philosophy who came to ask him not to forget his *Moses*. One of the visitors who impressed him most was brought by Stefan Zweig. This was Salvador Dali, the 'fiery young Spaniard with the candid, fanatical eyes' who made a sketch of him on the spot and made him modify his views on surrealists who, although they had adopted him as their patron saint, had struck him as being a dangerously unbalanced crowd.[2] Salvador Dali's sketch still adorns the study in Maresfield Gardens where Freud's desk, settee, statuettes and personal treasures have been left just as they were during their owner's lifetime.

Freud managed to complete his book on Moses before the operation he underwent at the end of the year. The German edition came out in Amsterdam in August 1938.

[1] To Eitingon, June 6, 1938, *Letters,* p. 446.

[2] To Stefan Zweig, July 20, 1938, *Letters,* p. 449.

The English edition, for which Freud waited impatiently, appeared in March 1939. However, the operation left him completely exhausted and shortly afterwards a tumour appeared which the doctors considered to be inoperable. After that, his days were nothing more than a slow and appalling death struggle which no one, not even his family, could wish to see drag on. During the whole sixteen years he was ill Freud never took a sedative, saying that he 'preferred to think in torment rather than not to be able to think clearly'. Now he agreed to take a little aspirin and, with this poor aid, continued his fight against illness and neurosis which had lasted more than forty years.

During August his condition continued to deteriorate. He could no longer feed himself, the cancer which had affected his jaw and palate now invaded his cheek and blood-poisoning was feared. The declaration of war found him worn out but lucid, with no feeling of self-pity and as realistic as ever. When his physician, Dr Schur, asked him if he thought this war would be the last he answered: '*My* last!' On September 19th Ernest Jones was called to his bedside to say goodbye. On the 21st Freud reminded his doctor of the promise he had made at the outset to help him to 'leave this world decently' when his pain became unbearable. The time had come. Schur assured him that he had not forgotten and Freud thanked him.

The next day the doctor gave him a small dose of morphia which, in view of his extreme weakness, was enough. In the night of September 23, 1939, his long life finally came to an end. He died without saying a word, except what he left in his work, and without any other consolation than the immortality which he perhaps expected from his arduous labour and which only man has the power to grant to genius for a brief eternity.

INDEX